the

PERFECT

ENDING

for the

WORLD

JOHN NOĒ, Ph.D.

What People Are Saying about John Noē and This book . . .

"Noē's book just could be the spark that ignites the next reformation of Christianity." – Dr. James Earl Massey, Former Sr. Editor, *Christianity Today*, Dean Emeritus, School of Theology, Anderson University & Distinguished Professor-at-Large

"Your treatment of the 'end of the world' is the best treatment of this idea . . . . Your book could really open the eyes of a lot of people." – Walter C. Hibbard, Former Chairman, Great Christian Books

"You have developed this theory in more detail than anyone else I know . . . . I am encouraging my students and colleagues to carefully consider the preterist view." – L. Rush Bush, former past-President, The Evangelical Theological Society

This book, in its original form and title, *Beyond the End Times*, was named by *Christianity Today* magazine one of the top three books in its article, **"The Millennial Book Awards,"** – October 25, 1999 issue.

"Noe . . . argues, with no little energy, against traditional views . . . [it] does have an internal logic that makes for exegetically interesting reading." – Mark Galli, Book Review Editor, *Christianity Today*

"John Noē has provided a fresh, open-minded look to the questions concerning the end times. His new work . . . is a thoughtful and carefully reasoned interpretation of biblical prophecy. Many, like myself, will not be fully persuaded of his conclusions, but all will be challenged to read the biblical text more faithfully. Noē's work deserves very serious consideration." – David S. Dockery, President, Union University

"It surely is a message that is desperately needed . . . . So often, God has given his special gifts on understanding to lay people. John Calvin was a layman. John Noe is a layman. And both of them have left writings which the Church must read and 'come to grips with.'" – Robert H. Schuller, Former Senior Pastor, The Crystal Cathedral

"God has given you a prophetic message for our time . . . . What you are doing will shape the church for decades to come if not for centuries. Many people will be quoting you over the years to come."
– Bruce Larson, Former Co-Pastor, The Crystal Cathedral, Adjunct Professor, Fuller Theological Seminary

"The premise . . . is right on target . . . . I enjoyed reading this . . . immensely. You are a good writer, an excellent communicator, and an incisive thinker . . . I am intensely interested in the unfolding of this approach." – Knofel Staton, former President of Pacific Christian College, Professor, Hope International University

"You make an impressive case. One being made practically no where else in evangelical Christianity . . . and one that deserves to be made and discussed . . . I can see this book attracting a lot of interest." – Ronald J. Allen, Associate Professor, Christian Theological Seminary

"I predict this book will be a classic!"– John L. Bray, Evangelist

"Your handling of Daniel's prophecies is revolutionary and needs as much exposure as it can get." – Pastor Joe Lewis

"It's a masterful treatment of the entire spectrum of biblical prophetic revelation. Every Christian pastor, teacher, and layperson will benefit from studying it with careful scrutiny of the details presented." – H. Edward Rowe, former Executive Director, Coral Ridge Ministries

"It is a terrific, well-researched work which justly clobbers the chops off the last-days, end-times scare mongering profiteers." – John W. Chalfant, author of *Abandonment Theology / America – A Call To Greatness*

The Perfect Ending for the World

By John Noē, Ph.D.

An updated, revised, expanded, and re-titled new edition of the author's original work, Beyond the End Times © 1999, 2000.

Published by:

East2West Press
Publishing arm of the Prophecy Reformation Institute

5236 East 72nd Street
Indianapolis, IN 46250 USA
(317)-842-3411

Cover: Tom Haulter

ISBN: 978-0-9834303-0-8

Library of Congress Control Number: 2011926384

Prophecy. End Times. Bible. New Testament Revelation.

Dedication

To my colleagues, past and present
on whose shoulders I am standing.
Thank you for helping me see these truths in God's Word.

To my wife, Cindy,
for her invaluable contributions.
Thank you for being frank and honest with me.

To those over the years
who have listened to my teachings, participated in my Bible
study groups, and questioned and challenged me.
Thank you for your encouragement to publish this updated, revised
expanded, and re-titled new edition and other materials.

In preparing this new edition, I have made considerable
additions and, I trust, improvements in hope
of making it more worthy, effective, and useful.
I send it forth again to do whatever work
the Lord may have in store and in believing
that truth will ultimately prevail.

Contact Us:

EAST2WEST PRESS

Pioneering the next reformation

www.east2westpress.org

Publishing arm of . . .

PRI

PROPHECY
REFORMATION
INSTITUTE

5236 East 72nd Street
Indianapolis, IN 46250
www.prophecyrefi.org
jnoe@prophecyrefi.org
Ph. # 317-842-3411

Contents

Author's Note

My Quest for the Rest

A strange thing happened when I became a Christian for sure in 1980. I and my family became victims of the end-saying tradition (saying, "The end is near!").

Back then, all that we were hearing was, "Time is short. We don't have much time left."

"How do you know?" I asked.

"We are living in the 'last days!'" they exclaimed. "These are the end times. Soon it will be all over. Jesus is coming back. We're leaving this world."

It was the heyday of Hal Lindsey's book, *The Late Great Planet Earth*. And this end-times-gospel was everywhere, at least everywhere in the circles I was traveling. For me, however, this was not good news.

I remember thinking at the time, "Oh, no!" I had just become a Christian. The business my wife and I started five years ago was starting to make money. Our two children were attending grade school. I wanted to see them grow up. I didn't want everything to end, at least not yet.

When my daughter, Elise, transferred to a Christian school, she was hearing so much of this end-saying message that for several years she was convinced she would never have to make plans to go to college and would never get married. Today, she is happily married, has four wonderful children, and has earned a both a bachelor's and master's degree. How sad, in retrospect, that she had to undergo all this confusion and needless anxiety when she was young.

As a new Christian, I was also being told and taught to read and study my Bible. That's when another strange thing started happening. Verses began popping out, like these two verses from the New Testament book of Hebrews 1:1-2. "In the past God spoke to our forefathers through the prophets at many times and in various ways, but in these last days he has spoken to us by his Son."

So I started asking more questions of those I deemed to be in the know like . . . "Doesn't the writer of Hebrews state here that the biblical timeframe known as the 'last days' was taking place, back then and there—i.e. during the earthly ministry of Jesus and during the time he was writing? And if that is true, how can we possibly say that we are now living in the 'last days?'"

"Well, we just are! Look around," I was bluntly informed. "It doesn't take a genius to figure this out. Just look at the moral decay in society and world events—especially those in Israel. How could anyone come up with any other conclusion? Everybody knows we are living in the 'last days.'"

But I found this response quite unsatisfying. The answer of another Christian leader seemed to make more sense. He assured me that the "last days" were, indeed, present in the 1st century. But they stopped.

"When and how?" I queried.

"When the Jews rejected the kingdom Jesus was bringing and crucified Him, God's prophetic time clock stopped ticking and everything—the kingdom and 'these last days'—was postponed and put on hold" he replied with confidence. "But the 'last days' started up again."

"When was that?" I responded.

"In 1948 when Israel was re-birthed as a nation. And soon, Jesus will return and set up his kingdom here on earth, in Jerusalem," he further explained.

His answers seemed plausible, until I got home. Then it hit me. The writer of Hebrews was writing some 35 years after Jesus' crucifixion and this claimed postponement of the kingdom and interruption of the "last days." I also discovered that other inspired Scriptures, written some 20 to 30 years after Jesus' crucifixion, were still presenting the kingdom as a then-present and viable reality. For example, the Apostle Paul after his three missionary journeys was "boldly and without hindrance" preaching "the kingdom of God" and teaching "about the Lord Jesus Christ" (Acts

28:31 – also see Acts 1:3; 19:8; Heb. 12:28). Furthermore, and fifty days after Jesus' resurrection, the Apostle Peter proclaimed that the outpouring of the Holy Spirit at Pentecost was "in the last days" (Acts 2:17).

Apparently, if what I was being told was correct, somebody, like the Apostle John or the Holy Spirit, forgot to clue either Paul or Peter in that the kingdom had been postponed and the "last days" put on hold. Besides, I pondered, how are Christians today supposed to follow Jesus' admonition to "But seek first his kingdom and his righteousness" (Matt. 6:33), if this kingdom is in a postponed status and not even here?

A few months later, I discovered another view. "Sure, they were living in the 'last days' back then," one pastor agreed. "And we have been living in them ever since."

This view seemed much more credible, until I started asking questions like, these are the lasts days of what? "The end of the world, the end of time," they told me. Yet in almost every Sunday worship service we dutifully either sang or recited in unison this famous doxology and confessional of the historic Church:

> Glory be to the Father, and to the Son, and to the Holy Ghost.
> As it was in the beginning, is now and ever shall be.
> World without end, Amen.
>
> (*Gloria Patri*)

Once again, I was confused. A lot of things weren't matching up.

Needless to say, the more questions I raised about "these last days" and other related topics, the more I began to sense that most of my Christian leaders and friends did not appreciate my inquisitiveness.

"If you keep this up," my Bible study leader warned me, "you'll only get more confused and confuse many others."

I confess his warning intimidate me. Maybe, I was being too critical. After all, I was a new Christian and, at the time, had no formal theological training. What did I know? And everyone I knew believed this end-time-gospel message. All the popular Christian books proclaimed it. The TV preachers preached it. It seemed that almost everything I heard or read was proclaiming a message of an impending global cataclysm. We must be living in the "end times, the "last days." It seemed so logical. But I also knew that the answers I was getting simply did not match up to what the Bible actually said.

What's more, the imminent destruction teaching I was being fed seemed to poke holes in other teachings I was expected to accept. I wondered, for example, why I should be such a good steward over my possessions and invest my time and resources in future generations when I was living in the "final generation" and when everything I owned and invested in was going to be wiped out anyway? Why should I be concerned about spreading the gospel around a world that was soon going to be blown out of existence? And how could I live in joy, peace, and hope when people I dearly loved were about to be annihilated?

---

the more questions I raised . . . the more I began to sense that most of my Christian leaders and friends did not appreciate my inquisitiveness.

When I asked these questions, I got all the trite answers most Christians have come to accept without challenge. "Just do it because God's Word commands it," "You just can't worry about all those things," and so on. But my curiosity continued on, unabated.

My Rest of the Story

Over the past many years, my wife, family, and I, like many millions of others around the world, have gathered almost every week to hear a story. For two thousand years this story has been told and retold. It has been dubbed "the greatest story ever told." It is about a man called Jesus of Nazareth—his birth, death, and resurrection.

In 1949, Fulton Oursler penned his timeless best-selling book, *The Greatest Story Ever Told*. In 1965, it was made into a movie with the same title. I have seen it several times. Perhaps, you have, too. Both the book and movie present a fictionalized narrative of the life of Jesus Christ and cover the time between the betrothal of Mary and Joseph, around 4 B.C., through Jesus' death and rumors of his resurrection in A.D. 30.

Make no mistake, that story is important—very important. It's about a real historical human being—the historical Jesus—Who walked, breathed, and left huge footprints in the sand of history and in the lives of countless millions ever since. But as I have increasingly discovered, there is more to this story, much more.

Some might consider it a separate story. I prefer to frame it in the words of one of my favorite radio commentators, the late Paul Harvey, and his famous signature and sign-on phrase—"the rest of the story."

As a result, over the past thirty years, I have been on a quest for truth and understanding regarding what I now term "the rest of the greatest story ever foretold." This quest has taken me into the theological area known as eschatology (a branch of theology that focuses on the study of the end times and last things). My pursuit has led me around the country and across the paths of many people. During this time, I have continued asking tough questions. Some whom I have asked tried to discourage me, several to dissuade me, and a few precious others have encouraged me. In retrospect, my journey has taken me to new heights of understanding, practical relevancy, and spiritual appreciation. This book and its title are a product of my quest. And, Lord willing, there will be more books.

In this book you will travel along with me on my journey of discovery. As we proceed, I hope you will re-evaluate what you have been taught or have heard thus far about "the end" for the world and its so-called "end times" and "last days." Also like me, I hope you will make new discoveries and find a new peace and greater motivation in the knowledge of these two profound and yet seemingly paradoxical truths:

1. Our physical world and cosmos are without end.

2. "The end" proclaimed for the world throughout the Bible (and so frequently and falsely prophesied by so many for centuries) is not near and getting nearer; nor is it hanging over our heads like a guillotine blade poised to drop at any moment and chop off our future. Rather, it already came, perfectly and precisely; it's behind us not ahead of us; past not future. We moderns, consequently and currently, are living on the other side of the end appointed by God for the world—i.e., beyond the end. It's *The Perfect Ending for the World*.

As we travel this journey together, please be assured that I believe every word of the Bible is the living Word of God, totally true, and dependable (not including translation deficiencies). Hence, you will find this book well-grounded in the Bible's ancient authority. I also believe it clearly and emphatically supports the position I am presenting that the so-called "end times" or biblical phrase the "last days" (interchangeable terms) are also past and not future. In this book, I will lay out the evidence and ask you to carefully consider it. Even if you don't initially agree, test and prove everything I present (1 Thess. 5:21).

In this book you will travel along with me on my journey of discovery.

Likewise, I believe *The Perfect Ending for the World* is a book whose time has come. It is the account of the fulfillment of the greatest prophecies ever made and the most significant cataclysmic events ever experienced. Taken together, and arguably so, these realities changed our world more than anything else in the past or yet to come in the future. And yet, this rest of the story and these events are the most ignored, denied, and opposed in human history. No more! But you be the judge.

What Has Greatest Authority?

One of my textbooks in a doctoral course on hermeneutics (the science/art of interpretation) was titled, *Introduction to Biblical Interpretation*, by Drs. William W. Klein, Craig L. Blomberg, and Robert L. Hubbard, Jr. In it, they confirmed the validity of my two-pronged approach, thusly:

> The historically defensible interpretation has greatest authority. That is, interpreters can have maximum confidence in their understanding of a text when they base that understanding on historically defensible arguments . . . . We should seek the most likely *time* for the fulfillment of a prophecy in history.[1]

Not only is this book, the one you hold in your hand, well-grounded throughout in Scripture, it's also deeply rooted in documented history.

Why I Wrote This Book

This book confronts, head on, major hot-button issues of our modern day and time, as well as issues that have caused much needless confusion and anxiety over many centuries. That's why I feel compelled to share with you some of my thoughts and reasons behind its writing.

First and foremost, this book is a synopsis of some of the most relevant truths and empowering realities I have discovered during my thirty-year quest for truth and understanding and research into the prophetic Scriptures and historical accounts.

Secondly, this book is timely because a new apocalyptic, doomsday date is rapidly approaching for the proverbial "end-of-the-world-as-we-know-it"—December 21, 2012 (based on predictions from the Mayan calendar). Several books have already been published promoting this date, a big-screen movie made and released, and media coverage is intensifying.

Thirdly, my goal has been to demythologize the four major icons of the end-saying tradition (addressed in Parts II-V) by taking my corrective out of the ivory tower and put it into the general marketplace where it belongs. After all, it is in our families, schools, churches, and neighborhoods where this centuries-long, pop-culture, and termination tradition has inflicted the most damage.

Fourthly, this book is designed to break through old mindsets and transition us away from a worn-out and destructive paradigm. My hope is, readers will find my methodology and logic, clear and convincing, and this reformational message compelling and a breath of fresh air.

Fifthly, I've had to face the possibility that this book may have the opposite effect from what I desire. During the latter years of my quest, a few prominent church leaders and theologians have branded me a heretic simply because the position I present is so different from what they've been told and taught. I know it is a threat to them and their livelihood. During these testing times, I have found comfort in the fact that the dictionary defines heresy as "any belief that is against a belief of a church or most people." By that definition, Jesus was a heretic, and so was every New Testament writer. In their day, they were also iconoclasts and anti-establishment. Of course, I am not and would not compare myself to them. But I do feel I must stand up for what I believe God has shown me in his Word and in the historical accounts over these many years.

Sixthly, I believe the timing is perfect for you to discover the biblical and historical truth about the proverbial "end of the world," "the end times," Christ's so-called "second coming" or "return," the "time of the end," "the end," and the Bible's "a new heaven and a new earth." Lack of proper knowledge in these areas over the centuries and continuing today has misled many and destroyed much. No more! But you be the judge.

Seventhly, my overriding premise is that by seeing ourselves as long-term residents of this planet, we can translate this faith into a more serious commitment for making our world a better place. In other words, "ideas have consequences." And the driving idea behind this book is for it to be a call to action as we re-imagine the way we see ourselves, our world, and our responsibilities in it.

Exciting discoveries await you in the pages ahead. So, take your time. Be critical. Think it through. And, please, carefully consider all the contents before rushing to judgment.

If you are ready for a great and exciting adventure of challenge and discovery, buckle up, read on, and enjoy!

Introduction

Divine Perfection Once upon a Time

The God of the Bible is the God of order and design. Everything He created He did so with a plan, purpose, timeframe, and mathematical precision. For those who have eyes to see, his guiding hand is evident in every part of his creation—from macro to micro, the largest to the smallest. This attribute of God has been called the stamp or fingerprint of divinity. I chose to call it simply divine perfection.

So how do you feel when you gaze up into clear, star-studded, night sky with no man-made light to obscure the view? What do you think about when you contemplate this dazzling array, its immensity, its complexity, its beauty, and all that's up there and beyond—a hundred-billion-trillion stars, the planets, the Milky Way, the sun, the moon, and multiple galaxies? They aren't just up there twinkling and floating around. All are in motion spinning through the vastness of space at astronomical speeds, and with such mathematical precision and in such intricate and predictable patterns that people all over the world set their clocks by it.

The word *cosmos* literally means "order." The dependability of this order and its mathematical perfection is totally rational. That's the only reason why space flight is possible. It allows us moderns to calculate a trajectory, launch a space craft, and land it on the moon or Mars, or fly it past other planets, precisely at the right time. But if the universe was a product of unintelligent, unguided, impersonal, random forces and chance, what would be rational and dependable about that?

To the contrary, this part of creation is so perfect and dependable that Albert Einstein said, "I cannot believe that God plays dice with the cosmos."[1] And the ancient psalmist was inspired to write in awe:

> The heavens declare the glory of God;
> the skies proclaim the work of his hands.
> Day after day they pour forth speech;
> night after night they display knowledge.
> (Psalm 19:1-2)

Not only do the heavens spin in mathematical precision, so do the smallest subatomic particles. And they comprise everything created: the chair you sit on, this book you hold in your hands, and the clothes you are wearing, even your own body.

Tremendous advancements in scientific technology over the past one hundred years have enabled scientists of all kinds to discover and study the breadth and depth of the perfection that exists all around us. One of the realities they have increasingly discovered is physical matter is not solid and still. It only appears that way. Everything material is made out of atoms and inside each atom is ceaseless, mathematically precise order and motion.

But if the universe was a product of unintelligent, unguided, impersonal, random forces and chance, what would be rational and dependable about that?

Powered by rapidly improving technology, it has become increasingly more difficult to defend the notion that anything or everything in the universe and on the earth just evolved from chaos, over billions of years, through millions of mutations, via natural selection, random chance, and unintelligent forces.

Below are some dramatic examples of hard, empirical, and scientific evidence of this perfection from both the macro and micro creations.

Macro Evidence

Launched into orbit in 1990, the Hubble telescope has provided scientists an unprecedented opportunity to search our solar system, the universe, and distant stars and galaxies. Increasingly, they have discovered that we humans, indeed, live on a very privileged planet.

The two scientist-authors of the book, *The Privileged Planet* (2004) assure us that in our now more widely observable universe "mounting evidence suggests that the conditions necessary for complex life are exceedingly rare, and that the probability of them all converging at the same place and time is minute."[2]

Astrophysicist, Hugh Ross, calculates that, to date, 128 finely tuned, inter-dependent conditions or constants have been identified.[3] Each is necessary for life as we know it to exist on planet earth. Others agree and have calculated that "just a slight variation in any one of these values would render life impossible."[4] These finely tuned constants encompass the earth's location in the universe, in our galaxy, and in our solar system, along with the conditions present on the earth itself.

Here is a small sample of areas and factors which must be just right in order for life to exist on earth: the unique properties of water, the composition of earth's atmosphere, its magnetic field, its axis tilt, its rotation speed, its density and size, its crust, its distance to the sun and moon, its oceans-to-continents ratio, the color/size/heat of our sun, and size of our moon, etc. On no other planet or star in our observable universe possesses even a few of these 128 constants. For an elaboration of some of these constants familiar to most of us non-scientists, see *Exhibit A* below:

Exhibit A:

Today, school children and college students are taught that we live in a universe and on a planet that just happened, accidentally, naturally, and spontaneously, over billions of years. Notwithstanding, let's take a closer look at part of this precise creation, the earth. This magnificent sphere on which we live presents dramatic evidence of deliberate order, so that life on it would not only be possible but enjoyable:

- The earth spins on its axis at about 1,000 miles per hour at the equator. At mid-latitudes, the speed of rotation decreases to 700 to 900 miles per hour. This gives us our 24-hour day. If it were to spin at 100 miles per hour, we'd have ten "days" of daylight and ten "nights" of darkness. At night we'd freeze and during the day we'd roast.
- The earth moves in an elliptical, but almost circular, obit around the sun at around 67,000 miles per hour. It maintains a mean distance of 93 million miles.

  – "If it were a few % closer to the sun, we'd surely be in trouble but if it were 2% further away we would probably be ok,"[5] but it would be colder, perhaps freezing. But Hugh Ross insists "a change in the distance from the sun as small as 2% would rid the planet of all life."[6]

  – If the earth "had formed 1% farther from the sun . . . sometime during its history . . . Earth would have experienced runaway glaciation . . . if it had formed 5% closer to the sun . . . [it] would have experienced runaway greenhouse heating."[7]

  – "If the Earth was just 5% closer to the Sun it would be subject to the same fate as Venus—a runaway greenhouse effect with temperature rising to nearly 900 degrees. Conversely, if the Earth was 20% farther . . . CO_2 clouds would form in its upper atmosphere, initiating the cycle of ice and cold that has sterilized Mars."[8]
- If the sun was not exactly the right temperature and distance—a few degrees higher or lower, or a small percentage closer or farther away—there might not be life on this planet, or life as we know it (i.e., us).
- The moon (2000 miles in diameter) orbits the earth at an average but constant distance of 239,000 miles away. Sometimes, when a full moon peers over the horizon, it seems so close we could reach out and touch it. But if it were a little closer, we'd have tidal waves that would engulf and soon wash away most of our land mass. And "without the Moon, Earth's tides would be only about one-third as strong; we would experience only the regular solar tides."[9]

- The moon stabilizes the earth's rotation axis [23.5 degrees], "yielding a more stable, life-friendly climate . . . . a larger tilt would cause larger climate fluctuations . . . . If our Moon were as small as . . . Martian moons, Earth's tilt would vary not 3 degrees but more than 30 degrees . . . [producing] a 60 degree tilt. When the North Pole was leaning sunward . . . half of the year, most of the Northern Hemisphere would experience months of perpetually scorching daylight. High northern latitudes would be subjected to searing heat, hot enough to make Death Valley in July feel like a shady spring picnic. Any survivors would suffer viciously cold months of perpetual night during the other half of the year."[10] Conversely, "a planet with little or no tilt would probably have large swaths of arid land."[11] "Without a large moon, Earth's spin axis might vary by as much as 90 degrees"[12] . . . . [and result in] "a very unstable atmosphere."[13]

- "If the Earth was 25% larger, we would . . . weigh 25% more if the density stayed constant."[14] If it was much larger than that, our muscles would not be strong enough to lift us or get us around. Some hefty people might manage. But life would be difficult if not impossible.

- If the earth was smaller, gravity would be less and the air would be lighter and rarer. The earth's nitrogen-oxygen atmosphere would also be affected. If it was not just the right width and composition (oxygen 21%, nitrogen 77%, and traces of argon, carbon dioxide, and water), the earth's daily heat gain and loss would be out of balance and our present-day climates would be drastically altered.

- If three-fourths of the earth's surface were land rather than water (70.8% water vs. 29.2% land), the land masses would be mostly desert with only fringes of vegetation around the seas; and temperature variations would be so great it would be difficult, if not impossible, for humankind to live.

- "The oceans contain enough water to cover a spherical Earth to a depth of about 4000 meters. If the surface of the planet varied only a few kilometers in elevation, Earth would be devoid of land . . . . Thus, the planet's remarkable mixture of land and oceans is a balancing act."[15] . . . . "the volume of water was sufficiently large to buffer global temperatures, but small enough so that shallow seas could be formed by the uplifting of continents"[16] .... "It appears that Earth got it just right."[17]

- If the strong nuclear force (one of the four basic forces in nature that holds atomic nuclei together—the others being gravity, the electromagnetic force, and the weak nuclear force) was "just 2% weaker or 0.3% stronger than it actually is, life would be impossible at any time and any place within the universe."[18]

- "If the value of the coupling constant for electromagnetism were 4% smaller or 4% larger than what we observe, then life would be impossible. In the case of the coupling constant for the strong nuclear force, if it were 0.5% smaller or larger, life would be impossible."[19]

Some scientists affectionately call this convergence of finely tuned constants the "Goldilocks" story. Why? For the reason that "alone among planets, earth supports human life, because it is 'not too hot and not too cold, not too hard and not too soft, but just right.'"[20] In contrast, "most of the Universe is too cold, too hot, too dense, too vacuous, too dark, too bright, or not composed of the right elements to support life."[21]

What must be emphasized, once again, is this fine-tuned realization was only recently and increasingly made possible by "the unprecedented scientific knowledge acquired in the last century, enabled by equally unprecedented technological achievements . . . [that] when properly interpreted, contribute to a deeper appreciation of our place in the cosmos."[22]

---

the "Goldilocks" story .... it is 'not too hot and not too cold, not too hard and not too soft, but just right.'

Jonathan Wells, who holds two Ph.D.s—one in biology and one in theology, recognizes another significant factor:

> Not only is Earth especially suited for life, but it is also well situated for scientific discovery. Because the Milky Way is a spiral galaxy [most galaxies are elliptical], it is relatively flat, so we can observe distant galaxies that would otherwise be obscured by dust and stars in our own galaxy. And Earth's position in the Milky Way, about halfway between the galactic center and its visible edge, is just about ideal for making astronomical observations, giving us a fairly clear view of nearby stars as well as distant galaxies.[23]

Hence, and more and more, scientists are discovering that "the conditions necessary for complex life . . . . takes a lot of factors to have a habitable planet."[24]

In 1973 this unique convergence of finely tuned constants was dubbed, "the anthropic principle" (from the Greek word *anthropo* meaning "human" or "human existence"). The adjective anthropic means "of or relating to human beings." It is the name given by scientists to the observation that the universe and our earth were designed specifically and ideally to support human life. Notably, "the probability that all [this] would exist today *for any planet in the universe* has been calculated at 'one chance in 10 to the 138th.'"[25] In other words, the likelihood is almost if not totally impossible.

So what might we conclude from all this perfection? The two scientist-authors of *The Privileged Planet* book surmise that these fine-tuned factors "beg for a better explanation than mere chance"[26] and further conjecture that "there's more to the cosmos than we have been willing to entertain or even imagine."[27] Scientist, Paul Davis, in this book, *The Cosmic Blueprint: New Discoveries in Nature's Creative Ability to Order the Universe*, suggests, "There is for me powerful evidence that there is something going on behind it all . . . . It seems as though somebody has fine-tuned nature's numbers to make the Universe . . . . The impression of design is overwhelming."[28]

Get the picture—the big picture? We live in the midst of a vast and hostile universe that is finely tuned and mathematically precise. And our earth is perfectly located in the only place in our solar system, galaxy, and perhaps the universe, suited for life and tailor-made for our existence. What's the best explanation?

The Privileged Planet scientist-authors reckon that "the Earth's position in the universe with its physical laws and constants" and the fact that it has been uniquely "fine-tuned for the existence of life"[29] strongly suggests a "conspiracy . . . the product of a mind . . . an intelligent being . . . a supremely good and orderly Creator . . . for our sake . . . . the universe is ordered in an intelligent way."[30]

Hugh Ross is more specific, "The strength of the case for the God of the Bible can be judged by the direction of the trend line. Through the years, as we learn more and more about the universe, the longer—not shorter—grows the list of features that reflect fine-tuning *and* the more exquisite that fine-tuning appears."[31] Next, he adds this tidbit, "the Entity who brought the universe into existence must be a personal Being, for only a person can design with anywhere near this degree of precision."[32] Ross is, therefore, compelled to conclude that "God designed the universe for the benefit of humanity."[33]

Intuitively, most us know that design requires a designer. No one, for instance, would ever propose that the computer just evolved by random chance through many unguided mutations. But there's more hard evidence for us to consider before we come to a conclusion.

Micro Evidence

Let's now turn our gaze for divine perfection from upward through a telescope to downward through an electron microscope (invented in 1930). As with telescopes, recent advancements in microscopic technology have also opened up new vistas of study and discovery for scientists.[34] But whether one peers up or looks down, intricate order, design, plan, purpose, and mathematical precision are readily evident. Thus, scientists are increasingly finding that divine perfection is exhibited throughout all creation.

In 1996, Michael Behe (Ph.D. in Biochemistry from the University of Pennsylvania and Professor of Biological Sciences at Lehigh University) challenged the scientific community and its Darwinian theory of evolution on purely scientific grounds. With the publication of his best-selling book, *Darwin's Black Box*, Behe popularized the concept of and term "irreducible complexity."[35] In defense of his book's title, Behe correctly pointed out that "to Darwin . . . as to every other scientist of the time, the cell was a black box" (i.e., its contents were unknown) and Darwin was only able to try and make sense of "biology above the level of the cell."[36] And as was true for the macro evidence cited above, "the black box of the cell could not be opened without further technological improvements."[37]

To set the stage, Behe launched his challenge by quoting Darwin's own admission that his theory of gradual evolution by natural selection carried a heavy burden:

> If it could be demonstrated that any complex organ existed which could not possibly have been formed by numerous successive, slight modifications, my theory would absolutely break down.[38]

Behe then proceeded to do just that. But he did so by going all the way down into the micro, single cell level.

First, he defined *irreducible complexity* to mean: "a single system composed of several well-matched, interacting parts that contribute to the basic function, wherein the removal of any one of the parts causes the system to effectively cease functioning."[39]

Secondly, he theorized, "an irreducibly complex system cannot be produced directly (that is, by continuously improving the initial function, which continues to work by the same mechanism) by slight, successive modifications of a precursor system, because any precursor to an irreducibly complex system that is missing a part is by definition nonfunctional."[40]

Thirdly, he presented numerous examples of irreducibly complex biological, biochemical life systems where evolution is an impossible explanation for their formation. Next, he documented scientific reasons why the whole system had to have been created all at once—which, again, is impossible in the Darwin's theory of gradualism.

Starting with an Elvis poster, a mousetrap, and a Scrabble-message as simple illustrations for demonstrating this hallmark, his highly technical examples included: 1) Details of single cilium or cilia (oar devices) that some cells used for propulsion. 2) The intricacies of the rotary propeller device termed a flagellum—a long, hair-like filament and rotating whip by which some bacteria swim. 3) The intricately woven blood clotting system. 4) The many different compartments in a single cell in which different tasks are performed, including the nucleus where the information-laden DNA resides. 5) The body's immune system. 6) The formation of proteins, amino acids, nucleic acids (DNA), and nucleotides.

Fourthly, he hypothesized that "an irreducibly complex biological system, if there is such a thing, would be a powerful challenge to Darwinian evolution. Since natural selection can only choose systems that are already working, then if a biological system cannot be produced gradually it would have to arise as an integrated unit, in one fell swoop, for natural selection to have anything to act on."[41]

Fifthly, he questioned that "in the face of the enormous complexity that modern biochemistry has uncovered in the cell" and the fact that "no one at all can give a detailed account of how . . . . [any of these] might have developed in a Darwinian fashion . . . . [Yet] all these things got here somehow: if not in a Darwinian fashion, then how?"

Sixthly, he reasoned, they "must have been put together quickly or even suddenly"[42] . . . . not by the laws of nature, not by chance and necessity; rather they were *planned* . . . . Life on earth at its most fundamental level, in its most critical components, is the product of intelligent activity." This conclusion, he emphasized, "flows naturally from the data itself—not from sacred books or sectarian beliefs."[43] Therefore, "over the past four decades modern biochemistry has uncovered the secrets of the cell . . . . The result of these cumulative efforts to investigate . . . life at the molecular level—is a loud, clear, piercing cry of "*design!*" In his opinion, "the result is so unambiguous and so significant that it must be ranked as one of the greatest achievements in the history of science."[44] Behe called it, "intelligent design."[45]

So what has been the response of the scientific and educational communities? The bulk of them have not embraced Behe's startling discoveries, reasoning, and conclusions. Why not? Behe believes it's because of their "one overriding and defining rule . . . *Rule No. 1,*" which is to "explain the behavior of the physical and material universe in terms of purely physical and material causes, without invoking the supernatural"[46] or a "higher intelligence."[47] It seems, he further commented, that "many important and well-respected scientists just don't *want* there to be anything beyond nature. They don't want a supernatural being to affect nature, no matter how brief or constructive the interaction may have been."[48] So the vast majority in the scientific community have roundly denounced Behe and his book to discredit his conclusion of intelligent design.

Writing ten years later in his book's new edition, Behe notes that "the scientific argument for design is stronger than ever" because of "the enormous progress of biochemistry in the intervening years.[49]" He further prognosticates that "as science advances relentlessly . . . . the case for intelligent design of life becomes exponentially stronger."[50] In other words, and like a simple mousetrap or a more sophisticated wrist watch or computer, complex living organisms could not have functioned until all their intricately interwoven components were assembled.

Also during these ten intervening years Behe records that the scientific community has done little, if anything, to refute his claim of "intelligent design" or "to show that the Darwinian process really can do [explain] what its boosters claim it can do—account for the functional complexity of the molecular foundation of life"[51] and how such systems "could have evolved . . . by random mutation and natural selection, with each tiny mutational step improving on the last, without causing more problems . . . and without veering off into temporarily-advantageous-but-dead-end structures."[52]

So today, "the situation remains unchanged from what it was ten years ago." According to Behe, there have been no detailed Darwinian account "in the scientific literature . . . that describes how molecular evolution or any real, complex, biochemical system either did occur or even might have occurred . . . [only] assertions . . . but absolutely none are supported by pertinent experiments or calculations."[53]

Christian apologist and author Charles Colson concurs that "nearly ten years after the publication of, no one has successfully challenged his arguments."[54] Marvin Olasky, publisher of *World* magazine, also agrees that no one has been able to credibly refute Behe's emphasis on "irreducible complexity" and "why chance mutations could not be the driving engine of macroevolutionary change."[55]

In retrospect and fairness, Charles Darwin did not have the advantage of the great advances in scientific technology for understanding life that we have today. This technology has been increasingly showing that the physical creation is far more intricate and marvelous than Darwin could ever have imagined. Thus today, evolution's almost stranglehold in scientific and educational circles is a theory in crisis. Its plausibility grows more and more implausible as scientists continue to discover more and more about "irreducible complexity" and the beauty and order of "intelligent design."

But I like to call all this micro, hard-physical, empirical evidence for what it truly is, in my opinion—more proof of divine perfection.

So Who's the Fool?

In the midst of overwhelming evidence—found not only in the largeness of the universe but throughout its smallness—and given the insurmountable odds of all this perfection occurring without design and a designer, an atheistic folly prevails in most scientific and educational communities. In these circles, people who believe the "god-myth" are ridiculed as hopelessly ignorant and outmoded. This latter and ridiculed group comprises more than half of Americans. Surveys show that's how many believe in a special creation by God as opposed to Darwin's theory of evolution by natural selection—a view that has "produced one of the bleakest views of human life imaginable."[56]

Darwin was only able to try and make sense of "biology above the level of the cell" . . . . "the black box of the cell could not be opened without further technological improvements."

But once again, most of us when we see design, we infer—via everyday logic—a designer. Who of us when we visit a place like Mount Rushmore would assume these carved faces are actually the result of unguided, unintelligent, and random forces?

Of course, the existence of God cannot be proved or disproved.[57] But the precision in the sky, in the cell, in biochemical systems, and at the subatomic level is hard, stunning, and compelling evidence. Scientifically, it can be rationally viewed and weighed. Even so, some are compelled by misguided pride to believe that "nothing times nobody plus random change over billions of years equals everything in perfection."[58] In the perplexing words of the first precept of the *Humanist Manifesto* that John Dewey, the so-called "Father of American

Education" signed: "Religious humanists regard the universe as self-existing and not created."

But when it comes to origins or causes, the bottom line is, how do we explain the beauty, order, and complexity we see all around us? There are only two possible explanations—natural or supernatural. Practically speaking, and in this author's opinion, it takes less faith to believe that than "In the beginning God created the heavens and the earth" (Gen. 1:1; also see Isa. 40:26-28).

Of course, those who feel no need of God will always find ways to ignore, discount, or explain away the view of a supernatural creation as they grope around for alternative explanations to avoid the "god-myth." They want no part of God. So they must disassociate Him from *both* the plainest hard evidence up in the sky as well as all that's around us here on the earth.

So how, you may ask, can two scientists look at the same evidence and come up with radically divergent conclusions? Perhaps, it's like the old saw says:

> Two men looked through prison bars;
>
> One saw mud; the other saw stars.

But I believe there is a greater and more basic answer. Since everything that exists exists in a vast storehouse of order, knowledge, precision, perfection and even beauty; and since design inspires most of us to infer if not seek its Designer, those who despise God must distort this truth. And so they have. In my opinion, to believe that all this perfection circling around us in mathematical precision just happened by chance is the folly of the fool who "says in his heart 'there is no God'" (Psa. 14:1a; Isa. 53:1).

To the contrary, this evidence of divine perfection is one of the most powerful arguments for the existence of God. Once again, the ancient psalmist is right on as he proclaims, "the earth is the Lord's and everything in it" (Psa. 24:1). And it shows. "For since the creation of the world God's invisible qualities—his eternal powers and divine nature—have been clearly seen, being understood from what has been made, so that men [and women] are without excuse" (Rom. 1:20). Thankfully, this Lord of creation allows and encourages us humans to explore, study, and discover how incredibly wise, powerful, skillful, and purposeful He was in creating it all. Moreover, He created it all within a fixed and specified timeframe of "six days" (Gen. 1:1-2:3).[59]

In our continually enhanced and advancing explorations, however, an ever increasing irony keeps manifesting itself. The more explainable our complex and precise universe has become, the more baffling its innermost workings appear. This irony reinforces the probable involvement of an all-knowing, all-powerful, creative Being—as opposed to vague or mysterious cosmic force(s) operating by chance.

Many scientific giants of history, such as: Bacon, Boyle, Copernicus, Descartes, Einstein, Faraday, Galileo, Kepler, Mendel, Newton, Pascal, and Planck, believed in an infinite and personal God, Who created a uniform universe and earth with pattern and purpose. They felt their task as scientists was to observe, discover, and explain his handiwork, not to invent it, create it, or deny it.

Today, some are terming this new and increasingly being-uncovered perfection in creation "the new apologetic" (defense of the faith). They see it as best hope for the resurgence or revival of Christianity in face of recent and bold atheistic challenges.[60] But there is another venue of order and mathematical precision for us to re-explore.

Another Venue of Divine Perfection

The God of order and design in creation is the same God of order and design in redemption. As He did in the physical creation, He created his plan of redemption with a design, purpose, and a fixed and specified timeframe leading up to and culminating with its goal—the "appointed time of the end." Then, He progressively completed it with timely and mathematical precision. As we shall see in the pages ahead, every event in the orderly unfolding of his plan falls with exactness in its proper time and place—no delays, no postponements, no unexpected interruptions, as we have been traditionally told and taught.

This is why the Apostle Paul was prompted by God's Spirit to write these time-sensitive words: Jesus Christ was born "when the time had fully come . . . to redeem those under the law" (Gal. 4:4); that He died "at just the right time" (Rom. 5:6); and "who gave himself as a ransom for all men – the testimony given in its proper time" (1 Tim. 2:6). The Greek word translated "time" in the first verse is *chronos* and denotes a space or span of time. But in the latter two verses the word is *kairos* and is more specific. It means a fixed, definite, or set time.

According to God Himself, the timely and precise fulfillment of prophecies foretold long ago "from the distant past"—and not the perfection in the physical creation—is how we humans can know Who the one true God truly is. This demonstrated factor of divine authenticity is so important that the God of the Bible inspired the Old Testament prophet Isaiah to write about it six times and in various ways. You can read all about this in Isaiah 41:21-24; 42:8-9; 44:6-7; 45:20-22; 46:9-11; and 48:3-6.

Fact is, the God of the Bible foretold—many times and in many ways—what was going to happen in the future. And it all happened. No other god, faith, religion, or ideology in the world can claim this phenomenon of predictive and prophetic precision. Nor do they have anything to compare with the subsequent and validating evidence of fulfilled prophecies.

The God of order and perfection in creation is the same God of order and perfection in redemption.

As I will present for your consideration throughout the rest of this book, everything else the God of the Bible promised and prophesied via his prophets regarding his plan of redemption (saving us human beings from sin and restoring our fellowship with Him) *also* happened "at just the right time" and "in its proper time."

Unfortunately, this reality of timely, mathematical, and precise past-fulfillment has been largely ignored, resisted, or denied by most Christian and non-Christian traditions. But as was true with the physical creation, evidence of divine perfection in this other venue abounds. How can this be, you may ask?

The Appointed Time of the End

We are a time-oriented people. God is time-oriented, too. After all, He created time—the "two great lights" in the sky, the sun and moon, to "serve as signs to mark seasons and days and years" (Gen. 1:14, 16).

They travel across our sky at astronomical speed and with mathematical precision. God also knows how to tell time. And He has communicated to us human beings in time-restrictive language we can easily understand. We can rest assured in the revelation, as the Hebrew prophet Amos announced long ago, "Surely the Sovereign Lord does nothing without revealing his plan to his servants the prophets" (Amos 3:7). That is why, seven centuries before Christ, the God of the Bible inspired the ancient prophet Habakkuk to write:

> For the revelation awaits an appointed time; it speaks of the end and will not prove false. Though it linger, wait for it; it will certainly come and will not delay.   (Habakkuk 2:3)

One century later, God gave another Old Testament prophet, Daniel, two specific time prophecies that pinpointed the exact time in human history for the future coming of the Messiah and this "appointed time . . . of the end." Daniel also perfectly foretold the end's historical setting, nature, and defining characteristic. As you will see, this end is the only end the Bible consistently proclaims. But its time is not near and getting nearer; nor is it hanging over our heads today like a guillotine blade poised to drop at any moment and chop off our future. Rather, its time did not prove false, was not delayed, but certainly came, right on time, and just as Habakkuk had precisely prophesied.[61]

Consequently and currently, we moderns are living on the other side of the "appointed time . . . of the end." In other words, the end proclaimed is behind us, and not ahead of us; is past, and not future; and is far and getting farther away with each passing day. This book will present the biblical and historical evidence that we are living beyond the end. If true (I believe it is), this truly is *the perfect ending for the world as well as the climax for the rest of the greatest story ever foretold.* It is also, in my opinion, "the ultimate apologetic" and will change how we talk to people about the claims of the Christian faith. But I'll leave that appraisal up to you.

You may be surprised or even shocked, however, by this part of the "rest of the story." That's to be expected. But to date (as far as this author knows), no one has effectively challenged the centuries-long, ever-recurring, and pop-culture tradition of endsaying and its termination consensus with the breadth and depth of evidence that you will encounter herein.

Yet thousands of books focusing on universal fatalism and feeding on apocalyptic fears have sold by the millions. More are on the way. And the next new doomsday date being promoted is 2012. But before you get swept away by another termination tirade, join the company of the alarmed, detach yourself from society, or seek a cave in which to hide, let us seriously reconsider together the Bible's "appointed time . . . of the end" and the demonstrable reality that God kept his promise and accomplished it all right on time!

For some of you, this unlearning and relearning experience may be uncomfortable, upsetting, or even threatening. For others, it will be exciting and rewarding. For all, it should be an awakening. Please be assured, once again, as we go about this task, we will uphold the Bible as the divinely inspired, inerrant, and infallible Word of God. Its prophetic revelations together with the historical accounts of fulfillment reveal God's divine perfection, once again, in this other venue of redemption.

What's in Store for You?

Many exciting discoveries await you in the pages ahead. And in this author's opinion, the world and its inhabitants should be better off after absorbing and acting upon the revelations contained herein. But one thing is for sure. This book should greatly appeal to peace seekers, truth seekers, environmentalists, intellectuals, and every day people who want to save and improve our world, not just for ourselves, but for our children, our grandchildren, and future generations. For the greater good, the disheartening impact of the end-saying tradition upon human thought and practical living must be challenged and if proven false, ended.

Don't expect this long-standing fascination and pervasive pop-culture tradition to be easily overturned, however. Perhaps no other subject has captured the imagination and raised the fears of more people than this widely accepted apocalyptic practice and belief system. Similarly, no other subject has been the focus of more books, media products, entertainment ventures, as well as Internet chatter.

And despite the fact that over and over again, for almost two-thousand years, the Church (primarily) has been made to look like a joke in the eyes of the world as predictions of "the end of the world," "the end times," the "last days," the "second coming," and other end-saying events have come and gone without supposed fulfillment, many millions of Americans, and others worldwide, continue to believe that world-ending events and the so-called end times are here or soon coming.

Maybe you too have wondered what's in store for us. Should we be heeding the words of the latest end-saying prophecy pundit? Is Jesus' so-called "second coming" or "return" near? Will the world soon end? As you will see, many think so.

But I believe the time is ripe and the climate prime for a comprehensive breakthrough and a significant challenge to the long-standing tradition of endsaying. Now, after centuries of confusion, thousands of failed predictions, and the recent bombardment of millennial madness (Y2K), you may be about to make an exciting, paradigm-changing discovery that the end really is past and not future; and that we moderns actually are living on the other side of the end—i.e., beyond the end. If true, this truly is great good news. Its ramifications could change the perspectives of many people and groups, and possibly nations.

On the other hand, if after considering the biblical and historical evidence I have lain out herein and in a systematic, easy-to-understand, and progressive fashion, your verdict still is, we are not living on the other side of the end, then thanks for your time in reading this book. My hope, however, is that as we journey together through this book's five progressive parts and re-address the four major icons of the end-saying tradition, you will increasingly come to the same conclusion and realizations as have I.

Therefore, in <u>Part I</u>, we'll explore some of the major problems with the end-saying tradition.

In <u>Part II</u> – we'll re-address the popular notion of "the end *of* the world."

In <u>Part III</u> – we'll lay out the divinely determined timeframe of the end *for* the world.

In <u>Part IV</u> – we'll document the "end times" or "last days" that were and re-evaluate the so-called "second coming" or "return" of Christ.

In <u>Part V</u> – we'll unveil the present reality of the new heaven and new earth.

So, if you are ready for better answers than have been given in the past, let's look at several reasons why clearly, something is wrong.

PART I: IDEAS HAVE CONSEQUENCES

Chapter 1

Clearly, Something Is Wrong

"**M**ommy, Daddy, is the world going to end like everyone says?" A familiar question? Perhaps too familiar? How do you answer it, how do you explain it, especially when asked by ones you love and care for?"

Apocalyptic warnings and predictions of the past several decades have brought forth all sorts of questions about "the End." Some are broad in scope, but other questions are quite personal and intimate. What about you? Do you think the world is going to end someday? Perhaps someday soon? If so, you're not alone.

Endsaying is not a "Johnny-come-lately" activity. Ever since the first caveman poked his head out of his hole in the ground, peered up into a starry night sky, and witnessed a long-tailed comet blazing across the heavens, we humans have been convinced that the world, or at least the world as we know it, would someday end.

Thus, for eons—especially during the past fifty years—this pop-culture tradition has plagued the world. And since words have meaning and ideas have consequences, frankly put, endsaying must be characterized for what it has become—an age-old crime against humanity. This practice of saying "the end *of* the world is near," along with its supposed associated events, has been and still is being perpetrated primarily, but not exclusively, by Christians misreading their Bibles and, unwittingly or consciously, disseminating disinformation.

It's not hard to see how any one growing up during the last half of the 20th century could become pessimistic and fearful about the future.

A Late Great Victim

"I got really scared when I started reading Hal Lindsey's *The Late Great Planet Earth*," a deeply troubled young man recently told a counselor.

"I couldn't put it down! All that stuff about Israel becoming a nation in 1948 . . . and Russia . . . and the European Common Market . . . the final generation and the end times made me stop and think. . . . I'd never read anything about prophecy . . . . It really got to me," he continued.

"I started going to End Times conferences, reading the *Left Behind* books and other books on prophecy, and listening to CDs. The more I heard about Jesus' coming back, the more uptight I got. I dropped out of college, all but abandoned my family, and just bummed around the country, listening to any prophecy teacher who seemed to know what he was talking about. I even went to Israel to try to sort it all out."

"Then, I began to notice something strange," he observed. "No two prophecy teachers seemed to agree. I mean, they'd argue over which came first the rapture or the great tribulation. Then, when the year 2000 was coming, they were one hundred percent sure this was it and they were right and the others were all wrong. But Y2K came and nothing happened."

---

endsaying must be characterized for what it has become—an age-old crime against humanity.

"So, what came of all that?" asked the counselor.

"I just got more and more confused," he lamented. "Eventually, I had to push the whole thing out of my mind and get on with my life."

"Are you still frightened about Jesus' return?" the counselor asked.

"I don't know what to think," came the quick response. "I just try not to think about those kinds of things anymore."

Is There Really No Hope for the Future?

Recent surveys show that many millions of Americans continue to believe "the end of the world" is coming, the "second coming" or "return" of Jesus could occur at any time, and that we are now living in so-called "end times:"

- **In 1990**, the *Chicago Tribune* reported that "at least **50 million** Americans buy the 'end is near forecasts,'"[1] That's a lot of people!
- **In 1993**, a *Time/CNN* poll found that **20% of Americans** agree that ". . . the second coming of Jesus Christ will occur sometime around the year 2000. 49%** answered no, and **31%** didn't know."[2]
- **In 1994,** a *U.S. News & World Report* poll found **61%** of Americans believe Jesus Christ will return to Earth—of those: **34%** believe it will be within a few years or a few decades; **37%** believe it will be longer than that. **59%** of Americans believe the world will come to an end—of those: **12%** within a few years, **21%** a few decades, **16%** a few hundred years, **28%** longer than that.[3]
- **In 1997**, an *Associated Press* poll found that **24%** of adult American Christians believed that Jesus Christ will return to earth within their lifetime.[4]
- **In 1997**, another *U.S News & World Report* poll revealed that **66%** of Americans say that they believe Jesus Christ will return to earth some day—an increase from the **61%** in its poll three years earlier.[5]
- **In 1999**, a *Newsweek magazine* poll found the following percentage of adults believed that the world will end with the battle of Armageddon as described in the biblical book of Revelation: **40%** of American adults; **45%** of Christian adults; **71%** of Evangelical Protestants; **28%** of non-Evangelical Protestants; **18%** of Roman Catholics. Of those who believed that Armageddon will happen, **45%** believe that Jesus will return during their lifetime—that would be **18%** of American adults, or roughly **36 million** people who so believe.[6]

- **In 2003**, and post-Y2K, *Chicago Sun-Times* reports that "Recent polls show that about **40%** of Americans . . . believe the physical world will come to an end. [Of those] **40%** believe it will happen in their lifetime . . . . apocalyptic visions are dancing in our heads like sugarplums on Christmas Eve."[7]
- **In 2004**, a *Newsweek* poll gauges that **17%** of Americans believe the end of the world will occur in their lifetime.[8]
- **In 2006**, *Christianity Today* magazine cites a survey by Pew Forum on Religion & Public Life claiming that "**59%** White evangelicals . . . say modern Israel fulfills part of the biblical prophecy about the Second Coming" and "**33%** Those who expect Jesus to return in their lifetime."[9]
- **In 2006**, an end-of-the-year, Associated Press-AOL News poll noted "one in four, 25% of Americans, anticipated the second coming of Jesus Christ . . . . in 2007."[10]
- Many others are in a quandary about what to think of all this. And who can blame them?

There Are Legitimate Concerns

As we approached the latest frenzy of end-saying activity associated with Y2K and the turn of millennium—questions about the end of the world, the end times, Jesus' second coming/return, and what's going to happen in the future reached an almost feverish pitch. Predictions of dire events and an impending global disaster associated with our dependency on computers were intermixed with other apocalyptic ravings. Gloom-n-doomers from all directions rushed forward to cash in on these burgeoning fears and uncertainties. Publishers brought out a spate of new books linking current events to the fulfillment of end-time prophecy. TV evangelists gave weekly analysis of news events interpreting them as signs of what was foretold in the Bible. But, once again, nothing happened.

This apocalyptic furor might be brushed aside were it not for an overabundance of legitimate political, economic, and scientific concerns that seem to grow in frequency, intensity, drama, and scope every day.

- Events in Israel and Middle East wars, political upheavals, and terrorism come and go but keep the end-times' pot boiling and the world on edge.
- Worldwide terrorism, especially post the catastrophic events of 9/11, is a ticking bomb that now inflicts fear on millions of citizens and travelers, and is creating major problems for the world's transportation, food and drug supplies, and water systems.
- Add to this the frightening possibility of loose nukes from the former Soviet Union, Iran, or North Korea falling into the hands terrorists from desperate rogue nations.
- Illegal drug trafficking threatens to destroy whole nations, including the United States.
- The most recent collapsing global economy, as well as the overwhelming debt burden in Third World countries and even in America, poses the threat of worldwide economic collapse and widespread depression termed by some as a coming "financial Armageddon."[11]
- The AIDS problem appears totally out of control, and many reputable medical experts predict that it is only going to get worse and worse.
- Numerous ecological disasters and many scientists generally agreeing that our environment is reaching a pollution saturation point.
- Medical and scientific advances continue to raise moral issues like genetic manipulation, cloning, and mind control.
- The moral fabric of society, the values of family, and the relevancy of the Church continue to deteriorate at an accelerating pace.

With all of these concerns parading across our television and computer screens day after day, along with an abundance of natural and man-made disasters, it's easy to see why so many people feel that we are living in the biblical timeframe known as the "last days," and that something cataclysmic is about to happen. No doubt, this is why many publishers and TV pundits will keep promoting end-of-the-world fears, merchandizing end-time prophecy, and pumping out gloom-n-doom sensationalism.

Are we then living in the final generation that will see the return of Christ? Many today are asking this question more frequently and with greater intensity than ever before. But let's take a look back in time and see if there is something to be learned from the past. As you read through the selected examples in this next section, ask yourself two questions: Why have so many been so wrong for so long? What can we learn from this list of failures? The correct answer(s) may surprise you.

Centuries of Confusion and Needless Anxiety

Traditionally, people have looked to the Church for answers in confusing and troubled times. After all, if anybody should understand where the future is going, how the world is going to end, and when Jesus is coming back, it should be the institution that claims to have an inside track with the Creator and Controller of our universe.

It makes sense, doesn't it, that people would turn to the one source which should be able to interpret the confusing language of biblical writings to give them some clues about what to expect? Unfortunately, when people turn to the Church for answers to these questions, they simply find centuries of confusion and much needless anxiety. Below are some prominent examples. Yet they are merely the tip of the iceberg. Perhaps, we should characterize this list as a "hall of shame." Bestselling author Jonathan Kirsch negatively terms it "the history of a delusion."[12] But you be the judge:

A.D. 500. Church father Hippolytus of Rome (A.D. 170 - 236) predicted that the second coming of Christ and the end would take place around A.D. 500, based on his analysis of days and years in the Bible.[13]

A.D. 513. In A.D. 313, Church father Lactantius (c. A.D. 250 - c.325) succumbs to the prevalent belief of his time and makes what would become an all-too-familiar observation about the signs of "the extreme old age of . . . a tired and tottering world." He calculates that "the end of the world" and the "last day of the final conclusion is already approaching . . . . the entire expectation or length of time left seems to be no greater than two hundred years."[14]

A.D. 999. When the change of millennium drew near, hardly anyone knew it, since most of the world of that day did not use the Christian-based calendar, and could not read. Europe was the exception, and Christian expectations of an imminent end of the world flooded the continent. Accounts vary, but terrified masses feared the 1,000 years spoken of in the prophetic book of Revelation would be up and Jesus would reappear to end it all. Signs and warnings were eagerly sought in the final months leading up to A.D. 1000. It is said that activity in European monasteries nearly ground to a halt as A.D. 999 wound down. Some believed the Battle of Armageddon would take place on Christmas Eve.[15]

A.D. 1033. When Jesus didn't make an appearance in A.D. 1000, quick recalculations were made on the premise that Revelation's 1,000 years should be figured from his ascension and not from his birth. But A.D. 1033 was also a bust.

A.D. 1200s. Joachim of Fiore, an Italian monk and leading biblical prophecy scholar of his day, challenged the allegorical interpretations of Augustinian origin and brought back a literal perspective. According to his date-setting technique, the end was to come between A.D. 1200 and 1260.[16]

A.D. 1500. The English bishop John Hooper believed that he was living in the very "last days" in writing, "But we are fallen into the last times and the End of the world."[17]

A.D. 1501. Christopher Columbus allowed 155 years for all mankind to be converted to Christianity, after which the world would end.[18]

A.D. 1536. Martin Luther believed the end of the world would take place within a hundred years, or by about 1636. He wrote, "We have reached the time of the white horse of the Apocalypse. This world will not last any more, if God wills, than another hundred years . . . at the outside."[19]

A.D. 1546. Before he died, Martin Luther stated many times that "verily the day of judgment [or end of the world] is not far off; yea, will not be absent three hundred years longer." He also believed that "all the signs which are to proceed the last days have already appeared."[20]

A.D. 1606. German visionary, Nicholas Raimarus, first published in Nuremberg a long narrative title laying out plain evidence that the end of the world was inevitable and imminent: *Chronological, Certain, and Irrefutable Proof, from the Holy Scripture and Fathers, That the World Will Perish and the Last Day Will Come Within 77 Years.*[21]

A.D. 1692. American Puritan minister Cotton Mather wrote about the nearness of the end, saying, "I am verily persuaded, 'The judge is at the door'; I do without any hesitation venture to say, 'The Great Day of the Lord is near,' it is near, and it hastens greatly."[22]

A.D. 1717. Mather next predicted the second coming of Christ would take place in this year.[23]

A.D. 1717. Sir Isaac Newton, in his book entitled *Observations upon the Prophecies of Daniel and the Apocalypse of St. John*, believed he was living in the end times, "the last age."[24]

A.D. 1736. Cotton Mather, who predicted the second coming would take place in 1717, changed his prediction to 1736.[25]

A.D. 1736. William Whiston, the English writer best known for his translation of the works of Josephus (the 1st-century Jewish scribe for the Romans), predicted that London would be destroyed on October 13, 1736, and that this would mark the beginning of the end.[26]

A.D. 1766. Richard Clark, an Anglican clergyman in South Carolina, set 1766 as the date for the end of the world.[27]

A.D. 1831. Joseph Smith father of Mormonism (The Church of Jesus Christ of the Latter Day Saints), prophesied that some of his closest followers would live to see the Second Coming."[28]

A.D. 1835. Smith wrote that the second coming of Christ was 56 years away and would occur by 1891, "even fifty-six years should wind up the scene."[29]

A.D. 1832. Utopian socialist Robert Owen announced the second coming of Christ would take place in 1834 in writing, "This . . . is the great advent of the world, the Second Coming of Christ . . . . The time is therefore arrived . . . ."[30]

A.D. 1835. "Our lot has fallen under the solemn period emphatically designated in Daniel as the time of the end!" declared Archdeacon Browne, of England, as quoted in *The Last Times*, by Joseph A. Seiss, D.D.

A.D. 1843. William Miller, founder of the Millerite movement in America, predicted that Christ would come and the world would end sometime between March 21, 1843, and March 21, 1844. Stressing the systematic nature of his methodology and rationality of his conclusions, Miller's end-times mass movement swept through the United States and generated much excitement. The date was later revised to October 22, 1844.

A.D. 1848. "Had the present state of Europe been prophesied fifty years ago, would any have credited the prophecy? We believe that in this year we have seen the beginning of the end." *The New York Evangelist*, as quoted in the book, *The Last Times*.

A.D. 1852. "No well-informed man can look upon the world as it is, without coming to the conclusion that some great consummation is about to take place." Dr. Baird, in Rochester, as quoted in *The Last Times*.

A.D. 1856. "It is agreed, by all believers in the Bible, that mysterious scenes await our world . . . . God's purposes are fixed, and the wheel of his wonderful providence is rolling us on to the funeral of the world that now is." *The Last Times*.

A.D. 1860. The renowned British Reformed Baptist preacher, Charles H. Spurgeon, asserted in a sermon delivered on Sabbath Morning, October 7th that he and his hearers were "now [living] in these last days" because of the new prominence in Europe of "certain modern theologians" who were espousing the "negative theology" of "the Universal Fatherhood of God"—i.e., that "all men [are] universal sons" of God.[31]

A.D. 1874. Claiming to be the sole possessors of God's revealed truth, the Jehovah's Witnesses began a string of prophecies for the end of the world which continued through the years 1874, 1878, 1881, 1910, 1914, 1918, 1925, and 1975.

A.D. 1914. "War! War! War!!! proclaimed a Pentecostal journal at the outbreak of World War I. "The Nations of Europe Battle and Unconsciously Prepare the Way for the Return of the Lord Jesus."[32]

A.D. 1917. Three dramatic visitations of the Virgin Mary occurred in Fatima, Portugal. The first unveiled a terrifying vision of hell and prophesied the end of World War I. The second visitation warned of another major conflict (WWII), the rise of communist Russia, and its collapse and conversion to Christianity if enough people prayed and consecrated it to Mary. The content of the third visitation, whose outward visual manifestations in the sky were witnessed by 50,000 – 70,000 people, was kept secret by the Catholic Church for 83 years. During that time speculation swirled that it predicted a fiery end to the world at Jesus' return and was being kept secret for fear of setting off worldwide panic. But on June 26, 2000, the Catholic Church decided to reveal the secret and published its text. It foretold an event that had already happened—the assassination attempt on Pope John Paul II in 1981.

A.D. 1926. Oswald J. Smith, one of the leading missionary statesmen of his day, wrote in his book, *Is The Antichrist At Hand?* that "the Great Tribulation, the arrival of the Roman Empire, the reign of the Antichrist and the Battle of Armageddon must take place before the year 1933."[33]

A.D. 1950. A youthful Dr. Billy Graham announced at a rally in Los Angeles, "Two years and it's all going to be over." In a December 19,

1994 article reflecting on this quote and chalking it up to Dr. Graham's "youthful exuberance," *U.S. News & World Report* noted that "Since then, Graham has become more cautious regarding apocalyptic timetables."

A.D. 1970s. Hal Lindsey's *The Late Great Planet Earth*, a title that speaks for itself, outsells everything. The *New York Times* declares it "the book of the decade." Total sales reportedly now top 40 million. In it, Lindsey cites the rebirth of Israel in 1948 as *the* prophetic sign. Within one generation (forty years, i.e., by 1988) we would witness the end of the present world and the return of Christ. He envisioned the new interpretative idea of a nuclear war starting in Israel, resulting in radioactive fallout and a melted earth. The dust jacket of the book's 1977 edition warned readers not to make plans beyond 1985. Lindsey wrote:

> The Bible foretold modern man's *countdown to extinction*. I believe this generation is overlooking the most authentic voice of all, and that's the voice of the Hebrew prophets. They predicted that as man neared the end for history as we know it that there would be a precise pattern of events . . . . And all of this would be around the most important sign of all—that is the Jew returning to the land of Israel after thousands of years of being dispersed.

A.D. 1972. Tim LaHaye releases his prophecy book titled *The Beginning of the End*. Regarding the "key generation" of Matthew 24:34, he wrote on page-165: "Carefully putting all this together, we now recognize this strategic generation. It is the generation that 'sees' the four-part sign of verse 7 [of Matthew 24], or the people who saw the First World War." (See A.D. 1991 for the "revised and expanded" edition and changed version of his "prophecy.")

A.D. 1978. "The world must end within one generation from the birth of the State of Israel. Any opinion of world affairs that does not dovetail with this prophecy is dismissed," wrote Gary Wilburn in a *Christianity Today* magazine article titled, "The Doomsday Chic."[34]

A.D. 1978. "We are already living in the *age of Antichrist*! The world is on the threshold of catastrophe." Salem Kirban, *The Rise of Antichrist*.

A.D. 1978. Popular west coast pastor Chuck Smith writes in his book *Future Survival* that he is "convinced that the Lord is coming for his Church before the end of 1981."

A.D. 1980. "Many people will be shocked by what will happen in the very near future. The decade of the 1980s could very well be the last decade of history as we know it . . . . We are the generation that will see the end times . . . and the return of Christ." Hal Lindsey, *The 1980s: Countdown to Armageddon*

A.D. 1988. Edgar C. Whisenant, a retired NASA rocket engineer and prophecy teacher, sends shock waves through fundamentalist circles with his 4.5 million copies of *88 Reasons Why the Rapture Will Be in 1988*. A revised sequel came out the next year: *89 Reasons Why the Rapture Will Be in 1989*. His first book was front-page news around the U.S. His second one wasn't.

A.D. 1989. In a mass mailer, evangelist Jerry Falwell wrote, "With all of my heart–I believe–in just a few days we will enter what may very well be . . . . THE FINAL DECADE! . . . Jesus is coming soon. And I want you to be ready."

A.D. 1990. Dallas Seminary President John F. Walvoord re-releases his 1974 book, *Armageddon, Oil and the Middle East Crisis*. It sold over one and a half million copies playing off the apocalyptic fears of an American war with Iraq leading into the final Battle of Armageddon. When the war was over, so were its sales.

A.D. 1991. The "revised and expanded" edition of Tim LaHaye's 1972 book, *The Beginning of the End* is released. He changes his "prophecy" about Jesus' "key generation" of Matthew 24:34 without informing his readers of his new view (a common slide-of-hand trick of the end-saying trade). He now writes on page-193: "Carefully putting all this together, we now recognize this strategic generation. It is the generation that 'sees' the events of 1948"—i.e., Israel's re-birth as a nation.

A.D. 1991. Dallas Seminary professor Charles Dyer releases his book *The Rise of Babylon: Sign of the End Time*, in which he argues that Iraq's

Saddam Hussein was rebuilding the ancient city of Babylon, whose end-time destruction is prophesied in the book of Revelation. His thesis was blown apart by the United States' defeat of Iraq in the first Persian Gulf War. But it will resurface.

A.D. 1991. War with Iraq brought forth a fevered pitch of cries from church leaders, teachers, and writers about the nearness of fulfillment of biblical prophecies regarding "Armageddon," "Apocalypse," and "the end of the world." Major newsmagazines featured headlines like: "Is This the Battle of Armageddon?" "Is The End Near?" "Apocalypse Now?" "Revelations in the Middle East." Another spate of doomsday books came out from respected church leaders touting, once again, end-of-the-world, Jesus-is-coming proclamations. The national television networks gave them prime-time coverage. Many wondered if this was a prelude to the second coming of Jesus.

A.D. 1992.

> "Rapture Oct 28 '92.
> Jesus Is Coming.
> Don't Receive The 666 Mark!"

Front-page pictures of this sign were splashed around the world by the news media. The source was a Seoul, South Korean church with 20,000 members. Shortly thereafter, its pastor, Lee Jang Rim, was sentenced to a two-year jail term for defrauding members of over $4 million.

A.D. 1993. In the midst of David Koresh's apocalyptic ravings during the peak of the Waco crisis, radio evangelist and founder of Family Radio network, Harold Camping, and I debated on CNN's *Larry King Live*. Camping, in keeping with the title of his book, *1994*, affirmed the return of Christ and the end of the world for September 1994. I opposed his position for some of the reasons you will read in this book. Guess who was right.

A.D. 1994. Jack Van Impe, popular television Bible prophecy teacher, spreads the "good news" of Armageddon. On his nationally televised program of June 22, 1994, he prognosticated "everything is winding up within the next ten years." On his February 5, 1997 show he changed his timetable to between "2001 and 2012."

A.D. 1994. Televangelist Paul Crouch of TBN declared during his internationally televised "Spring '94 Praise-A-Thon" fundraiser, "we are in the last moments of grace before the wrath of God is revealed. This is the windup. The curtain is about to come down. We don't have much time left . . . . If Jesus hasn't come back by the year 2000 A.D., then we [he and his guest preachers] have misread the Scriptures." Crouch and Hal Lindsey, a frequent guest, discussed how they certainly don't see "it [this world] can go beyond 2005 or 2010" at the most.

A.D. 1994. In another of his doomsday books, *Planet Earth – 2000 A.D: Will Mankind Survive?* Hal Lindsey warned, "Never before have all these signs come together like this." In a section titled "Gone by 2000?," Lindsey advised, "I wouldn't make any long-term earthly plans . . . *the end times are almost here.*"

A.D. 1994. *US News & World Report's* December 19th cover story reported, "The approach of a new millennium in the year 2000 is unleashing a flood of doomsday prophecies, not only from zealous Christians who are convinced that Christ's return is imminent and will end history and inaugurate a divine kingdom . . . but also from those . . . far removed from Christian belief."

A.D. 1995. Televangelist Pat Robertson, during a week-long fundraiser on CBN's *The 700 Club*, with the theme "Signs of the Times 1995," pleaded with viewers:

> All is being set up for us just like the book of Revelation said . . . . All signs point to the end of the world and the end of life as we have known it . . . . Nobody knows the day or the hour . . . . What all this means is we're coming up on the time of the end . . . . Now the time is urgent to bolster the resources of CBN. . . . This world is not going to get any better . . . . The worst is yet to come . . . . Now is the lull before the storm . . . . Your dollars may not do any good in five years or so.

During the previous year's fundraiser Robertson told viewers (May 12, 1994), "We are possibly talking about the final age of humankind, right now. Let's work together while we have a chance. Please call and make a pledge."

A.D. 1995. The Reverend Billy Graham wrote in a front-cover article titled "Are You Ready for the Last Days?" in the Billy Graham Evangelical Association's *Decision* magazine:

> There are 'signs of the times' given to us in Scripture, and each day, as we read our newspapers or watch the news on television, we are reminded of some of the signs Jesus told us to look for . . . famines . . . earthquakes . . . weapons that can destroy the entire world with fire. . . . 'nation shall rise against nation.' We are seeing that today . . . . When will the end be? We don't know . . . . But every indication is that it will be sooner than we think.

A.D. 1995. The first of fourteen fictional books—in what would become the widely popular, 65-million worldwide sales,[35] Christian-themed, *Left Behind* series of novels—is released. It's titled: *Left Behind: A Novel of the Earth's Last Days* (Tyndale House Publishers). These books are co-authored by Tim LaHaye and Jerry Jenkins and reflect the popular end-time view of most evangelical Christians. Three years later, Focus on the Family's *Citizen* magazine called this series "the hottest trend in apocalyptic literature since author Hal Lindsey's million-selling *The Late Great Planet Earth*."[36]

A.D. 1996. Not to be outdone, the largest Christian publisher, ThomasNelson, released *The Beginning of the End* by TV preacher John Hagee. This end-times book marched to the top of the Christian bestseller list. In it, Hagee connected the November 4, 1995 assassination of Israel's Yitzhak Rabin with "the beginning of the end and the coming Antichrist." He contends that the end-time countdown to the Rapture, Tribulation and Armageddon has already begun. As of 2006, "over 1 million sold."[37]

A.D. 1997. ThomasNelson released a new Bible, called the *Prophecy Study Bible*, edited by John Hagee. In it, he identifies ten prophetic signs indicating that our generation today is the "terminal generation."

A.D. 1997. Front-page, top headline in *The Indianapolis Star* reads, "Is the Second Coming at hand?" and reports that "Millions of Christians believe Christ will return soon after next millennium."[38]

A.D. 1998. On October 4th, the *New York Times* ran a front page feature story about the phenomenal success of the *Left Behind* series and reported, "In an instant, millions of people [will] disappear from the face of the earth, shedding their clothing, shoes, eyeglasses and jewelry."

A.D. 1998. *CBA Marketplace*, the Christian Bookseller Association's magazine, headlined in its November issue: "No End to Success for End-Time Videos . . . Book momentum builds as the year 2000 approaches."

A.D. 2000. Leading up to this monumental year computer experts conjured images of a secular Armageddon and predicted January 1, 2000, as "The Day the World Shuts Down" and "The end of the world as we 00 it" (that's "oh-it"). Some Christians recast the "Y2K" problem in religious terms, seeing it paving the way for an end-time Antichrist and portending the return of Christ and the end of the world. But Y2K came and went and nothing of any significance whatsoever happened.

A.D. 2000. In a news article immediately following the Y2K fiasco, *World* magazine related how many Y2K doomsayers, including the *Left Behind* authors, were forced to backpedal away from failed predictions:

> Tim LaHaye and Jerry Jenkins . . . had claimed online that the bug would wreak havoc, "making it possible for the Antichrist . . . to dominate the world commercially until it is destroyed." By the end of the year, the quote came back to haunt them. "We regret having talked about it," Mr. Jenkins blushed to *The Washington Post*.[39]

A.D. 2001. 9/11 – the day of infamy. Prophecy expert, Tim LaHaye reports that "Before September 11 was over, the phones of prophecy scholars rang off the hook. People in media were looking to spiritual leaders for answers . . . . Like people everywhere, they wanted to know 'Is this the end of the age?' or 'What is the prophetic significance of this national tragedy?' All of which confirms that even many of the most godless among us fear the end of the age as outlined in the Bible."[40]

A.D. 2002. Harold Camping, whom I debated in 1993 (see above), and despite missing his 1994-end-times deadline, tells Christians to stay away from churches. He claims "the Church Age" is over. Satan has now set up his throne in the Church. It's part of the end-times apostasy and Jesus is coming soon. But this time he names no date.

A.D. 2003. Going solo, Jerry Jenkins, the best-selling co-author of the *Left Behind* series, and Tyndale House, the publisher of the series, release a new prophecy book appropriately titled, *Soon: The Beginning of the End*. It's backed by a million-dollar marketing and promotion budget and claims to be "the end-times thriller for our times." Jenkins signed an eight-figure contract for three end-time thrillers in this series.

A.D. 2003. Tim LaHaye, the other co-author the *Left Behind* series, but now with a new co-author Greg Dinallo, releases the first of four novels in a new end-time, fictional series. It's titled *Babylon Rising* (Bantam). It, too, is backed by a million-dollar marketing campaign and is based upon LaHaye's futuristic view of Bible prophecy. According to LaHaye, the books in this series are "based on prophecies that are not covered in the *Left Behind* books and that have great relevance to the events of today." LaHaye signed for a $45-million advance, as this series promises to take readers on "a countdown to what the Bible calls 'the time of the end'" and will help them "understand that end times prophecy could be fulfilled in our lifetime."[41]

A.D. 2005. Carol Eisenberg of *Newsday* reports in a syndicated newspaper article titled, "Fundamentalists link disasters to 'end times'":

> Every morning the Rev. Michael Mitchell, senior pastor of New Life Tabernacle United Pentecostal Church in New York City, prays that if today is the beginning of the end of the world as we know it, he will be ready . . . . Mitchell's belief that he is watching biblical prophecy unfold in the form of modern-day famines, floods and earthquakes has grown increasingly urgent . . . . Set against a backdrop of terror threats and worries that avian flu may morph into a pandemic, it's no wonder that talk of a biblical-scale reckoning is cropping up in all sorts of conversations.[42]

A.D. 2007. Celebrity, Hugh Downs, gathers responses from over 100 personalities—including presidents, scientists, artists, writers, and religious leaders—who talk about how they think the world will end. Published by W Publishing Group (a ThomasNelson imprint), the book is appropriately titled, *The Last Days of Planet Earth*.

A.D. 2008. Again, the fellow Christian I debated in 1993, Harold Camping, publishes a new book with a new date for the proverbial "end of the world." Titled, *We Are Almost There!*, this persistent endsayer now figures—using a combination of numbers from throughout the Bible—that the Rapture will take place on May 21, 2011 with the end of the world following five months later on October 21, 2011. On the front cover he announces:

> With no apologies, it is the intent of this book to warn as many people as possible about the abundant biblical evidence that the end of the world is almost here. The end of the world is that awesome and terrible moment when Jesus Christ, the supreme ruler of mankind, will complete the judgment process that began in the Garden of Eden when Adam and Eve disobeyed God.[43]

Non-Christian Endsayers

Doomsday prophesying is not the exclusive domain of Christians. Although others are not deemed as "credible" or as influential, their end-saying predictions are nevertheless widely reported:

Nostradamians. The 16th-century Jewish-French physician and psychic, Nostradamus, purportedly predicted the great fire and plague of London, the execution of Charles I, the rise of Oliver Cromwell, the French Revolution, Napoleon's campaigns, both World Wars, the ravages of Hitler, and even the deposing of the Shah of Iran. Relying on this impressive track record, Nostradamians in the 1990s keyed in on July 1999 as the rapidly approaching end. They cited Nostradamus' Quatrain X:72 in his massive volume of verses known as the *Centuries*, which says, "In the year 1999, the seven months, from the sky will come the great King of Terror. He will bring back to life the great king of the Mongols. Before and after War reigns happily."

The opening line of a full-page ad in *Publisher's Weekly* magazine, December 9, 1996, for the book, *Nostradamus 1999* ('96) by Stefan Paulus, reads:

> On the evening of November 15, 1996, author Stefan Paulus generated such tremendous interest that 32,000 radio listeners in New Orleans jammed the phone lines–all because they wanted to know how to survive the end of the world.

Following this failure, Nostradamians are now re-exploring their prophet's 942 obscured quatrains looking for more dire and relevant predictions. One of their web sites features this quatrain:

> At forty-five degrees, the sky will burn,
> Fire approaches the great new city,
> Immediately a huge scattered flame leaps up,
> When they want to have verification from the Norman
> (Century VI, Quatrain 97)

Nostradamians now ask, "Does this reference the destruction of New York City? By War? Earth Changes?" They claim it does, stating "this phrase . . . refers to a great city in the new world of America near forty-five degrees latitude. Experts agree this could only be New York."

Another quatrain has a familiar 9/11 ring to it and is offered in support of the above interpretation:

> Earth-shaking fire from the center of the earth,
> Will cause the towers around the New City to shake,
> Two great rocks for a long time will make war,
> And then Arethusa will color a new river red.
> (Century 1, Quatrain 87)[44]

Another Nostradamian web site has announced the "amazing discovery" of "an unknown manuscript by the famed . . . Nostradamus." It is said to reveal details about "Osama bin Laden, the next major terrorist attack in the US, the resulting war with Iran, a confrontation between the US and China/Russia, and . . . the hidden timeline . . . and the course of World War III." Their new book is title, *The Nostradamus Code: World War III* and covers "the years 2006 through 2012."

Look for even more predictions of doomsday calamities and catastrophes from this source as Nostradamians become more "sophisticated" in finding new modern-day meanings in these old and obscured quatrains.[45]

Pyramidians. Claiming one-inch equals one-year from measurements taken within the chambers of the mystical Great Pyramid of Giza in Egypt, they believe . . .

> There is a prophetic timeline encoded within the measurements of the Great Pyramid of Giza, which is derived from its geometrical features. When retro-viewed, the dates indicated by this timeline and geometry appear to correlate with significant historical events, including the birth of Jesus Christ, the development of the atomic bomb, and the two world wars of the last century. This timeline is calculated to have begun in 3999 B.C., and ended on September 17, 2001.[46]

This timeline also predicted the second coming of Christ in 1934 and 1953.[47] Despite this failure, Pyramidians warn that there are virtually no measurement prophecies for anything beyond the year 2000 or 2001. What does the end of this timeline mean? Pyramidians say it means we are approaching "the ending of the present world Age." They further point out that "all major prophetic traditions point to this time in history."[48]

Scientists. "An avalanche of books chronicles Earth's 'impending' doom" headlined a syndicated newspaper article in 2004. Books cited were: "Our Final Hour," "The End of the World," "Catastrophe," "Imagining the Unthinkable." But the article clarifies that these are not "the ravings of wild-eyed doomsday prophets. Rather, they're titles in a recent spate of scientific books and reports calling attention to various perils facing our plant."[49]

On February 26, 1997, *National Geographic* aired a television special titled, *Asteroids: Deadly Impact* in which they chillingly said, "the question is when, not if, Earth will receive a big-time, possibly fatal black eye from an asteroid knockout."[50]

The House of Yahweh, a Jewish-oriented doomsday group, in their February 1998 newsletter headlined, "World Destruction in Only Three

Years." Previously, front-page headlines in the November 1997 issue proclaimed, "Nuclear War Through The Hebrew Year 5760" (which corresponds with the Roman year 2000). Inside they wrote, "All nations will be affected . . . the time of destruction is here." At the time, they believed the Arab-Israeli peace treaty signed by Prime Minister Yitzhak Rabin on September 13, 1993, was the "confirmation of the covenant" prophesied by the Old Testament prophet Daniel. This supposedly started God's prophetic time clock ticking again and gave humankind just seven years preceding the world's last war—the infamous Battle of Armageddon. This seven-year period "will end in destruction for all nations." Obviously, their starting point was wrong. No doubt, they will update it and recalculate their seven-year period.

In 1990, **Elizabeth Clare Prophet**, a New Age guru who claims she communicates with Jesus and Buddha, moved her followers onto a thirty-three-thousand-acre range in Montana to prepare for the coming Armageddon and imminent end. According to their The Summit Lighthouse web site, they are still there and waiting. Their site optimistically advises, "Prophecy is a warning; it is not set in stone. So we can actually change the course of events and make this new millennium what we want it to be!"[51]

The militia group the **Patriots** held their 1995 "End of the World" Expo in Dallas, exhibiting anti-government and conspiracy literature, and the latest in survivalist gear. At "Preparedness Expo '96" in Indianapolis, Bo Gritz, a former Green Beret turned negotiator in the Montana Freeman standoff, conducted the featured seminar, titled, "Are We in the Biblical End Times?" His answer? "Yes." A common thread in the patriot and militia movements is an apocalyptic vision from the Bible that they still view as an imminent and threatening scenario.

In Cheiry, Switzerland, 48 members of **The Order of the Solar Temple**, a bizarre doomsday cult, are found dead in October of 1994 in the burning rubble of two Swiss villages. Their leader, Luc Jouret, had urged his members to stockpile an arsenal and prepare for the end of the world. Oddly, the apocalyptic beliefs of this religious fanatic group are quite similar to those of Waco's David Koresh (1993), as well as the popular evangelical Christian view.

Some **astrologers** had pointed to *5/5/2000*, the title of a book from Crown (1997), and the date on which Mercury, Venus, Mars, Jupiter, and Saturn aligned with Earth for the first time in 6,000 years, as a time of great cataclysm. More upcoming cosmic convergences are sure to reinvigorate future doomsday claims.

Six-day Theorists, using "the six-day, world-age theory" from the Genesis creation account, have long been predicting that all sorts of things are to happen in or around the year 2000. They assume that God created the universe in 4004 B.C.[52] and within six literal days. Then they add the theory that God's plan for ending the world is similar, but equated by the time scale of "one day is as a thousand years" (Psa. 90:4 and 2 Pet. 3:8). Therefore, their 6-day, 6,000-year time line was up around 1996. But some admit they may have been off by a few years and something big is still about to happen. This six-day theory is also another reason many Christians warn that we are living in the apocalyptic "End Times," in the biblical "Last Days."

Prior to the turn of millennium, the **Mount of Olives Hotel** in Jerusalem advertised itself as "the best place to be for the anticipated second coming." According to reports, nearly a hundred Americans were living on this hill, located just across a small valley from the old city. They had destroyed their American passports and sold their earthly possessions, and were watching and praying for history's climactic event from the vantage point of this ringside seat. In the meantime, Israel girded itself for a deluge of Christian pilgrims as the year 2000 approached.[53] $12 million was budgeted by the Israeli government to upgrade security, especially around the Temple Mount, "fearing extremists might undertake suicidal attacks in Jerusalem as a way to bring about the fulfillment of end-times prophecy."[54] THESE GOOD SEATS ARE STILL AVAILABLE!

Furthering the status of and capitalizing on the widespread fascination associated with this pop-culture tradition, popular singer/songwriter/ performer **Jimmy Buffet & the Coral Reefer Band** named their upcoming summer concert tour "Party at the End of the World 2006."[55]

The next major new date now being touted for the world to come to an end, and which is receiving increasing media and publishing attention, is December 21, 2012. This exact end-date for doomsday is based on predictions supposedly made in the ancient Mayan calendar more than 2,000 years ago. (More on this in our next chapter.)

Other dates being espoused for the end by various groups or individuals are (as I write): 2011, 2014, 2016, 2022, 2029, 2030, 2033, 2038, 2040, 2048, 2056, 2060, 2694, 2914, 2993, 3836.[56]

What Can We Learn?

Can there be anything more foolish than this stream of end-saying prophets (Christian and non-Christian, alike) whose announced times, dates, and urgent warnings for the end of the world and/or the second coming, etc. have passed away without incident? Examine their record. Laugh if you will; cry if you must. But better, ask yourself how could so many respected leaders and their followers have been so mistaken? Surely something is wrong. Yet this is exactly how millions are being programmed today. If there is a lesson to be learned here, why not learn it now?

One thing most of these endsayers already have in common is they have been proven wrong. Yet I have given these examples not to impugn anyone's character or demean the faith they represent, but to illustrate the problem. Many of them we know as people of sincerity and integrity. I have only reported what they have said or written publicly, or what was written about them. But there is a lesson to be learned from this long trail of failed predictions as many of these times and missed dates have already come and gone.

Of course, more examples could have been given. And, no doubt, more will be coming in the years ahead—if this tradition is not suitably terminated. A few things, however, should already be obvious:

- The merchandising of the end-of-the-world, end-time Bible prophecy, and Jesus-is-coming-soon predictions has become big business and a growth industry. But at what cost?

- Almost every generation since Jesus' time has believed that their end-time expectations were the correct ones.
- Embarrassments are quickly forgotten. In their wake, new time-liners, date-setters, and endsayers come on the scene, adjust their scenarios, and recalculate their figures. The unsuspecting hearer, encountering endsaying for the first time, may easily be seduced by its use of current events. And on it has gone into our post-Y2K, new millennium world.

Should We Heed the Words of the Next 'Prophets'?

With so many voices coming from so many sources and with so much uniformity, let's face it; we are being bombarded as never before. And these prophetic visions and cataclysmic warnings fascinate us. But are they true? Is "the end of the world" near? Are we now living in the apocalyptic "end times," the biblical "last days"? Is history drawing to a close? Will Jesus soon return? Or, is this all a fantasy perpetuated by profit-hungry media and self-serving ministries cashing in on the public's almost insatiable appetite for apocalypse?

Perhaps you too have wondered what's in store for us. Could our generation actually be it? Should we be heeding the words of the next set of "prophets?" Worldwide, people want to know what's going to happen. Are things going to get worse? Is there hope for the future? If there is, what is the basis for that hope? Two things, however, are certain: uncertainty about the future is running at an all-time high and apocalypticism is still burgeoning.

As we've seen, when the 20th century and 2nd millennium drew to a close a few years ago the conviction grew, more than ever before, that "the End" was surely coming, and coming very soon. Others tried to avoid thinking about it or only paid a degree of uneasy attention to the doomsday pundits until Y2K passed. After the heat was off they forgot about it . . . until the next time of global crisis. Some, on the other hand, spend a lifetime harboring secret doubts and worries. A few simply dismiss the whole thing as ignorance gone to seed, but lack an authoritative reason for doing so. Whatever we try to do with it, the destructive tradition of endsaying is always there, waiting to rear its ugly head and spread its gloom-n-doom message.

If the "end of the world" were an established fact, it would be tragic for most, if not all, people alive at the time. But, as we shall see, this is not biblical truth. Still, the pop-culture tradition of endsaying will not go away easily. The whole ideology that the end is coming soon, whether rooted in religion, science, and/or nature, is also an effective marketing and fund-raising tool. Those who profit by it will not want to let it go. Sensationalism, fear-mongering, scare tactics, and crisis-oriented pleas are the tools of the trade in the end-saying game in many arenas:

- *Environmentalists* sound alarmist trumpets of impending ecological disasters which threaten our lives and life on earth itself. The culprits are global warming, global cooling, ozone depletion, deforestation, acid rain, toxic waste, and shifting weather patterns. We are headed for disaster, they tell us.
- *Economists* preach global economic apocalypse, worldwide famine, overpopulation, plagues (AIDS), and pandemic diseases. The earth cannot support indefinite expansion, they plead. The stage is set. This is how the world ends.
- *Astronomers* project how all life could end by an asteroid or comet colliding with earth. After the impact and subsequent shockwaves, dust clouds will obscure the sun resulting in falling temperatures all over the planet, expansion of the polar ice caps, and radical shift in weather patterns—all affecting crops, vegetation, migrations and extinctions of numerous species. After all, this is how the dinosaurs became extinct, they reason. It could happen to us, too.
- *Scientists* measure the motion of a million galaxies. Some say that the cosmos is expanding in different directions and the whole thing could snap like a rubber band. Others warn the universe is winding down or decaying via the Second Law of Thermodynamics (entropy). Everything could implode. Either way spells doom.
- *Psychics* and *astrologers* galore "see" unimaginably horrific cataclysms coming our way very soon.
- *Best-selling authors* cash in on our fear of and fascination with apocalypse. They look for any excuse to bring out another doomsday book and find more reasons to be pessimistic about the future.

- *Nuclear scientists* grip us in an extended anxiety attack. They warn of the growing threats of a nuclear Holocaust—everything from global war, mad dictators, power plant accidents, and disarmament fiascoes, to nuclear proliferation, accidental launches, mishandling of nuclear waste, and loose nuclear material in the hands of terrorists. The minute hand on the Doomsday Clock at the *Bulletin of the Atomic Scientists* Building in Chicago was recently changed from 11:53 P.M. to 11:55 P.M.—five minutes to midnight. When it strikes midnight, it's all over. The justification for the latest change is, in the words of the Board of Directors of the *Bulletin of the Atomic Scientists*:

  > **"Chicago, January 17, 2007** – "The world stands at the brink of a second nuclear age. The United States and Russia remain ready to stage a nuclear attack within minutes, North Korea conducts a nuclear test, and many in the international community worry that Iran plans to acquire the Bomb. Climate change also presents a dire challenge to humanity. Damage to ecosystems is already taking place; flooding, destructive storms, increased drought, and polar ice melt are causing loss of life and property."[57]

  Since the end of the Cold War in 1991, this is the fourth time the hand has moved forward.

  > In 2002 – 7 minutes to midnight
  > In 1998 – 9 minutes to midnight
  > In 1995 – 14 minutes to midnight
  > In 1991 – 17 minutes to midnight
  > In 1947 – 7 minutes to midnight"[58]

- *Religious extremists*, like David Koresh in Waco, Texas, garner major headlines and tragically lead gullible followers astray with end-of-the-world views and bunker-mentality lifestyles.
- *Self-proclaimed prophecy experts* assure us that "history's hourglass is almost empty" and that "it will all be over soon." Many base their predictions on personal calculations from the

Bible. Others base them on the frequency of natural calamities like earthquakes, floods, plagues, and famines, which are supposedly occurring more than ever before. Almost every major, global crisis is regarded as a sign of the end. In the popular style, they assure us that "it's all happening just like the Good Book says it would."

- Saddest of all, in this author's opinion, are the *devout, well-known, respected, and gifted church leaders* who have and are still echoing the termination refrains they learned in their particular tradition. They were told and taught that God determined a specific plan for history's last days and the earth's demise, a plan now coming to fruition. For many, it's a driving force behind their ministries. Armed with detailed prophecy charts, they are *increasingly* asserting that Jesus will soon return and bring an end to the world, as we know it. Their failed prophecies in the past, however, have given rich material to those who mock the Christian faith. They have also greatly damaged the credibility of Christianity in the eyes of the world, distracted many Christians, and emasculated the effectiveness of the Church, especially here in America.

Meanwhile we, as a society, pay an enormous price. The constantly perpetuating stream of termination tirades and pessimistic predictions is far more damaging than most people think. Again, in this author's opinion, it's not only an age-old crime against humanity; it's one of the cruelest psychological and theological travesties of our times.

Some good news is, however, that growing numbers of people are rightly sensing that there might be something wrong with this message. Unfortunately, they don't know what it is or how to combat it. Something is indeed very wrong with the end-saying message. I will show you in this book where the errors lie and why you can count on the future.

But next, let's look at one other significant aspect of this pervasive endsaying tradition and practice—its disastrous power and effects.

Chapter 2

The Disastrous Power of Cataclysmic Imagery

Where I live, in the Midwest, I love to take a drive on the back roads out into the countryside on a pleasant summer's evening. Then, roll down the windows and feel the breeze sweep across my face and through my hair. As I pass quaint little family farms and fields nestled among the gently rolling hills, the freshness of the air smells sweet. Occasionally, I catch the scent of new-mown hay. Then suddenly, I hit a patch of something that stinks. It's the manure some farmers spread on their fields.

Down on the farm, one learns to count on the future. Each year farmers plow the ground, sow seed, and fertilize. The plants grow and are harvested. It's nature's basic pattern. Of course, some years are better than others, but there is always next year. Farmers have learned to count on the future.

Not so for masses of people in our world today. They have been programmed, by church people and non-church people alike, not to count on the future. Chalk it up to our seemingly insatiable appetite for the apocalypse, if you will. As we've partially seen in the last chapter, never before have so many prophets from so many perspectives bombarded humankind with so much gloom-n-doom. Termination tirades and end-times predictions are pervasive. They have infected the whole world. Like my drives into the countryside, every so often you get a whiff of it. It's the awful stench of our future being fried.

Pictures and Ideas

Educators, psychologists, and communication experts tell us the world runs on ideas. And ideas are crucial to all of life. They are the foundation upon which our lives are shaped, our dreams are generated, and our nations are built. Conversely, ideas can ruin lives, devastate dreams, and crumble kingdoms.

Perceptions shape our ideas. And perceptions are fragile; they are formed by both the words we hear and the pictures we see. This is how we humans process information. Of course, words are important. But if a picture is worth a thousand words, then pictures have a greater effect on us than words. The advertising industry is built on this principle.

Let's face it, we are susceptible to what we both hear and see. But more and more we moderns have become a people governed by pictures. The experts tell us that we think in terms of pictures, so our ideas are most often shaped by the pictures we see.

If you were asked to name the one picture that has had the most influence on humanity in the past hundred years, what picture would you pick? In this author's opinion, the picture with the greatest impact is this one:

This image of an atomic fireball and its mushroom cloud first flashed around the globe on July 16, 1945. In a remote area of New Mexico, during the predawn hours, the incredible destructive power of the atom was first unleashed. What had been mere theory became reality. This event forever changed our world. Since then, we have had to live with the possibility of an impending and man-made, apocalyptic disaster of global proportions. This picture, along with its associated images of mass destruction and nuclear winter, has been deeply and repeatedly etched inside most of our minds.

The psychological power of cataclysmic imagery should not be underestimated by anyone seeking to understand 20th and now 21st-century American culture and mentality. A whole generation of "nuclear kids" has been raised under the haunting reality of nuclear confrontation. We have learned to live with its prospect of annihilation. And "picturing" this destruction casts a numbing spell as many of us tend to dwell on negatives and not positives. The news media latched onto this fact long ago. Bad news sells and good news doesn't, so they bombard us with bad news. The entertainment industry capitalizes on the addictive power of doom as well.

The fact is, for the first time in human history, a godless, man-made "end of the world" seems like a real, technological possibility. And once that idea is accepted, our minds are ripe soil for other apocalyptic scenarios. Fear breeds more fear. Threats breed more threats. Consequently, other images of the world getting worse and worse are imprinted upon our minds, feed our insecurities, and sap our emotions. Many of us find ourselves imagining the end much too often. The cumulative effect is, we become casualties of a fatalistic mood.

Why is this impending sense of an end so harmful? It's because our concept of the future determines our philosophy of life. It affects how we live in the here and now. And unlike anything ever before, the advent of the nuclear age drastically changed humanity's vision of its earthly future. The threat of a nuclear cataclysm symbolizes our era.

---

our concept of the future determines our philosophy of life. It affects how we live in the here and now.

Not surprisingly, end-time Bible prophecy experts readily jumped on the atomic theme. Before 1945, they interpreted the Bible's use of "burning, melting, and shaking" language in terms of earthquakes, comets, or volcanoes. But Hiroshima and Nagasaki changed all that.

Now, nuclear disasters are incorporated into prophetic passages. A torrent of modern-day prophecy writers and preachers now insist that the Scriptures not only foretold atomic and nuclear weapons, but also their ultimate "end-time" use. In their opinion, the reality of nuclear war confirms the inerrancy and divine inspiration of the Bible. The earth is doomed, and the only way out is the salvation claims of the Bible and a possible mass escape for Christians (the Rapture).

As a result of our nuclear age, Christianity and all of civilization are under the siege of a nuclear Armageddon mentality. It's the latest language of doom. Even Dr. Billy Graham, the highly respected evangelist, in his 1984 book titled, *Approaching Hoofbeats:The Four Horsemen of the Apocalypse*, used this new language in warning that "there will be nuclear conflagrations, biological holocausts and chemical apocalypses rolling over earth, bringing man to the edge of the precipice."[1]

The ominous image he depicted still hangs heavy. His unsurpassed credibility only gives this popular scenario more credence in the eyes of millions. And, of course, the prospects of a nuclear war and a resultant holocaust are real and would be disastrous. Add to this the "new" possibility of small nuclear weapons or dirty bombs being smuggled into U.S. or other world cities and exploded, and we have a threat that will not go away. If one of these nuclear attacks were to occur, one thing is for sure. In the words of a 2004 Homeland Security Council report, a nuclear attack "would forever change the American psyche, its politics and worldview."[2] But with all due respect and appreciation for Dr. Graham, and as we shall see in subsequent chapters, I believe he has subscribed to a flawed interpretation of end-time Bible prophecy. Negative consequences of this popular belief system, however, are real and disastrous.

Pessimism for the Future

"For many Americans, the future seems about as secure as a dandelion puff," reported The *Wall Street Journal* in a front page story.[3]

An entire generation has grown up in despair of the future. Underlying this fear is our concept of the end, not so much the end of our lives, which is certain, but the so-called "end of the world."

Make no mistake; the incessant pounding of doom-n-gloom scenarios and the cumulative effects of urgent warnings and apocalyptic crises take their toll and leave their mark on the human psyche. Many have "seen" the future and believe that its name is "doom." When a fatalistic perception internalizes itself, it's like a slow-working poison; it colors one's thinking and infects all we feel, say, and do. Call it a bunker mentality, a future funk, global gloom, or hanging on the edge; the bottom line is depression and defeat.

Nevertheless, the media loves our insatiable appetite for apocalypse and has jumped on the end-of-the-world-is-coming-soon bandwagon:

Network and Cable Television.

The opening for **NBC's** two-hour, prime-time show, *Ancient Prophecies III, New Visions of the Future*, the third in a four-part series, which aired February 28, 1996, teased:

> The clock is ticking and time may be running out! Over the centuries prophets have seen the close of this millennium as the end of time as we know it. Some trace the warnings back to the prophets of the Bible. Others find evidence in the book of Psalms. And then there are voices alive today from mystics and visionaries, seemingly blessed with supernatural insight, to the more common seers, ordinary men and women, some of them forever changed after a brush with death. But whatever the source, the prophecy remains the same. Something cataclysmic seems headed in our direction. Is our world doomed by fate? Or is our future conditioned? The answers may come sooner than we think.

ABC's weekend show *Sightings*, which aired on April 22, 1995, included a segment that asked, "Is the end really near?" Featured were:

- Dire predictions of a diverse group of "modern prophets" claiming that half of the world's population will soon be killed.
- Visions of an impending "end of the world" given by "ascended-master" spirit beings.
- A foreboding alignment of all nine planets due to occur on May 5, 2000.

- A segment on using the Bible's book of Revelation as "blueprint for imminent disaster."

The **History Channel** marks the new resurgence of endsaying (post Y2K). If they are to be believed, humankind's fate is facing a looming certainty. We are about to suffer a violent extinction. Citing sources like Nostradamus, the Mayan calendar, and the Bible, this cable channel frequently televises features on various potential apocalypses as if they were a given. On October 22 and 23, 2008, for instance, three hour-long programs once again proved that fascination with the apocalypse is not limited to Christian zealots:

- "Decoding The Past: Countdown to Armageddon" warned of "asteroids on a collision course with Earth, super volcanoes, global warming, killer viruses—all are potential catastrophes that threaten to wipe out life on our planet."
- "The Universe: Cosmic Apocalypse" touted "the universe as we know it is condemned to death. Space, matter and even time will one day cease to exist and there's nothing we can do about it."
- "Decoding The Past: Mayan Doomsday Prophecy" examined "in detail how the Maya calculated the exact date of doomsday." Using their ancient calendar "made more than 2,000 years ago . . . the world is coming to an end on December 21, 2012."[4]

Syndicated Radio.

"**Coast to Coast AM,**"—rated by *The New York Times* as the highest rated radio program in the country once the lights go out—late one night in February, 2006, billed their program as "a scientific investigation into civilization's end." It featured guest Lawrence E. Joseph, the author of the book *Apocalypse 2012*. "What followed was a graphic recitation of disaster scenarios for 2012, including hurricanes, earthquakes and volcanic eruptions caused by solar storms, cracks forming in the earth's magnetic field and mass extinction brought on by nuclear winter . . . . As 2012 approaches, 'Coast to Coast AM' has been devoting more and more programming to prophecies of doom and signs and wonders that are thought to be harbingers of the coming end time."[5]

Magazines.

Newsweek magazine's cover of November 23, 1992, portrayed a large, burning, and menacing comet speeding toward a collision with the Earth. It headlined, "Doomsday Science: New Theories About Comets, Asteroids and How the World Might End."

Newsweek magazine's cover of November 1, 1999, depicted a bearded God-figure with baby angels at his side and headlined, "Prophecy: What the Bible says about the end of the World."

U.S. News & World Report magazine's cover December 15, 1997 pictured an angel with sword in hand and captioned, "Prophecy: Religious scholars' new insights into predictions about the Second Coming and the end of the world."

Time magazine, in the fall of 1992, published a special issue devoted entirely to the mystical year 2000 and the new millennium. It stated that "no symbol of the future has sparked more anticipation and mystery than the year 2000 . . . . It promises a new age, or an apocalypse."

The April 2009 cover of *Newsmax* headlines "The Jesus Question—will he ever return?" Inside, David A. Patten writes that "Experts of various stripes tell Newsmax that public buzz about the biblical last days is at its highest level since 9/11 . . . . Overall, Americans are pretty sure that reality's clock is winding down rapidly . . . . the idea that creation's clock could strike midnight at any time turns out to be as American as apple pie, pink slips, and debt collectors."

The October 2009 cover of *Charisma* heralds "Last Days Fever—Some Christians say the world is coming to an end. Others reject that fear. What can we know for sure about the end times?" Inside writer Troy Anderson cites Israel being back in their land (1948) as "one of the key signs" of the soon-coming end.

Supermarket Tabloids.

The June 24, 1997 issue of the supermarket tabloid *Weekly World News*, cited Dr. Robert Calke, a doomsday expert, and reported that the Battle of Armageddon will start when China and Iraq attack Israel on May 3, 2000, and that the world will come to an end on or before May 13, 2000. The issue also reported that the U.S. Government is hiding the information and suppressing the Bible prophecies that prove it.

Another tabloid, *Sun* magazine, on April 26, 2004 featured a fiery picture of the twin towers of the New York World Trade Center just before they collapsed and headlined, "Last Days Have Begun." On its August 23, 2004 cover, *Sun* displayed a rising Jesus figure and captioned, "Signs Last Days Have Begun." Its June 14, 2010 issue elaborates further with the headline, "Lost Gospel reveals the shocking truth . . . Last Days What Really Happens." Its February, 21, 2011 issue headlines, "Jesus returns . . . Exactly where and when! . . . New Bible code predictions for the next 100 days."

In front-page headlines in its January 5, 2009 issue, *Weekly World News* announces, "Nostradamus Lost Book Predicts Earth's Final Days—They're coming much sooner than you think!" This newly found book pinpointed "sometime between July 23 and August 22 of 2009."

Nationally Syndicated Cartoon Strips.

Beetle Bailey, cartoon strip, in *The Indianapolis Star*, June 12, 1995 echoed this popular sense of foreboding.

Used by permission.

Frank & Earnest, cartoon strip, in *The Indianapolis* Star, June 30, 1995, captured a crucial question of the end-saying tradition. Two angels ask God:

Used by permission.

Secular Apocalypse Books.

The Celestine Prophecy (1995 Warner Books), playing off of apocalyptic themes, shoots to the top of the *New York Times* best-seller list and stays there for an astonishing 152 weeks, selling 8 million copies worldwide, once again proving the power and appeal of the apocalyptic.

The Bible Code (1997 Simon & Schuster) jumps onto the *New York Times* best- seller list with a controversial claim, a secret code hidden in the Hebrew text of the Bible's first five books. The code has just now been unlocked by computers, and supposedly reveals future world events. It warns that the Bible foretold disasters set to come upon the world. Among the cataclysms, both past and future, are the rise of Hitler, the Holocaust, the atomic bomb, President Kennedy's assassination, the Gulf War, and Yitzhak Rabin's assassination. According to author Michael Drosnin, this hidden code also reveals the time predicted for the biblical "time of the end" should have begun in September, 1996, with Armageddon to follow in 2000.

2008 books promote the next new apocalypse date, 2012 – a full-page, two-column article in *Publishers Weekly* (Sept. 22, 2008 issue) featured four new end-saying books (based on predictions from the Mayan calendar). Three have 2012 in their title and one has 2013. The magazine reported "sales on this topic have been through the roof."[6] In their March 26, 2007, issue, *PW* previously noted that "there's a lot of fringe stuff that is latching onto the 2012 theme."[7]

The End of the World: Stories of the Apocalypse (Skyhorse / Norton, dist., 2010) – this book thematically presents "19 varied glimpses of humankind's ending."[8]

Christian Apocalypse Books.

What in the World Is Going On?: 10 Prophetic Clues You Cannot Afford to Ignore (ThomasNelson, 2008) Dr. David Jeremiah again assures us that events unfolding in today's world are leading up to Armageddon and the return of Christ.

Can America Survive?: 10 Prophetic Signs That We Are the Terminal Generation (Howard Books – S&S, 2010). Prolific and best-selling, end-times author and pastor, John Hagee, once again sounds the doomsday siren citing on the book's back cover:

- "The impending nuclear war in the Middle East
- The coming death of the dollar
- The consequences of rejecting Israel
- The absolute accuracy of biblical prophecy
- The coming Fourth Reich
- The Year 2012: The Beginning of the End?"
  (In 1996, Hagee thought *The Beginning of the End* (his former book title) was on November 4, 1995—see chapter one, page 35)

Edge of Apocalypse (Zondervan, 2010). Not to be "left behind" and with plenty of time left to capitalize on the 2012 hype, Tim LaHaye (co-author of the phenomenal best-selling "Left Behind" series of books) and Craig Parshall release this first novel of their new series of apocalyptic thrillers provocatively titled "The End." This book's back cover lays the groundwork for this title and series, thusly, "as world events begin setting the stage for the 'end of days' foretold in Revelation."

Time Has an End: A Biblical History of the World 11,013 B.C. - 2011 A.D. (Vantage Press, 2005). Harold Camping, "President of the California-based Family Radio, "a ministry with worldwide broadcast facilities, including more that 150 outlets in the United States"[9] and the Christian I opposed and debated on *Larry King Live* back in 1993 and his book, *1994*, is back at it again. A civil engineer by trade, Camping has re-crunched the numbers and is now predicting the end of the world on October 21, 2011—beating the Mayan date. He re-published this book in 2008 with a new title, ***We Are Almost There!*** (See again chapter one, p-33.)

Big-Screen Hollywood Movies.

In November, 2009, the tentpole movie ***2012*** hit theatres. "Apocalypse Wow" headlined *The Hollywood Reporter* (Nov. 16, 2009) as the spectacular, special-effects-laden movie depicting massive earthquakes, gargantuan tidal waves, and exploding volcanoes wiping out most all of the earth's population and rocked worldwide box office sales with a blockbusting $225 million opening weekend. FX has snapped up the TV rights to show this apocalyptic blockbuster in the year, you guessed it, 2012. The preliminary copy in a one-minute trailer on the movie's website: "2012 Official Movie Site" teased:

HOW WOULD THE GOVERNMENTS OF OUR PLANET
PREPARE SIX BILLION PEOPLE
FOR THE END OF THE WORLD?
THEY WOULDN'T
2012
FIND OUT THE TRUTH

Hollywood loves these end-of-the-world tales. Other recent movies exploiting this ultimate-termination theme include: *Terminator Salvation, District 9, The Road, The Book of Eli,* and *Legion* to name a few. According to a *Christianity Today* magazine article titled, "It's the End of the World and We Love It" . . . "more such films—pre- and post-apocalyptic—are on the 2010 tap"[10] and soon-coming to a theater near you.

Let's not be so naïve or gullible. Even though end-saying predictions have come and gone, more are on the way. Making predictions is the stock and trade of the end-saying profession. Like a madness their end-of-the-world rumblings impact our daily existence, affecting our behavior, and undermining our dreams and goals. Like a flood, termination tirades drown out our willingness to make commitments and get involved. Like a cancer, apocalyptic rumors spread and kill the fabric of a progressive society. Like a guillotine's blade, endsaying hangs poised to drop and chop off our future. For too many young people despair for the future has wiped their great plans of life right off the drawing boards.

Endsaying, in all its various forms, plays a prominent role. Even when it's viewed as nonsense, it still takes a toll. And none of us is immune. Its proliferation in American life is, in my opinion, a most significant reason why the optimism and activism of the 19th and early part of the 20th century have changed to pessimism and withdrawal.

Is it any wonder then that millions of young people today are burdened with cynicism, loss of direction, dashed hopes, and a sense of futility? They see themselves as disenfranchised, with the future drawn up before them like a gangplank. Many are angry. Some are rebellious. Others seek solace in an unproductive otherworldliness, passively waiting for the life to come. Some drop out, get hooked on drugs, or hide out in isolation. A fatalistic rationale reinforces their lack of interest and neglect of responsibility. Thankfully, a fraction of our youth has refused to succumb to the notion that their lives will likely be cut short by an apocalyptic disaster. Yet the message that there really is no hope for the future, at least here on *this* earth, is the one being actively presented by many influential groups and prominent people.

What's needed is a sound and solid rebuttal to stem the tide of world-terminating scenarios and end-saying predictions. This age-old crime against humanity must be refuted, reformed, and replaced with substance, positive hope, and confidence in the future. That is exactly what you'll find in this book. So, let's continue our journey by learning *the* most important lesson we can learn from this sad trail of failed predictions.

Failed Prophets of a False Premise

In our last chapter, we laid out a multi-centuries-long list of both Christian and non-Christian end-saying examples. Likewise, you might remember the round of apocalyptic ravings which accompanied the first Persian Gulf War and the latest round which led up to Y2K and the turn of millennium. Once again, what has happened over all these centuries? Nothing! Absolutely, nothing! Is it possible that the only thing these prophets had wrong was their timing? Or, is more involved here?

The following cartoon satirically captures this farce of failure. It appeared in the *Wall Street Journal*, August 6, 1991, shortly after the first Persian Gulf War and the failed apocalyptic outbursts and doomsday predictions subsided without explanation:

Used by permission.

This next syndicated cartoon that appeared in *The Indianapolis Star*, September 18, 2006. It, too, sends a similar and sarcastic message:

Used by permission.

What impression do these cartoons give you? "There go those religious nuts again." Rarely if ever do endsayers explain or apologize when they're proven wrong. Some followers become confused, others frustrated, and a few disillusioned. Surprisingly, many others don't seem to mind and rarely, if ever, hold their leaders accountable.

As we've seen, history is littered with good and godly people who've claimed certain knowledge of the end and tried to fit the events of their day into the fulfillment of end-time prophecy. The examples given in the last chapter was only a partial list of thousands of past mistakes. But as times for the end and Jesus' return have come and gone, and predicted events have failed to materialize, embarrassments are quickly forgotten. New endsayers come on the scene, re-adapt their scenarios to changing world conditions, and recalculate their figures. Soon a new wave washes ashore, proclaiming humankind's bleak and frightening future. It's the highly adaptive mechanism by which the end-saying trade survives. The next wave of "prophets" proves just as effective at stirring up their brand of sensationalism and fanning it from an ember into a flame. Unsuspecting hearers, encountering endsaying for the first time, can easily be sucked in. And on and on it has gone and goes.

All these endsayers have one major error in common. And sooner or later, they all will be proven wrong—100 percent dead wrong—and their names added to a long and growing list of failed prophets. Why? It's because their error is not one of timing, as is commonly assumed. Rather:

~

All endsayers will be proven wrong within their due time, the same as their predecessors. Why? It's not because their timing was or is wrong. It's their concept that's wrong. They are simply failed prophets of a false premise. They are trying to predict a non-event. If we are slow to learn this truth, then we are doomed to repeat their folly.

~

Let's be honest. It's a wonder the age-old, end-saying tradition and doomsday-peddling trade has any credibility left. But if there is another thing we can learn from the past, it's that we too seldom learn from the past. "Hitler always said, 'the bigger the lie, the more people who will believe it.'"[11]

Incredibly, we keep falling for it. Urgent warnings, prophetic certainties, date setting, termination tirades, the latest doomsday scenario—we're addicted. The specter of an apocalypse fascinates us. Many are thrilled by the notion that the end is near and are more than willing to overlook its long history of prediction and non-occurrence. So as old waves of discredited prophets wash out to sea, new ones roll in to take their place and break onto shore—heavy on assertion and light on proof. But only for a short stay. What suddenly would make today's latest speculation about the end any more reliable or trustworthy? The explanation usually offered as to why past predictions failed is the claim those past prophets didn't have the advantage of knowing what we now know. So here we go again. Don't be surprised, for example, if Hal Lindsey's "terminal generation," the *one generation* following Israel's rebirth as a nation in 1948, is re-figured to be seventy years in length instead of forty. That would place his predicted end date any time between now and 2018.

But why do we keep getting sucked in by these end-times peddlers? Perhaps we don't like to admit that we were duped by the last one. Besides, endsaying has been a sucker's game for centuries, and we like apocalyptic thrills and chills. We are charmed by the secret insights these prophets so attractively package and sell. Admittedly, finding hidden meanings in a world of uncertainty soothes us with a sense of power and elitism. It has an addictive, insider appeal. But this pastime also has consequences—undesirable consequences.

Our brief review of the end-saying legacy through history should have been a sobering exercise. Yet many of us still find ourselves wondering, is it possible some new prediction might finally be right? The answer we will be exploring in the chapters ahead is, "No." They are not now finally right. They are not inexact guesses either; they are just another repetition of the same fundamental error. Here's another critical point for you to consider. All the endsayers we have reviewed so far have completely missed the divinely determined time period for and proper meaning of the Bible's "appointed time . . . of the end." In my opinion, and as you will see in the chapters ahead, it will greatly be to our advantage to progress up this learning curve.

The Consequences of Untruth—Four Critical Areas

Midwestern farmers love to tell the story about the man who bought a long-abandoned farm. For years, he worked hard putting the farm back in shape and making it productive and a showplace. One day the preacher stopped by, looked around and said, "My, hasn't the Lord blessed you with a beautiful farm."

To which the hard-working farmer replied, "Oh yeah, you should have seen it when the Lord had it by Himself."

Farming is a demanding way of life. Try slacking off on your duties and see what happens. Soon your fields will be overrun with weeds, your equipment rusted and broken down, and if you don't sow in the spring, you don't reap in the fall. Traditionally, most farm families feel a sense of responsibility to pass the farm along to other family members in better shape than they received it.

The cumulative effect of end-of-the-world beliefs has the opposite effect; it creates an "abandon-the-farm" attitude and takes the significance out of human action. After all, if the future is fixed and terminal, why bother?

Both beliefs and ideas have consequences. That's why endsaying is far more than an attempt to foresee the future; it actually conditions it. As multitudes conjure up every possible worry and terminating scenario, those who otherwise would be diligent stewards and productive workers tend to sink into helplessness. They may resort to piety and isolation. But the bottom line is a shirking of responsibility.

Incredibly, we keep falling for it . . . we're addicted. The specter of apocalypse fascinates us.

Below are four critical areas in our society today where end-saying beliefs and ideas have had major negative consequences.

Eclipsing Environmental Issues

If there is no future for the future, and our planet is soon going to be destroyed, why work to "save the Earth"—if its end is just around the corner?

This is a major reason why environmentalists face an uphill struggle. They warn us that if our environment doesn't receive top priority, dire consequences will result. Such warnings fall on deaf ears among "end-of-the-worlders." Theirs in effect is a world-hating theology and antithetical to the Christian faith's highest callings. Therefore, they have little interest in environmental concerns. In their view, the world is supposed to get worse and worse before the end comes. "It's inevitable, it's desirable, and it hastens the day. Anyway, we're getting out of here.

So why bother? This world is a miserable place. It's not worth fighting for. And God is going to destroy it all very soon, anyway."

Someone has said, "If there's no faith in the future, there is no power in the present." Consequently, there is no desire to pass our planet along to future generations in a better condition than we found it. No question about it. Endsaying negatively influences and conditions our attitudes against ecological responsibility. The earth is doomed, and the sooner it goes, the better.

David Neff, the Editor in Chief of *Christianity Today* magazine in a July 2008 issue encapsulated this stewardship-escapist immersion in which many Christians find themselves in a recent article titled, "Second Coming Ecology." First, he acknowledged that "Christians have consistently been end-of-the-world people." Next, he cited a well-traveled account of James Watt, an evangelical believer and former Secretary of the Interior during the Reagan administration, who supposedly once told the U.S. Congress that "'protecting natural resources was unimportant in light of the imminent return of Jesus Christ . . . . After the last tree is felled, Christ will come back.'" What Watt actually said was, "I do not know how many future generations we can count on before the Lord returns, whatever it is we have to manage with a skill to leave the resources needed for future generations."

Even so, Neff admits that "It's often said that many Christians—particularly evangelical Christians—don't care for the environment precisely because they are so focused on end times. If God is going to come and destroy all this anyway, why should we invest our energies in preserving it?" He also recognized "a fear among theologians who specialize in thinking about the environment that too much talk about the End (for that matter, any talk at all) will undermine care for the Creation."

So what was Neff's solution? It is to de-emphasize the End by recalling that "Jesus and the apostles played down the time element and even the manner of the End."[12]

As we shall see later in this book, Jesus and the New Testament writers did not "play down" things concerning "the End." They did the exact opposite.

Shirking Social Responsibility

Our concept of the future also has a powerful influence in shaping our attitude toward other people and social responsibility. After all, and once again, if the world is soon coming to an end, what is the point in trying to solve social injustice problems and human need issues, or working for the betterment of humankind by investing in long-term efforts to transform institutional structures?

Another major culprit in this evasion schema is a portion of Christendom involving millions of Americans. For this group, the appeal of a great escape from the difficulties and responsibilities of this world is very attractive. Therefore, they would rather ponder "the End" than pitch in with the job at hand. Typically, they don't care much about the welfare of the next generation, since they aren't going to be here anyhow. Add to this the negative mindset that nothing we can do will put this world on a positive course, that all our reform efforts are a waste of time, and that earthly enthusiasm is pointless and in vain, and what do you get? You get the natural conclusion that there's nothing we should do to stop the inevitable downfall. Their only job is to get people ready for the next world, not to fix up this one.

As a result, masses of sanitized souls sit, soak, and sour paralyzed in pews, consoled by the preaching of demise, and increasingly isolated from society. More and more, as "the End" looms, they see themselves as cultural outsiders reluctant to plunge into social, moral, or political activism. Their plans for this life have a short horizon. In the armed services, we called it a "short-timer's attitude." It's too late to patch up this old troubled world, so they long for "the End" to come. The only hope is for Christ to come back and get them out of here. Then, let Him take care of the mess. Basically, this group has abandoned this world for the next.

A radio talk show host, interviewing me a few years ago, hit the nail on the head. He said, "this 'end-of-the-world' stuff just creates 'Chicken Little' people—people hiding under rocks waiting for the sky to fall, unwilling to come out and help the rest of us clean up the mess."

He's right. Endsaying is the ultimate social downer for those called to be the salt and light of the earth. Searching the headlines for more signs of "the End," they wring their hands, slink into their corners to hide, and shrink away from social evils and contemporary issues—all the while hoping and praying that Jesus will come back real soon and get them out of this mess. Their withdrawal plays right into the hands of those hostile to the Christian faith, who are more than willing to rush in and fill the vacuum they have created. All of which is interpreted as just another sign that "the End" is nearer. Beliefs do have consequences. And whether we realize it or not, endsaying affects our personal lives, community life, national life, and even our international life.

Plaguing Foreign Policy

Why were we glued to our television sets during the two recent Persian Gulf Wars? One compelling reason is the effect it could have on the entire world. When you add modern-day destruction technology to a belief system that everything will get worse and worse just before the world comes to an end, what do you get? You get the possibility that personal views of Bible prophecy might influence the policy decisions of a President of the United States. And the problems of the Middle East always end up on the American President's desk. How far-fetched is this? An article in the Nov. 19, 1990 issue of *U.S. News and World Report* stated, "The idea that foreign policy can sometimes be influenced by interpretations of Biblical prophecy is not as far-fetched as it may seem."

In April of 1984, a story in the *Washington Post* stated that President Reagan had a long-standing interest in Bible prophecy. He appeared to accept the popular evangelical view of inevitable nuclear war and the imminence of the Battle of Armageddon. Citing various kinds of evidence, the *Post* story concluded that the President's policies toward Israel, the Soviet Union, and nuclear arms were closely tied to his understanding of Bible prophecy. Shortly thereafter, a documentary on "Ronald Reagan and the Prophecy of Armageddon" was aired on 175 public radio stations nationwide. As Reagan believed and said, ". . . the day of Armageddon isn't far off . . . . Everything's falling into place. It can't be long now."[13]

During the first Persian Gulf War, the media reported that the White House ordered nine copies of the end-saying book, *Armageddon, Oil, and the Middle East Crisis*, by John Walvoord. The night before the American led an air-strike against Iraq it was also reported that President

Bush requested the presence of evangelist and "Armageddon theology" author, Dr. Billy Graham.

In his 2006 book, *American Theocracy*, author Kevin Phillips charges that "commitment to theories of Armageddon and the inerrancy of the Bible has already made the GOP into America's first religious party."[14] He reports that "George W. Bush has averred this belief on many occasions . . . . [and] has embraced . . . war hawkishness, Armageddon prophecy . . . ."[15] He further charges that this end-times view "has taken an unprecedented role under George W. Bush, as more and more Republicans think in apocalyptic terms and seek to shape domestic and foreign policy around religion."[16]

Privately-held, end-times, end-of-world beliefs can lead to possible foreign and military policy follies, according to David Neff, when he was managing editor of *Christianity Today* magazine:

> First, it may tempt us to help bring on Armageddon (by arming one side in the conflict). Second, it may offer the opposite temptation, to think that foreign policy doesn't matter since the Earth will be destroyed (leading us to ignore issues of justice and human rights).[17]

Currently, as I write this chapter, Barack Obama is in the third year of his presidency and fighting once again is raging between Israel and Palestine. Also, other Middle East and North African nations are engaged in domino rebellions. Even more threatening, the President of Iran has vowed to "wipe Israel off the map." It remains to be seen how Obama will handle the Middle East and what actions he will or will not take.

But what do modern-day wars in the Middle East, the present nation of Israel, America's involvement in Iraq and Afghanistan, famines, and earthquakes mean for the fulfillment of end-time biblical prophecy? As we shall see, *nothing! Absolutely nothing*!

"Wait a minute," the pro-Israel, end-saying contingent protests. Isn't end-time prophecy happening right before our eyes? Aren't the pieces of prophecy falling into place in Israel, fulfilling God's plan as revealed in the Bible? Won't Russia, Muslims, or somebody from the "north" invade Israel and begin the final Battle of Armageddon? The answer, I suggest, is no! But "the scary thing is that millions of Americans view politics through the foggy lens of prophetic inevitability."[18] Later in chapter six, we'll see who this "invader from the north" actually *was* (past tense).

So let me ask you. Do you not find it strange that not one "prophet" forecast the fall of the Berlin Wall in 1989, the demise of communism, the breaking apart of the Soviet Union, or the speedy victory of American forces against Iraq in both the first and second Persian Gulf Wars (despite our lengthy entanglement in the later)? They were all taken by surprise. Perhaps, as Hal Lindsey later admitted, "modern-day prophecy teachers have been a little too quick on the Armageddon trigger."

Moreover, have you ever wondered about how "pro-Israel" some Christians are, when—according to their end-time scenario—two-thirds of the Jews will be killed during a future, seven-year tribulation period and final Battle of Armageddon? This mass slaughter more than rivals the Nazi Holocaust and places Israel's most tragic days still ahead of them. Ironically, this view is rooted in the idea that God still "loves" the Jews and has a special future in store for them. Some of my Jewish friends don't think this view is so "pro-Israel." But this prevalent belief system (which originated in the 19th century) has major foreign policy and political implications. And its proponents have had the ear of several recent presidents of the United States.

... if the world is soon coming to an end, what is the point in trying to solve social injustice problems ...?

On September 5, 2003, I experienced a once-in-a-lifetime opportunity. I met, face-to-face, with the President of the United States and spoke with him for about fifty seconds. George W. Bush was in town for an election fundraiser. And since my wife is a state representative, she and I were invited to attend. After his speech and while he was signing autographs our paths crossed.

At the time, I was concerned because the press had been reporting that many high-profiled Christian endsayers had been meeting with him in the White House and trying to dissuade him from pursuing his plans for peace in Israel and the Middle East. So I began my conversation with him by saying, "I want to encourage you, Mr. President, and your 'Road Map for Peace' in Israel and the Middle East."

He briefly glanced up at me and said, "Thank you," as he continued signing autographs.

Then I plead, "Please do not be influenced by some Christians who do not think that peace is possible."

He stopped signing and looked directly into my eyes. "Oh, I believe it is possible," he assured me, nodding his head.

I mentioned to him that I had delivered a theological paper, titled *The Israel Illusion*, which supports this position and asked if he'd like a copy.[19] He said he would. I handed a copy to one of the Secret Service men. As we concluded our conversation, twice I assured him, "Blessed are the peacemakers, Mr. President. Blessed are the peacemakers."

He smiled and moved on down the line. Five months later, I received a personal letter from him (probably from someone on his staff) thanking me for the paper and my thoughtfulness. For me, it was quite an experience!

"This 'end-of-the-world' stuff just creates 'Chicken Little' people—people hiding under rocks waiting for the sky to fall, unwilling to come out and help the rest of us clean up the mess."

In this book, we will challenge many of the popular end-saying notions upon which Armageddon theology is based. Hopefully, you will see that our situation is not hopeless and that we, indeed, can help shape the course of history. You will also see why I do not think our efforts are in vain when we confront troubling world trends, strive to avoid or resolve wars, and deal with environmental and human justice issues.

In contrast to the views of historical fatalism, I will offer for your consideration a positive worldview that could blast us out of our complacency and motivate us to make a viable and significant difference in our world. Remember, as I reminded President Bush, Jesus said, "blessed are the peacemakers . . . ." (Matt. 5:9). And while our world is a dangerous place, peace and not destruction is God's modern-day program for our planet. And our world leaders need to know that there are solid biblical and historical reasons to strive for peace, and not be misguided by any view that says it is not attainable and that their efforts are in vain.

Compromising the Church

The foolish predictions that have been cascading off the shelves of Christian bookstores, contaminating Christian TV and radio programs, and spewing forth from many pulpits not only have been an embarrassment for the Church, but they have brought both the Bible and the Christian faith into disrepute. By and large, that is why secular media regard most Christians as prophecy junkies. They see us as psychologically addicted to Jesus-is-coming-soon beliefs and cataclysmic endsaying, much as the millions of supermarket tabloid readers are attracted to astrology and psychic sensationalism.

Sad to say, these next two cartoons, the first from *Christianity Today* magazine[20] and the second from *The Indianapolis Star*, September 25, 2004, portray our compromising addiction quite well:

Used by permission.

Used by permission.

Notably, the reestablishment of modern Israel in 1948 was the catalyst for the recent upsurge in the end-saying trend within Christianity. For many modern-day endsayers in the Church, it was the beginning of the biblical last days, and the first step in the final countdown to the end of the world. Hal Lindsey's bestseller, *The Late Great Planet Earth*, burst on the scene in 1970 and "confirmed" this event as the authentication of his end-time view. Lindsey then claimed that we are living in the last generation, the terminal generation. He assured his readers that the next event on God's prophetic timetable would be their "blessed-hope" (i.e., the "Rapture"—their removal from planet Earth just before horrible, too frightening-to-imagine, final events took place).

Although this view is advocated by a minority in Christendom, they are the most vocal, most televised, most broadcast, and most published. Therefore, this view is the one most often heard. It dominates Christian media, publishing, and marketing today for a good reason—millions of Christians love this sensationalism. They can't seem to get enough of it. They're obsessed with it. And Lindsey and others like him are sensational. But they have one severe drawback; when their prophecies do not come true, they simply revise them. We scarcely know what to expect next. But failed prophecies have a backlash—it can trigger laughter, scorn, disbelief, and discredit the entire faith.

Another satirical cartoon that appeared in the *Wall Street Journal* [21] shortly after the first Persian Gulf War illustrates a sad but undeniable truth; the Christian Church's end-saying tradition, and consequently the Church itself, has become a joke.

"Hey – you win some – you lose some . . ."

Used by permission.

In the eyes of the world, the whole Church is commonly lumped together with its failed prophets of doom. What's worse, the assumption is made that if the Church isn't right on its facts, it probably isn't right on its faith, either. Therefore, why take it seriously about anything at all? This is a major reason the Church is have difficulty being a relevant player and effective communicator in modern society.

What's even more troubling, Christianity—one of the major religions in the world—is in danger of being labeled a false religion. Repeated failures to predict Jesus' return and incessant endsaying by high-profile spokespersons are perceived as false promises, and false promises are perceived as lies. This is why a growing number of non-Christians have relegated the whole of Christianity to a failed cause. They continually mock and openly remind Christians that our founder "failed" to come again as and when He said He would, and as and when He was expected to by his supposedly Holy-Spirit-guided followers and writers of the New Testament (John 16:13). This leads to the perception that Christianity is an illusion, or worse, a delusion.

If you're a Christian, as I am, these accusations hurt. But let's face it; they are valid. And if truth sets you free, as Jesus said (John 8:32), what do you think error does? Fact is, few Christians have any idea how to combat or refute these criticisms. So before we get caught up, once again, in the cosmic curtain coming down in the Holy Land, or turn to another prophecy pundit for insight into "signs of the times," we'd be well advised to take another look at what the Bible really says or doesn't say about the end of the world, the end times, Jesus' second coming or return, and the new heaven and new earth. These are the four major foundational icons of the end-saying tradition that we'll address in the next four parts of this book.

Of course, all Christian endsayers claim the Bible as their authority. Many are reputable church leaders. An end-time urgency underscores their final-push pitches to frighten people into submission. Some think this approach will spur missionary efforts and cause people to run after God and eternal values as never before. But nowadays it's not working as well as it used to. In reality, this fear-based approach has had more of an opposite effect—paralyzing millions in end-time obsessions and fostering complacency, ineptness, and laziness. Fact is, most people unconsciously react to a message of doom with a feeling that nothing earthly really matters. In my opinion, it can no longer be claimed that endsaying inspires faith, hope, and outreach ministry. Rather, it inspires anxiety, paranoia, and surrender.

Christianity—one of the major religions in the world—is in danger of being labeled a false religion.

With its centuries-long legacy of failed and revised predictions, and wolf-cries of nearness, the whole Jesus-is-coming-soon, end-saying message does great harm and little good. What's more, the all-too-silent majority in the Church are offended by it. They consider these end-time claims outlandish and their scare tactics as cheap theatrics. "It's a 'sky is falling,' 'last days' religion," complained one pastor. "Its focus is on frantic appeals and quick fixes. Scare people into salvation, into giving money, into staying in church. It's one of the cruelest con games ever perpetrated on a lost world and in the Church itself."

Another pastor lamented, "Any religion that uses fear is questionable. Fear is the devil's tool. Too many of our brethren have tried to turn the 'good news' that Christ came to bring salvation to the world into the 'bad news' that He's poised ready at any moment to return and destroy it all."[22]

Another point that must be emphasized here is, in America and prior to the 20th century, the Church was culturally relevant, involved, and positive. Not so anymore. After the turn of the century, Hal Lindsey's pop-cultural brand of endsaying and its doomsday mentality spread like a wildfire through Christianity's evangelical ranks and devastated previous gains. Consequently, millions of Christians sit around defeated awaiting the so-called "rapture" and/or Christ's "second coming," or simply to die and go to Heaven—the seemingly major purpose for being a Christian, anyway. In this author's opinion, if the Church is to regain its influential and prominent role in modern society, what's needed is an impulse, a breakthrough, a reformational impetus backed by sound biblical and historical substance that will jolt us out of our termination mindset, scriptural confusion, and cultural complacency.

Kevin Phillips in his recent book *American Theocracy* surveys this territory and sums it up well. In his chapter titled "Radicalized Religion" he writes:

> In consequence, believers have time and time again had to work out elaborate explanations for why Jesus did not appear; why . . . claims had not been borne out. Books and videos detailing and amplifying these relentless embarrassments and disappointments—as far as I know, few such exist—might offer a useful counterpoint to the end-times and second-coming materials marketed in such profusion by current fundamentalist drummers.[23]

Now, one such book does exist. You hold it in your hands. I hope you will soon come to see this book as a voice of reason, a counterpoint, and a corrective in a sea of end-saying tumult. I believe it offers a fresh look at what God had in mind when He gave prophetic scriptures to humankind. Therefore, starting with our next chapter, we'll see how end-time Bible prophecy has been mishandled and misunderstood. We'll explore the basic flaw in the popular interpretive methods that has led to many false conclusions and other flaws—all of which attempt to cover up for the basic flaw.

In closing this chapter, three things must be changed. First, we in the Church must be true to Scripture and get our faith straightened out regarding the four foundational icons of endsaying—especially if we are going to legitimately profess the Bible as authoritative. Secondly, we need to craft a credible and effective apologetic (defense) in response to both our end-saying brethren and outside critics. Thirdly, we need to replace the negative, destructive, and unscriptural message of futuristic endsaying that has so infiltrated the Church with a positive, constructive, and scripturally accurate message. Once these changes are heard and tested (1 Thess. 5:21), I believe the face of Christianity will drastically change for the better—i.e., the way it's preached, practiced, and perceived. Should these changes happen, they may well lead to a greater (in effect) reformation than the Protestant Reformation of the 16th century.

But isn't the world really going to end someday? In our next chapter, we'll sift the wheat from the chaff, cut to the chase, and confront this popular-iconic myth, head-on, as we uncover the long and seemingly lost truth about the proverbial end of the world.

PART II: WHAT ABOUT THE END OF THE WORLD?

Chapter 3

Why the World Will Never End

As we've seen, endsaying (saying, "the end is near!") is nothing new. This long-standing, widespread, pop-culture tradition can be traced back for millennia. Never has there been a time when both intelligent and not-so-intelligent human beings didn't look around and become convinced that the world was going to end in their lifetime. We've heard it for so long and from so many different sources that the world is going to end; we assume it must be true. But is it?

Where can we turn for the truth about the end of the world? To a scientific theory? To another endsaying prophet? To a psychic's latest revelation? At best, human opinions come and go like waves lapping on the shore. Some might suggest that we turn to the historic creeds of the Church. But no creed mentions an end of the world, an end to human history, an end of time, or a demise of the planet. So where can we turn?

Since the end of the world concerns the creation made by God, we should go to the one book that tells us about his creation, the Bible. Down through the ages the majority of people have always wanted to know what the Bible has to say about the important issues of life. Modern-day polls indicate the same desire. Christians turn to the Bible because they believe that "all Scripture is God-breathed" (2 Tim. 3:16). Scholars turn to the Bible because of its literary prominence and great spiritual wisdom. By far, the Bible is the world's most popular book. For these reasons alone, the Bible should be our first source of information in this matter.

But the Bible is also the single most popular source of end-of-the-world speculations. From within its pages come a wide variety of cosmic-cataclysm and earth-catastrophe language. Nevertheless, only the Bible can provide solid answers to our questions. Yet we must let the Bible speak for itself. And as we shall soon see, *it's not the timing of the Bible-reading endsayers that has been wrong, it's the concept itself.*

In this chapter, we are about to discover a simple, yet profound, if not revolutionary idea, and one long overdue.

What the Bible Actually Says

What the Bible says about the end of the world is *nothing*! That's right—just like the historic creeds. *Nothing*! Many Bible teachers qualify "the End" by telling us that the world and human history will certainly end in its present form, or as we know it. What do these qualifying phrases mean? They don't know. Nobody knows. Yet they keep telling us this. The fact is, the world is always changing or coming to an end in its present form or as we know it, and a new one is continually coming into existence. Ask your parents or grandparents, if they are alive, if the world as they knew it hasn't changed.

What does the Bible say about the world ending as we know it or in its present form? Again, *nothing*! What did Jesus say about it? *Nothing*! What does the Bible say about an end of time or end of human history? Again, *nothing*! Not a single text, taken in a literal, plain, straightforward context, declares the world will ever end. As unpleasant as this truth may be for some, the end of the world is simply a false and pagan doctrine that's been dragged into the Church and read into the Bible. This revelation should be a major wake-up call to all endsayers.

But wait a minute! you protest. I've been reading Dr. Billy Graham's newspaper column for years and he says the Bible says:

- "everything we see around us has had a beginning (and will have an end);"[1]
- "the world will definitely end some day."[2]
- "Heaven is real – more real than the ground you walk on or the stars you see at night, because some day they'll all come to an end, but heaven will remain."[3]

With all due respect, once again, to this revered man of God, and one with whom I agree on so many other points of faith, the emphatic answer to that assertion is, *it does not!*

Moreover, relying on who says what will not settle this matter. Only specific statements from Scripture will do, as we agree to "test everything. Hold on to the good . . . ." (1 Thess. 5:21). Nothing is exempt from this scriptural admonishment. And the fact is, there is no clear statement that teaches an end of the world, an end of time, or an end of human history. *None!*[4]

Likewise, not one iota of evidence exists that 1st-century Jews, the early Christians, or any New Testament writer (men guided by the Holy Spirit, according to John 16:13) anticipated an end to the human race or the demise of planet Earth. It is not, as some believe, a profound and glorious doctrine of the Church, even though many throughout church history have espoused it. This terminal belief must be exposed for what it is—again, a false assumption that has been arbitrarily read into Scripture.

The biblical truth about the end of the world is contained within the biblical phrase "world without end, Amen." The Bible says that the world had a beginning, but is without end . . . "from the beginning of the world . . . . throughout all ages, world without end. A-men" (Eph. 3:9, 21, KJV).

As we have seen, the *Gloria Patri*, the famous doxology and confessional of the historic Church, emphasizes and confirms this biblical truth and understanding:

> Glory be to the Father, and to the Son, and to the Holy Ghost.
> As it was in the beginning, is now and ever shall be.
> World without end, Amen.

A pastor friend of mine declared in astonishment one day, "I've said and sung this doxology so often in church and never stopped to realize what it meant." He added, "it's tragic that so many of us, so often, have repeated this biblical phrase in our services without ever stopping to consider what it means."

What does "world without end, Amen" mean, anyway? It means exactly what it says: the world (or age) is not going to end! It's endless. Earlier I said that the truth about the end of the world is contained within this biblical phrase. I stated it this way because in the original Greek language of the New Testament, the phrase translated as "world without end" in the King James Bible is an idiom and is translated differently in other, more modern translations. Some versions read, "throughout all generations (ages) for ever and ever!" Literally in the Greek, it reads "into all generations of the age of the ages." As an idiom, the actual meaning of the phrase is greater than, and cannot be directly understood, from its literal words. But every translation of this Greek idiomatic phrase contains the same basic truth.

The meaning of the word translated as "age" (*olam* in Hebrew and *aion* in the Greek) is "an indefinite and/or unknown period of time." And, of course, every age has a beginning and an end and a duration that could be either long or short. Therefore, an age does not mean "forever." In Ephesians 3:21, however, the verse contains both the singular "age" and the plural "ages." The reason for this double employment is because neither the Hebrew nor Greek language had a separate word for the concept of eternity, foreverness, or endlessness. That's why throughout the Old and New Testaments both of these ancient languages used a range of phrases employing the word "age" in a hyperbolic and idiomatic fashion.[5] The more this word was employed in a phrase, the more intensified was the meaning of what might best be translated as *forever*. Examples of these phrases in an increasing and intensifying order are:

- "unto the age" (singular)
- "unto the ages" (plural)
- "unto the age of the age" (double singular)
- "unto the age of ages" (singular and plural)
- "unto the ages of the ages" (double plural)

Hence, this double use of age (singular) and ages (plural) in Ephesians 3:21 is a way of saying forever. One thing, however, is for sure. This idiom cannot mean its opposite. Therefore, "world without end" or "forever and ever" are preferred translations that emphasize the concept of permanence, eternalness, endlessness, everlastingness, perpetuity. These translations clash with any idea of an end of the world, end of human history, or end of time.[6] The world, time, and the present new-covenant age simply do not have an end.[7]

The translation "world without end" is also a contra positive. In literary style, a contra positive is used to make the meaning more emphatic, like John F. Kennedy's famous phrase, "ask not what your country can do for you . . . ." Biblical statements, too, are sometimes made more powerful by using a negative. Are they not? Instead of strengthening a point by using a superlative, the statement is emphasized by using a negative. "I am not ashamed of the gospel of Christ" (Rom. 1:16 KJV) is an example. What it really means is, I am exulting in it, I am proud of it.

The "amen" following "world without end" makes the phrase even more emphatic. Amen affirms the contrapositive proclamation and adds the meaning, "so may it be in accordance with the will of God." What we end up with, then, is a double strengthening and emphasis of the certainty of this Greek idiom that the world (or age) is without end (i.e., is going to continue forever and ever).

Over the centuries, many attempts have been made to evade the plain meaning of certain biblical phrases. This one is no exception. Contrast this message from God's Word to the many voices that keep trying to predict the end of the world. Doesn't this explain the reason why endsaying prophets of doom throughout history have continually been proven wrong? As I've stated before, it's not their timing that is wrong. It's their concept that is wrong. As failed prophets of a false premise, they have been continually trying to predict something that's not going to happen. In their folly, they've ignored or rejected the transcendent truth of the Bible and the historic proclamation of the Church that "the world is without end, Amen."

Consequently, endsaying can be compared to crying wolf when there is no wolf. In this case, they've been crying, "End! End!" but there is no end of the world. It's a basic foundational flaw of all endsaying and a concept that's headed for the scrap heap of history. Moreover, we've been programmed by it for too long. The world is never, repeat never-ever, going to end. We live in a never-ending world. How can we be so sure? We can repeat the old rhyme, "How do I know? The Bible tells me so."

A few hundred years ago, according to myth, some in Europe believed that the world was flat, had an edge, and that if you sailed far enough, you would fall off and die.[8] This flat earth concept is clearly contradicted by the Bible. Eight centuries before Christ, the prophet

Isaiah declared that the earth is a "circle" (Isa. 40:22). Twenty-three centuries later with this revelation and other convictions from the Bible, Christopher Columbus set sail and discovered the New World. We're glad he did.

---

it's not their timing that is wrong. It's their concept that is wrong. As failed prophets of a false premise, they have been continually trying to predict something that's not going to happen.

Now, in our day and time, everyone knows that the earth is a sphere. We've seen the pictures of it from outer space! Perhaps centuries from now the inhabitants of planet Earth will be glad that we have rediscovered the age-old, biblical truth of "world without end, Amen." Unfortunately, many people have trouble accepting new ideas. They raise objections and issue threats against those who bring them. I, however, believe the world is without end because the Bible says it is, and will continue proving it. "World without end, Amen" is a strong, direct statement from God's Word. It cannot be ignored or diminished. We can count on it, Hal Lindsey *et al's* opinions notwithstanding.

Yet this declaration does not exhaust the biblical evidence that the world is without end—far from it.

God Promised Never Again to Destroy the World

Twice, since the flood in Noah's day, God has promised not to destroy the world. He made these two promises to Noah on behalf of all humanity for all time. They are recorded in the Old Testament and the Torah book of Genesis as a record of his faithfulness and trustworthiness.

Promise 1: "Never again will I [God] curse the ground because of man, even though every inclination of his heart is evil from childhood. And never again will I destroy all living creatures, as I have done. As long as the earth endures [remains], seedtime and harvest, cold and heat, summer and winter, day and night will never cease." (Gen. 8:21b-22)

Promise 2: "Never again will all life be cut off by the waters of a flood; never again will there be a flood to destroy the earth." (Gen. 9:11b)

For centuries, theologians have debated what these two promises really mean. Most agree they are eternal promises and depend solely upon the reliability of God. But most also surmise that the second one is a disclaimer or qualifier of the first. They assume God placed this later restriction on his first promise, and argue that since God "destroyed" the world once by a flood, the sum total of these two promises is that He has only limited Himself by how He can destroy it the next time. That is, He is supposedly free to use any method other than water (such as fire, colliding planets, nuclear bombs, or even bowling balls) to destroy it all or end it as we know it. Or, is He free to do this? After all, what is the value of a promise?

What is at stake here is the fundamental question of the reliability of God. Nowhere else in the Bible does God take away from any of his other eternal promises. If God or you or I can make a promise and then come back a little while later and diminish what we promised, can this be considered trustworthy or faithful?

Let me illustrate this point by being absurd. Suppose I go on a mad rampage and destroy my house by hacking up some of or all the furniture and chopping holes in the walls with a long-handle ax. Then I promise my wife and kids that "Never again will I destroy all the furniture and the walls, as I have done. As long as the house endures [remains]." A few days later, however, I tell them, "Never again will all the furniture be cut to pieces and holes poked in the walls by a long-handle ax; never again will there be a long-handled ax to destroy the house."

What will I have promised? Would my second promise reduce the commitment of the first? Would the first greater promise be diminished by the lesser second one? Would the first one then be null and void, freeing me to choose any other method (fire, bulldozer, bombs, chainsaw, or bowling balls)? How could my wife and kids ever again trust any promise if all I had to do was come back a little later and change things by making a lesser promise or issuing a qualifying disclaimer? My family would never buy it. Neither would yours, and neither should we. God is trustworthy and faithful. He is not playing games with his promises. We can rely fully on both of them.

Why not just take God's Word at face value here? If we do, his second promise does not compromise his first. He simply made two independent promises about the same topic separated by ten verses of scripture—not one promise plus a disclaimer. Each one stands on its own merits and is subject to its own contingencies.

Granted, God's second promise is contingent upon a flood method. There's no question about that. Special notice should be given, however, to the fact that planet Earth remained intact both during and after the flood; nor did time end, even though the world was said to have been destroyed.

God's first promise, conversely, is not contingent upon the phrase, "as I have done," but upon the conditional phrase, "as long as the earth endures [remains]." Please notice that God did not say "as long as I allow the earth to endure." So how long does the earth endure [remain]? Elsewhere, the Bible tells us, "Generations come and generations go, but the earth endures [remains] forever" (Eccl. 1:4).

God's promise is contingent upon the earth's immortality, which is forever.[9] The Psalmist further confirms that the earth is established forever (Psa. 78:69) and that the earth and its foundations shall not be removed, ever (Psa. 104:5; see also Psa. 93:1; 96:10; 119:90). This applies to the whole material universe that He created, as well. Both moon and sun are eternally established as faithful witnesses in the sky (Psa. 89:36-37), as are the highest heavens (Psa. 148:4, 6). Eternalness is not only an attribute ascribed to God and his glory, it's also an attribute ascribed to his creation. That's one reason why Psalm 19:1 states, "The heavens declare the glory of God; the skies proclaim the work of his hands."

It is important to note again that God has never diminished any of his promises in the Bible, but only enhanced them. Likewise, no scripture can be used to negate or diminish another scripture. They all fit together in harmony and consistency. We have many corroborating scriptures stating that not only is the world without end, but the moon, the sun, and the heavens endure [remain] forever, as well.

**Eternalness is not only an attribute
ascribed to God and his glory,
it's also an attribute ascribed to his creation.**

The second stanza of the classic hymn of the Church, "Great Is Thy Faithfulness," picks up on a portion of this great enduring truth from God's first promise to never again destroy the world:

> Summer and winter, and springtime and harvest,
> Sun, moon and stars in their courses above.
> Join with all nature in manifold witness,
> To Thy great faithfulness, mercy and love.
> Great is Thy faithfulness, Great is Thy faithfulness . . .[10]

The Psalmist further writes, "Your faithfulness continues through all generations; you established the earth and it endures [forever]" (Psa. 119:90).

Moses, in the 14th century B.C., wrote, "Know therefore that the Lord your God is God; he is the faithful God, keeping his covenant of love to a thousand generations of those who love him and keep his commands" (Deut. 7:9; also 1 Chron. 16:15-17; Psa. 105:7-10).

This passage is to be understood figuratively and as an understatement. But even if we reduce Moses' thousand generations to a literal level and assume that a generation is forty years, then that equals 40,000 years. Approximately 3,400 years have transpired since God directed Moses to write these words in the book of Deuteronomy. If my mathematics are correct, that leaves us with at least 36,600 years yet to go. What do you think people 100, 200, 5,000, 7,000 and 10,000 years from now will think of our 21st-century, end-of-the-world musings? Someday future generations may view our 21st century as a primitive and unenlightened time, especially on this topic of the end of the world.

God's plan since the flood has not been to deal with human sin by eliminating the human race or by destroying his creation. If we think otherwise, we've misunderstood his plan of redemption. "For God so loved the world that he gave his one and only Son . . . . For God did not send his Son into the world to condemn the world . . . ." (John 3:16a, 17a). And neither should we condemn it by saying it's going to end, when Scripture clearly states that it's without end and therefore not ever going to end.[11]

Rest assured that the future stability and everlasting nature of the earth and the cosmos are secure. They are grounded in the trustworthiness of the Almighty God who "perfectly" created the universe in the first place. As the Creator and Controller of the universe, He has personally pledged to forever sustain and protect all life from total destruction by his grace and his great faithfulness. This includes all animal life, as well. So, in whom shall we believe? In God's promises, grace, and great faithfulness? Or, in Hal Lindsey, Nostradamus, the Mayans, and other endsayers who are trying to predict worldwide catastrophe and destruction of all living things, even the whole universe (which certainly isn't contaminated by sin)?

Apocalyptic Language and Its Fulfillments

Falling stars, bloody moons, darkened sun, shaking earth, signs in the sky . . . this collapsing-universe, cosmic-cataclysm language is employed throughout the Bible. In our modern-day minds it sounds like the end of the world. But scattered throughout biblical history, and mostly overlooked by the pop-culture prophecy writers, are numerous uses and fulfillments of this apocalyptic language. Determining and knowing the non-literal but real nature of these previous uses and fulfillments will enable us to make proper sense of this biblical language.

Nonetheless, the popular stream of endsayers has ignored this consistent string of scriptural precedents. Instead, they have assumed that the Bible's apocalyptic language must be interpreted literally and physically, and that since no one has witnessed a cataclysmic, earth-ending event of this nature, its time must lie in the future. The shock value of earthquakes, exploding stars, cosmic eclipses, and nuclear holocausts is awesome. Thus, a literal/physical rendering of the Bible's apocalyptic texts serves the purpose of endsayers, and has become fixed in the minds of millions of Americans.

The problem with this line of thought is that no biblical grounds exist for this assumption. What's worse, it's an obviously flawed method of interpretation. It ignores the biblical precedent and pattern of fulfillment. This is not the way to approach the Scriptures. When we fail to give proper attention to the historical usages and fulfillments, we do a grave injustice to understanding the Bible's use of apocalyptic language.

Let us look at some of the Bible's apocalyptic descriptions of cosmic disaster and see how they were actually fulfilled. This type of language has always been associated with another major, Old Testament theme:

the coming of "the day of the Lord." Only when we view these poetic figures of speech from within their numerous historical contexts can we properly apply them to our own time. Without this historical perspective, we are guaranteed to misinterpret their meaning, committing the error of eisegesis—reading one's own preconceived ideas back into the text. This is not wise if one sincerely desires to know what the text is talking about.

When we fail to give proper attention to the historical usages and fulfillments, we do a grave injustice to understanding the Bible's use of apocalyptic language . . . . this is not wise . . . .

As we allow the Bible to shed light on itself, we'll see that this type of apocalyptic language always depicted a coming judgment of God. Its use and this mindset were in full bloom in Bible times. Jesus used this same language, as did many New Testament writers, and added no disclaimers that they were using it any differently. Its roots are in the Old Testament, and 1st-century Jews were steeped in it, not only from ancient Scriptures but also from inter-testament literature dating back to the 4th century B.C. Consequently, they expected apocalyptic fulfillments to be quite different from what most of us today have been led to believe. Here are some examples from the Old Testament:

Isaiah 13:10, 13. "The stars of heaven and their constellations will not show their light. The rising sun will be darkened and the moon will not give its light . . . . Therefore I will make the heavens tremble; and the earth will shake from its place at the wrath of the Lord Almighty, in the day of his burning anger."

Fulfillment. The prophet was *not* speaking of the end of the world, a final judgment, or a solar or lunar eclipse. He was giving a figurative prediction of the literal destruction of Babylon by the Medes in 539 B.C. (Isa. 13:1). The use of cosmic language means the Presence of God was involved and revealed in this judgment upon these people.

Isaiah 34:4. "All the stars of heaven will be dissolved and the sky rolled up like a scroll; all the starry host will fall like withered leaves from the vine, like shriveled figs from the fig tree."

Fulfillment. This was *not* the end of the world, or the end of the cosmos, but a figurative description of the coming divine destruction of Edom in the late 6th century B.C. (Isa. 34:5).

Ezekiel 32:7, 8a. ". . . I will cover the heavens and darken their stars; I will cover the sun with a cloud, and the moon will not give its light. All the shining lights in the heavens I will darken over you."

Fulfillment. This prophecy was God's warning to the Pharaoh of Egypt of his impending fall in the mid-6th century B.C. (Ezek. 32:2).

Nahum 1:5. "The mountains quake before him and the hills melt away. The earth trembles at his presence, the world, and all who live in it."

Fulfillment. The subject is God's coming in judgment on the city of Nineveh, and not the physical world, in 612 B.C. (Nahum 1:1).

Isaiah 40:4. "Every valley shall be raised up, every mountain and hill made low; the rough ground shall become level, the rugged places a plain."

Fulfillment. This is not a reference to a giant excavation job, but a description of the 1st-century ministry of John the Baptist (Matt. 3:1-3; Isa. 40:3).

Joel 2:30, 31. "I will show wonders in the heavens and on the earth, blood and fire and billows of smoke. The sun will be turned to darkness and the moon to blood before the coming of the great and dreadful day of the Lord."

Fulfillment. Joel was not describing the end of the world. He was giving a figurative description of the actual events accompanying the coming of the Holy Spirit on the day of Pentecost. Peter said it was fulfilled in their day (Acts 2:16-21). We'll see that this "day of the Lord" (actually, "the day of Christ") followed less than forty years later.

The Old Testament pattern of figurative language usage and numerous fulfillments by literal, real, momentous, and divine judgment events sets the precedent. If the words of these passages were to be taken literally, it would mean that massive changes or destructions of the cosmos and earth occurred numerous times. But the language transcends its literalism and has to be understood figuratively. It's associated with and really and truly describes the literal coming of God's judgment upon a people or nation.

Next let's look at some uses found in the New Testament. These prophesied another, soon-coming-judgment event:

Matthew 24:29. ". . . the sun will be darkened, the moon will not give its light; the stars will fall from the sky, and the heavenly bodies will be shaken."

Fulfillment. Jesus is speaking in the same apocalyptic terms drawn from the language of the prophets cited above, a language very familiar to 1st-century Jews. As we shall see in subsequent chapters, He was figuratively describing the coming judgment and fall of Jerusalem in A.D. 66-70—an event as serious and severe as God's judgments upon people and nations in the Old Testament.

2 Peter 3:10, 11a. "But the day of the Lord will come like a thief. The heavens will disappear with a roar; the elements will be destroyed by fire, and the earth and everything in it will be laid bare. Since everything will be destroyed in this way, what kind of people ought you to be?"

Fulfillment. Again, Peter is employing the same common apocalyptic terminology of his day (2 Pet. 3:2). His words are no more to be taken literally/physically than are any of the others above. As we shall see later in this book, the figurative fulfillment about which he was warning came upon his contemporaries in a way [nature] totally consistent with all the other apocalyptic fulfillments cited above.

So what should we learn from the above perspective? One thing is for sure—the Bible's use of this collapsing-universe, cosmic-cataclysm, apocalyptic language is well-developed, consistently employed, and highly pragmatic! No disclaimers, qualifications, or changes are ever recorded or hinted at by Jesus or any New Testament writer who used this identical language. What, then, would cause us to interpret this apocalyptic symbolism differently today? If we do so, without legitimate justification, isn't this interpretation by exception and a violation of proper and honest interpretation methodology?

Many more examples could be cited, but that would belabor the point. Even though it sounds like the end of the world, this apocalyptic language of the Bible is a common and frequently used linguistic style. It's the language of the prophets and it's employed throughout the Old and New Testaments in an identical manner. It's the Bible's method of metaphorically describing actual, literal events—specifically, God's coming judgments upon nations, peoples, or cities that have been enemies of his people; or his judgment upon his own people, Israel. The physical means employed are always those of invading foreign armies or natural disasters. These many biblical judgments are also events of international and/or eschatological importance. In every instance, the "worlds" (social, political, and religious) of those receiving this judgment of God were ended or dramatically changed. So complete and comprehensive was each judgment event that it was appropriately spoken of in hyperbolic, world-ending terms. Speaking appropriately does not require that one speak literally. Please note that in none of these historical fulfillments did the physical nature of literal heavenly bodies or the earth change *one iota*.

And yet you might legitimately ask if it is possible that a literal/physical, time-ending, universe-destroying, cosmic-crashing event can be an additional fulfillment? Can apocalyptic language using symbolism and poetic imagery be taken both figuratively and literally? Some theologians argue that they can, terming such a case a double or multiple fulfillment. But is this possible here?

Certainly, a future cosmic destruction could be within the sovereignty and capability of a God who many believe spoke the world into existence in the first place (see Gen. 1). But to break the pattern of biblical precedent by suddenly literalizing apocalyptic terms and phrases and applying them to the destruction of the physical universe, *without an expressed biblical warrant to do so*, is to misunderstand the Bible on the Bible's own terms.

The Jews of the 1st century did not understand apocalyptic phraseology as literally ending the world. And neither Jesus nor any New Testament writer amended this common Jewish understanding when employing this linguistic form. Doing so in our day is totally arbitrary and completely reprehensible. It only confuses and leads readers away from what this kind of language always meant and how it was consistently fulfilled when it was used. Nor is a literal rendering in harmony with the scriptures we have cited that proclaim eternalness.

On the other hand, when God wanted to express his blessings upon a nation or a people, the same apocalyptic language is used, but in positive terms. Instead of the earth or the universe pictured as collapsing or destroyed, they're shown to be abundant, flourishing, and more strongly established. Note the following.

Isaiah 30:26; 60:19-20. "The moon will shine like the sun, and the sunlight will be seven times brighter, like the light of seven full days, when the Lord binds up the bruises of his people and heals the wounds he inflicted . . . . The sun will no more be your light by day, nor will the brightness of the moon shine on you, for the Lord will be your everlasting light, and your God will be your glory. Your sun will never set again, and your moon will wane no more; The Lord will be your everlasting light, and your days of sorrow will end."

Fulfillment. Portrays the blessings promised to Old Covenant Israel if they submitted to God and were obedient.

Isaiah 35:1, 6. "The desert and the parched land will be glad; the wilderness will rejoice and blossom. Like the crocus, it will burst into bloom; it will rejoice greatly and shout for joy . . . . Then will the lame leap like a deer and the tongue of the dumb shout for joy. Water will gush forth in the wilderness and streams in the desert."

Fulfillment. The figurative language describes actual kingdom blessings brought by Jesus. He proclaimed them in like manner when He declared, "'Whoever believes in me, as the Scripture has said, streams of living water will flow from within him.' By this he meant the Spirit, whom those who believed in him were later to receive." (John 7:38, 39a).

Both positive (blessing) and negative (judgment) symbolism were well understood in the synagogues of the 1st century. We Americans use symbols today, too. For example, if I said that I love the Colts, the Bears, the Bulls, or the Dolphins, would you think I was an animal lover? Or, if I showed you a cartoon of an elephant and a donkey fighting each other, what would that mean to you?

On the other hand, when God wanted to express his blessings upon a nation or a people, the same apocalyptic language is used, but in positive terms.

The interpretation of apocalyptic language is taught to us by the Bible itself. This precedent should serve as a caution to any modern-day interpreter toying with the idea of breaking this long-established pattern.[12] With a proper historical understanding of the Bible's consistent use of apocalyptic language in mind, we moderns would be wise to follow it. We must conclude from the Bible itself that God isn't going to destroy the world. That leaves only us.

Could We Really End the World If We Planned It?

Psalm 24:1 declares that "The earth is the Lord's and the fullness thereof" (KJV; see also 1 Cor. 10:26; Exod. 9:29). In Job 38:33, God states that He is the one who has "dominion over the earth." These passages are meant to remind us that we live in God's world, not ours. He created it. He owns it. He sustains it (Heb. 1:3). We are not the owners, but mere stewards, and we're only here for a short stay.

Therefore, it is legitimately debatable whether we humans, as irresponsible stewards, could really end the world even if we sat down and planned it. Allow me to illustrate this point by being absurd, again.

If we:

- Exploded all our nuclear bombs at one time, or in a chain reaction? It's doubtful we could blow up the world once, let alone four-times-over,[13] or affect its orbit, axis, or rotation. How much of all life would be permanently impacted? Remember Bikini in the Marshall Islands? It has recovered rather nicely after 23 nuclear explosions in the 1940s and 1950s.
- Took a direct hit by a massive asteroid? Would that do the job? The other side of the world would probably notice no difference. After all, Jupiter seems to be surviving rather well after massive, multi-comet crashes in 1994.

- Poured all our waste directly into the waters, onto the land, or spewed it into the air. Sure, this would be terrible. But could we really destroy all life before contravening variables intervened?
- Melted the polar ice caps or started a new ice-age? It's reasonably arguable how much of humanity would be lost, given our high-tech knowledge and survival capabilities nowadays.
- Let the population explosion grow on unabated? Again, how far would it go before contravening variables began to interfere?

Absurd statements? Of course. And best-case scenarios would be catastrophic. But could we humans really destroy, terminate, and end God's world?

Let us bear in mind that the scientific community greatly disagrees about possible environmental apocalyptic scenarios. For example, many reputable scientists tell us that most pollution arises from natural causes, like volcanic eruptions, geysers, and forest fires, which vastly outdo people in producing major pollutants. They contend that the earth has far more power to destroy itself than we do, and the earth has been doing this for eons. It also keeps regenerating itself.

Furthermore, the earth's fullness is much bigger than we tend to think. It is so easy to underestimate the earth's immensity and resiliency to heal itself when we're sitting inside our four-walled buildings. It's not that "little globe" sitting on the shelf. Those of us who have climbed mountains, sailed the seas, or gazed into spacious skies over fruited plains may have a small sense for how large our planet truly is and how impossible it would be for us tiny surface dwellers to destroy it, even if we tried.

But the clincher in this author's opinion is God would thwart our plans. If we human beings ever sat down and attempted to plan out "our" planet's demise, or even started coming close due to gross mismanagement (assuming we could destroy it), I suspect God would confound our plans, just as He confused the builders of the tower of Babel (Gen. 11:1-9). After all, the earth belongs to Him. He has dominion over it. And his stated will and purpose is that the earth be filled with his glory, not destroyed (Num. 14:21; Isa. 6:3; Hab. 2:14).

But what about the Second Law of Thermodynamics, also termed "entropy" or "energy degradation?" some one may object. This law (actually, it's only a theory or conclusion[14]) states that any order in a closed system will eventually wind down, move toward decay, and dissipate.   Some scientists using the Hubble Space Telescope "confirmed" this suspicion for the universe. They reported that the sun is burning out and that we may only have five billion years to figure out what to do about it. But let's think about this possibility further.

First, it has not been proven that earth resides in a closed thermodynamic system—nor our universe, for that matter. And "strong new evidence" presented by other astronomers also using the Hubble Space Telescope contradicts this leading theory/law. They now claim the universe is expanding and "will continue expanding forever instead of snapping back in a 'big crunch.'"[15]

Secondly and most importantly, if it's true that God originally spoke the entire universe into existence—and the majority if not all the scientific evidence points to this type of creation event—then He certainly should be able to transcend or override the Second Law of Thermodynamics any time He desires, shouldn't He? After all, God is sovereign over the laws of thermodynamics, as He is over everything. If a little more sun or cosmic substance of any kind is someday needed, all He need do is simply speak a little more of it into existence. Likewise, if the speed of light slows down too much—as some scientists worry about—He could give it a boost. These divine acts would be minor tweaks compared to the task of creating it all out of nothing in the first place, wouldn't they?

The bottom line is that it's legitimately debatable—make that doubtful—that we small specks of dust confined to the earth's massive surface as it spins and flies through outer space at astronomical speed could terminate this planet and/or kill all life upon it. Sure, we can inflict great harm, perhaps even irrevocable harm in our so-called exploitation of God's world. But, and once again, He created it. He owns it. He sustains it (Heb. 1:3). Contained in its "fullness" is a strongly entrenched resiliency, full of contravening variables.

Another point worth reconsidering is, while it's true that earth's limits are finite, we most likely are not close to pressing against those limits or surpassing the planet's so-called carrying capacity. And contrary to some opinions, the earth's health is not fragilely balanced, delicately poised, or precariously teetering on a knife's edge.

In the best-selling book and blockbuster movie *Jurassic Park*, the character of Malcolm said it quite well:

> Let me tell you about our planet . . . . Our planet [has] . . . a background of continuous and violent upheaval, mountain ranges thrust up and eroded away, cometary impacts, volcanic eruptions, oceans rising and falling, whole continents moving . . . . Endless, constant and violent change . . . . Even today, the greatest geographical feature on the planet comes from two great continents colliding, buckling to make the Himalayan mountain range . . . . The planet has survived everything, in its time. It will certainly survive us . . . . This planet is not in jeopardy. We are in jeopardy. We haven't got the power to destroy the planet—or to save it. [16]

Please Don't Misunderstand

In this chapter, I do not intend to send an anti-environmentalist message. To the contrary, irresponsible stewardship of any type (war, pollution, overuse of resources, short food supplies, etc.) can severely damage the quality and quantity of life on this planet, or on portions of it. But the rain will still fall and the sun will still shine. Life as we know it would be different, inhospitable, perhaps unthinkable, but eventually the earth would recover. It is legitimately debatable whether we humans, intentionally or unintentionally, could destroy this amazing sphere on which we live so briefly, even if we wanted to. We can't come close to duplicating the powerful forces of nature which have been polluting and damaging earth's environment for eons of time. And the earth has survived it all. More than likely, it will survive you, me, our kids, and endless generations to come.

There is a Latin saying worth noting: *Nemo contra mundum nisi deus ipse.* "Nothing can destroy the world but God Himself," and He has promised not to!

Chapter 4

What a 'World without End' Message Could Mean

There is one thing stronger than all the armies in the world;
and that is an idea whose time has come.
Victor Hugo

The recovery of a world that is "without end, Amen" is an idea whose time has come. Its power to influence the human psyche and thus the future course of history cannot be overestimated. In this author's opinion, the unleashing of this truth is destined to change the cultural and theological landscape. Entire schemes of religious and non-religious teaching focusing on a future end of the world have run their course; their prophecies have not come true. Instead of striving to hang on till the end, we can have a strong reason to undertake dynamic roles in the present, both individually and corporately, for a better future and for the benefit of current and coming generations.

Pioneering a new idea, however, is rarely a popular work, at least at first. Historically, the "powers that be" usually reacted angrily whenever confronted with an upsetting truth. Voltaire, the 18th-century French philosopher, hit it on the head when he surmised, "Our wretched species is so made that those who walk on the well-trodden path always throw stones at those who are showing a new road."

Our road is really not new, but so old and so neglected that it seems new. Thus, it will likely suffer the usual reactions of anger and disbelief. Admittedly, the idea of a world without end is a threat to the status quo, which is dominated by a traditional termination futurism, be it Roman Catholics or Protestants. They view "evil" as simply too much for God to overturn and transform. Therefore, God "must" destroy the planet before He makes it "anew" (more on this in our last chapter). But after a reformational idea bursts onto the public scene and awareness spreads, a paradigm shift begins to take place as people at the grassroots level begin to realize how much the value of the new outweighs the detriments of the old.

A New Paradigm Shift

The word paradigm comes from the Greek *pardeigma* (*para*, side by side + *deiknynai*, to show, point out). A paradigm is a model, a pattern, a frame of reference, a worldview, or simply a way of thinking for understanding and interpreting external reality. It's the way we "see" the world, not visually but by perception. It is the mental framework by which we construe reality, process information, make decisions, and determine actions. For individuals, it brings order and meaning to our experiences. It's also at the very heart of any culture.

Pioneering a new idea, however, is rarely a popular work, at least at first. Historically, the "powers that be" usually reacted angrily whenever confronted with an upsetting truth.

Our paradigm answers our most basic question: what is real? If one's paradigm is the correct way of seeing the world, then one's judgments, decisions, and actions will be correlated and productive. If it's distorted or incorrect, they will be skewed. In practice, a person may not live what he or she professes, but that person will always live in accordance with his or her paradigm. In other words, we live out what we truly believe and think. Consequently, when our paradigm shifts, many things will change.

Our view of the world and the future is a paradigm. As we've seen, millions have been programmed into believing in an end-of-the-world paradigm. Most of them are simply following the way they have been raised or parroting what they've heard others say. But many are in bondage to this paradigm, venerating it as a religious icon. They are afraid to raise questions. Some actually want the world to end and even imagine it as a wondrous happening. Call it a termination wish. They see "the End" as God's, and their own, final vindication, and as their best opportunity to escape from the toils and responsibilities of this life, even from death itself. For them the idea that "the world's going to end" sounds so right. They are comfortable with it. Few have bothered to check the Scripture for themselves, and most are unaware of the Bible's clear and concise promises to the contrary.

It's time this future-destroying deception and fear-mongering crime against humanity was stopped. We need to let go of this myth and stand up against this icon with something of substance. It's time for a paradigm shift—a mental transformation for how we imagine our world—that offers a new, optimistic, and opportunistic perspective on the future of the future. Yet changes of this nature are never easy, often take time, and are usually achieved incrementally. But now, after the inconsequential turn of millennium, I predict a paradigm shift away from the tyranny of termination and into the hopeful, scriptural truth of a world without end.

This new, open-ended paradigm will force us to reexamine and rethink other end-time assumptions, prophecies, and beliefs, and our role in an unending world. We'll address three more of these end-associated icons in this book's next three Parts. But if this world is, indeed, a world without end, and eternally established by a Creator God, isn't our role in taking care of it, and of each other, even more significant? Doesn't this provide more reason, motivation, and responsibility to pass it along to future generations in a better condition than we found it?

A Greater Responsibility Recap

Ideas and beliefs have consequences. And, as we've seen, 'end-of-the-world' predictions and tirades are pervasive. They have infected the whole world. Even when viewed as nonsense, the cumulative effects of this incessant pounding and their urgent warnings still take a toll. Few are immune. And incredibly, millions keep falling for it. So check this highlighting recap out:

- ✓ Socially, it leaves its mark on the human psyche and on our dreams and goals— especially on those of our youth.
- ✓ Culturally, it diminishes our willingness to make commitments and get involved in social injustice and human needs issues, or to invest in long-term efforts to transform institutional structures. After all, if the future is fixed and terminal, why bother? So many who otherwise would be diligent stewards and productive workers tend to sink into helplessness, piety, and/or isolation.
- ✓ Politically, many fear the personal views of end-time Bible prophecy might influence the foreign policy decisions of the President of the United States and other world leaders— especially concerning the Middle East.
- ✓ Environmentally, it's a major reason why environmentalists face an uphill struggle—again, if there is no future for the future, why bother "polishing-brass-on-a-sinking-ship?"
- ✓ Theologically, wolf-cries of nearness and missed times and dates have been an embarrassment and discredited the Bible and the whole Church, making it appear like a joke in the eyes of the world. Therefore, many reason, why take Christianity seriously about anything?

The alternative and positive worldview of a world that never ends could blast many out of their complacency and motivate us to make a more viable and significant difference in our world for the benefit of present and future generations. Why so?

- ✓ Socially, because one's view of the future determines one's philosophy of life.
- ✓ Culturally, because the proliferation of end-of-the-world tirades and dates in American life is a significant reason why the optimism and activism of the 19th and early 20th century has changed to pessimism and withdrawal today.
- ✓ Politically, because world leaders need to know their efforts for world peace are not in vain but attainable, and have solid reasons to support that optimism.

✓ Environmentally, because a world that never ends demands we earthlings take better care of it than a world that's about to end, which is what we keep hearing from so many different sources, nowadays.

✓ Theologically, because the Church's long string of end-saying, fatalistic pundits is in dramatic contrast to and flies directly in the face of the optimistic beliefs of our forefathers in the faith who came to this country and founded its great institutions under Judeo-Christians principles. Sad to say, many Christians today would rather contemplate "the End" than pitch in with the job at hand.

In conclusion, endsaying (crying out "the end is near") must be termed for what it is—not just a deceptive con game but an age-old crime against humanity. Hence, it must be refuted, reformed, and replaced with solid substance, positive hope, and confidence in the future. This is exactly what readers of this book will find throughout the rest of these pages.

Not surprisingly, this dramatic change of paradigms in thought and belief herein being proposed will necessitate that we moderns become more responsible for passing our world onto future generations in better condition than we found it—socially, culturally, politically, environmentally, and theologically.

What This Paradigm Shift Means for the Church

For centuries, people in the Church have imposed on generation after generation of believers, and the rest of the world as well, the view that this world is doomed. Like the tobacco industry, we've been pulling the wool over everyone's eyes, including our own. But now we must face the biblical fact that what we have done is wrong—scripturally wrong! Our first task, therefore, must be to get our faith back in order. If the Church is to be taken seriously, it must clamp down on the steady drone of endsayers misinterpreting and exploiting Bible prophecy. It must lay aside these distractions. Then we can take this corrected faith to the world and expect much better results.

To begin this reformation process, let's summarize by comparing what the Bible actually says with what our traditions say on the issue we've been discussing so far:

The Bible Says:	The Endsaying Tradition Says:
World without end, Amen	The world's going to end
The earth remains forever	The earth shall be destroyed
Generations come and go	We may be the last generation

So who's right? A Christian should believe that the Bible is right. But, paradoxically, the Bible also teaches that an "appointed time . . . of the end" will "come," will "not prove false" and will "not delay" (Hab. 2:3). What's this end all about? How does this end relate to a world without end? It might be comforting to know that Jesus understood the difference. The writers of the New Testament understood the difference, as well.

Before we can teach a true and corrected faith to the world, we will need to understand the true, biblical meaning and fulfillment of Habakkuk's "appointed time . . . of the end." As we shall see, it's something quite different from the traditionally posited, cataclysmic end of the world. For this revelation, we must begin with the Old Testament book of Daniel. The timely, precise, and complete fulfillment of its key end-time prophecies will be the subject of our next three chapters.

PART III: THE DIVINE TIMEFRAME

Chapter 5

Don't Monkey with Daniel[*]

S omething was up, back then in Bible times. Something so big and so near that it prompted the 1st-century, Holy-Spirit-guided writers of the New Testament (John 16:13) to make or record such startling statements as . . .

- …the end of all things is at hand (1 Pet. 4:7 KJV)
- …the fullness of time was come (Gal. 4:4 KJV)
- …the time is fulfilled (Mark 1:15 KJV)
- …the fulfillment of the ages has come (1 Cor. 10:11)
- …the ends of the world [ages] are come (1 Cor. 10:11 KJV)
- …for these be the days of vengeance, that all things which are written may be fulfilled (Luke 21:22 KJV)
- …the time is short (1 Cor. 7:29)
- …for the world in its present form is passing away (1 Cor. 7:31)
- …it is the last hour (1 John 2:18)

What's the scoop? Why were they talking like this? Is it possible that these words literally mean what they say and, therefore, these writers said what they meant? If so, what could have been so monumental and so

---

[*] Much of the material in this and the next chapter was originally presented by the author in a paper delivered at the Evangelical Theological Society's Midwestern Region Meeting in March 1996 in Fort Wayne, Indiana.

impending, right there and then and in their lifetime, to justify such emphatic and strong claims? The thoughtful answer to that question is, in this author's opinion, what should be termed the *climax for the rest of the greatest story ever foretold.*

No question about it, the 1st-century followers of Christ lived in expectation of something big about to happen, very soon. For them, it was the "last hour." But the last hour of what? Was this big event the proverbial end of the world? The end of time? Or, the conclusion of human history? Obviously, it was not. So it had to be something else. If nothing of radical magnitude happened, befitting this language and imminency (nearness), then these statements were misleading or mistaken, at best—which is exactly the interpretation that has been given to us by many modern interpreters!

No question about it, the 1st-century followers of Christ lived in expectation of something big about to happen, very soon.

Their popular methods of interpretation qualify or change the meanings of these simple words to remove their nearness and relevance from the time period in which they were penned. But this sort of imposition upon the text will not do if we believe God's Word is authoritative and relevant. Each statement cited above uses common, easily understood words. They are not just sayings that could be used at any time, anywhere, under any circumstance, up until the end. They specify an event or events that have a specific timeframe. They cannot be dragged out over the course of thousands of years. Instead of being puzzled or resorting to constant qualifying, we'd be well-advised to honor these inspired statements as God-given, clear, and precise. Therefore, let's consider the possibility that they meant exactly what they said for that particular time—a most important time when "the time" of something extremely significant had grown very "short."

If the event was that important, and supposed to happen soon, what could it have been?

The Two-age Jewish View of Time

To help us discover what was going on, let's put ourselves inside the 1st-century scene. Foundational to both Judaic and Christian thought in that century was the division of time between two consecutive periods—"this present age," and "the age to come." Back then, they were living in "this present age," the age of Moses, the Old Covenant age of the Temple system. "The age to come" was being anticipated. It was to be a golden age of God in which all of God's promises to Israel would be fully realized, and God's power would operate in a new and better way.

This dual concept of time represented the Jewish expectation for God's plan of redemptive history here on earth. They did not view history as a series of unending ages, but stressed these two distinct and contrasting periods. No parenthetical age, third age, or interruption between the two ages was ever envisioned. The line of demarcation, or transition, between the two ages would be accomplished by a visitation of God. Specifically, it was to be ushered in by the coming of the Messiah (Savior) into human history, along with a terrible coming of "the day of the Lord," and the establishment of the everlasting kingdom here on earth.

Although these two-age expressions are not found in the Old Testament, they are found in the New. Jesus reinforced this Jewish differentiation of time (Matt. 12:32; Luke 20:34-35), and especially drew attention to it in his famous prophecy of "the end of the age" (see Matt. 24; Luke 21; Mark 13). He also equated "the end of the age" with the harvest of the kingdom (Matt. 13:39), and "the age to come" with eternal life (Mark 10:30; Luke. 18:30). Paul and the Hebrews' writer also spoke of this age division (Gal. 1:4; Eph. 1:21; Heb. 6:5). These expressions were well-known to 1st-century hearers.

Furthermore, the Jewish religious society of that day had been well-schooled, and clearly understood that the Messiah, at his coming, would end "this present age" and usher in "the age to come" (the Messianic age). Most rabbis believed that this period of transition between the two ages would last about 40 years, like the wilderness wandering, the reigns of David and Solomon, and the three 40-year periods of Moses' life. They also believed it would take place within the confines of history.[1] But Jesus didn't usher in this new age during his earthly ministry, or so most traditions have assumed. Therefore, reasoned the Jews—from that day to the present—Jesus could not be the promised Messiah. Nevertheless, Peter, a 1st-century Jew who believed that Jesus *was* the Messiah, penned these quintessential words naming time and consummation, "the end of all things is at hand" (1 Pet. 4:7 KJV). What did he mean?

Habakkuk's Appointed Time of the End

We modern-day mortals have not been left to wonder about the timing, duration, or nature of this most important, age-changing, transition, and consummatory period. It's variously termed the end times, the eschaton,[2] or, biblically, "the last days," "the last time(s)", "the time of the end" or just "the end." Hence, the biblical meaning for "the end" is the place for us to begin.

Two of several Old-Testament prophets who specifically prophesied of "the time of the end" were Habakkuk and Daniel.[3] They are in agreement, and one prophecy gives light to the other. As we saw in the Introduction, in the 7th century B.C., God inspired the Old Testament prophet Habakkuk to prophesy:

> For the revelation awaits an appointed time; it speaks of the end and will not prove false. Though it linger, wait for it; it will certainly come and will not delay. (Hab. 2:3)

At that time, neither Habakkuk nor any one else had any idea when this "appointed time . . . of the end" (not "end of time"—big difference[4]) would come, or what events would accompany it. All Habakkuk knew was that there was such a thing as an appointed time, that it would "not prove false," that it would "certainly come," and that it would "not delay."

One century later, in the 6th century B.C., God supernaturally gave another Old Testament prophet, Daniel, the two most spectacular and explicit time prophecies ever given to humankind. They are "Daniel's 70 weeks" and the "time of the end." You'll find them in Daniel 9:24-27 and 12:4-12, respectively. Like bookends, these two prophetic time periods bracketed the exact time in history for this coming of the Messiah and Habakkuk's "appointed time . . . of the end." They foretold the climactic events that would signal the consummation—i.e., the end or goal (Greek word, *telos*) of God's redemptive plan for humankind.

Unfortunately, much disagreement has arisen among both Christian and Jewish scholars over how and when Daniel's prophecy occurred. Some deny its prophetic element and say that Daniel's book was a "contemporary" forgery composed after-the-fact in the 2nd century B.C. and falsely attributed to a fictitious character of the sixth century B.C. in order to give it prophetic authority. This, they claim, accounts for its accuracy—it was "predicting" events that had already occurred during the persecutions of Antiochus Epiphanes (175-163 B.C.) and the Jewish revolt led by Judas Maccabaeus that defeated Antiochus.[5] This degrading view seems illogical when we note the reverence given to the book of Daniel in Jewish Scripture. It was so prized, revered, and accepted by the 1st-century B.C. scribes in the Qumran community that they made more copies of it than any other Old Testament book. These two factors indicate their regard of Daniel as authoritative. Furthermore, and as we shall soon see, there is no possible way even one of the six purpose statements encapsulated in this prophecy could have been fulfilled during that time of Antiochus (see Dan. 9:24).

Nonetheless, two indisputable facts remain. First, Jesus gave no credence to any kind of a fulfillment or typological "double reference" in Antiochus Epiphanes' time. As we shall see in chapter eight, He did just the opposite, bypassing Antiochus' time entirely. Secondly, many Jews back in Jesus' day and time were expecting the Messiah. Why was this? They had been reading Daniel's scroll and figuring out its time prophecies. Thus, "Messiah fever" was running high back then and there.

In a similar degrading fashion, Daniel's two time prophecies, elaborating on Habakkuk's "appointed time . . . of the end," are (it is almost needless to say) some of the most misunderstood and misapplied passages of Scripture. The popular view among Christian evangelicals in our day and time is that this "appointed time" has been delayed (or put on hold), and is yet future. But this is in direct contradiction to Habakkuk's text, and invalidates the very inspiration these proponents seek to uphold. As we are about to see, there is a better, more fitting, and simpler fulfillment framework that keeps the biblical inspiration intact.

Daniel Is the Key to the End Times

Because Daniel provides the key to understanding the "end times," we will give it close attention. It is the basis upon which all other end-time prophecies and events rise or fall. Our main point will be that God is not ambiguous or deceptive with his use of time prophecies or time statements in Scripture, and Daniel proves this point. There are no hidden or secretly encoded meanings in Daniel's two time prophecies. They are plainly written and Daniel got it exactly right. Nothing illustrates the supernatural character of the Bible and the divine perfection of God better than this ability to predict the time and nature of end-time events and see them fulfilled, precisely and perfectly.

Daniel's two time prophecies . . . are (it is almost needless to say) some of the most misunderstood and misapplied passages of Scripture.

In this chapter and the next, we will examine the historical evidence supporting the literal, exact, chronological, and sequential fulfillment of Daniel's two time prophecies. We will see that:

- God doesn't play word games with these time prophecies. They are his self-imposed boundaries and his framework for the end-times. No artificial interpretative devices such as gaps, interruptions, delays, elongations, twisted dates, flip-flopped segments, symbolic appeals, non-literal tampering, or esoteric qualifying methods of any kind are required to properly understand this fulfillment. God intended that Daniel's time prophecies be clearly understood, not confusing and divisive.
- They present the "big picture" and central theme of the whole Bible—man's problem and God's solution—i.e., redemption. They contain God's predetermined blueprint for this course of human and redemptive history. These fulfilling events lead up to and include Habakkuk's appointed time of the end. As we shall soon see, it was all precisely pinpointed, did not prove false, certainly came, and did not delay (see again Hab. 2:3).

- Like bookends, Daniel's two prophecies identify the front end (70th week) and the back end (time of the end) of Habakkuk's appointed time of the end. Daniel covers the complete and indivisible transition period between "this present age" and "the age to come," and not the demise of planet Earth or the end of human existence.
- This fulfillment in literal timing and in two unbroken time periods is *the overriding precedent* for the proper interpretation of all other end-time prophecies and time statements, and *the starting point for total prophecy reform.*
- God's time trustworthiness throughout his Word is totally consistent with his divine perfection in creation of the physical universe. It is the discipline to which all interpretations of the consummation must adhere. It's also *the ultimate apologetic*—the final proof in defense of the faith.

In Daniel's day, the 6th century B.C., this transitional period of history was still in the "distant future" (Dan. 8:19, 26). Daniel was told to go his way because "the words are closed up and sealed until the time of the end" (Dan. 12:9). In stark contrast, John, in his 1st-century book of Revelation is instructed by an angel to leave his book unsealed. The angel tells John, "Do not seal up the words of the prophecy of this book, because the time is at hand" (Rev. 22:10). Note the significant difference.

A word of caution. Over the centuries many scholars have offered a wide variety of conflicting and manipulative interpretations of Daniel's prophecies. Using questionable techniques, they have built a wide array of different end-time expectations and scenarios. No doubt this methodology is behind the reason many feel that Daniel's time prophecies are "one of the most puzzling prophetic texts to decipher."[6] The problem here, as we shall continue to see, is not what or how Daniel prophesied. The problem is with the presuppositions, assumptions, and expectations modern-day interpreters bring to this text.

In my opinion, the understanding outlined in this and the next chapter is the most straightforward, clearest, historically documentable, and inspirationally impressive and defensible. Even a hard-boiled skeptic must be impressed by its unaltered, uninterrupted, chronological exactness, and its historically significant context. As you read, keep in mind that it's not all-important to agree with every detail in order to grasp the totality of what exactly transpired during these two interrelated time periods and the transition in between. Keep in mind that if some aspects were not fulfilled and still lie in the future, as most popular futuristic endsaying views hold, then Habakkuk's "appointed time of the end" failed to arrive on time; it proved false. But such truncated views violate the integrity of Scripture. If it was delayed, then Habakkuk prophesied falsely, for he said it would certainly come, and would not be delayed. We'd be well advised not to monkey with Daniel and his two time prophecies. Instead, let's see how they can be understood in a straightforward sense.

Daniel's Time Prophecy of 70 Weeks

Around the year 538 B.C., some 2,500 years ago, many Jews were living in captivity in Babylon. At this time the prophet Daniel prayed to the God of Israel for his people. He knew that God had decreed beforehand, through the prophet Jeremiah, a precise 70-year period of captivity during which no mention was made of any interruptions or gaps of time (Dan. 9:1-2; Jer. 25:11-12; 29:10; also Zech. 1:12; 2 Chron. 36:20-23).[7] Since Daniel and a first group of captives were deported in 605 B.C., he realized that Jeremiah's prophecy was near completion. It was time for their release and return to their homeland.

As he prayed, the angel Gabriel appeared to him. In answer to his petition for the forgiveness and restoration of a repeatedly rebellious Israel, Gabriel gave Daniel a powerful prophetic vision. He was to have clear "insight and understanding" (Dan. 9:22) of the extended future that God had determined for the Jews. Part of that vision was this time prophecy of "seventy sevens" or 70 weeks of years (Dan. 9:24-27 [KJV]):

> Seventy 'sevens' are decreed [determined] for your people and your holy city to finish transgression, to put an end to sin, to atone for wickedness, to bring in everlasting righteousness, to seal up vision and prophecy and to anoint the most holy.

> Know and understand this: From the issuing of the decree to restore and rebuild Jerusalem until the Anointed One, the ruler, comes, there will be seven 'sevens,' and sixty-two 'sevens.' It will be rebuilt with

streets and a trench, but in times of trouble. After the sixty-two 'sevens,' the Anointed One will be cut off and will have nothing. The people of the ruler who will come will destroy the city and the sanctuary. The end will come like a flood: War will continue until the end, and desolations have been decreed [are determined]. He will confirm a covenant with many for one 'seven,' but in the middle of that 'seven' he will put an end to sacrifice and offering. And one who causes desolation will place abominations on a wing of the temple until the end that is decreed [determined] is poured out on him.

The Hebrew word (*sha bu'a*), translated above as "sevens," or "weeks" in some versions, literally means a unit, a period or a group of seven of something. It's akin to our English word *dozen*, which means a unit of twelve of something. The word by itself does not tell us what the units are. Most interpreters agree that Daniel's sevens of something was sevens of years. They have two good reasons for this understanding:

1) Jeremiah's original prophecy of "seventy" was an explicit period of 70 years of Babylonian captivity. This time of deportation was to serve as both the setting (2 Chron. 36:21) and an uninterrupted (no gaps) archetype for Daniel's 70 weeks.

2) This concept of time was not new. God had used the same biblical concept of "weeks of years" from the beginning of Israel's history under Moses (Lev. 25:8). He had equated days to years for determining their period of wandering in the wilderness (Num. 14:34). He had divided the Hebrew calendar into seven-year periods with every seventh year being a sabbatical year. Also, the seven years that Jacob worked for Rachel was called "the fulfilling of her week" (Gen. 29:27, 28 KJV). I agree with the standard interpretation that "seventy sevens" means "seventy times seven *years*." As we shall see, this total time span equates to 490 consecutive years without any gaps or interrupts.

The angel Gabriel further stated that both the duration and contents of this divinely fixed time period of 490 years were "decreed [or determined] for your people (the Jews) and your holy city (Jerusalem)." This time period's express purpose was to reveal the exact time in human history when God would send the "Anointed One, the ruler" or "Messiah the Prince" to Israel, begin his public ministry, and confirm a covenant for one week of years (seven years). Thus, Daniel's 70 weeks prophecy historically links the Old Covenant, Judaic period to the New Covenant, Christian period.

The total elapsed time of 490 years further demonstrates that the course of events was already decided. It had a specific starting and finishing point, and was subdivided into three time segments: 1) an initial period of "seven sevens" or 49 years, 2) a period of "sixty-two sevens" or 434 years, and 3) a final period of "one seven" or 7 years.

Scripturally, we can examine this prophesied 490-year period and verify its determinism and accuracy. Historically, we can see it transpire as a firm, unbroken sequence of chronological time and events leading to the Christ. For those accustomed to a postponement tradition, the following exposition may be disturbing or even threatening. For others, it will be quite illuminating. For all, it is important validation of the biblical faith that must not be overlooked or truncated. I hope you'll be convinced that this explanation demonstrates that the God of the Bible is the God of divine perfection, exactness, and history told in advance. As the one, true, and proven God (Isa. 44:6-8; 41:22-23, 26; 42:9; 44:7-8; 46:9-10; 45:21-22; 48:3-6; Amos 3:7). He has spoken through his prophets to all humanity. The sincere seeker of truth will surely recognize and understand the precision and drama of Daniel's prophecy.

Beginning at 457 B.C. and using the ancient dating chronology of Ptolemy,[8] I will present for your consideration a section-by-section, historic, and mathematically precise fulfillment of Daniel's 70 weeks with no gaps and no gimmicks:

The Starting Point

457 B.C. ... *from the issuing of the decree to restore and rebuild Jerusalem* ... (Dan. 9:25).

The Bible records three decrees by Gentile kings that affected the restoration and rebuilding of Jerusalem (Ezra 6:14):

- Cyrus' Decree in 538 B.C. (Ezra 1:2-4).
- Darius' Decree around 520 B.C. (Ezra 6:3-12).
- Artaxerxes' Decree, dated by the majority of historians and Bible scholars at 457 B.C. (Ezra 7:11-26).

Which is the right one for the starting-point of Daniel's 70 weeks of years?

The decree and date which best begins the grand countdown of 490 years is the last one, Artaxerxes' in 457 B.C.[9] It is the best for three reasons:

1) In retrospect, dating from the first two decrees has no literal, future, or chronological significance, or historical prophetic value. In other words, numbering from these starting points does not add up. But dating from Artaxerxes' Decree does.

2) Some interpreters feel Cyrus' Decree should be the starting point, since the prophet Isaiah, a century and a half before, had foretold that a man by that name would decree the rebuilding of Jerusalem and the Temple (Isa. 44:26-28; 45:1-4). But for some unknown reason, both Cyrus' and Darius' decrees, as recorded in Scripture, only called for the rebuilding of the Temple in Jerusalem and made no mention of the city or the restoration of Israel as a people.[10] Big difference. A rebuilt Temple would enable the Jews to offer sacrifices and pray for the well-being of the king (Ezra 6:10). But a rebuilt city would provide the Jews with a military fortress. They could then rebel again, and this was a concern of Israel's enemies, as seen in the letter to the king of Persia (Ezra 4:12, 15). Using the 538 B.C. date as the starting point would require either a time gap or a symbolic reading of the numbers for the time period to come out with any significant meaning. Note that 538 B.C. plus 490 years only works out to 48 B.C., and nothing of significance occurred then.

3) Artaxerxes' Decree nearly one hundred years later in 457 B.C., and his subsequent letters of passage issued in 445-444 B.C. (mentioned in Nehemiah 2:5-8), covered everything.[11] This is the latest possible date for the beginning of Daniel's 70 weeks. In addition, these associated letters specifically mentioned both the rebuilding of the city and the Temple.

First Segment: the Seven Sevens

457 – 408 B.C. . . . It will be rebuilt with streets and a trench, but in times of trouble . . . (Dan. 9:25).

The first segment of 49 years spanned the restoring and rebuilding of Jerusalem under the administration of Ezra and Nehemiah. You can read about it in the book of Nehemiah, especially chapters 2-6. Nehemiah records how the Jews returned from captivity and worked "in times of trouble," just as Daniel had prophesied. Carrying materials with one hand and a weapon in the other, returning Jews rebuilt the walls in 52 days (Neh. 4:17-18; 6:15). This was only part of the restoration. They also restored the streets and houses (Neh. 7:4); instituted laws, civil ordinances (Neh. 7:5), and religious reforms (Neh. 13:30); and finished settling in Jerusalem within this 49-year time segment (Neh. 11:1).[12]

Second Segment: Sixty-two Sevens

408 B.C. – A.D. 27

Sixty-two sevens, (i.e., 434 more consecutive years) pass. Note that no interval or interruptive gap between the 7-week and 62-week segments is suggested in the text. Toward the close of this second segment, messianic expectations began running high in the Promised Land, and for good reason. Daniel's time prophecy was well known, and its fulfillment was being anticipated. In addition, Jesus Christ was born, most probably in 4 B.C., not A.D. 0, as is sometimes assumed. (Mistakes made in transposing dates into the commonly accepted Christian calendar by the 6th century A.D. Roman monk, Dionysius Exiguus, account for this dating discrepancy.)

Third Segment: One Seven—the First Half

A.D. 27 – 30. . . . until the Anointed One, the ruler, comes, there will be seven 'sevens' and sixty-two 'sevens' . . . (Dan. 9:25).

This one week is the most significant and the most misunderstood. It will require special attention. To help our understanding, I have divided it into four sections: first half, middle, second half, and finishing point. An "anointing" event marks both the conclusion of the second 62-week segment and the beginning of Daniel's 70th and final week of unbroken and uninterrupted years.

Again, there is no suggestion in the text of any interval or interruptive gap between the 62-week and 1-week segments. Simple arithmetic shows 483 years (49 + 434 years) had elapsed since Artaxerxes' Decree in 457 B.C. It's now A.D. 27. Jesus Christ, "the Anointed One, the ruler" (or "Messiah the Prince"),[13] who had emptied Himself of his glory, authority, and power to become like other men (Phil. 2:7-8; Heb. 2:17), is hereby publicly identified as the Messiah with his baptism in the Jordan River. At that moment he is *anointed* by the Holy Spirit. No previous or subsequent event in Jesus' earthly life could be taken as the fulfillment of these words of Gabriel to Daniel (see Acts 10:38; Heb. 1:9). Luke reports that Jesus was about 30 years of age at that time (Luke 3:22-23). As was the Jewish custom, the 30th year was the age at which men of Israel were permitted to become active in temple or tabernacle service. Next, Jesus departed and went into the wilderness for a period of forty days (Luke 4:1-2). Luke 4:13-21 records that after Jesus had been tempted in the wilderness, He went to Nazareth where He had been raised, stood up in the synagogue, and read the messianic prophecy from Isaiah 61:1-2 regarding the coming of an "anointed one" and "the year of the Lord's favor." Then Jesus said, "Today this scripture is fulfilled in your hearing."

Something else, however, is especially noteworthy about Jesus' quotation from Isaiah. He stopped in mid-verse. He did not quote the last half of Isaiah 61:2 concerning "the day of vengeance of our God." Why not? Because the time period for the fulfillment of that day of judgment was not yet present. Its fulfillment awaited the future time of Daniel's "time of the end," which we'll cover in the next chapter.

From the day of his anointing, Jesus moved in the power and authority of the New Covenant. During the next 3½ years of his earthly ministry, Jesus taught and demonstrated the new in-breaking kingdom of God (Dan. 2:44; 7:14, 18, 22, 27) and modeled its "powers of the age to come" (Heb. 6:5). Also, He trained and commanded his followers to do likewise. Thus, "Jesus came into Galilee, preaching and manifesting the gospel of the kingdom of God, and saying, the time is fulfilled . . ." (Mark 1:14-15 KJV). What time was He talking about? It was the fullness of Daniel's 70 weeks time prophecy.[14] The 70th week was upon them, precisely, right on time.

Next, we must read this verse closely. What is to happen *after* the sixty-two sevens is crucial to our understanding.

> After sixty-two' sevens' the Anointed One will be cut off and will have nothing. The people of the ruler who will come will destroy the city and the sanctuary. The end will come like a flood: War will continue until the end, and desolations have been decreed [determined] .... And one who causes desolation will place abominations on a wing of the temple until the end that is decreed [determined] is poured out on him. (Dan. 9:26 [KJV])

The only time restriction here is "after" sixty-two sevens (the 69th week, 483 years). It is not predicting that all this will happen during the 70th week of years. It is simply saying "after" the 69th week. Nor does it say how long after— just after. However, we know that the final week began with Jesus' anointing some 3 years earlier. So, the Messiah being "cut off"[15] so as to "have nothing" meant He was crucified and had nothing befitting the Messiah. This did occur during the middle of that 70th week in A.D. 30. He was without his messianic kingdom. This event is time-restricted in the next verse, and will be addressed in our next section on the middle of the 70th week.

Hence, we have separated the "cutting off" (the crucifixion), which is time-restricted to the middle of the final week, from the other events of Daniel 9:26, which are not so restricted, but only named as coming "after" the sixty-two weeks. We know from history that these events occurred some 37 years after the crucifixion.

The other events that were to come "after" the sixty-two weeks are the destruction of Jerusalem and the Temple, and desolations and abominations. They were "decreed" or "determined" (meaning fixed and unable to be changed) *within* Daniel's 70th week, when most of Israel did not or would not recognize the time of its visitation by Messiah, just as Jesus had warned (Luke 19:41-44). These latter events did not take place until around A.D. 66 - 73 because they were part of *the end* and were associated with Daniel's other time prophecy, the *time of the end*. In Daniel's last chapter, Gabriel gave Daniel this second time prophecy for the chronological fulfillment of those "determined," time-of-the-end events. As we shall discover, it has its own, separate timeframe, different time parameters, and different terminology.

How can we be so sure these end-time events were only "decreed" or "determined" *within* Daniel's 70th week and not fulfilled in that time segment? The answer is found in the way the Hebrew word is used elsewhere. In Daniel 11:36, the same Hebrew word [*charats*], translated as "decreed" or "determined," is used in a future fulfillment sense, ". . . for what has been determined must take place." Hence, "decreed" or "determined" [past tense] does not require that all events "happen" during that same timeframe, although some did. Others were only set, or locked into motion (determined) for future fulfillment. *This distinction must be understood.* It enables us to maintain the integrity of Daniel's two interrelated and interconnected timeframes without resorting to gaps, interruptions, or other manipulative gimmicks.

Middle of the Final Week

A.D. 30. . . . He will confirm a covenant with many for one 'seven,' but in the middle of that seven, he [Jesus, the Messiah] *shall put an end to sacrifice and offering . . .* (Dan. 9:27).

Note that this event is in the middle of the last week, the same time as the previous "cutting off." The crucifixion of the Messiah is hereby time restricted to the middle of the 70th week, and so is the end of sacrifice and offering. Even though the Jews continued the practice of animal sacrifices and offerings for another 40 years, Christ's death and resurrection ended that Old Covenant obligation. It no longer had value and acceptability. It had been superseded by the "once-for-all . . . sacrifice" of Christ (Heb. 9:26, 10:10; 1 Pet. 3:18). What's more, it sealed or "determined" the fulfillment of all six of the redemptive purposes and promises for Daniel's 70 weeks time prophecy stated in verse 24:

1. To finish transgression;
2. To make an end of sin;
3. To atone for wickedness;
4. To bring in everlasting righteousness;
5. To seal up the vision and prophecy;
6. To anoint the most holy (place).

This is restoration language. It speaks of the final portion of God's plan for redeeming humankind from the consequences of sin. With his death on the cross, Jesus set in motion this restorative and consummatory process. But, as we shall see throughout this book, the new could not fully come, nor all six of these purposes and promises be fully brought in and totally fulfilled, until the old was completely removed at the "time of the end." That time was still in the future for those living in A.D. 30. But it would "not prove false, it would "certainly come," and would "not delay," just as Habakkuk had prophesied.

Second Half of the Final Week

A.D. 30 – 34. After the Messiah was "cut off," or crucified, as the prophet Isaiah had also foretold (Isa. 53:8), his disciples and followers obediently stayed in Jerusalem awaiting and then experiencing the events of Pentecost (Luke 24:49). But after Pentecost they did *not* disperse and "Go . . . and teach all nations" or "make disciples of all nations," as Jesus had commanded (Matt. 28:19 KJV - NIV). Why didn't they? Because the covenant was to be confirmed for "one seven" (one week of years), first and exclusively upon the Jews (Dan. 9:24; Rom. 1:16; John 4:22). The purpose and focus of Daniel's last week of years was to be a 7-year period of covenant confirmation for the Jews. Half of this final "one-seven" segment still remained. The covenant to be confirmed was the one promised through the prophet Jeremiah (Jer. 31:31-33). The first half of 3½ years was fulfilled by the earthly ministry of Jesus Christ and his disciples. That meant that 3½ more years were yet to be fulfilled before Jesus' followers would be free to take the Gospel outside the Jewish realm. To this day, most Jews don't recognize that their prophet Isaiah said the Servant (the Messiah) would also be sent to the Gentiles (Isa. 49:6f.).

The biblical fact of Jewish preeminence is frequently emphasized throughout the Gospels. God set it up that way. Remember, Jesus did not minister to the Gentiles (with a few notable foreshadowing exceptions). He had commanded his disciples, "Go not into the way of the Gentiles, and into any city of the Samaritans enter ye not; but go rather to the lost sheep of the house of Israel" (Matt. 10:5-6; 15:24 KJV). Is Jesus' command here in contradiction to his Great Commission command to go and teach [make] disciples of all nations (Matt. 28:18-29)? No, it is not. Why not? Because there was a time-restricted waiting period in which the New Covenant was to be confirmed with the Jews exclusively. That time was during the seven years of Daniel's 70th and final week.

Jesus' disciples knew this. How did they know? Quite simply; in Luke we are told that Jesus expounded and explained in all the Scriptures the things concerning Himself. He began at Moses and proceeded through all the prophets (Luke 24:27). Jesus' teaching would have most certainly included Daniel, the Jews' most copied book, and Daniel's prophecy of 70 weeks pertaining to the Messiah. Further, "He opened their minds so they could understand the Scriptures" (Luke 24:45). The Bible says that Jesus' teaching caused their hearts to burn within them (Luke 24:32). This is how they knew that they were prohibited in where and to whom they could go until the time restriction ran its course. Consequently, they remained in Jerusalem and preached exclusively to the Jews until the time was up.

Finishing Point of the Final Week

A.D. 34. Toward the end of A.D. 33, Jewish persecution of Christians in Jerusalem reached a climax with the stoning death of Stephen (Acts 7:54-60). The Bible says that all except the apostles were scattered throughout Judea and Samaria (Acts 8:1).

The event that documents the finishing point of Daniel's 70th week occurred when "Philip went down to a city in Samaria, and proclaimed Christ there" (Acts 8:5). How could he do this? Hadn't Christ forbidden it? What's more, the apostles in Jerusalem sent Peter and John to Samaria as a support team to build on what Philip had started (Acts 8:14 ff.). Were they disobeying Jesus' prohibition on going to the Gentiles? The answer is no, because was now A.D. 34.

The time restriction for confirming the New Covenant exclusively for the Jews was now chronologically over.[16] The Gospel of the New Covenant had come first to the Jews, then to the Samaritans, who, as half breeds, were despised by the Jews (Acts 8), and finally to the Gentiles (Acts 10; 11:18-20) and the whole world. In this manner, the mystery of God uniting Jew and Gentile into one body was phased into human history (John 4:22; Eph. 3:3-6, 9; Col. 1:26-27; 2:2; 4:3; Rom. 3:29-23;

15:26-27). God's grand purpose was never to make boundaries between peoples or nations, but to make all one.

In retrospect, then, the prophecy of Daniel's 70 weeks:

- *Commenced* in 457 B.C. with the decree of Artaxerxes.
- Was *determined* in A.D. 30 at the cross.
- Was *confirmed* by the New Covenant for 3½ years before and 3½ years after the cross.
- *Concluded* in A.D. 34 when the Gospel had been preached to the Jews and was now freed to go to the Gentiles.

The entire prophecy transpired in an uninterrupted 490-year period. No valid rationale exists for interrupting the time segments, splitting apart the years, inserting gaps, elongating weeks, or postponing, delaying, minimizing or tampering with the fixed time period in any manner. Thus, the front bookend of the end-time, age-changing transition period—Daniel's 70th week—certainly came and was perfectly fulfilled. Perfectly! It's a mainstay of messianic authentication, a mathematical demonstration for the divine inspiration of the Bible, and an unanswerable argument for critics of the Christian faith.

The time restriction for confirming the New Covenant exclusively for the Jews was now chronologically over.

Even so, all was not complete. More that had been "decreed" or "determined" remained to be accomplished; a fact which brings us to our back bookend, our final time period, and the grand finale of the end that would shortly come to pass. *(See Appendix A for a timeline of the events outlined in this chapter.)*

Chapter 6

Daniel's Time of the End

We find Daniel's second time prophecy in his very last chapter, Daniel 12, verses 4-13. It serves as the back bookend or boundary of the age-changing transition we call the "end times." The biblical term is the "time of the end" (Dan. 12:4, 9; 11:35; 8:19), not the "end of time." Big difference! The Bible never speaks of an end of time. Changing the order of these words has led many into gross error, such as end-of-the-world misconceptions.

But you, Daniel, close up and seal the words of the scroll until the time of the end. Many will go here and there to increase knowledge.

Then, I Daniel, looked, and there before me stood two others, one on this bank of the river and one on the opposite bank. One of them said to the man clothed in linen, who was above the waters of the river, "How long will it be before these astonishing things are fulfilled?"

The man clothed in linen, who was above the waters of the river, lifted his right hand and his left hand toward heaven, and I heard him swear by him who lives forever, saying, "It will be for a time, times and half a time. When the power of the holy people has been finally broken, all these things will be complete."

He replied, "Go your way, Daniel, because the words are closed up and sealed until the time of the end. Many will be purified, made spotless and refined, but the wicked will continue to be wicked. None of the wicked will understand, but those who are wise will understand.

"From the time that the daily sacrifice is abolished and the abomination that causes desolation is set up, there will be 1,290 days. Blessed is the one who waits for and reaches the end of the 1,335 days.

"As for you, go your way till the end. You will rest, and then at the end of the days you will rise to receive your allowed inheritance."

In his previous 70-week prophecy, Daniel referred to some of the events that would take place during this "time of the end," including the fall of Jerusalem, the destruction of the Jewish Temple, and many other desolations of war (see Dan. 9:26). But these events were only "decreed" or "determined" within Daniel's 70th week. Their actual occurrence (fulfillment) lies outside that time period. But how can we be sure this interpretation is correct?

In his last vision, Daniel sees two others (angels) standing on the bank of a river and talking. One asks the other, "How long will it be before these astonishing things are fulfilled" (Dan. 12:6b). The asking of this time question subsequent to Daniel receiving his 70 week prophecy strongly suggests that the events of this fulfillment were not included in that previous time period. This is evidently why Daniel is given another time prophecy for another sovereignly determined time period. Note that this one uses different time terminology, which differentiates it from the 490-year time span covered by Daniel's 70 weeks (see previous chapter).

This second prophecy speaks in terms of straight days (1,290 and 1,335) instead of "sevens" or "weeks" of years. As we shall see, the two sets of days are not two separate time periods, but rather the shorter period is inclusive within the longer. This can also be legitimately surmised since it was specified that the "time of the end" would be "for a time, times and half a time," or approximately a year, two years, and half a year. This phrase links back to the same terminology used in Daniel 7:25-28 and was the standard Jewish interpretation contained in their rabbinical writings and commentaries. Further, it compares with the 2,300 evenings and mornings (Dan. 8:14) of temporary cessation of Temple services occurring during the three-year and two-month period of occupation by Antiochus Epiphanes in 167-164 B.C. (more on this in chapter nine).

Daniel's "time of the end" would be a time of intensified trouble and divine judgment. That judgment would be poured out upon Daniel's people (Israel) "in the latter days" (Dan. 10:14 KJV) because of their continual breaking of the covenant and rebellion against God and his plan of redemption via the Messiah. The climax would occur "when the power of the holy people (the Jews) has been finally broken." At that time, "all these things" concerning the "time of the end" would "be complete" (Dan. 12:7). So, what was this "power of the holy people?" It was the biggest power God had ever given anyone at that time—the power of biblical Judaism (i.e., their exclusive relationship with God as manifested by the Temple complex [Isa. 2:2-5; 56:7]). The final breaking of this power was to be both the *historical setting* and *defining characteristic* for Daniel's "time of the end." Note that this distinguishing element was *not* to be the demise of planet Earth, the end of time, the end of human existence, the removal of believers from the world (rapture), a 1,000-year reign of Christ, or any of the other traditional end-time notions.

The climax would occur "when the power of the holy people (the Jews) has been finally broken." At that time, "all these things" concerning the "time of the end" would "be complete" (Dan. 12:7).

In contrast, however, to the wealth of Scripture supporting the fulfillment of Daniel's 70-weeks time prophecy, none exists for the fulfillment of Daniel's "time of the end." Why not? A strong case can be made that all the books later included in the New Testament canon were written before the "time of the end."[1] However, with the help of Josephus (A.D. 37 - c.100),[2] the 1st-century Jewish priest and renowned historian for the Romans and who was an eyewitness to the end time, we have authentication for the fulfillment of Daniel's final, "time-of-the-end" prophecy—again, no gaps and no gimmicks, but literal, exact, chronological and sequential fulfillment.

The Starting Point

A.D. 66. (Dan. 12:11) . . . from the time that the daily sacrifice is abolished . . . .

In July of A.D. 66, Josephus records that, as part of the Jewish rebellion against Rome, Jewish Zealots stormed Jerusalem and burned the palace of Agrippa and Bernice (the Roman ruler and his sister). They also burned the palace of the Jewish High Priest, Ananias, and killed him in retaliation for his liberal affiliation with the Romans. Next, they massacred a garrison of Roman soldiers. And to top it off, they stopped performing the twice-daily Temple sacrifices for Caesar and the Roman people. Josephus states that this cessation of the daily sacrifice was the true beginning of the Roman-Jewish War.[3] Both the Romans and the revolting Jews viewed it as a formal declaration of war. The total cessation of all sacrifices didn't take place until the Jews ran out of priests and animals in August of A.D. 70, just prior to the fall of Jerusalem and the destruction of the Temple by the Roman army.

1,290 Days Later *(Dan. 12:11) . . . and the abomination that causes desolation is set up, there will be 1,290 days.*

Earlier, Daniel had referred to "desolations" (note the plural) that had been "decreed" or "determined" (Dan. 9:26b), and stated that "one who causes desolation (note the singular) will place abominations on a wing of the temple until the end that is decreed is poured out on him" (Dan 9:27b).[4] "Wing" refers to a pinnacle or an extremity point of abominations. Again, the determination was done during the 70 weeks, but their fulfillments were not a chronological part of the 70 weeks' timeframe. As we saw in the last chapter, the only restriction was "after" the second 62-week segment, and not "during" that third segment.

Early in the year of A.D. 70 (approximately—if not exactly—three years and six months, or 1,290 days, after the cessation of the twice-daily sacrifice for Caesar and Rome), Josephus reports that a major abomination took place in the Temple that all in Jerusalem could see. While the Roman Army (under the leadership of Titus) was encamped in Caesarea on the Mediterranean Sea, approximately 55 miles northwest of Jerusalem, and marshaling its forces for the final campaign against Jerusalem, civil strife between three rival, Jewish factions inside the city walls reached a climax. Rival Zealot factions defiled the Temple's innermost courts with murders as fierce fighting raged between the Jews struggling for control. The Temple was their battleground and was defiled with carnage at every corner. Even worshipers were killed while trying to offer their sacrifices.[5]

There can be no doubt that the warring of the three Jewish factions inside the city walls (and particularly in the Temple area) was one of the many abominations and desolations spoken of by Daniel. But even this was not the worst or the pinnacle one. Josephus details how the Jews frequently and blatantly desecrated their own Temple during the time of the Roman-Jewish War. As a Jewish priest himself, and speaking from a priestly point of view, he felt that these Temple atrocities and their impact on the rest of the Jewish people were what eventually led to the complete desolation of Jerusalem and the Temple by the Roman legions.

A strong argument can be made that the Jews brought the final desolation upon themselves. When all the facts are known, the Jews were "the people of the ruler [i.e., the people of Jesus, and not the Roman army under Titus' command or some future Antichrist ruler] who will come and destroy the city and the sanctuary" (Dan. 9:26). The question of who destroyed Jerusalem has been equated with the age-old question of who crucified Christ?" In both cases, the Romans tried to avoid the final action. But the Jews' abominable and self-destructive activities forced the Romans to act. You can read about it in Josephus' eyewitness accounts of the Jewish rebellion and the subsequent Roman-Jewish War in A.D. 66 - 73.[6]

The Finishing Point

1335 Days Later
A.D. 70 (Dan. 12:12) Blessed is the one who waits for and reaches the end of the 1,335 days.

Jesus warned his first followers, "When you see Jerusalem surrounded by armies, you will know that its desolation is near . . . . For this is the time of punishment in fulfillment of all that has been written" (Luke 21:20, 22; see also Luke 19:43-44).

Shortly before Passover in the spring of A.D. 70 (approximately—if not exactly—45 days following the previously-cited Temple desecration), Titus' Roman legions advanced toward Jerusalem from the

Northwest through Samaria (just as Antiochus Epiphanes, the king of Syria, had done in 167 B.C. as the invader from the "north" of Ezekiel 38 and 39). He "set up" three encampments within three miles of the walls on the hills surrounding and overlooking Jerusalem. This was the fourth and final encampment of armies around Jerusalem during the Roman-Jewish War period. Although it is not possible to know the final "day or hour" (Matt. 24:36; 25:13), this "setting up" occurred precisely within the 1,335-day time period prophesied to Daniel. The "time of the end" was now at hand. And, as we'll see in chapters eight and nine, Jesus had given the Jews ample signs and warnings that this end was coming upon them within their lifetime. And come it did.

In April of A.D. 70, the Roman army began the fourth and final siege of the war. In September, it was over. Not only the city and the Temple but the whole of biblical Judaism was utterly destroyed and left desolated. This Roman siege, using 1st-century warfare technology, was precisely the form of judgment Jesus had promised was coming (Luke 19:41-44). It was also the fulfillment of "the day of vengeance of God." This was the portion of Isaiah 61:1-2 which Jesus, 43 years earlier, auspiciously did not quote while reading the scroll in the synagogue (Luke 4:13-21). But at just the right time, the "appointed time of the end" had "certainly come," it did "not prove false," and did "not delay," just as God's prophet, Habakkuk, had prophesied almost eight centuries earlier.

All the events cited in this and the last chapter as fulfillment of Daniel's two time prophecies (the 70 weeks and "time of the end") took place literally, exactly, chronologically, and sequentially within their two respective time periods, and precisely as foretold, with no gaps or gimmicks. As a result, both the *historical setting* and *defining characteristic* of Daniel's "time of the end" achieved fulfillment in A.D. 66 - 73 when the "the power of the holy people" was "finally broken." The Jews' exclusive relationship with God, as manifested by the Temple complex, was finally terminated. Ever since and yet today, rabbis speak about the destruction of the Temple in A.D. 70 as "the end of biblical Judaism." Even they recognize that something extremely significant happened back then. Since then, it has not been reversed and, contrary to popular Jewish and Christian views, will never be restored.

However, we will miss the greater significance of these events if all we see in them is the destruction of a local city and its Temple. As we shall see throughout the remainder of this book, the time of the end involved much more. "All these things," including the accomplishment of Daniel's six purpose clauses (Dan. 9:24), were fully "completed" (Dan 12:7). Plus, the transition between the two ages was finished at the fall of Jerusalem circa A.D. 70 - 73.

Thus, the end the Bible proclaims is *past*. Habakkuk's "appointed time . . . of the end" certainly came and is over. It did not demand the end of human history, the end of time, or the destruction of the physical creation. This end, its end times, and the biblical last days are behind us, not ahead of us. They are in the past, not in the future. Note especially that every New Testament reference to the "last days" or equivalent "last times, last hour," refers to the time its writers were living in—the 1st century. They weren't the last days of planet Earth, or the end of time. They were the last days of the Old Covenant Jewish system and age. There are no exceptions (see Heb 1:2; Acts 2:17; 1 Tim. 4:1; 2 Tim. 3:1; Jas. 5:3; 2 Pet. 3:3; 1 Pet. 1:5, 20; Jude 18; 1 John 2:18).

Therefore, and like two bookends, Daniel's two time prophecies provide the front and a back for the biblical end-times period. Like a picture frame, they provide the divine and perfect framework in which all end-time events took place and the appointed time of the end certainly came.

THE END TIMES

| Daniel's 70th Week A.D. 27 - 34 FRONT BOOKEND | The Last Days
The Fullness of Time
The Eschaton
Days of the Messiah
Age-changing Transition Period | Daniel's Time of the End A.D. 66 - 70 BACK BOOKEND |

(See Appendix A for a complete timeline.)

Chapter 7

Is God's Word Trustworthy?

One of the most divisive elements in recent Christian history...
Few doctrines unite and separate Christians as much as
eschatology [end-time prophecy]. [1]

After reading many books on the end times and realizing that there are so many different views coming from the same Bible, one must conclude that there is a glitch somewhere. Not only have the endsayers misled generations of people about the end *of* the world and the time of the end *for* the world, they have seriously compromised the integrity of God's Word on other related matters as well. The result is that many Christians and non-Christians, alike, don't really know what to believe about Bible prophecy, or even about the Bible itself!

But God is not the author of confusion, nor of this confusion (1 Cor. 14:33). His demonstrated attribute of divine perfection means his Word is trustworthy—totally trustworthy. For example:

- God's Word says the earth is a "circle" (Isa. 40:22). We can count on it.
- God's Word declares, "Generations come and generations go, but the earth remains (endures) forever" (Eccl. 1:4). We can count on it.

- God told Noah, "Seven days from now I will send rain on the earth for forty days and forty nights" (Gen. 7:4). We can rest assured that these were two precise timeframes.
- God's prophet, Jeremiah, prophesied the duration of Babylonian captivity at 70 years. That was its exact length—no gaps, no gimmicks.
- God commissioned the angel Gabriel and the Lord Jesus Himself to show Daniel the beginning and ending of the period we call the end times or the "last days." This time-framed period encompassed the coming and cutting off of the Messiah, the cessation of the daily sacrifice, the power of the holy people being finally broken, and much more that was perfectly prophesied to occur. We can trust the precise timing and integrity of this prophecy as well. It is God's Word.

God is not ambiguous. He doesn't play word games with any of his Word, and certainly not with his time statements. No artificial interpretative devices of any kind—gaps, gimmicks, interruptions, postponements, delays, or tampering of any type—are required to understand the intended meaning. All of God's time periods given to humankind are reliable, accurate, and literally precise. Each commenced, transpired, and was fulfilled in chronological and sequential exactness.

All of God's time periods given to humankind are reliable, accurate, and literally precise.

As further proof, God also set his end-times events into the definite context of world history. Daniel was also given the famous apocalyptic view of four world kingdoms. In two parallel dream-visions, Daniel isolated, this book-ended, age-changing, end-time period to be *within* the days of the old Roman Empire (which ended in A.D. 476):

- In Daniel 2, Daniel both declared and interpreted the king's dream of a statue with four sections (head of gold, chest and arms of silver, belly and thighs of bronze, and legs and feet of iron and clay) to symbolize four earthly kingdoms.

- In Daniel 7, Daniel's prophetic dream of four beasts (a lion, a bear, a leopard, and a ten-horned beast) symbolizes the identical scenario—four earthly kingdoms.

I agree with the majority of biblical scholars that these two dream-visions portray the same thing. Four—not five—Gentile kingdoms or world empires with control over the Promised Land would transpire during this divinely predetermined course of history. They began in Daniel's day and successively unfolded. They were Babylon, Medo-Persia, Greece, and the old Roman Empire, respectively.[2] Again, since Daniel prophesied the rise and fall of these kingdoms so accurately, some scholars insist that these sections must have been written after-the-fact, in the 2nd century B.C. Even if that were true, this would still leave a two-hundred-year-plus foretelling factor to explain (see again footnote 5, chapter five).

Daniel records that during—not after—the time of the fourth beast/kingdom (the old Roman Empire) one like the Son of Man (the Messiah) was to come on the clouds and establish his everlasting kingdom. It would happen "in the times [days] of those kings" (Dan. 7:13-14; 2:44). This divine placement in world history perfectly harmonizes with the fulfillment of Daniel's 70 weeks and time of the end prophecies I have presented (see Jesus' declaration in Mark 1:14-15). Twice in these dream-visions, and more than 600 years in advance, Daniel unerringly foretold the general time when the Messiah would come and God's appointed end for Israel would be carried out by the power of Rome. It all happened in the 1st century A.D. exactly *as* and *when* it was supposed to happen, and precisely *as* and *when* it was expected as God's Spirit came and guided Jesus' first followers "into all truth" and told them "what is yet to come" (John 16:13).

What Should We Learn from This Divine Perfection?

We of biblical faith could solve many of our disagreements by reconsidering the time-integrity of Daniel's time prophecies, and by becoming better acquainted with the nature and historical accuracy of their fulfillment. To help us further, here are seven principles for "making sense" of God's divine perfection and time trustworthiness.

***Principle 1. When the Normal Sense Makes Sense,
            Seek No Other Sense.***

Doesn't a straightforward approach to Daniel's prophecies and the preciseness of their literal, exact, chronological, and sequential fulfillment make more sense than a view that interrupts the time context? By the straightforward method, Daniel's prophecies were fulfilled long ago. Only by tampering with the text can we force a postponement and get a yet-future fulfillment.

Most Christian endsayers, however, insist that the prophetic time clock stopped ticking when the Jews rejected the Messiah and crucified Him on the cross. So they interrupt Daniel's 70 weeks and insert a time gap of indeterminable length between the 69th and the 70th week. Next, they lift the 70th week out of its 1st-century, time-period context, stretch it like a rubber band over 19 centuries and counting, and plop it down somewhere out in the future. This seven-year period, which was designated by the text as the time the Messiah would confirm a covenant with the Jews, is now recast into being a future 7-year period of tribulation upon the Jews, who are then ruled by the Antichrist. In this bizarre scheme, the Antichrist rises from one of the nations of a so-called revived Roman Empire and confirms a supposed covenant with the geopolitical and secular nation of Israel.

The biblical fact is, no scriptural warrant or valid precedent exists for such abusive treatment or manipulative handling of God's Word. No imposition of gaps, interruptions, or delays can be scripturally or historically justified.[3] This type of tampering with Scripture has crippled the Church and resulted in erroneous and disastrous date-setting.

Ironically, the futurist-literalist endsayers profess a good and valid phrase: "when the normal sense makes sense, seek no other sense." It's unfortunate that those who subscribe to this bit of good sense are doctrinally and/or emotionally committed to violating it here. But times are changing. A new paradigm and reformation is underway.

Principle 2. The 'Once For All Delivered' Faith.

    . . . *Contend for the faith that was once for all delivered to the saints.* (Jude 3). The vast majority of Christians and Jews do not do this. They contend for a faith that has only been partially delivered. Sad to say, they are woefully ignorant of the past-fulfillment heritage of our once-for-all-delivered faith.

Through the Jewish prophet Daniel, God provided four clear time parameters—two specific and two general—for when the Messiah would come, the time determined upon the Jews would be over, and when Habakkuk's "appointed time . . . of the end" would take place. Both biblical Judaism and Christianity spring from these same deep roots and shared scriptures. And there is no Messiah apart from Israel's Messiah.

The literal, exact, chronological, and sequential fulfillment of Daniel's historical time prophecies presents a powerful argument that Jesus of Nazareth was and is Israel's promised Messiah, the Christ. He came at "just the right time" (Rom. 5:6), the appointed time, or He is not the Messiah. The renowned Jewish historian for the Romans, Josephus, wrote these astonishing words about Jesus being the Messiah:

> About this time lived Jesus, a wise man, if indeed one ought to call him a man. For he was the achiever of extraordinary deeds and was a teacher of those who accept the truth gladly. He won over many Jews and many of the Greeks. He was the Messiah.[4]

Unfortunately, when "the appointed time of the end" is taken out of its 1st-century context, the biggest victim is truth. Part of God's grand purpose was to draw Jews and Gentiles into one people. This He accomplished during this divinely-determined, fixed end-time period. It cannot be changed, amended, or protracted to an unscriptural "end of time." Nor should we ignore it, suppress it, or hold it in contempt. The stakes are too high. Both Christians and Jews dilute and diminish the credibility of their separated faiths by failing to recognize the historical fulfillment outlined in our last two chapters. Let us now sincerely reconsider our full, joint, and historical heritage, and stop deferring it as a yet-future hope.

Principle 3. The Foolishness of Antichrist Speculation.

It's almost unbelievable how some Christians speculate that some future and final Antichrist is the one who confirms the covenant in Daniel's 70th week. What is their textual proof? There is none.

First, in Scripture, there is no such thing as a "final Antichrist." Antichrists (note the plural, see 1 John 2:18) were present in the midst of 1st-century saints, and have been present ever since (1 John 2:22; 2 John 7). Moreover, they don't confirm covenants. Only God makes and confirms covenants. If anything, antichrists break them. Speculation about some future, final Antichrist is just that—pure speculation that has been read into prophecy.[5]

Second, Jesus was the One who, through his crucifixion and resurrection, put a stop to the Jewish sacrifices. It was not some future Antichrist in some distant revived Roman Empire inside a rebuilt Jewish temple in Jerusalem. Moreover, there is no possible way a future Antichrist could fulfill even one of the six purpose statements encapsulated in this prophecy (see again Dan. 9:24). Likewise, there is no need to reconstruct the same socio-political conditions of that 1st century, or revive the days of Rome, or reestablish any of the obsoleted institutions of the old Judaic system (Heb. 8:13) in order for them to be destroyed again. Nor is there any need to forecast these repetitions of fulfilled end-time prophecy. It need never again be repeated.

This redundancy idea is terrible scholarship. The Bible says nothing about the Jews building a third temple in our day or in the future. Let's call this theology for what it truly is—the re-Judaizing of biblical faith (Christianity). Sadly, it has great appeal, if not a strange hypnotic power, over many who claim they are the ones who are "rightly dividing the Word of truth" (2 Tim. 2:15). If we have ever wondered how "the elect" could possibly be deceived in our day as Jesus warned (Matt. 24:24), here is one way. This delayed and deferment view does not serve the work of the Church or the purposes of God one *iota*.

Principle 4. Shifting the Burden of Proof.

The chronological exactness of Daniel's two time prophecies is, at the least, thought provoking. Their prophetic fulfillment has perfectly come to pass (see Deut. 18:22). Isn't this perfection and precision just like God? Isn't this exactness more logical than interrupting timeframes and extending fulfillment far outside of its divinely determined time context?

If we have ever wondered how "the elect" could possibly be deceived in our day as Jesus warned (Matt. 24:24), here is one way.

Increasingly, Bible scholars are recognizing, as did Klien, Blomberg, and Hubbard in their textbook, *Introduction to Biblical Interpretation*, that "the historically defensible interpretation has greatest authority. That is, interpreters can have maximum confidence in their understanding of a text when they base that understanding on historically defensible arguments."[6] They also further suggest that we "should seek the most likely time for the fulfillment of a prophecy in history."[7] Others advise that our understandings "must be historical as well as grammatical, and must always seek the meaning intended, not any meaning that can be tortured out of a passage."[8] This is exactly the interpretative methodology we have employed in the last two chapters and will follow throughout this book. As you will continue to see, my perfect-fulfillment contentions are certainly historically defensible.

When the realization of the historical fulfillment of Daniel's two time prophecies becomes better known, then the burden of proof, or rather disproof, will shift. Rightly, it must fall on those who argue that these scriptures and their fulfillments should be interpreted in unique ways:

- Those who insert a gap on their own initiative and maintain that Daniel's time prophecies are not successive, but interrupted, and who break off the fixed 70th week, leap over a gap of at least two millennia and counting, and stick it out in the future somewhere. Although this dismantling tactic provides material for sensational endsaying preaching (i.e., Israel's worst days are still ahead of them via a contrived and soon-coming, 7-year period of great tribulation), it has no known scriptural justification and undermines the credibility of those who support it.

- Those who arbitrarily stretch out Daniel's final week, or its last half, to embrace a long period of time termed the Church age (i.e., between Christ's supposed first and second comings).

- Those who tell us that the fulfillment of these end-time events cannot be found anywhere in known history—and therefore must be yet future.

- Those who claim that the timing for end-time events cannot be known by man and place it just before the proverbial and unscriptural end of the world.

- Those who believe that God's Word does not communicate to us in terms of time tables and time contexts which we can understand or trust, and that God is therefore not limited by our understanding of their normal-sense meanings.
- Those who neglect this prophecy's historical context and say that we moderns are now living in the end times, or biblical last days, and who attempt to fit present-day world circumstances and events into their end-time scenario.
- Those who shrink the 490 years to a lesser time span, or use a starting point prior to 538 B.C. (the date when Daniel received this vision) in order to make these prophecies fit into a 2nd-century B.C. fulfillment in the time of Antiochus Epiphanes and the Maccabean rededication of the Temple. Again, if this was the true fulfillment, how could all six purpose clauses of Daniel 9:24 possibly have been fulfilled in those events?
- Those who claim that Daniel's time prophesies should not and cannot be pressed to yield literal exactness or chronological reliability.

The bottom line is, no interpreter has the freedom to weave in and out of time-restricted contexts at will. We'd be well advised to honor what God has put together and let no man presume to put asunder, divide, or separate this divine and perfect ending (Matt. 19:6). Let us also heed Jesus' warning that "the Scriptures cannot be broken" (John 10:35).

Principle 5. Only One 'End' and One Indivisible 'End Time.'

Some still may be wondering, "which end was up at the time of the end?" They've been led to believe that there may be two ends, or one end split in half and only partially fulfilled back circa A.D. 70.

Please be advised that the Bible is a divinely constructed unity. Therefore, and consistently, it proclaims only *one end* (from the Greek word *telos,* meaning "goal," "destination," or "definite point," and not a "termination") and *one indivisible end-time,* or age-changing period. It may have different names, such as the "last days," "the fullness of time," "the eschaton," or "the days of the Messiah," but it is the same end. This was also the same end that Job prophesied about in writing, "my Redeemer lives and that in the end he will stand upon the earth" (Job 19:25). It's the end-time period when God completed his plan of redemption for humankind through Jesus Christ. Its historical setting and defining characteristic was "when the power of the holy people has been [was] finally broken" (Dan. 12:7). Note, once again, it was not the end of the material world, human civilization, or of time, but the end of biblical Judaism and its Old Covenant age. Hence, "the end" of which the Bible consistently speaks was covenantal and not cosmic in nature. It was and is, as they say in Latin, both a *terminus ad quem* – "the end to which, a finishing point" and a *terminus a quo* – "the end from which, a starting point." As promised, it was a "short work" (Rom. 9:28; Isa. 10:22, 23), and is long past.

This one-and-only end is also confirmed by John in the Bible's last book of Revelation. How so, you may wonder? Daniel was told to "seal up the words of the scroll until the time of the end" (Dan. 12:4). But some six hundred years later, as John was writing down the words of the prophecy of Revelation, he is told by an angel, "do not seal up the words of the prophecy of this book, because the time is at hand" (Rev. 22:10).[9] Revelation, Daniel, and all of Scripture speak of this same end.

Its historical setting and defining characteristic was "when the power of the holy people has been [was] finally broken" (Dan. 12:7).

Today, we have nothing to fear from the end that's behind us and not ahead of us—only positive things to gain. For one, it's the foundation for a better understanding of all end-time prophecy and the whole of biblical faith as well. No longer can we credibly preach a pre-end message in a post-end world.

Hence, the end the Bible proclaims lies within history rather than outside of history or at history's conclusion (there is no such thing). Outside this finished end-time framework, neither the Bible nor the end can be properly understood. Doesn't this explain why we have so many conflicting and competing views today? They naturally arise whenever the foundation of eschatological and redemptive history is torn from its God-ordained, 1st-century setting and forced to fit a timeframe God never intended.

I believe with all my heart and mind that the realization and acceptance of this fulfilled truth and historically defensible paradigm is the starting point for a new and the next reformation. As we shall continue to see, all promised end-time events were fulfilled and all redemptive realities fully established within this divinely determined time context.

Principle 6. Exact Timing Demonstrates God's Sovereignty and Perfection Better Than Gaps and Gimmicks.

The God of the Bible accurately foretold and time-restricted the course of human history through the arrival of the time of the end. This exactness demonstrates his existence, sovereignty, and divine perfection. It reveals the God of the Bible as the one, true, and proven God, Who is wise, powerful and orderly, because He accurately foretold and fulfilled these and many other things long ago (again see Isa. 44:6-8; 41:22-23, 26; 42:9; 44:7-8; 45:21-22; 48:3-6; Amos 3:7). This realization should be comforting, and not disturbing. The precise fulfillment of a predetermined end secures our faith and lends credibility and superiority to the Bible's claim of supernatural origin. No other faith, religion, or philosophy has this authenticating quality and quantity of evidence.

No longer can we credibly preach a pre-end message in a post-end world.

At other times in Scripture when God foretold through his prophets a period of time within which something significant would happen, He used familiar time language. And in every case, that event occurred precisely on time. Here are some examples:

- The 430 years of sojourning of Abraham's posterity were accomplished to the day (Gen. 15:13; Exod. 12:40-41; Gal. 3:17).
- Joseph foretold the chief baker three days would pass and then Pharaoh would hang him (Gen. 40:18-22).
- The seven years of plenty and seven years of famine that Joseph prophesied were fulfilled exactly (Gen. 41:25-32; 45:6).
- The forty-year wanderings of the Israelites in the wilderness (Num. 14:34).

- The "third day," or "in three days," or "after three days," when Jesus would be raised from the dead (numerous times in the Gospels).

Surely, the honest reader will concede that exactness glorifies God more than postponement gaps and other side-stepping gimmicks? As we shall also soon see, it honors and secures our trust in the words of Jesus and in the writings of the New Testament. By clear and conclusive proof, exactness certifies that the Bible is the inspired, infallible Word of the living God, that the world is governed by divine providence and perfection, and that biblical faith is the most reliable of all faiths. God kept all his promises, right on time. That's part of his divine perfection and the stamp of divinity. It's also an absolute and irresistible proof of the divine origin of Christianity—the *ultimate apologetic* for biblical faith. When one compares this demonstrated perfection of foretelling and precise mathematical fulfillment with the folly of various postponement, manipulation, and fabrication tactics employed by most interpreters, there is no comparison.

Principle 7. The Harmony of Consistency as a Standard for Agreement.

A truly amazing harmony of consistency runs throughout end-time Bible prophecy. For example, Daniel's time prophecies are in perfect agreement and synchronization with all the verses cited at the start of chapter five, and many more yet to be cited, including the literal rendering of Peter's consummatory statement, "The end of all things is at hand," (1 Pet. 4:7). As we shall continue to see, all were literally fulfilled in that 1st-century time context "when the power of the holy people has been [was] finally broken" (Dan. 12:7). But that harmony is lost when fulfillment is deferred to a later century. It was biblical Judaism whose time was "short" and ending, not the end of planet Earth, of human existence or the end of time—to which there is no end.

Thus, biblical faith is not a blind faith, a confused faith, or an ambiguous hard-to-understand faith. It's true, clear, technically accurate, and perfectly harmonized when kept within its 1st-century fulfillment context. The bottom line is, we can stand firm on the trustworthiness of God's Word and his literal, exact, chronological, and sequential linkage between two covenants, the Old Covenant and the New Covenant. This is the full foundation of the Christian faith upon which we are to build (Eph. 2:20), and not upon some other foundation (1 Cor. 3:10-11).

When one compares this demonstrated perfection of foretelling and precise mathematical fulfillment with the folly of various postponement, manipulation, and fabrication tactics employed by most interpreters, there is no comparison.

2,500 years ago, the Bible precisely foretold Jewish history—from Babylonian captivity to the cross, to the destruction of Jerusalem, to the end of the Old Covenant system and consummation of the new in A.D. 70. That's the way God announced it through the prophets in the Bible and performed it in history. All the pieces fit together in one harmonious whole, with no gaps, no gimmicks, and no inconsistencies when left in this divinely determined time context. Again, isn't that just like God?

In our next PART IV, we'll further discover how Jesus' and the New Testament writers' amazing predictions and their Holy-Spirit-guided expectations (John 16:13) of the end *directly* and *perfectly* tie into and connect the time between Daniel's two time prophecies. You will also see how other pieces of the end-time scenario fit this past-fulfillment paradigm better than futuristic, deferment paradigms. Once again, I implore you not to dismiss anything you read here without first testing the Scriptures and all the evidence to be presented herein (1 Thess. 5:21).

If you're ready for more, read on!

PART IV: THE 1ST-CENTURY WITNESS

Chapter 8

Jesus' Most Dramatic Prophecy Revisited

The week before He was crucified, Jesus made some startling statements about the end. He left no doubt that something truly significant was about to happen. His prophetic words are paramount to understanding end-time prophecy. Although they have puzzled and perplexed humankind for nearly 2,000 years, they need not. We have only to compare his prophecy with Habakkuk's and Daniel's—and take Him at this word—to arrive at his proper meaning.

While sitting on the Mount of Olives, looking across the valley at the beautiful Jewish Temple, Jesus stunned his disciples by prophesying that this entire complex of buildings, an awesome structure "famous throughout the world" (2 Maccabees 2:22 NRSV), would be totally destroyed. "I tell you the truth, not one stone here will be left on another; every one will be thrown down" (Matt. 24:2).

His disciples asked, "When will this happen?" (Matt. 24:3) and He answered, "I tell you the truth, this generation will certainly not pass away until all these things have happened" (Matt. 24:34). Not only was something significant about to happen, it was to happen in their lifetime. To top it off, He told them about many other end-time events that would take place within that same time period. Included in Jesus' "all these things" were:

- The end of the age and the sign of his coming (*parousia*) (vs. 3)
- The gospel preached in all the world . . . to all nations (vs. 14)
- The end will come (vs. 14)
- The abomination of desolation standing in the holy place (vs. 15)
- The hearers fleeing for their lives (vs. 16-20)
- A great tribulation, unequaled in history before or after (vs. 21)
- False Christs and false prophets appearing, performing great signs and miracles and deceiving even the elect—if that were possible (vs. 24)
- The coming (*parousia*) of the Son of Man (vs. 27)
- The sun and the moon darkened, stars falling from the sky and the heavenly bodies shaken (vs. 29)
- The sign of the Son of Man appearing in the sky (vs. 30)
- Them seeing the Son of Man coming on the clouds (vs. 30)

This passage of Scripture is recognized as Jesus' longest and most dramatic prophecy. It is also his most problematic and contested teaching. It contains the promise of what many considered to be his biggest, baddest, and best coming of all. Scholars call it the Olivet Discourse, since Jesus gave this end-time prophecy while sitting on the Mount of Olives during the last week of this life. I suggest you read Jesus' prophetic words for yourself before continuing this chapter. Three similar but slightly different versions are recorded in Matthew 24, Mark 13, and Luke 21.

Today, millions of Bible readers and scholars continue to be baffled and confused by Jesus' allegedly cryptic words and his emphasis that some of those who were there with Him at the time would witness all these climactic end-time events—i.e., "all these things." Most debate centers on what generation Jesus was really talking about when He referred to "this generation." Let's also note that He emphatically warned his first hearers, "Watch out that no one deceives you" (Matt. 24:4). As we shall see, his warning is just as relevant today as it was back then. So, if we take Jesus at his literal word (as they did) and hold to an authoritative view of Scripture, "all these things" must have occurred within the lifetime of his disciples exactly *as* and *when* He said. Nothing short of the credibility of Jesus Christ is at stake. Surely Jesus didn't make a mistake or intend to mislead his disciples. The only other alternative is that He spoke truly—just as He said He did.

Skeptics contend that Jesus' Olivet Discourse is an empty prophecy, since neither Jesus' generation, nor any generation since, has seen its "complete" fulfillment. However, his prophesied stone-by-stone destruction of the Temple complex is historical fact. It occurred in A.D. 70 - 73, precisely within the time period Jesus said. Yet most people of the world have been led to believe that the rest, and most, of Jesus' other prophetic words are still to be fulfilled.

Nothing short of the credibility of Jesus Christ is at stake. Surely Jesus didn't make a mistake or intend to mislead his disciples.

To side-step the plain meaning and utmost importance of Jesus' words, prophecy teachers and futuristic theologians have devised every kind of strained exegesis (an explanation or interpretation of a word, sentence, or passage), linguistic gymnastics, and sophisticated arguments imaginable. Not surprisingly, every attempt over the centuries to evade the force of this passage and place its fulfillment beyond the 1st-century timeframe Jesus specified has brought nothing but embarrassment and discreditation to the Church as well as undermined the deity of Christ and the integrity of the Scriptures.

Five Side-stepping Devices

Traditionalists assure us that when Jesus "returns" at his so-called "Second Coming" at some point in the future, He will fulfill the rest of his prophecy and destroy this physical world. But is this really what Jesus taught? For those raised in postponement traditions, most have never considered that Jesus might have been speaking of events (note the plural) which were *all* to transpire during the lives of his 1st-century hearers. Consequently, to cover up for Jesus' apparent failure to produce what He promised, and to defend their futuristic-deferment positions, they have employed one or more of five side-stepping devices.

These interpretative techniques usually fall under the guise of "traditional explanations." And many of us have naively accepted one or more of them as orthodox. Each device, however, is a ploy born of theological necessity—this is what they want to believe and are required to believe despite what the text plainly says. Yet none of these devices is textually, exegetically, or grammatically justifiable. They are simply "necessary" to evade, finesse around, distort, or neutralize the plain, face-value meaning and clear relevance of Jesus' prophetic words and time restriction. In other words, they are tied to agendas, and therefore "absolutely demanded." Here are the five, most-widely used, side-stepping devices to wrestle away Jesus' intended meaning from the text:

Device 1: "Generation" must refer to a future generation. Interpreters in the most popular, postponing tradition (premillennial dispensationalism) try to escape the plain meaning of Jesus' time-restrictive phrase "this generation" (and also the "you" who would experience "all these things") by claiming that Jesus' words were meant for some other, yet-unborn generation in the distant future. They maintain that the phrase "this generation" is qualified by the phrase "not pass away until all these things have happened." The latter phrase, they say, governs the timing of the former. Since they can't fathom how "all these things" could possibly have occurred during the lifetime of Jesus' contemporaries or been fulfilled in any subsequent generation, they conclude that they must occur in the lifetime of some future generation—now almost 2,000 years and counting away from when Jesus' spoke these words.

This postponement device was popularized by C.I. Scofield in the 1900s. In the reference notes for Matthew 24:34 in his *Scofield Bible*, he writes:

> The word 'generation' (Gk. *genea*), though commonly used in Scripture of those living at one time, *could not mean* those alive at the time of Christ, as none of 'these things'—i.e. the world-wide preaching of the Kingdom, the tribulation, the return of the Lord in visible glory, and the regathering of the elect—occurred then. The expression 'this generation' here (1) *may mean* that the *future generation* which will endure the tribulation and see the signs, will also see the consummation, the return of the Lord . . . . (italics mine)

Hal Lindsey, today's best-known end-time prophecy writer of this same tradition, claims that Jesus' "this generation" began in 1948 with the rebirth of the nation of Israel. In Lindsey's vernacular, this means our current generation is "the terminal generation." Several red flags wave against this popular but misleading interpretative device.

First, it's circular reasoning as well as double talk to say that whatever generation sees these things happen will be Jesus' "this generation." What must rightly be emphasized is that at the time He spoke these words, Jesus was sitting face-to-face with his disciples on the Mount of Olives. He spoke directly to them. Naturally, He used first-person speech (now printed in red letters in some Bibles) and the commonly used, normally understood language of ordinary people of that time: "And the common people heard Him gladly" (Mark 12:37 KJV). His strong sense of directness and imminence would not have led them to believe that He was addressing distant matters or a future, far-removed generation of people. Furthermore, Matthew expected them to "understand" (see Matthew's insert editorial note in Matt. 24:15; also in Mark 13:14).

Second, no other or future generation is mentioned or even hinted at anywhere in this chapter's context or in any of the chapters leading up to or following Jesus' prophecy. That's why the demonstrative pronoun Jesus used is *this* and not *that*. Since "this" has no textual antecedent, the generation Jesus was speaking to personally is its first-person object. Hence, "this generation" carries the grammatical idea of present existence. To divorce this time-indicator phrase from its natural first-person context is both a grammatical abuse and an interpretive violation.

Third, a simple word study of the seventeen other New Testament uses of the identical word construction reveals that "this generation" always means the generation then living.[1] Since no textual justification exists for abandoning its consistent use, the standard, natural, and plain grammatical meaning should be the one accepted.

Fourth, let's recall that the vast majority in the first generation of the nation of Israel, who came out of Egyptian bondage with Moses and wandered through the wilderness, never entered the Promise Land. They had treated God with contempt and disobeyed Him. Hence, God pronounced judgment on *that* generation and the adults of *that* generation perished in the wilderness. Their children also suffered for the unfaithfulness of their parents. For forty years they were confined as shepherds to the wilderness (see Num. 14:23-35). Likewise, and over a long time in biblical history, judgment had been prophesied upon the last generation of national and biblical Israel (see Deut. 31:26-29; 32:1-43; Isa. 5:1-7; Dan. 9:24-27; 12:1-13). That generation was Jesus' "this generation." They suffered the desolating judgment of the destruction of Jerusalem and the Temple. It all happened within the span of forty years from the time Jesus Himself pronounced this same, age-ending judgment upon his contemporaries.

Fifth, Jesus' many uses of the personal pronoun "you" always relate to the same time period and group of people He is speaking to. His plural "you(s)" consistently refer to the ones living then and there, and the ones hearing his words. Jesus told them, "*you* will be handed over and put to death . . ." (Matt. 24:9; see also Matt. 10:16-23 and Paul's similar words in 1 Thess. 3:3-4). "*You* will see . . ." (Matt. 24:15), "*Your* flight . . ." (Matt. 24:20), "I have told *you* ahead of time" (Matt. 24:25), "*You* know . . ." (Matt. 24:32, 33), and "I tell *you* the truth . . . " (Matt. 24:34), "And so upon *you* will come all the righteous blood that has been shed on earth . . . ." (Matt. 23:35), "Look, your house is left to *you* desolate" (Matt. 23:38). He used "you" in a personal way for both his followers and his adversaries, a factor that must not be ignored or denied. This is the simplest and plainest understanding of the text and the most conventional use of the word "you"—i.e., applying it to a present audience. Jesus was not trying to misguide those early Christians or the unbelieving Jews to keep them in line. They were the "you" He meant. To *them* He applied the fulfillment of his prophecy. Their generation would be the one that would not pass away until "all these things" took place. They would personally witness and experience all these end-time events. This is the most logical and harmonious understanding of this supposed "difficult" text. It only becomes difficult when we try to circumvent its original audience and make its relevancy fit into a still-future time and nature context.

As we shall see, in our next chapter, Jesus' hearers and first readers took this relevancy to heart. For them it became a matter of life and death. Furthermore, while Jesus' prophetic words were spoken and written *to* them, and not to us or some future generation, they were certainly written *for* us. Big difference!

Device 2: "Generation" must mean "race," "nation," or "a kind of people." Some Bibles add a footnote next to Jesus' word "generation"[2] indicating that the word could mean "race or nation (Israel)." The Scofield Bible's reference note for Matthew 24:34 gives this possibility as a second meaning:

> . . . it may be used in the sense of *race* or *family*, meaning that the nation or family of Israel will be preserved "until all these things have happened . . . .

This device stretches Jesus' words "this generation" from being a contemporary group to being a long line of successive generations. But by substituting these alternative meanings, all time relevance is lost. Especially note, however, that the *only* place the word "generation" is footnoted with these alternative meanings is in the three gospel accounts of Jesus' Olivet Discourse. In all its other thirty-three identical uses in the New Testament, *no footnote* is attached and no alternative meaning added! And, this word is never interpreted nor translated as race, nation, Israel, or the Jewish people. Could there be any more blatant evidence of bias-interpreting among translators? This arbitrary device is a classic example of the inconsistencies some will resort to in order to defend their agenda-driven, futuristic, postponing, end-time-scenario schemes. Yet no scriptural warrant exists for this intrusive and distortive attempt to make generation mean race or nation.

Could there be any more blatant evidence of bias-interpreting among translators?

Others attempt to avoid the temporal meaning of the word "generation" by claiming that it refers to a kind of people possessing similar attributes (such as unbelief and bad character and headed toward judgment). Proponents of this interpretation argue that Jesus' wick, adulterous, and evil generation will last as long as wickedness, adultery, and evil remain and persist. Obviously, they contend that such a period has not passed away. Some warrant does exist for this application. It is a possible but also a secondary meaning that is recognized in most Greek reference books. Like most words, generation has more than one meaning. Even today, English dictionaries list ten or more possible meanings for the word generation. This other meaning, once again however, is not its primary meaning.

A simple study of the Greek word *genea*, translated "generation," should clear things up. The primary meaning of *genea* is a people living at the same time. Most scholars agree that *genea's* use in the Bible refers to a chronological association, and not ethnicity or personal characteristics, nor to an unlimited duration of time. The Bible says that forty-two "generations" were between Abraham and Christ (Matt. 1:1-17), and these obviously are not forty-two races of Israel or forty-two kinds of people carrying Abraham's blood. Likewise, in the Old Testament, God's chronological timing for Israel to come out of Egyptian bondage was in the "fourth generation" of exiled Israelites, and not in some elongated unknowable time of a race or kind of people (Gen. 15:16). Similarly, God told Noah to get himself and his family into the ark "because I have found you righteous in this generation" (Gen. 7:1). Conclusively and consistently, the Bible reckons a generation to be a contemporary group of people. Scripture also implies that the length of a biblical generation is forty years (Heb. 3:9-10).

If Jesus had meant to convey any other meaning, the inspired writers of his words could have chosen from several more appropriate Greek words such as *ethnos* (translated as "nation" in Matt. 24:7, 9, 14), or *genos* (translated as "generation" in 1 Pet. 2:9 and having more of a meaning of "kin" or "kind"), or *suggenes* (translated as "race" in Rom. 9:3 NIV and meaning "kinsmen, fellow countrymen or a relative by blood)," or *gennema* (translated as "generation" in the KJV and as "brood" in the NIV in Matt. 3:7; 12:34; 23:33 and meaning a type or progeny of people with like character and attributes).

If we are so lax or willing to be so undisciplined that we'll allow some hard-pressed postponement interpreters and Bible translators such latitude and freedom in changing the meanings of simple words, why don't we change the meaning of some other simple words, as well? What would happen if we changed the definite article "the" to the indefinite "a" in "I [Jesus] am *the* way and *the* truth and *the* life . . ." (John 14:6)? What would be the justification for this change? It would be the same as changing "generation" from a definite contemporary group to an indefinite "race" or endless type of people. There is *no justification* for this change or device—*absolutely none.*

In all honesty, the biblical phrase "this generation" should cause no difficulty. After all, Jesus was answering a *when* question from his disciples (Matt. 24:3). These proposed other meanings would be non-answers and basically leave the disciple's time question unanswered. But Jesus consistently and repeatedly used this same key phrase and time-context statement elsewhere. In Matthew 23, Jesus sets the stage and historical context for his Matthew 24 prophecy. He pronounces seven "messianic woes" on the Pharisees. He calls them "You snakes! You brood of vipers!" (Matt. 23:33). He says, "upon you will come all the righteous blood that has been shed on earth . . ." (Matt. 23:35). Then He makes the identical time statement, "I tell you the truth, all this will come upon this generation" (Matt. 23:36). What generation did He mean? The answer is, the same one He intended in all his other identical uses of the word and phrase—his contemporaries. Here are a few more examples:

- The same "wicked and adulterous generation" who was asking for a sign (Matt. 12: 39; 16:4).
- The same one He calls an "unbelieving and perverse generation" and asks "how long shall I stay with you? How long shall I put up with you?" (Matt. 17:17).
- The same one that would reject God's only Son: "But first he must suffer many things and be rejected by this generation" (Luke 17:25).
- The same one to whom John the Baptist came and about which Jesus lamented, "To what shall I compare this generation?" (Matt. 11:16-24).
- The same one who would crucify Him: "Therefore, this generation will be held responsible for the blood of all the prophets that has been shed since the beginning of the world . . . Yes, I tell you, this generation will be held responsible for it all" (Luke 11:50, 51b).
- They were worse than all previous generations: "more wicked . . . . That is how it will be with this wicked generation" (Matt. 12:45).
- And the same one Peter warned his contemporaries about: "Save yourselves from this corrupt [perverse] generation" (Acts 2:40; from Deut. 32:5, 20).

The Pharisees knew that Jesus was speaking to them and prophesying a judgment that was to come upon them (see Matt. 21:45; 23:29-38; Mark 12:12). They were the generation who shouted out, "Crucify him . . . crucify him" and "let his blood be on us and on our children" (Matt. 27:22-25).[3] They were the ones who would personally experience the horrors of the end-time events. They were the ones upon who would "come all the righteous blood shed upon the earth . . ." (Matt. 23:35), not some unborn yet-future generation or people of the Jewish race in a far distant time. Jesus further told them, "Look, your house is left to you desolate" (Matt. 23:38). There is no need to explain away Jesus' use of the word generation, or mutilate its normally understood, consistent meaning. Nor is there a need to extend it beyond a scriptural forty-year period. History records that circa A.D. 70 exactly forty years and within one generation after Jesus gave his powerful end-time prophecy, Jerusalem, the Temple, and the whole of biblical Judaism were utterly destroyed and left desolated.

Only one generation in history was Jesus' "this generation." That generation was a contemporary group who had become the most evil, ungodly, rebellious generation of Jews ever. That generation of Jewish people filled up their cup of iniquity by rejecting and crucifying the promised Messiah and persecuting God's emerging new people. No other generation comes close. No other generation makes sense of the time-limited and time-sensitive meaning that Jesus gave it.

Only one generation in history was Jesus' "this generation." That generation was a contemporary group . . . .

Who are we to add some 19 centuries and counting? The Bible defines its own limitations. And no interpreter has the freedom or the right to weave in and out of time contexts at will. Jesus' "this generation" must be taken literally, consistently, and within the commonly used and normally understood meaning of his words. Outside this historical context, the end that the Bible proclaims, with all its associated events, cannot be understood. Therefore, postponement beyond the generation in which Jesus lived must be called what it truly is—unscriptural.

Device 3: Dividing Jesus' prophecy into two sections. Reformed, amillennial, and postmillennial circles use this side-stepping device. It, too, causes great harm to the intended understanding of Jesus' prophetic truths. And it bears a striking resemblance to the interruption and dismemberment treatment of Daniel's 70 weeks that we exposed in chapters five and seven.

To their credit, most reformed scholars agree that Jesus' "this generation" means exactly what it plainly says. But then they divide his prophetic words into two sections. One section is associated with events fulfilled circa A.D. 70. The other events, however, are ascribed to a second, yet-to-be-fulfilled "end of time" (a phrase the Bible never uses) section, which is equated to be the "real" end of the age (i.e., the end of the Christian age, which is without end—see Eph. 3:21; Luke 1:33; Isa. 9:7). How can they do this?

They allege that Jesus did not structure his Matthew 24 discourse according to the three questions asked by his disciples (Matt. 24:3). Rather, they contend, He "clearly separated" his answer to their first question about the destruction of the Temple and the fall of Jerusalem from their two other questions regarding his coming (return) and the end of the age. Of course, they concede that the first part occurred in A.D. 70. But they argue that his return and the end of the age (i.e., again, the end of the Christian age and not the age of Moses) still await the end of the physical world at the end of time. Thus, the whole of Jesus' predicted events must span two different end-time periods separated by a 19-centuries-and-counting gap of time. Sound familiar? Although totally unannounced in the text, and without any clear biblical warrant, the dividing line between the two time sections is usually placed between verses 34 and 35, or 35 and 36, and for *some very strained reasons.* Those reasons, followed by my rebuttals, are:

1. *Verse 36 begins with the word "but" (in some translation—see Matt. 24 KJV) and is, obviously, a transitional verse.* The word "but" is used here as a conjunction, not a preposition. It joins and does not change subjects, alter context, or contrast with what Jesus has just said. If the use of the word "but" at the beginning of a phrase *does* introduce a new subject—and we insist on consistency—then there are at least 15 subject changes in Matthew 24 and 25 in the KJV. That is clearly ridiculous!

2. *Signs are given in the first section but not in the second.* This is an argument from silence and proves nothing. Why must Jesus repeat what He's already stated? Isn't it possible that He had given all the signs He intended to give at that point?

3. *The text "demands" this division, but the events described in verses 14 and 27 belong in the second section.* There is no scriptural authorization for making such an exception. While clinging to their two-end program, Reformed dividers seem to have no qualms whatsoever about cherry-picking verses from one time section and applying them to the other.

4. *Or, the parousia mentioned in the first section (verse 27) is metaphorical and occurred in A.D. 70 but the one in the second section (verses 37 and 39) refers to another coming or the final return of the Lord at the end of time.* That means there are two *parousias,* two returns. The former one Jesus' disciples could know about. The other they could not. Then why in the second section would Jesus, by inspiration, command his disciples there with Him to "watch" (Matt. 24:42) and "be ready" (Matt. 24:44) for something that wasn't to take place until more than 1,900 years after their deaths? Or, why would He confuse them—and us—by telling his disciples about two age-ending comings when they only asked about one (Matt. 24:3)?

Moreover, how would Jesus' original audience have ever figured this out? The truth is Jesus' Olivet Discourse (Matthew 24) cannot be divided. He did not jump millennia in one breath or suddenly change subjects in midstream. Nor did He introduce a different coming, or ambiguously discuss a local minor coming versus a universal major coming centuries later. His terminology never changed. Nowhere does the text support this division. It's purely a devised and imaginary dividing line forced by a deferment agenda.

Here's more proof that every attempt to identify an unannounced point of division between any two verses is scripturally in error. Notice that neither of the accounts found in Luke 21 and Mark 13 lend themselves to any such division, nor does the parallel teaching in Luke 17:20-37. While this latter passage covers the same end-time events, it speaks of them all happening in one time period, "on the day the Son of Man is revealed" (Luke 17:30). Like the others, this passage cannot be divided into a two-section format. But, and even more interesting, its listing of events is in a totally different and intermingled order from that of Matthew's account. The graphic in Appendix B illustrates the fallacy of attempting to divide the events of Matthew 24 and Luke 17 into two different and time-separated sections.[4]

There is no escaping the obvious truth that the integrity and prophetic unity of Jesus' Olivet Discourse (Matt. 24, Mark 13, Luke 21) must stand undivided. His powerful prophecy is a united, end-times discourse discussing only *one* subject and *one* fulfillment. No announced or unannounced time division exists. Jesus plainly intended it to be one interconnected, interrelated, interdependent context. Contextually, "all these things" were to occur within Jesus' time-indicator phrase of "this generation" (i.e., the contemporary "you" group at the end of that Jewish age).

Isn't it time we ceased putting asunder, separating, or dividing what God (in Christ) has joined together (Matt. 19:6; Mark 10:9)? Let's affirm here too that "the Scripture cannot be broken" (John 10:35). Also worth mentioning is the biblical lesson of the two women who argued over possession of a baby. Solomon's proposed solution was a division—cutting the baby in half (1 Kgs. 3:16-28). But this was unbearable. Let's keep this story in mind the next time someone suggests dividing Matthew 24 into two parts. Lastly, let's also honor "rightly dividing the word of truth" (2 Tim. 2:15), with our emphasis on "rightly," not on "dividing."

Device 4: Change the meaning of the apocalyptic language. Again, without any scriptural justification, Jesus' descriptive phraseology of the sun and moon darkening, of stars falling from the sky, and heavenly bodies shaken (Matt. 24:29) is suddenly declared to mean something different from its time-honored figurative usages and its many historical fulfillments.

As we saw in chapter three, this figurative language is the language of the Prophets. In all its numerous uses and fulfillments throughout the Bible, never once was the physical creation ever altered or affected to this extent. Instead, this vivid cosmic-collapsing, earth-shaking language always prophesied a coming divine judgment and destruction of wicked nations. Here, in his New Testament prophecy, Jesus is quoting from the prophet Isaiah (Matt. 24:29; from Isa. 13:10; 34:4). Let's recall that

Isaiah used this same phraseology and apocalyptic imagery in foretelling a coming "day of the Lord" in judgment against Babylon in the 6th century B.C. (Isa. 13:10) and another against Edom in the 6th century B.C. (Isa. 34:4). Jesus gave no indication He was using this figurative language any differently.[5] In a similar fashion, He was announcing the coming judgment and destruction upon Jerusalem and the Temple, and the passing away of the Judaic system and age. The imagery and parallel are far too striking and strong to avoid.

For some strange and unknown reason, however, postponement interpreters arbitrarily declare that this type of language now means something it has never meant before (i.e., a literal and catastrophic end of the world). Such a shift in meaning without any legitimate textual justification betrays an ignorance and/or avoidance of biblical history and the nature of its many historical fulfillments. This fourth device is another serious interpretive error that's in opposition to the entire witness of Scripture. Almost verbatim, Jesus appropriated this apocalyptic language. Its scriptural precedents demand that we understand it in exactly the same way as it was fulfilled many times before in Old Testament history.

Device 5: Jesus was mistaken or never said these words. To their credit, atheists, critics of Christianity, and liberal-tradition Christians, alike, recognize the time limitation of Jesus' "this generation" and his pronounced emphasis on the fulfillment of all end-time events within the lifetime of his hearers. Rightly, they conclude that if "all these things" did not take place *as* and *when* Jesus said, something is dreadfully amiss.

This nonoccurrence factor is a legitimate complaint and an inescapable dilemma for Christians. It has opened wide the door for liberal Christians to invent some equally strained but disastrous twists in an attempt to discount or explain away the implications of Christ's Olivet Discourse. They handle the supposed nonoccurrence problem by contending that Jesus was mistaken and made erroneous pronouncements. Or, they contend that He never spoke some or many of the words attributed to Him, theorizing that these words must have been fabricated and added to Scripture after A.D. 70 by his zealous followers—including the prophecies about the invasion of Judea and destruction of the Temple.[6]

Thus, Jesus' embarrassing time and imminency statements in his Olivet Discourse became the crack that let the liberals in the door in the 19th century. Once in, they systematically began questioning and dismantling all of Scripture. Their assumption was, and still is, that if the Bible is wrong here, it's surely wrong elsewhere. They even call into question the divinity of Jesus and attempt to discredit large portions of his teachings and ministry by searching for the real historical Jesus. What's even more amazing is that conservative evangelicals have had no effective response to these liberal assertions and discrediting inroads, except to say that someday Jesus will come back and finish the job, which only proves the liberals' point.

This nonoccurrence factor is a legitimate complaint and an inescapable dilemma for Christians.

The imminence of Jesus' "this generation," and whom He meant by "you," lie at the heart of his message on the Mount of Olives. These two chronological and relevancy keys are indispensable to the proper understanding of his prophecy, and all New Testament end-time statements as well. His words were not vague or ambiguous. They were clear and time-sensitive. They qualified the time context and nature of fulfillment, and therefore absolutely demanded a 1st-century fulfillment. It's the most natural way of reading and understanding the text.

If, however, Jesus was mistaken, or even partially mistaken, about something this central and this dramatic, how can we trust anything else He said? Or, if we allow that He never made these statements, how can we defend the Bible as authoritative or inerrant? If the Bible is wrong here, might it not also be mistaken on any number of spiritual matters? This problem is a serious one. If any of these liberal assertions is true, biblical faith becomes extremely vulnerable. And this is precisely where the liberal methodology of historical criticism logically leads. All liberals in the Christian tradition need to squarely face the consequences of their approach—the bankrupting of the faith. All conservative evangelicals, on the other hand, need to squarely recognize that their cover-up attempts don't and won't work. There is only one credible and effective solution to the dilemma of nonoccurrence. It's *occurrence*. Perhaps this book will help both groups wake up. (More on this in chapter eleven.)

In sum, the five side-stepping devices are nothing more than exegetic gymnastics designed to evade, explain away, or cover up. The result is the same, however. The relevance and force of Jesus' prophetic words are undermined. These are simply blatant and desperate ploys born of theological necessity from those compelled by their particular traditions. At best, these avoidance and tampering techniques are serious errors. At worst, they constitute "handling the word of God deceitfully" (2 Cor. 4:2 KJV). None of these devices should be tolerated by responsible handlers of God's Word. When undisciplined manipulation of Scripture like this is allowed, any number of conflicting and confusing fulfillment claims can be advanced. This is precisely how most prophetic disagreements and confusion have come about. These devices have plagued the field of end-time Bible prophecy for far too long. They prevent an honest reader from grasping the true meaning and relevance of Jesus' powerful prophetic words. We must guard against these destructive tendencies and allow the Bible to speak plainly for itself. But there is another and extra-biblical witness that bears a hearing.

Enoch's '70th Generation' Prophecy

During the four hundred year period after the writing of the last Old Testament book (circa 400 B.C.) and prior to the birth of Jesus, other prophetic books were written that were never later canonized by the Church—i.e., made part of the Bible. One of these was the Book of Enoch. It is also called 1 Enoch or the Lost Book of Enoch. Most likely, it was preserved by oral tradition from an ancient date and written down by an unknown scribe some time between 200 - 80 B.C.

In New Testament times, this Book of Enoch was a well-known prophecy in Jewish circles. Fragments of at least eight separate copies have been found among the Dead Sea Scrolls. Interestingly, the early Church held it in high regard and gave it almost canonical status. More than fifty verses throughout the New Testament appear to come word-for-word from or were possibly influenced by the Book of Enoch.[7] Several early church writers quoted from it. And, it was used in the Church until the 3rd century, when it disappeared.

The book begins like the book of Revelation with an angel speaking to Enoch predicting "the day of tribulation," the coming of "the Holy

Great One," and the "judgment upon all." The angel, however, tells Enoch that this prophecy is "not for this generation, but for a remote one which is for to come" (1 Enoch 1:1-3).

Most Christian scholars maintain that this "remote" time still is in our future. But according to 1 Enoch 10:12, this judgment would occur exactly "seventy generations" from the man Enoch's generation (see Gen. 5.18-24).

In the New Testament book of Jude, Jude both cites the man Enoch of Genesis 5 and quotes directly from the prophecy of the Book of Enoch. Hence, Jude intimates that the origin of this prophecy was the seventh patriarch, Enoch. Contextually, the book of Jude discuss "certain men," there and then present in that 1st century, "whose condemnation was written about long ago" (Jude 4, 11-13). It refers to Enoch's same impending "judgment on the great Day" (Jude 6). By inspiration, Jude writes and quotes 1 Enoch 1:9, thusly:

> Enoch, the seventh from Adam, prophesied about these men: "See, the Lord is coming with thousands upon thousands of his holy ones to judge everyone . . . ." (Jude 14-15)

The question is, when would this coming and the judgment of all take place? It's not difficult to figure out. The Book of Enoch had said it would be "seventy generations" from Enoch's time. These generations are chronologically listed in Luke's gospel (see Luke 3:23-37). Since Luke said he had "carefully investigated everything from the beginning" and desired "to write an orderly account . . . so that you may know the certainty of the things you have been taught" (Luke 1:3-4), we can have confidence in his records. If we count backward through Luke's "the-sons-of" generations, starting with Jesus' generation, we discover that there were exactly seventy generations back to Enoch. *Thus, Jesus' generation was that 70th generation from Enoch's generation.* That means Jesus' generation was the time period predicted by the Book of Enoch for the Lord's coming in judgment and the judgment of all.

So what happened to this highly esteemed Book of Enoch? It was never canonized and disappeared around the 3rd or 4th century A.D. Consequently, it became known as the Lost Book of Enoch. A complete manuscript wasn't discovered until A.D. 1768 in Ethiopia.

Some theorize that its precise time prophecy was too radical (and past in fulfillment) for the Church's futuristic-oriented canon committees. It surely didn't fit with their idea that Jesus' coming in judgment was still future. It is further speculated that the Catholic Church destroyed all copies and that is why it only survived in Ethiopia. Others reason that it contains contradictions with other church doctrines and that its origin was the work of several writers. Therefore, it couldn't pass canonization requirements.

Of course, the Book of Enoch has not been considered inspired Scripture. But there are two significant exceptions: 1) It was somewhat regarded as inspired in Jude's time. 2) Jude's direct quote turned 1 Enoch 1:9 into Scripture. So surely it has some merit.

Thus, Jesus' generation was that 70th generation from Enoch's generation. **That means that Jesus' generation was the time** *period . . .* **for the Lord's coming in judgment and the judgment of all.**

What cannot be overemphasized is that the Book of Enoch's 70th-generation prophecy is in complete harmony and perfect consistency with the plain, natural, and literal understanding of Jesus' "this generation" time prophecy, and with the contemporary expectations of the inspired New Testament writers. All three sources bear a powerful and uniform witness to the 1st-century A.D. as the time of Jesus' coming on the clouds in age-ending judgment.

Restoring Jesus' Original Meaning

Any time someone has to create new definitions of familiar words, find exceptions to normal meanings, discount the reliability of Scripture, or go to any of the lengths outlined above, something is wrong. If allowed to stand, these traditions of men cast aspersion on Jesus' other sayings, destroy the authenticity, authority and inerrancy of Scripture, and make the Word of God of little or no effect (Matt. 15:6; Mark 7:13). It's time we stopped reading the text of Jesus' Olivet Discourse through the distorted eyes of these traditions and restored his powerful prophetic words to their original meaning. Consider these attributes of Jesus:

He is clear and emphatic. How could Jesus have been any more clear or emphatic? What other words or phrases could He have used to communicate any better? Moreover, how could He, Matthew, and Mark have expected his original hearers and readers to understand (Matt. 24:15; Mark 13:14) if He was being deceptive? Why don't we sincerely consider the possibility that maybe, just maybe, Jesus *said what He meant and meant what He said*? As we shall see, most but not all of his followers understood exactly what He literally intended and the utmost importance of his words in their lives.

Simplicity is the key for solving the majority of our end-time confusions and conflicts. In the words of the old hymn,

> Tis so sweet to trust in Jesus,
> Just to take Him at His word,
> Just to rest upon His promise,
> Just to know, "Thus saith the Lord."

Why should it be so hard for us to believe exactly what Jesus and the Bible say? What a contrast this presents to the inconsistencies, abuses, and errors of the five contrived, side-stepping devices used by most traditional interpreters and their postponing views.

He is in perfect harmony. The literal timeframe of Jesus' "this generation" perfectly correlates with the literal, exact, chronological, and sequential fulfillment of Daniel's two time prophecies previously covered. (Again, see the timeline in Appendix A.) This transition period transpired over exactly forty years—one biblical generation. It perfectly connected Daniel's last and 70th week to his 1,290 – 1,335 days "time of the end." That's why Jesus tapped directly into Daniel's time of "unequaled distress" or "tribulation" (Matt. 24:21 from Dan. 12:1) and the coming of "the abomination that causes desolation" (Matt. 24:15 from Dan. 12:11). The end in Jesus' prophetic discourse and the end in Daniel 12 are the *same end*. They speak of an identical scenario—"when the power of the holy people has been finally broken all these things will be completed" (Dan. 12:7). This breaking of power is the defining characteristic of the nature and historical setting for the one and only end the Bible consistently proclaims. It can refer to no other time or event other than the fall of Jerusalem circa A.D. 70. What's more, this perfect harmony of literal prophetic convergence in that 1st-century time period is beyond coincidence and human manipulation. Its pinpointed divine perfection should conclusively demonstrate that the end-focus of the Bible was covenantal change, not cosmic catastrophe.

> maybe, just maybe, Jesus *said what He meant and meant what He said*? ... most but not all of his followers understood exactly what He literally intended and the utmost importance of his words in their lives.

Furthermore, Jesus' words are in perfect harmony with the other time and imminence statements made by New Testament writers (or perhaps we should say that they are in perfect harmony with Him). Guided by the Holy Spirit into all truth, and shown the things that were to come (John 16:13), the New Testament writers spoke of the same end-time events and soon-coming end. Hence, Peter spoke in plain terms and in a 1st-century context when he warned that "the end of all things is at hand" (1 Pet. 4:7) and "it is time for judgment to begin with the family of God" (1 Pet. 4:17).

No evidence supports the contention that Jesus, the New Testament writers, or the early Church were looking beyond their day and time and the fate of Jerusalem to a world-ending catastrophe as the "end of all things." How much more perfectly must the time prophecies and imminency statements of Scripture agree and harmoniously align before men and women of faith bow to their authority? Postponing fulfillment of "these last days" (Heb. 1:2), or "last times" (1 Pet. 1:20) beyond the generation in which Jesus lived must be seen for what it truly is—unscriptural.

He is an infallible Prophet. According to the standard of Deuteronomy 18:22:

> If what a prophet proclaims in the name of the Lord does not take place or come true, that is a message the Lord has not spoken.

This Old Testament statement was the acid test for prophets in Israel. If "all these things" didn't come to pass *as* and *when* Jesus said, He should be considered a false prophet, or, at the very least, a fallible prophet, as many atheists, critics of Christianity, and liberals maintain. There is no other alternative. Conversely, we must give the name "false" to the failed end-saying prophets of subsequent generations and our generation. The remainder of the verse from Deuteronomy also says that such a prophet has spoken presumptuously, and that no one need fear him.

We are therefore left with two options: 1) continue with our various side-stepping devices, or 2) take a positive approach as we seek to understand the possibility of 1st-century fulfillment. Let's take the latter and submit to the absolute authority of Jesus and his prophetic words, and to the full and complete inspiration and divine perfection of the Bible. In so doing, I challenge you, as I have been challenged, to search the scriptures carefully for the real fulfillment of Jesus' most dramatic prophecy and its real "end time."

This is exactly what we will do throughout the remaining chapters of this book. Next, therefore, let's explore in more depth the historical and scriptural fulfillment of the end that was, the last days that were.

Chapter 9

The End that Was, the Last Days that Were

Much of what you are about to read in this chapter was common knowledge among Christians in the 18th century. But with the advent of modern futuristic prophecy views in the 19th and 20th centuries, this history has been largely ignored and forgotten.

History records that circa A.D. 70, exactly forty years after Jesus prophesied on the Mount of Olives and within the span of one biblical generation, Roman armies led by Titus destroyed the city of Jerusalem and the Jewish Temple. This was the same Temple that was standing when Jesus foretold its destruction—not some third (or fourth), rebuilt temple centuries removed.

Make no mistake—Jesus was no false or fallible prophet. He was the greatest Prophet of all. And even though many may have dealt loosely, if not treacherously, with Jesus' words, He set a definite time limit for the "last days," of biblical Judaism. Every New Testament reference to the "last days" or to equivalent terms such as "last times" or "last hour," confirms the same. These times were not a 19-centuries-and-counting extended period. Without exception, they literally refer to that 1st-century timeframe in which these writers were living, there and then. Hebrews 1:1-2 clearly and firmly affixes Jesus' earthly ministry, as well as the time in which the writer of Hebrews was writing, to the historic and biblical time period termed the "last days:"

In the past God spoke to our forefathers through the prophets at many times and in various ways, but in these last days he has spoken to us by his Son . . . . (also see: Acts 2:17; 1 Tim. 4:1; 2 Tim. 3:1; Jas. 5:3; 1 Pet. 1:5, 20; 2 Pet. 3:3; Jude 18; 1 John 2:18).

This time-restricted period of "these last days" was to encompass the full redemptive work of the Messiah: his birth, anointing, teaching, ushering in of the everlasting kingdom of God, death, resurrection, sending of the Holy Spirit, ending of the Jewish age, and much more, as we shall see.

These biblical "last days" were never to be the last days of the world, planet Earth, human history, or the Church. They *were* also the beginning days of the Church, as well as the last days of the biggest thing that was ending at the time or will ever end on Planet Earth—the ending of biblical Judaism and its Old Covenant age. That's why the Apostle Paul reminded his contemporaries that ". . . this world in its present form is [was] passing away" (1 Cor. 7:31) and that "the time is [was] short" (1 Cor. 7:29). For Paul the end was very close. Was he wrong? Or did he understand exactly what he was saying?

No doubt for most readers, what I have been presenting is a completely different understanding of end-times prophecy and its fulfillment. But crucial to our understanding are the proper identification of this end-time period and its literal fulfillments. It's a powerful vindication of the perfection of God's prophetic word. Daniel had prophesied that its historical setting and defining characteristic would be "when the power of the holy people has been [was] finally broken" (Dan. 12:7). And this is exactly what happened circa A.D. 70. Jesus' Olivet Discourse prophecy perfectly fits this scenario. Forty years—one biblical "this generation"—had been given to the Israelites to repent and accept their Messiah. Some did. Many didn't. But when the time of God's grace was over, "it is [was] time for judgment to begin with the family of God" or "at the house of God" (1 Pet. 4:17 NIV-KJV). This age-ending judgment certainly came during the final portion of Israel's "last days." After A.D. 70 -73, the "last days" were over.

As we saw in chapter six, the events leading up to and following this historic period are well-documented in the eyewitness accounts of Josephus, the 1st-century Jewish historian and Pharisee who led the Galilean army during the revolt of A.D. 66. His eyewitness account of the terrible sieges and the fall of Jerusalem is one of the most fascinating and reliable that can be found anywhere. Other non-eyewitness accounts were written by Tacitus, the Roman historian; Eusebius, the 4th-century Christian historian (A.D. 263 - 340.); and in the Talmud.

But crucial to our understanding are the proper identification of this end-time period and its literal fulfillments.

The existence of these historical accounts often comes as a surprise to many Christians. Let's especially note that Josephus was not a Christian, nor was he sympathetic to Christianity. He was a Jewish general who was captured by the Romans and later prophesied that Vespasian would become Emperor of Rome. When this happened, Josephus gained favor with the Romans and was released from prison. They appointed him their historian. So he wrote to please the Romans rather than the Christians. It is amazing how closely Josephus' recorded history illuminates and reflects the various details of Jesus' Mount Olivet prophecy as recorded in the three gospel accounts (Matt. 24, Mark 13, and Luke 21).

Below are eight confirmatory insights into key events fulfilling Jesus' prophecy of "all these things" within his literal time-constraint of "this generation." Once again, keep in mind these two directives: 1) Though not one word of Jesus' end-of-the-age prophecy was written *to* us, every word was written *for* us. 2) "The historically defensible interpretation has greatest authority."[1]

Eight Confirmatory Insights

1. Early confirmations. Jesus told his 1st-century disciples that they would be the ones to see "all these things" take place. Three early Church fathers confirmed that these things did indeed occur:

- Historian and church leader Eusebius (A.D. 260 - 340), in his patristic writings of the early 4th century, is our source for much information about the first three centuries of the Christian community. He understood that the "great tribulation" of Jesus' Olivet prophecy was fulfilled in the events leading up to and culminating circa A.D. 70:

> All this occurred in this manner, in the second year of the reign of Vespasian, according to the predictions of our Lord and Saviour Jesus Christ . . . .[2]

> The abomination of desolation, according to the prophetic declaration, stood in the very temple of God . . . which was approaching its total downfall and final destruction by fire.[3]

- St. Augustine, writing about this same topic, stated:

> For Luke (21:20) very clearly bears witness that the prophecy of Daniel was fulfilled when Jerusalem was overthrown.[4]

- Athanasius wrote:

> . . . in accordance with the injunction of the Apostles, let us go beyond the types and sing a new song of praise . . . For no longer were these things to be done which belonged to Jerusalem which is beneath . . . the things pertaining to that time were fulfilled, and those which belonged to shadows had passed away.[5]

2. Those who correctly read the signs and fled. Jesus spoke of a whole catalogue of signs (events) which would herald the coming of the end (Matt. 24:5-12, 21-25). Many modern-day interpreters call these "signs of the times" and argue that we are just now seeing them occur, or are seeing them occur with greater intensity and frequency. These signs include: social decay, wars, rumors of wars, famines, diseases, natural catastrophes, earthquakes, false prophets, and apostasy. While it's true that these signs are prevalent in our day, they were also prevalent in A.D. 60 - 69. In fact, they are continually characteristic of depraved humanity, human history, and/or the earth's physical dynamics. In and of themselves, Jesus said that they do *not* indicate the end. They were only "the beginning of sorrows" or "birth pains" (Matt. 24:8 KJV – NIV). So we must not be misled by the presence of these same signs today; rather we should focus on the two certain, recognizable, and indisputable signs of the end to which Jesus gave prime importance over all the others:

Prime sign #1: The abomination that causes desolation . . . . standing . . . ."

> So when you see standing in the holy place 'the abomination that causes desolation' spoken of through the prophet Daniel—let the reader understand—then let those who are in Judea flee to the mountains (Matt. 24:15-16; Mark 13:14).

The Jews of Jesus' time were the "you" group He was warning. And He, Matthew, and Mark expected them to "understand" what He was talking about without having to explain. How could they? Quite simply, most of them were well-schooled in Jewish history, like most Americans are or used to be about our history. They knew that the last abomination of desolation that "stood" or took place in the holy place was the Temple desecration and temporary cessation of religious rites caused by Antiochus Epiphanes in 167 - 164 B.C.

During the intertestament times, the Jews were taught that all of Daniel's prophecy concerning the abomination of desolation had been fulfilled by Antiochus Epiphanes. Jesus, to the contrary, prophesied that all had not yet been fulfilled. Rather, this 2nd-century B.C. abomination, as prophesied in Daniel 8 and 11, was a type and was going to happen again, as prophesied in Daniel 9 and 12. This next time, as before, the very "standing" or presence of unholy acts and pagans in the holy place would be the abominating offense. But unlike before, this next time would bring more than a temporary three-year period of desolation. It would bring the permanent and everlasting desolation. Here's a brief synopsis of what transpired.

Early in the decade of A.D. 60 - 69, an unqualified Jew, Phannias, was appointed to the position of high priest. Prior to that time, nothing secular or unholy was allowed in the Temple. This high priest and his staff of other priests failed to properly perform the daily sacrifices and many other required Temple duties. Instead, they made a mockery of the holy ordinances. In A.D. 66, priests and Zealots fought each other in the Temple courts. Josephus reports that the floors swam with the blood of more than eight thousand who stabbed each other. Many more atrocities (abominations) between the Zealots and other Jewish factions occurred in the holy place between A.D. 66 - 70. The final abomination that caused the final desolation was similar to that of Antiochus Epiphanes. What happened before, happened again. It came in the same way, when another foreign Gentile army, the Roman army, stood in the Temple, and raised and worshipped its standards, as was their custom. But then, the Romans destroyed the Temple and tore it down stone-by-stone.

Josephus readily saw this analogy in writing:

> And indeed it so came to pass, that our nation suffered these things under Antiochus Epiphanes, according to Daniel's vision, and what he wrote many years before they came to pass. In the very same manner Daniel also wrote concerning the Roman government, and that our country should be made desolate by them.[6]

Prime sign #2: Jerusalem surrounded by armies.

Luke's parallel account of Jesus' prophecy tells us exactly what the nature of this final abomination of desolation would be (was) by adding Jesus' words:

> When you see Jerusalem surrounded by armies, you will know that its desolation is near. Then let those who are in Judea flee to the mountains, let those in the city get out, and let those in the country not enter the city. For this is the time of punishment in fulfillment of all that has been written (Luke 21:20-22).

We must note that ". . . all that has been written" always and only referred to the Old Testament, biblical writings. This would certainly include Daniel's "time of the end," Isaiah's new heavens and new earth, and much more (see Luke 24:44; Matt. 4:4, 7, 10).

Again as in 167 B.C., foreign armies were God's instrument of judgment. Early in the decade of 60 - 69 A.D., skirmishes between Jews and Romans began to break out. Many false Christs appeared among the Jews. "Wars and rumors of wars" were rampant. When the twice-daily sacrifice for Caesar and the Roman people was stopped, the die was cast. Then, *four times*, shortly following this time-frame-starting event, and just as Jesus had warned, Jerusalem was surrounded by armies.[7]

First Time. In A.D. 66, Roman armies commanded by Cestius Gallus came to put down the Jewish rebellion. After surrounding

Jerusalem, they began their siege. But for no apparent reason, Cestius withdrew his troops and left in retreat. The Jews pursued the Romans, slaughtering many and capturing their abandoned war machinery. This humiliating withdrawal by the Romans gave the Jews a false sense of being unconquerable. In addition, it helped create an atmosphere of having "peace and safety" before the destruction of the day of the Lord which was soon to "come on them suddenly" (1 Thess. 5:3).

Second Time. When news of Rome's defeat at the hands of the Jews reached Nero, he was most upset with Cestius' "poor generalship." He ordered Vespasian, a veteran general, back to Jerusalem in A.D. 67 to completely crush the Jewish uprising and avenge Rome's humiliation and damage to its ruling prestige. Vespasian advanced into Galilee, a region north of Jerusalem. He conquered its major cities and subdued the land. After his Galilean campaign in the north, he marched south and encamped around Jerusalem. But when word came of Nero's death, Vespasian delayed his plan for taking Jerusalem, withdrew his troops, and returned to Rome to become Emperor. Again, the Jews prevailed.

Third Time. In A.D. 68, at the request of the Zealot faction inside Jerusalem, Idumaeans from the territory south of Judea camped outside the walls. The Zealots inside let the Idumaeans into the city to join their forces. In the ensuing battle, over 8,500 were killed in the Temple area. Shortly afterwards, the Idumaeans withdrew from the city, but the cruelties and killings of Jews by other Jews continued.

Fourth and final time. Shortly before Passover in A.D. 70, Titus, the son of Vespasian, arrived with his legions at the northern outskirts of Jerusalem to finally put an end to the Jewish revolt and finish the insurrection. He had marched from the north to the south through Galilee and set up three camps overlooking the city. During this final siege, those who sought to flee were either prevented from doing so, killed by the Jewish factions inside, or captured, tortured, and crucified by the Romans at the city wall so all could see. By this time, it was too late to flee. All inside the walls were entrapped by Titus and his Roman legions. Jerusalem's days were numbered (see again chapter six). Josephus details how the Romans encircled and built an embankment or rampart to breach the city walls, just as Jesus had foretold (Luke 19:43-44). He further notes that 500 or more were captured daily and that "the soldiers out of rage and hatred amused themselves by nailing their prisoners in different postures; and so great was their number, that space could not be found for the crosses nor crosses for the bodies."[8]

It's more than coincidental that sometime around A.D. 65 - 67, and perhaps just prior to the arrival of the first army, the Apostle Peter announced that judgment was about to begin at "the house of God" (1 Pet. 4:17 KJV). And John twice proclaimed, "this is the last hour . . . . it is the last hour" (1 John 2:18). Even John the Baptist in A.D. 27 warned his generation to "flee from the coming wrath" (Luke. 3:7). There is no need to side-step or try to explain away these passages. Nor should we believe that we have been living in this "last hour" for almost 2,000 years. Also, contrary to another very popular end-time notion, the king or invader from the north spoken of in Daniel 11 and Ezekiel 38 and 39 is not a modern-day Russian or Iraqi army invading from countries located directly north of Israel. Rather, it was the Roman army of that 1st century. In all three campaigns against the Jews, the Roman army came from the "north" and fought many battles as it systematically marched southward. It's both historically and prophetically significant that the Romans chose to invade from the same direction from which Babylon invaded in 579 B.C., just as Ezekiel and Daniel had prophesied.

By this time, it was too late to flee. All inside the walls were entrapped by Titus and his Roman legions. Jerusalem's days were numbered . . . .

Josephus recounts how Jewish war refugees and defeated defenders fled Israel's northern territories for the south and the "safety" of Jerusalem's high walls. They continually carried with them news of the fighting and the defeats of the fortified cities. Great mourning and fear swept over the inhabitants of Jerusalem as they prepared the city for the impending siege. Many Jerusalem Jews, however, felt that the city—with its massive fortifications and protection by God—could never be taken.

During the persecutions and the time between the four sieges, a great temptation arose for many to abandon the new Christian faith and return to the old ways of Judaism. Others remembered Jesus' solemn warning to "watch out no that one deceives you" (Matt. 24:4) and heeded his life-saving instruction to "flee" (Matt. 24:16). They were watching, and did what Jesus had told them to do. Around A.D. 66, when the two prime signs began to occur in tandem (Matt. 24:32-33), they didn't wait until the final stages but began fleeing from Jerusalem and Judea while they still could. This is the reverse of what the Jews normally did in troubled times before an impending battle. Always before, they had fled to the city and the protection of its walls. But as A.D. 70 drew nearer and anticipation of the end intensified, fleeing the city became more and more difficult. Then it was impossible. The days of warning and grace were over. Judgment was upon Jerusalem and the rebellious Jewish people.

But everyone should have known this. Jesus had emphatically warned that this destruction would happen in their "this generation." Those who believed Him and his timeframe were watching and were not taken by surprise. They escaped the slaughter, the horrors, and the total catastrophe that befell all others trapped inside the city walls. According to Jesus, no one at the time (including Jesus and the angels) knew or could know the final "day or hour" (Matt. 24:36; 25:13).[9] But that did not mean they, and we, could not know the time. This prohibition on knowing was only against knowing the day or hour, not the week, month, year, or generation. Therefore, knowing was not and is not a futile task. In A.D. 66 - 70, it was a matter of life and death, and claiming to not know was not a viable excuse. That's the reason Jesus gave these two prime signs.[10] Amazingly, however, some thirty-seven years after Jesus' death, resurrection, and ascension, in A.D. 67 - 68, and by the guidance of the Holy Spirit (John 16:13), John knew and twice proclaimed "this is last hour . . . . it is the last hour" (1 John 2:18).

On the other hand, Jesus' followers, in obedience, had watched for these two signs and knew when the end was near. And because they correctly recognized these signs and the urgency for flight, that day and hour (time) did not overtake them as a thief (1 Thess. 5:4-6); at various times during the first three sieges and times in between, they left in obedience to the Lord's instruction and were delivered from God's judgment and wrath. Eusebius records that many Christians fled to Pella in Transjordan around A.D. 68 after the first siege and before the second one.[11] Others fled to Alexandria in Egypt, and still others to Asia Minor. In this way, "Jerusalem will be [was] trampled on by the Gentiles [armies] until the times of the Gentiles are fulfilled" (Luke. 21:24b). Hence, "the times of the Gentiles" have been fulfilled.[12]

This explanation of the end proclaimed throughout the Bible is in stark contrast to the popular, modern-day view that these signs and warnings apply to a yet-future, time-ending, earth-destroying, great tribulation period. This period of great tribulation was and is not an event that the entire world was to experience. If this latter application were correct, Jesus' instruction to "flee to the mountains" would be meaningless. How could one flee from the traditionally posited end-of-the-world scenario if that was what Jesus had in mind?[13] To mishandle Jesus' teachings in this way is to eliminate what He said to his disciples in answer to their three questions (Matt. 24:3). Flee is what his Jewish and Gentile disciples did in that 1st-century time period. Remember, this instruction to flee was given to them, not to us. They properly read the two prime signs and were spared from the horrors of the fall of Jerusalem. There is therefore no longer a need to flee to the mountains if Jerusalem becomes surrounded by armies in our day (which it is). This directive was not and is not a worldwide phenomenon, but was a local and time-sensitive instruction.

Jesus kept his word. The Roman army was God's ordained instrument to destroy Jerusalem and bring about the end. One of the most remarkable and documented facts surrounding the fulfillment of Jesus' end-time prophecy is that none of his disciples is known to have perished in the siege and destruction of Jerusalem. The historian Eusebius actually recorded that no Christians were trapped and destroyed in the siege of Jerusalem which concluded in A.D.70 - 73.[14] Others weren't so fortunate.

3. Those who failed to read the signs. Two groups experienced the horrors of the fall of Jerusalem: the unbelieving Jews and former followers of Christ who were zealous for the law and fearful of being put out of the synagogue. Both groups chose to remain inside Jerusalem and failed or refused to read the signs. Members of both groups suffered the judgment, and many physically perished. Let's take a closer look:

The unbelieving Jews. Having rejected Jesus as the Messiah, this group naturally refused to follow his prophetic warnings. In their minds, Jesus was a disgrace and a failure. Since the Temple in Jerusalem was the only place in the entire world where acceptable worship could be offered (again this was "the power of the holy people" which would finally be broken—Dan. 12:7), the Jews wanted to continue their exclusive relationship with God, and viewed equality with the Gentiles as an insult. They also believed that God would someday make Israel politically supreme over all the nations. So they held fast to their supremacy hopes, and steadfastly believed to the end that God owed them deliverance from their current enemy, the Roman army. They had a good reason, they thought. As descendants of Abraham and God's chosen nation, the Jews had a long history of deliverance from their enemies—but not this time. And God had warned them about this time, again and again (see Deut 32; Isa. 5:1-7; Dan. 12; Matt. 24, etc.).

History records that by the time of the first Roman siege, unbelieving Jews had divided into three rival and warring factions. This continued to the very end with Jews slaughtering each other inside the city walls and in the Temple itself.

An unknown number of law-zealous followers of Christ who were unwilling to give up the old ways. For this group, the presence of the Temple, the priesthood, the daily sacrifice, and the appeal of the city itself were too much to leave. So they turned their backs on the crucified Messiah and reverted to their old faith. Their end-time apostasy is mentioned in several of Paul's letters and was forecast by Jesus Himself (Matt. 24:10, 12, 24). As "foolish virgins" (Matt. 25:1-13), they failed to heed Christ's warnings and to follow his instructions to flee.

There is therefore no longer a need to flee to the mountains if Jerusalem becomes surrounded by armies in our day (which it is).

Other warnings were given as well. Some were spectacular. Josephus writes of several strange, if not bizarre, oracles that appeared in the sky and in the city before the initial siege in A.D. 66 and foretold its impending devastation: a star in the shape of a sword that stood over the city; a comet that continued for a year; a brilliant light around the altar at night; a cow that gave birth to a lamb; the sighting of chariots and armed soldiers (angelic armies) in the sky; and the hearing of voices in the inner court of the Temple, saying, "We are departing hence."[15] These signs were also reported by the Roman historian Tacitus.[16] When those inside the city disregarded the prophesied signs (Acts. 2:19; Joel 2:30), ignored or misread the portending warnings, and rejected this final call from God, their fate was sealed. According to Josephus, 1.1 million Jews were killed in the fall and destruction of Jerusalem.[17] This tally does not include those killed in countless skirmishes against the Jews in foreign cities, or in the Galilean campaign, or those who died in the Diaspora of disease, famine and persecution. Ninety-seven thousand more Jews went into foreign captivity. Thus, members of both groups held onto false hopes, rejected Jesus as the Messiah, disregarded his prophetic words, and stayed in the city. They personally received the judgment of "the time of the end" in apt fulfillment of Jesus' words:

> This is how it will be at the coming of the Son of Man. Two men will be in the field; one will be taken [into captivity] and the other left [to die in the destruction]. Two women will be grinding with a hand mill; one will be taken and the other left (Matt. 24:39b-41; Luke 17:34-36).

4. The Temple complex torn down stone by stone. God had set Jerusalem "in the center of the nations, with countries all around her" (Ezek. 5:5), for a definite purpose (see Ezek. 5:8-17). The city's centerpiece was the Temple complex. Its grandeur was "famous throughout the world" (2 Maccabees 2:22 NRSV), and powerfully manifested the Jews' exclusive relationship with God. Again, this relationship was "the power of the holy people," which the Jews held over all the nations. But the prophet Daniel had prophesied that at "the time of the end" this power would be "finally broken" (Dan. 12:4, 7).

The earthly life of Jesus took place during the time of this magnificent second Temple. Isaiah had prophesied thusly of this last-days time, "In the last days the mountain of the Lord's temple will be established as chief among the mountains; it will be raised above the hills and all nations would stream to it" (Isa. 2:2ff; Acts 2: 17; Heb. 1:2; 2 Tim. 3:1; and compare 2 Pet. 3:3 with Jude 18-19). The small country of Israel sat strategically located in a geographic corridor at the crossroad of three continents. The expansion of the Roman Empire had brought peace (*Pax Romana)* and the Roman road system (Isa. 2:3-5). This enabled traders, travelers, and messengers throughout the ancient world to pass through Jerusalem.

The Jews thought their privileged position with God would never end, and that He would always protect them and their Temple. They therefore believed that it would remain the exclusive center of worship forever. But someday they expected God to remove the Romans and make their nation chief among the nations. Sadly, their expectations were not accurate and never fulfilled. Rather, they were dramatically altered when Titus and the conquering Roman legions removed almost every building stone from the Jews' second Temple, just as Jesus had perfectly prophesied when He warned, "I tell you the truth, not one stone here will be left on another, every one will be thrown down" (Matt. 24:2; Luke 19:44).[18] After this occurred, the Temple on the Holy Mountain in Jerusalem was no longer the exclusive center of acceptable worship, just as Jesus and Jeremiah had also prophesied (John. 4:19-26; Jer. 51:25-26). But why did the Romans go to such an extreme effort to dismantle the Temple stone-by-stone and raze the whole city to the ground?[19] They had four reasons:

- They were so enraged by the humiliations they had suffered during the 3 1/2 year campaign against the Jews and feared that news of this Roman weakness could trigger other uprisings in the provinces of their empire.
- They were driven by their hatred of the Jews and had sworn to make an example of them.
- They were concerned about the tenacity of the Jews and felt they would never cease their rebellion as long as the Temple stood as a focus of nationalistic pride, and the city provided a rallying point and a fortress to which they might return someday in times of trouble.
- They were hoping to recover melted gold. The Jews used gold to decorate the walls, furniture and fixtures in the Temple. During the intense heat from the fire which destroyed the Temple, this gold ornamentation melted and flowed down between the cracks of the huge stones.

After burning the city and removing the stones one-by-one over the next three years, the Romans plowed up the hill of the sanctuary. Thus was fulfilled the typologically prophecy of Micah: "Zion will be plowed like a field, Jerusalem will become a heap of rubble, the temple hill a mound overgrown with thickets" (Mic. 3:12; Jer. 26:18).[20] Josephus described the utter destruction and desolation of Jerusalem as follows:

Caesar gave orders that they should now demolish the entire city and
temple . . . . the city was so completely leveled to the ground as to leave
future visitors to the spot no ground for believing that it had ever been
inhabited. Such was the end to which the frenzy of revolutionaries
brought Jerusalem, that splendid city of world-wide renown.[21]

Amazing, isn't it? Jerusalem and its magnificent Temple complex,
known throughout the world, had been utterly destroyed, and biblical
Israel now ceased to exist. It all happened exactly *as* and *when* both Jesus
and Daniel had prophesied. Nevertheless, we must not fall into the trap
of thinking that the fall of Jerusalem was only a "localized" judgment, or
nothing more than the insignificant end of another ancient city. This was
no more the case than Jesus' crucifixion was only a "local" execution or
simply the end of another life on earth.
      These times were truly of paramount importance to the whole world.
It was the "time of the end" of the Jewish age. The rebellious Jewish
nation had filled up their "measure of sin" (Matt. 23:32; 1 Thess. 2:15-
16; Isa. 30:1). Her role in prefiguring the new people of God—the
Church—was over. God's age-ending "last days" judgment came. It was
a powerful witness! News quickly spread to all the nations that
something very significant had occurred. The city and the Temple, the
invincible centerpoint of Jewish religion and political clout—"the power
of the holy people"—was, indeed, "finally broken" (Dan. 12:7). And so,
"in the sight of the nations" (Ezek. 5:8), another end-time prophecy was
fulfilled: Israel was made ". . . a ruin and a reproach among the nations
around you, in the sight of all who pass by. You will be a reproach and a
taunt, a warning and an object of horror to the nations around you when I
inflict my punishment on you . . . ." (Ezek. 5:14-15).

      5. Christianity no longer a Jewish sect. In these "last days" of
biblical Judaism, God through his Messiah was calling out a new people
for Himself. John, in the book of Revelation, recorded it this way, "Then
I heard another voice from heaven say: 'Come out of her, my people, so
that you will not share in her sins, so you will not receive any of her
plagues" (Rev. 18:4). True, this passage speaks of Babylon the Great.
But Babylon is a sign and a symbol in a book filled with signs and
symbols. It points to the 1st-century city of Jerusalem. How do we know
this is the correct interpretation and understanding?

First, recall that at the time Revelation was written (A.D. 65 to 68), the ancient city of Babylon was nonexistent, having been deserted and destroyed by the literal sands of time several centuries earlier.

Next, the sign and symbol of Babylon in Revelation 18—which was yet to be destroyed—has been erroneously thought by many commentators to represent Rome, New York City, or any city anywhere. But by using the basic interpretative principle of letting "Scripture interpret Scripture," I can demonstrate that it actually represented, first and foremost, 1st-century Jerusalem. This can be aptly demonstrated with four simple syllogisms. (This material and format was first presented in an article by this author published in the *Journal of the Evangelical Theological Society*:[22])

Major premise #1: Five times this Babylon is called "O great city" (Rev. 18:10, 16, 19; 16:19; 17:18). Twice it is called "great city" (Rev. 18:18, 21).

Minor premise #1: "The great city" is "where also their Lord was crucified . . . which is figuratively called Sodom . . . ." (Rev. 11:8). And Jerusalem in the only city ever metaphorically called Sodom (Deut. 32:32; Isa. 1:10; Ezek. 16:44-58).

Conclusion: Jerusalem is Revelation's Babylon.

~

Major premise #2: Babylon was guilty of "the blood of the prophets" (Rev. 17:6; 18:24; 16:6).

Minor premise #2: According to Jesus and Paul, only Jerusalem killed the prophets (Matt. 23:34-37; Luke 13:33; 11:47-51; 1 Thess. 2:15-16).

Conclusion: Jerusalem is Revelation's Babylon.

Major premise #3: John's people are commanded to "Come out of her, my people, so that you will not share in her sins, so that you will not receive any of her plagues" (Rev. 18:4).

Minor premise #3: The only city Jesus ever commanded his followers to flee from is Jerusalem—when they saw two specific signs (Matt. 24:15-16; Luke 21:20-21). Early church Father, Eusebius recorded that this departure happened and no Christians were trapped and destroyed in the siege and destruction of Jerusalem in AD 70.[23]

Conclusion: Jerusalem is Revelation's Babylon.

~

Major premise #4: This Babylon would be destroyed (Rev. 18:2, 8, 10, 11, 17, 19-23).

Minor premise #4: The only city Jesus said would be destroyed was Jerusalem—it would be "left to you desolate" (Matt.23:38) with "not one stone . . . left on another" (Matt. 24:2).

Conclusion: Jerusalem is Revelation's Babylon.

Theologian Donald Guthrie suggests that "the symbol of Babylon was chosen because it stood for the oppressors of God's people."[24] This identification of the doomed harlot-city Babylon sets the fulfillment and understanding context for the whole book of Revelation. It was 1st-century Jerusalem and apostate Judaism that was persecuting God's emerging Church. And only one city in the world, at only one time in history, ever matched or will match this instruction and these descriptions. It was the city in which the "Lord was crucified." That city—and the apostate religious system it represented—was the city God was calling his people to "come out of."[25]

Another historical fact is, prior to circa A.D. 70, Christianity was regarded by the Jews, the Romans, and all other nations as a sect of Judaism (Acts 24:14; 28:22). The Temple and all it stood for had proven to be a stumbling block to many early followers of Jesus. Therefore, the destruction of the Temple was not only a judgment against an institution that had become "obsolete" (Heb. 8:13) and was being superseded by something better (Heb. 8:1-6; 9:8-14; 10:9), it was also a practical necessity for preventing God's new people from wanting to go back. Does this seem so far-fetched? Today this same attraction and re-judaizing tendency is still quite prevalent. Many modern-day Christians, along with orthodox Jews, long for a future time when, supposedly, the temple will be rebuilt in Jerusalem, its rituals reestablished, and its interior divinely re-inhabited. But this desire to go back is unworthy and an insult to Christ. It's similar to the desire of many Israelites who followed Moses out of Egyptian bondage and yet wanted to return to Egypt (Exod. 16 and 17). God's anger burned against them (Exod. 32:10-14), and they were not allowed to enter the Promised Land (Num. 14:22-23).

Likewise, a return to the old Judaic law system is not going to happen—unless God is schizophrenic. Schizophrenia is a condition of showing markedly inconsistent or contradictory qualities. In this case, God could be said to be schizophrenic if, after going from a lesser to a better, He decided to go back to the lesser (i.e., if He decided to go from the lesser types and shadows of the Old Covenant to the better substance of the New, and then back to the lesser types and shadows of the Old, again (see the whole book of Hebrews). Since God is consistent and "does not change like shifting shadows" (Jas. 1:17), we can safely say He's *not* schizophrenic!

Today this same attraction and re-judaizing tendency is still quite prevalent.

After circa A.D. 70, Christianity and Judaism were never again to be confused. Christians who had read the "signs" and heeded Jesus' warning to flee were never again considered to be a sect of the Jews. They had distinguished themselves from Judaism, and no longer served God under the Law of Moses. On the other side of the coin, unbelieving

Jews who survived the destruction cut off all connections with any of their countrymen who named the name of Jesus, and banned them from the synagogues. Christianity was thereby liberated from Judaism, freed to become its own worldwide movement, and compelled to develop mostly among the Gentiles. Thus was fulfilled God's Word through the prophet Hosea, "I will say to those called 'Not my people,' 'You are my people;' and they will say, 'You are my God'" (Hos. 2:23b).

Without a doubt, the destruction of Jerusalem and the Temple was the single most decisive and powerful "manifestation of the Sons of God" (Rom. 8:17 ff.). It was "a new creation . . . the Israel of God" (Gal. 6:15-16). This divine act of judgment fulfilled Jesus' words, "Therefore, I tell you that the kingdom of God will be taken away from you [Old Covenant Israel] and given to a people who will produce its fruit" [the Church] (Matt. 21:43).

6. The final abomination that caused desolation. Daniel's reference to a single "the abomination that causes desolation" (Dan. 11:31; 12:11) contrasts with his earlier plural reference to multiple "desolations" and "abominations" (Dan. 9:26-27). His two different usages have proven to be most difficult to understand for many modern-day interpreters. Jesus, however, only used the singular in his Olivet Discourse (Matt. 24:16). As we've seen, both during and after the Roman-Jewish War [A.D. 66 - 70] there were many different acts of abomination and desolation. But Daniel tells us that there was to be a pinnacle one (Dan. 9:27; 12:11). Here's a historical recap that should help us gain greater understanding into this apocalyptic phrase:

Abominations. The Jews clearly understood the meaning of all Hebrew words translated as "abomination," "detestable practices," and "desecrated," especially in reference to their city and Temple. In Jewish terminology, an "abomination" was anything that involved the worship of false gods or the false worship of their God in sacred places (see: 1 Kgs. 11:7; 2 Kgs. 23:13; Jer. 4:1; 13:27; Ezek. 5:11; 8:5-18; 22:1-16):

- The abomination which set the historical precedent and type for the final one was committed by the Syrian king Antiochus Epiphanes in the Maccabean period between 171-164 B.C. In 171 B.C., in fulfillment of the 2,300 evenings and mornings spoken of in Daniel 8:9-14, Antiochus Epiphanes replaced the Jewish high priest with Menelaus, who was not a priest, and began a severe oppression of all religious and political freedom. In 167 B.C. he captured Jerusalem, massacred many of its occupants, plundered the Temple and stopped the practices of the Jewish religion under the pain of death. In addition, He profaned the Temple by dragging in a pig—an unclean animal—and sacrificing it on the Jewish altar. He set up an altar to Zeus and erected a statue in the Holy Place. Licentious heathen rites were also conducted in the Temple courts and the Jews were required to take part. During this time, many Jews were put to death (1 Maccabees 1:29-64). Antiochus Epiphanes' abomination(s), however, only caused a three year and two month, temporary period of desolation (Figuring: 2,300 evenings and mornings as 1,150 evenings + 1,150 mornings = 1,150 days [see Gen. 1:5f; Lev. 6:9, 12, 20; 24:3]). In 164 B.C., the Jews revolted and drove Antiochus out of Jerusalem. They reconsecrated their Temple and reinstituted their religious practices.

Daniel had precisely prophesied both the length of this time period of desolation and the time in human history during which these events would occur—the time of the third world empire, the Grecian Empire, symbolized by a goat (Dan. 8:5-8). All this occurred after the Grecian Empire of Alexander the Great had been divided into four smaller kingdoms, symbolized by Daniel's four horns. One of those horns, a "little horn," caused this temporary abomination of desolation. History shows that the little horn was Antiochus Epiphanes, not a future "Antichrist." Two centuries later, Jesus would point back to this time and tell his disciples that a similar, but far worse, abomination would take place in their generation.

An irony of ironies is the modern-day Jewish Festival of Lights, or Hanukkah. It commemorates and celebrates the reconsecration of the Jewish Temple and the reestablishment of their faith, following the temporary abomination of desolation caused by Antiochus Epiphanes. Ironically, however, most Jews to this very day ignore or deny the significance of Daniel's pinnacle abomination and desolation, and Jesus' "abomination that causes desolation" which occurred circa A.D. 70. Nineteen centuries ago and counting, this last and worst abomination ended the practice of biblical Judaism forever.[26]

- Prior to A.D. 64, Christians were persecuted primarily by religious Jews, both in Jerusalem and throughout the Roman Empire (Gal. 1:13, 23). After A.D. 64—the year of the burning of Rome—the emperor Nero took over the persecution of Christians whom he blamed for this fire and sought as a scapegoat for this embarrassment. James, Peter, Paul, and others were martyred then.

- Before, during, and after the Jewish rebellion, a great falling away or apostasy from both Judaism and Christianity took place. Many forsook the better things in Christ and returned to Judaism. And biblical Judaism itself became grossly defiled in its last days. Even the Apostle Paul was accused of bringing Greeks (Gentiles) into and defiling the Holy Place (Acts 21:28).

- Animal sacrifices, made obsolete by Christ's crucifixion in A.D. 30, continued in the Temple until July 17, 70, when a lack of priests to offer them and animals to be offered forced discontinuance. God's attitude toward this detestable abomination was prophesied by Isaiah:

> But whoever sacrifices a bull is like one who kills a man, and whoever offers a lamb, like one who breaks a dog's neck; whoever makes a grain offering is like one who presents pig's blood, and whoever burns memorial incense, like one who worships an idol. They have chosen their own ways, and their souls delight in their abominations; so I also will choose harsh treatment for them and will bring upon them what they dread. For when I called, no one answered, when I spoke, no one listened. They did evil in my sight and chose what displeased me (Isa. 66:3-4).

- The Temple was repeatedly desecrated by the corruption and bloodshed of the Zealots who controlled the Temple from the beginning of the war until its end. First, they murdered Ananias, the high priest; then they chose a new high priest by casting lots.

The new priest was unworthy and ignorant of his priestly duties. He and his cohorts made a mockery of the Jewish law and Temple observances. Ceremonially impure, polluted, and bloodstained feet frequently invaded the sanctuary. Later, the Temple areas were turned into an armed fortress and headquarters for tyranny among the Jews.

Josephus reports another high priest, Annanus, as saying, "Certainly it had been good for me to die before I had seen the house of God full of so many abominations, or these sacred places that ought not to be trodden on at random, filled with the feet of these blood-shedding villains."[27] Concerning the "lawlessness" and "abominations" of the Zealots, Josephus himself said, "These men, therefore, trampled upon all the laws of man, and laughed at the laws of God; and for the oracles of the prophets, they ridiculed them as the tricks of jugglers."[28]

- The bitter strife that split the Jews into warring camps produced many brutal atrocities and thousands of killings within the Temple areas. Jews betrayed Jews and persecuted each other. Priests were even killed as they worshipped and administered their sacred duties. And, in violation of Jewish religious practice, the dead bodies were not buried, but thrown outside the city to rot. Obviously, this was part of the apostate Jews filling up their "measure of sin" (Matt. 23:32). Yet in spite of these ongoing abominations, Temple worship, daily sacrifices, and the celebration of the religious festivals continued.

During the last week of his earthly ministry, and in light of these future-coming, prophetic events, is it any wonder why Jesus did not speak of the Temple as being "my Father's house," or "my house," but instead changed this term when warned the Jews, "Look, *your* house is left to you desolate" (Matt. 23:38). (*italics mine*)

- During their internal battles, the apostate Jews not only killed and wore each other down, they also set fire to their own stocks of grain and other siege provisions. Josephus says that it was "as though they were purposely serving the Romans by destroying what the city had provided against a siege and severing the sinews of their own strength."[29]

- The famine and starvation forced Jews trapped inside the city walls to eat their own children. Josephus documents this abomination, which fulfilled Moses' dire prophecy in Deuteronomy 28:56-57 (also see Ezek. 5:10). Josephus tells of a certain woman named Mary who was at one time well-to-do, but whose house had been plundered several times and who was now dying of hunger. When no one would put her out of her misery, she killed her baby son, roasted his body, ate half of him, and buried the remainder. Jewish rebels, smelling the cooking aroma, rushed into her house and demanded that she show them what she had cooked. She uncovered the baby's second half and offered it to them.[30]

- The pinnacle and final abomination began when the Roman soldiers, driven by their hatred of the Jews, rushed into the Temple and set it on fire, in direct disobedience to the orders of their commander, Titus. Everyone they caught was butchered. Josephus says, "Around the altar a pile of corpses was accumulating; down the steps of the sanctuary flowed a stream of blood, and the bodies of the victims killed above went sliding to the bottom."[31]

- After the Temple was in ruins, the Romans paraded their emblems of deity into the Temple and worshipped and offered sacrifices to their pagan standards—a straight staff with a metallic eagle on top and a graven image of Caesar just below. In the Jews' very Temple area, they proclaimed Caesar as God (previous Caesars demanded and claimed to be divine). Later, they stripped the Temple treasury of its money, its raiment, and other spoils, such as the golden, seven-branched candlestick, the Menorah, and other implements. This booty of war was carried off and triumphantly paraded down the streets of Rome.

- In A.D. 75, a Roman temple was erected on the site where the Jewish Temple had stood. The Temple area was thereby transformed into a heathen shrine.

- In A.D. 361 - 363., the Roman Emperor Julian unsuccessfully attempted to rebuild the Jewish Temple at Jerusalem in order to cast doubts on the Christian claim to be the true Israel and discredit Jesus' divinity by proving false his prophecies that "not one stone here will be left on another" (Matt. 24:2), and that "Look, your house is left to you desolate" (Matt. 23:38).

Desolations. The above abominations produced these desolations:

- God had written consequences of disobedience into his covenant with Israel. If they broke the covenant, the greatest penalty would be the desolation of their land and sanctuary, and the scattering of their citizens among the nations (see Lev. 26 and Deut. 28). God kept his word. In 722 B.C., the ten northern tribes were taken captive into Assyria, although later they returned in obedience. In the 6th Century, the Babylonians destroyed Jerusalem and the first Temple, and took its citizens into captivity. They also returned in obedience. Most likely some time in August or September of A.D. 70, the end had come. Three years or so later, on the "last day" of the "last days," desolation became complete when the last stone was removed and the Temple ground plowed up by the Romans.
- All Judea became a scene of plunder and ruin. In their search for wood to build the earthworks against the city walls, the Romans stripped the beautiful suburbs outside the city of their trees and reduced them to "an utter desert." [32] Malachi had prophesied this desolation:

> "Surely the day is coming; it will burn like a furnace. All the arrogant and every evildoer will be stubble, and that day that is coming will set them on fire," says the Lord Almighty. "Not a root or a branch will be left to them . . . ." (Mal. 4:1).

The Jews knew that this time was coming. They frequently sang "the song of Moses" (Deut. 32:1-43) to remind them what would befall a "perverse generation" (vss. 5, 20) "in the latter days" or "end" (vs. 29). It would be their destruction by a consuming fire (vs. 22; see also Luke 3:9, 17; Heb. 12:29), "famine," "plague," and "bitter destruction" (vs. 24).

- Sometime during the many abominations, God forsook the Temple, thus fulfilling Ezekiel's tragic and midexilic vision of

God's Glory and Presence departing from the Jerusalem Temple (Ezek. 10:18-19; 5:11).[33] Perhaps this also reflects Jesus' tragic pronouncement, "Look, your house [the Temple] is left to you desolate" (Matt. 23:38; also see Matt. 21:13). Josephus writes, "Wherefore I cannot but suppose that God is fled out of his sanctuary, and stands on the side of those against whom you fight."[34]

- Biblical Judaism (not rabbinical Judaism) was so thoroughly destroyed that it has never been, nor ever will be, reestablished. Many rabbis refer to A.D. 70 as "the end of biblical Judaism" and "the end of days." God's judgment had to so completely destroy the Temple, the city, the genealogical records—everything—in order to demonstrate his repudiation of biblical Judaism as a religious system. There was, however, one exception to this destruction and desolation—a very important and the only remaining element which God had given the Jews. Jesus said, "but my words will never pass away"—i.e., the ancient Scriptures (Matt. 24:35).

- In Matthew 24:28, Jesus also prophesied, "Wherever there is a carcass (body), there the vultures (eagles) will gather." Although this and its parallel verse in Luke 17:28 and Revelation 19:21 have puzzled commentators for centuries, its meaning can now be logically deduced. First, let's note that the Greek word *aetos* can be rendered either eagle or vulture for both are fierce birds of prey, tear apart their victims, and devour dead flesh. Scholars, therefore, claim that neither the Jews nor Greeks distinguish between eagles and vultures. Perhaps then, this verse refers to physical vultures that literally gathered to feast on the dead bodies of the Roman-Jewish War. Or, figuratively, it may have been the Romans who were voracious vultures as they circled outside the walls of Jerusalem, awaited their dying prey as the Jews killed and wore each other out on the inside, and then swooped down to tear and devour their victim, only to fly away. Or it could be a reference to the eagles on the Roman standards which they literally planted in the soil of a destroyed Jerusalem (now a carcass or corpse of itself) and which were objects of worship. All three possibilities are quite descriptive and relevant!

- For over fifty years the entire country was left desolate and devoid of most of its inhabitants. The people had been killed, had died, or were sold into slavery. Everything was utterly destroyed—"to the uttermost" (1 Thess. 2:16 KJV). Sixty-five years after the fall of Jerusalem, the Roman army returned again and wiped out the entire state of Judea.
- No country or people ever suffered the magnitude of God's judgment and wrath as befell Old Covenant Israel. Not only did Israel cease being the nation of the living God, it ceased being a nation for 19 centuries until its rebirth as a secular nation in 1948. The world of biblical Judaism, however, perished forever. It all happened some forty years from the time Jesus told his disciples that "not one stone shall be left on another." This fulfillment is more than coincidence.

Without question, Josephus held his own countrymen responsible for the destruction they had brought upon themselves. He writes, "for by their madness it was that the people came to be destroyed."[35] Titus gave the Jews numerous opportunities to spare themselves, the Temple, and the city. Josephus pleaded with them, personally. But the rebellion spread "a madness" among the Jewish people, who appeared eager to go up against Rome and felt that their God would protect them as before. But He didn't.

No country or people ever suffered the magnitude of God's judgment and wrath as befell Old Covenant Israel.

Daniel 9 prophesied that the destruction of the city would be caused by "the people of the prince" or "the ruler" (Dan. 9:26). As discussed in chapter six, most likely Jesus Christ is "the Messiah the Prince" (Dan. 9:25 KJV), and "the people" were the Jews. The Jews brought on the judgment. The Romans carried it out.[36] And so abominations and desolations came upon God's chosen nation. In a collective fashion, the Jews' rejection of Jesus as their Messiah, their internal battles, and their desecrations of the Temple were some of the "abominations" spoken of by Daniel that culminated in the pinnacle one—the "wing" of "desolation" at the hands of the Roman army. What stronger proof could there be that "the time of the end" in Daniel 12 is identical to "the end of the age" in Matthew 24 and to Peter's "the end of all things is at hand" in 1 Peter 4:7 KJV? "The power of the holy people" had "been finally broken" (Dan. 12:7). It all fits together perfectly when we leave it in its divinely determined context. And it all took place before Jesus' "this generation" had passed away. It is the perfect ending!

Consequently, the abomination of desolation standing in the Temple is a thing of the past. It's not prophesied to occur again. Those words were written to them, not to us, although they are for us. No future Antichrist is necessary to erect a statue or instigate abomination(s) of desolation(s) in a rebuilt temple in Jerusalem during a cut-off 70th week of tribulation. A Jewish temple does not need to be destroyed again. God utterly destroyed that Temple centuries ago. It was the one that was standing when Jesus prophesied its destruction and desolation. The whole of biblical Judaism became obsolete (Heb. 8:13). It had ceased to shine for God and was darkened. A rebuilt temple in the modern-day secular city of Jerusalem would serve no eschatological or redemptive purpose whatsoever. None! The perfect ending had come, right on time!

7. The great tribulation objection. One objection that has prevented some from accepting a 1st-century fulfillment as the time of "great tribulation" or "great distress," is that Jesus said it would be "unequaled" (past) and "never to be equaled again" (future) (Matt. 24:21; also Dan. 12:1). Critics of Jesus' assertion are quick to point out that the Jewish Holocaust in the 20th century produced five times more Jewish deaths (5-6 million) than the circa A.D. 70 fall of Jerusalem. There are three valid responses to this objection.

1) The problem might be said to lie with the numerical assumption. The severity and significance of what happened to the Jews in the 1st century was greater than the death toll figure alone indicates. Indeed, it was and is unequaled and never to be equaled again in Jewish history. It was even worse than Noah's flood that destroyed all life on earth (Gen. 9:11). And its consequences and ramifications did "come upon the whole world to test those who live on the earth" (Rev. 3:10). They still do.

The Jewish people have suffered many tribulations since this destruction of Jerusalem, yet these other times of persecution and distress—as horrible as they have been—cannot compare with the utter destruction of Israel as the nation of God, the loss of their Temple, and the abolishment of biblical Judaism in A.D. 66 - 73. If this "great tribulation" is not yet fulfilled, then their worst days and an awful catastrophe still lie in the future for the Jews.

2) Others dilute the force of Jesus' words by explaining that this was stock-and-trade language or common dramatic speech (see Exod. 11:6; 2 Kgs. 18:5; 23:25; Ezek. 5:9).

3) A far better explanation, in this author's opinion, is that many equate or confuse the "great tribulation" with God's judgment and wrath. Contrary to the popular notion, Jesus' "great tribulation" or "great distress" did not come upon the rebellious Jewish nation. Rather, it came upon the early Church. Divine judgment and wrath came upon the apostate Jews; Jesus called it the "days of vengeance" (Luke 21:22 KJV). Big difference! Jesus also said, "for the sake of the elect those days will be shortened (Matt. 24:22). "The elect" were not the rebellious Jews upon whom Jesus pronounced seven "woes," and called "snakes" and "brood of vipers" (Matt. 23). "The elect" were the newly emerging people of God, or the Christians (both Jews and Gentiles) whom Jesus warned to get out of Jerusalem.

The term "unequaled" recognizes that the 60s, and especially the Roman-Jewish War of A.D. 66 - 70, was a totally unique and unparalleled time of tribulation *for the Church*. Never before and never again was the very existence of God's people (now the Church) more vulnerable and imperiled. The unbelieving Jews had been the greatest enemy of the early Church. They had crucified the Lord Jesus, violently opposed the preaching of the gospel, and wanted to stamp out the rival Christian sect not only in Jerusalem but in the other cities and countries of the Roman Empire as well (2 Thess. 1:4). That time had to be cut short for the Church's sake. But after the destruction in A.D. 70 - 73, neither the Jews nor anyone else has mounted such a threat to the very existence of "the elect"—the Church. Nor will they ever again.

8. The whole-world objection. Jesus emphatically specified that "this gospel of the kingdom will be preached in the whole world as a witness to all the nations, and then the end will come" (Matt. 24:14). No way around it, it's what He said. This condition was a prerequisite for "the end" to come.

How then could the end possibly have come circa A.D. 70, when the gospel had not yet been preached in the Western Hemisphere? The great missionary movement of the 18th and 19th centuries hadn't taken place, worldwide communications hadn't been developed, and many nations and people groups in remote tribes had yet to hear the gospel. This fact alone, critics contend, should stop dead in its tracks any idea that the end came circa A.D. 70.

As we've seen several times before, the Bible must be understood on its own terms and in the context of its original hearers. Only then can we properly understand what any portion really means for us today. Therefore, let's carefully note that the inspired writers of the New Testament confirmed, several times, that Jesus' prerequisite was accomplished in their day:

- Using hyperbole and in the context of the Jewish worldview, "every nation under heaven" was assembled on the day of Pentecost (Acts 2:5).
- The Apostle Paul, 31 years later, confirmed that "all over the world this gospel is producing fruit and growing . . ." (Col. 1:6) and that "the gospel that you heard . . . has been proclaimed to every creature under heaven" (Col. 1:23), and that "your faith is being reported all over the world" (Rom. 1:8). This was not Paul's opinion. It is inspired Scripture. A few years after Paul said these words, the end came, right on time.
- For more confirmations, read: Rom. 10:18; 16:26; Acts 1:8; 24:5; Jude 3; also compare with Dan. 2:39; 4:1, 22; 5:19; 7:23; Luke 2:1, 30-32; 24:47; Rev. 3:10.

Why is this scripturally-documented fulfillment of Jesus' prerequisite so hard to believe? The answer is simply the power of the traditions of men rides roughshod over the Word of God (Mark 7:13; Matt. 15:6). According to the Bible itself, and prior to A.D. 70, the gospel was preached to all nations and to the world. The Greek word translated "world" in Matthew 24:14 is *oikoumene*, meaning land (i.e., the [terrene part of the] globe, specifically the Roman Empire).[37] In this commonly used and restricted sense, the then-known Roman world, or the civilized world of that time, was also the "world" of the Jews into which they had been scattered. If the entire global earth was meant, the Greek word *kosmos* would have been used, as it is in Matthew 24:21. But it wasn't.

A Jewish temple does not need to be destroyed again. . . . The perfect ending had come, right on time!

Hence, Jesus' end-coming condition has been scripturally met. This is a truth that has been lost by many today. But early Church father Eusebius clearly understood this linkage and its significance. He confirmed that both the world-wide preaching of the gospel and this end of biblical Judaism were fulfilled:

> Moses had foretold this very thing and in due course Christ sojourned in this life, and the teaching of the new covenant was borne to all nations, and at once the Romans besieged Jerusalem and destroyed it and the Temple there. At once the whole of the Mosaic law was abolished, with all that remained of the Old Covenant . . . .[38]

Let's further note that the fulfillment of this world mission was an absolutely necessary part of God's plan. Since Jews had been scattered over the world (Jas. 1:1), they all had to have the opportunity to accept the gospel or reject it and persecute its proclaimers. In this way they would and did "fill up, then, the measure of sin of your forefathers" (Matt. 23:32; Isa. 65:6-12). That's why the gospel had to go out into "the whole world." The previously cited verses verify this accomplishment. They cannot be lightly dismissed. So let's just believe what inspired Scripture writers said. God had allowed one generation of time—Jesus' "this generation"—for the completion of this missionary task. Once completed, the stage was set. The end could now come. It did, perfectly. It was the end of the Old Covenant, biblical Judaic system, and not the physical creation, which will never end.

A Caution: Many Christian evangelists and preachers fear that the recognition of this scripturally-documented and 1st-century fulfillment of Jesus' worldwide, gospel-preaching prerequisite will cause the Church to lose motivation for evangelism and we will fail to complete its task in our day and time, or in the future. Of course, this fear is based on the belief that the preaching of the gospel to all the nations is necessary to hasten the so-called and futurized "return" of Christ—i.e., the sooner we get this done, the sooner He will return. As we shall see, this, too, is mistaken notion and concept.

But is the mission mandate a completable, once-for-all task? Let's recall that it neither originated nor terminated with Jesus' Matthew 24:14 statement or with his Great Commission "to make disciples of all nations" (Matt. 28:18-20). Why not? The mission mandate for world evangelism has always been the responsibility of those who are called to God, and always will be.

Four thousand years ago God called Abraham and made a covenant with him. Not only did God promise to bless Abraham, and all families of the earth through him (i.e., through his seed), He also instructed him and his descendants to actively be a blessing to others (Gen. 12:1-4). God's covenant with Abraham was the origin of the mission mandate. It is frequently referred to and enlarged upon throughout the Old Testament. For example, God's people were to be priests and to minister

---

The mission mandate for world evangelism has always been the responsibility of those who are called to God, and always will be.

---

to others (Exod. 19:4-6). Make "your [God's] ways known on earth, your salvation among all nations" (Psa. 67:2; also Psa. 98:3; Isa. 49:6; Acts 13:47). Be "a light for the Gentiles" (Isa. 42:6). "You are my witnesses" (Isa. 43:10, 12; 43:8), and "they will proclaim my glory among the nations" (Isa. 66:19). "Make known among the nations what he has done . . . tell of all his wonderful acts . . . proclaim his salvation day after day. Declare . . . his marvelous deeds among all peoples" (1 Chron. 16:8-9, 23-24). Thus, Israel's mandate to witness was grounded in her covenant with God and applies to every child of Abraham (Gal. 3:7)—by blood and/or by faith—and never ceases (Gal. 3:15-19f).

Sadly, the Old Covenant Jews failed to take God's blessings to the Gentiles. Instead, they hoarded these blessings for themselves. In our day, if God's people desire his promised Abrahamic blessings through Christ, we must not keep his blessings for ourselves, either. We, like them, are responsible to pass them on, to be a blessing to others and all nations, to be "witnesses" (Acts 1:8), to be "fishers of men" (Matt. 4:19), and to "produce the fruit" of the kingdom we've been given (Matt. 21:43). This missionary mandate hasn't changed since the days of Abraham. What has changed is that God's blessings are greater and the known civilized world is much bigger. We are to bless all the nations with "the eternal gospel" (Rev. 14:6), just as Jesus' contemporaries did in their time.

One More Biggie

Anyone seeking truth should hesitate to embrace any tradition that tampers with the words of Jesus Christ, that takes issue with his imminency, or that even hints that He might have been mistaken or never said these things. Let's also be cautious of accepting any method of biblical interpretation or listening to any end-time prophecy "expert" who un-anchors and lifts "last days" events out of their 1st-century, historical, and covenantal context and assumes that they are just beginning in our day. It's all too easy to drift off in any direction and attach speculative and subjective meanings that are grossly in error. Let's also be aware that the greatest threat to the Word of God comes not from without but from within the Church. Jesus lived, spoke, and died during the biblical "last days" or "last times" (Heb. 1:1-2). This was "the end" and the "last days" of the biggest thing that was ending at the time or will ever end—biblical Judaism, and not the cosmos. It's God's precise and perfect ending!

In conclusion, if Jesus was an infallible prophet and if we truly value the integrity of our faith and the authority of Scripture, then *everything* contained in Jesus' homogeneous prophecy of "all these things" *must have happened within the time span* He specified—"this generation." The destruction of Jerusalem and the Temple, and the end of the Judaic age are historical facts. But *there is one more end-time event that also must have occurred* during that generation. It's a biggie! We'll devote our next three chapters to it. If I can demonstrate to you, scripturally, historically, and effectively, that it was also fulfilled back then, then all futuristic postponement traditions fall to the ground. But, and not surprisingly, opposition and criticism abound here as well.

This was "the end" and the "last days" of the biggest thing that was ending at the time or will ever end—biblical Judaism, and not the cosmos. It's God's precise and perfect ending!

In closing this chapter, let's recall and recommit, again, to the methodology we are employing throughout this book that Drs. Klein, Blomberg, and Hubbard, Jr., affirm in their hermeneutics textbook, *Introduction to Biblical Interpretation*:

> The historically defensible interpretation has greatest authority. That is, interpreters can have maximum confidence in their understanding of a text when they base that understanding on historically defensible arguments . . . . We should seek the most likely *time* for the fulfillment of a prophecy in history.[39]

Chapter 10

What Do the Critics Charge?[*]

T he fall of Jerusalem circa 70 A.D. does not stand alone as an
isolated event of history. Nor does it compare with catastrophes
like the siege of Troy, the downfall of Carthage, the demise of the
Roman Empire, or even the collapse of Communism. Behind its visible
events is an unseen significance that is just as real and even more
relevant and more important than any other major event in history.

Until now, only a few scholars have recognized and appreciated what
we will discuss in this and the next chapter. Why is it so important?
Because God's Word tells us that "My people are destroyed from lack of
knowledge" (Hos. 4:6a). Lack of this knowledge has destroyed much and
hindered many. As a result, the Church has squandered much of its true
heritage and traded its sure foundation for a bowl of postponement
pottage (Gen. 25:19-34).

In addition to his astonishingly accurate prediction in A.D. 30 of the
destruction of the Temple, the fall of Jerusalem, and the end of the age,
Jesus included one other major eschatological event in his prophecy, his
parousia, or "coming on the clouds:"

---

[*] Much of the material in this and the next chapter was presented in two papers
by the author. The first was delivered at the Evangelical Theological Society's
48th Annual Meeting in November 1996 in Jackson, Mississippi and the second
delivered at the 54th Annual Meeting in Toronto, Canada, November 2002.

- *What will be the sign of your coming (parousia)?* (Matt. 24:3).
- *For as the lightning comes from the east and flashes to the west, so will be the coming (parousia) of the Son of Man (Matt. 24:27).*
- *At that time the sign of the Son of Man will appear in the sky, and all the nations of the earth will mourn. They will see the Son of Man coming (erchomai) on the clouds of the sky, with power and great glory* (Matt. 24:30).

With three short words, Jesus proclaimed that "all these things," everything from verse 3 through 33, would transpire before "this generation . . . passed away" (Matt. 24:34). At face value, these words of Jesus are so plain and grammatically precise that they should preclude any possibility of misunderstanding, especially of the timing issue. If not, then his words have no obvious or definite meaning. Like it or not, Jesus' Olivet Discourse is one continuous and homogeneous prophecy. And, once again, no interpreter has the freedom to weave in and out of its time-limited context at will. Likewise, no justification exists for either postponing its fulfillment to some distant future or exempting and extracting any of the things He said would happen from his time restriction of "this generation."

If Jesus meant what He said, said what He meant, and was an infallible Prophet, all the components of his prophecy must stand or fall together. This certainly includes his *parousia* and coming on the clouds with power and glory. The failure of any one component to occur within that existing generation would disqualify Jesus as a prophet and call into question the truth of Scripture. If He did not come in this manner—*as* and *when* He said He would—we have a dilemma of huge proportions.

The Enigma of 'Nonoccurrence'

No subject in the Bible generates more interest, speculation, or debate than the coming again, or "return" and "second coming" of Jesus Christ, as it is variously so-called.[1] Yet for nearly 2,000 years the vast majority of Christians has been eagerly expecting and predicting his soon-and-any-moment "return." Meanwhile, we've struggled with the enigma of "nonoccurrence," as we try to maintain a pretense of inerrancy, infallibility, inspiration, and authority of Scripture—an impossible and harmful balancing act.

Conservative scholarship postulates that Jesus' coming again has been delayed or postponed. This makes Jesus' time-frame references and the imminency expectations of the early Church major embarrassments that must be explained away. Liberal scholarship reckons that Jesus and the New Testament writers were simply mistaken or deluded. Some think that the statements were altered or added later by his frustrated followers. These questionable conclusions dismiss the authenticity of Christ and the whole issue of Bible inerrancy.

If He did not come in this manner —*as* and *when* He said He would— we have a dilemma of huge proportions.

Most Christians don't seem to realize the predicament we are in if Jesus Christ didn't fulfill his many promises to come or "return" within the time parameters He specified. Informed critics of Christianity, on the other hand, have no trouble seeing through the strained attempts of Church leaders to explain away "nonoccurrence" in order to protect the credibility and divinity of Jesus in the face of his supposed failure. But let's face it. These critics have a legitimate complaint if Jesus did not do something that He said He would, and within the timeframe He stated. They also are quite aware of both the enigma and dilemma that "nonoccurrence" presents for the Christian Church and the impossibility of escaping it without being disloyal to Christ.

- **Bertrand Russell.** Atheist Bertrand Russell, in his book *Why I Am Not A Christian*, discredits the inspiration of the New Testament by saying:

  > I am concerned with Christ as He appears in the Gospel narrative . . . He certainly thought that his second coming would occur in clouds of glory before the death of all the people who were living at the time. There are a great many texts that prove . . . He believed that his coming would happen during the lifetime of many then living. That was the belief of

his earlier followers, and it was the basis of a good deal of his moral teaching.[2]

- **Albert Schweitzer.** In his 19th-century book, *The Quest of the Historical Jesus,* liberal Schweitzer summarized the problem of "Parousia delay" as follows:

  > The whole history of Christianity down to the present day . . . is based on the delay of the Parousia, the nonoccurrence of the Parousia, the abandonment of eschatology, the process and completion of the 'de-eschatologizing' of religion which has been connected therewith.[3]

- **Jewish Critics.** Jewish critics contend that Jesus didn't complete the whole mission of the Messiah within the timeframe their prophets had predicted, although some admit He fulfilled some of it. They allege that Christians invented the idea of a "second coming" off in the future to cover up Jesus' failure to return as He promised. This is the Jews' primary excuse for rejecting Jesus and belittling Christianity. Prominent orthodox rabbis and Jewish scholars have written:

  > The main task of the Messiah was to bring the world back to G-d, and to abolish all war, suffering and injustice from the world. Clearly, Jesus did not accomplish this. In order to get around this failure on the part of Jesus, Christians invented the doctrine of the "Second Coming.". . . All the prophecies that Jesus did not fulfill the first time are supposed to be taken care of the second time around. However, the Jewish Bible offers absolutely no evidence to support the Christian doctrine of a "Second Coming."[4]

  > The idea of a second coming is a pure rationalization of Jesus' failure to function in any way as a messiah, or to fulfill any of the prophecies of the Torah or the Prophets. The idea is purely a Christian invention, with no foundation in the Bible.[5]

  This two-fold misapprehension of Jesus—the nearness of the kingdom of heaven and his Messiahship—perpetuated his memory and created Christianity. Had not the disciples expected his second coming Christianity could never have come into being: even as a Jewish sect . . . . The Jews as a whole could not, however, follow after a belief based on so slight a foundation . . . . Yet again, through the preaching of his messianic claims, after he had failed to manifest himself to the world again, in his power and glory, he became, in spite of himself, a "sacrifice," a "ransom for many."[6]

The success of the Christian claim or its failure rests to a very large extent on the theory of the second coming . . . . The Jews never had the concept of a second coming, and since it was the Jews themselves who first taught the notion of a Messiah, via the Jewish prophets, it seems quite reasonable to respect their opinion more than anyone else's . . . . the theory of the second coming is not based on Jewish tradition or sources, and is a theory born from desperation.[7]

- **Muslim Critics.** Many Muslim critics paint Christianity as a failed and false religion. They acknowledge that Jesus was a prophet, but discredit his divinity and destroy the credibility of the Bible by pointing out alleged errors and inconsistencies concerning his *perceived* non-return (among other things). They rightly recognize the logical implications of the Bible's time statements as having a direct bearing on the messianic and divine claims of Christ. They also believe that either Jesus never spoke any time-restricting words concerning his imminent "return" or the Apostles lied about it and other eschatological matters, and corrupted the New Testament by adding words to this effect. These arguments naturally seek to undermine the inspiration and authority of the Bible and open the door for the acceptance of the Qur'an/Koran and Islam. One of many Muslim web sites expresses their view thusly:

We will instead present the following verses with regard to WHEN Jesus' second coming is supposed to occur. They are self explanatory but this has not prevented some [Christians] from inventing new abstract meanings for them:

".... " Matthew 24:29-34. How many generations have passed since?

". . . ." Mark 13:23-30. How many generations have passed now?

". . . ." Matthew 10:22-23. They have not only gone over all the cities of Israel, but have dispersed throughout all of the Earth and we are still waiting.

". . . ." Matthew 16:27-28. Are there any of those who were standing who are alive to this day? Is this not further proof of mankind's tendency to put words in the mouth of Jesus (pbuh) which he never said?

At first, the Christian community expected an imminent return of Christ . . . . This hope carried on in the second century. When the second coming failed to occur, the church organized itself as a permanent institution under the leadership of its bishops. This, however, did not stop the predictions of "the second coming". . . . Muslims too believe in the second coming of Jesus (pbuh). However, Muslims are told that Jesus (pbuh) was not forsaken by God to the Jews to be killed, rather, he was raised by God and it was made to appear to those present that he was crucified (Jesus' apostle Barnabas tells us that it was Judas the traitor who was taken to be crucified) [see Qur'an 4:155-157]. Muslims are also told that he will not return to earth until just before the end of time, and not that he will return before the death of his own generation, as stated above. [8]

Paradoxically, the view most prevalent in Christian evangelical circles regarding the timing of Christ's supposed "second coming" is more aligned with this Muslim statement and view than with the numerous biblical references to Jesus' "return" being within the lifetime of his contemporaries. Likewise, most Christians are unaware that the Bible never mentions an "end of time"—the time for Christ's "return" also held by both the amillennial and postmillennial views. The Bible only mentions a "time of the end" (Hab. 2:3; Dn. 8:17; 11:35, 40; 12:4, 9). There is a big difference!

For these reasons and more, Muslims believe that the current Bible is not the true word of God. It has been corrupted. The Qur'an along with other Islamic sacred texts are more accurate testaments, make more sense, and are absent of contradictions:

> The accusation that Jews and Christians had falsified their Scriptures . . . is the most basic Muslim argument against both the Old and New Testaments . . . . In the Qur'an it is a central theme, used mainly to explain away the contradictions between the Bible and the Qur'an, and to establish that the coming of Muhammad and the rise of Islam had indeed been predicted in the uncorrupted "true" Bible.[9]

> The first generation of Christians were convinced that Jesus would shortly return in glory. Despite the fact that this did not happen in their lifetime, the belief that he would return for the final judgment lingered on and became enshrined in the creeds. Throughout the history of the Church this belief has been the subject of renewed speculation during times of social and political upheaval . . . . The Qur'an itself does not explicitly refer to Jesus' return but the classical commentators detected allusions to it in 4:159 and 43:61 and occasionally elsewhere.[10]

> In tradition, *Hadith*, the basic body of religious sources second to the Qur'an, Islam lives in the vivid expectation of Jesus' second coming, ushering in the realm of peace and justice at the end of time, in which Muhammad plays no part. At the end of time, Jesus will descend . . . to slay the Antichrist. He will go to Jerusalem, perform the prayer at dawn in Muslim fashion and rid the world of all unbelievers and their symbols. All peoples of the book will believe in him, forming only one community, Islam, and the reign of justice and complete peace will set in. The reign of Jesus, God's glorified servant, will last forty years, followed by the 'Hour', the end of the world on the day when God alone will sit in judgment at the universal resurrection.[11]

> It is the prophetic role of Muhammad . . . to witness the truth of Christ's Second Coming which alone can bring into being the "universal Messianic reconciliation" . . . of Jews, Christians, and Muslims.[12]

- **Scoffers.** In New Testament times, Jewish scoffers acknowledged the link between Jesus' "return" and the destruction of the Temple. They pointed to the continuation of everything—the Temple, city, and priesthood—as evidence that Jesus hadn't come back as He promised. No visible changes were evident. Therefore, these scoffers doubted the sureness of Jesus' promise, viewed Christianity as a perversion of Israel's future, and mockingly asked, "Where is this coming He promised?" (2 Pet. 3:3-4; Jude 16-19). Back then, Jesus' prophecies were only thirty-some years old. Currently, the "delay" is 19 centuries long and counting. Not surprisingly, the arguments of those early scoffers are looking pretty good now. If there has been a delay of this length, hasn't history proven those 1st-century scoffers were right after all?

- **Complicity in the Christian Camp.** Most Christian traditionalists have not faced or answered the challenge of Jesus' so-called non-return. In essence, they have aligned themselves with the 1st-century scoffers and become unwilling accomplices of Christianity's critics. Most agree that Jesus didn't "return" *as* and *when* He promised, in that generation or in that century. Standard Christian explanations for this posit that Jesus' coming has been delayed or postponed, or that the timing was misunderstood, and that He will come again (return) someday "soon" and finish the job. Sadly, these rebuttals only prove the critics' point that Jesus was incorrect about his time-restricted predictions and therefore cannot be the Messiah. The bottom line is that postponement theories directly contradict the teachings of Jesus, and nonoccurrence leaves Christianity vulnerable to all manner of critical and skeptical assaults. It gives critics all the license they need to blaspheme Jesus as not only a false prophet, but a deceiver as well. It opens wide the door to the dismissal of all Christian claims.

Even C.S. Lewis, the respected Christian apologist and author, I am embarrassed to report, said in 1960 about Jesus time-restrictive, "this-generation" statement in Matthew 24:34:

"Say what you like," we shall be told [by the skeptic], "the apocalyptic beliefs of the first Christians have been proved to be false. It is clear from the New Testament that they all expected the Second Coming in their own lifetime. And, worse still, they had a reason, and one which you will find very embarrassing. Their Master had told them so. He shared, and indeed created, their delusion. He said in so many words, 'this generation shall not pass till all these things be done.' And He was wrong. He clearly knew no more about the end of the world than anyone else."

It is certainly the most embarrassing verse in the Bible. Yet how teasing, also, that within fourteen words of it should come the statement, "but of that day and hour knoweth no man, no, not the angels which are in heaven, neither the Son, but the Father." The one exhibition of error and the one confession of ignorance grow side by side.[13]

As we shall see, the embarrassment belongs to C.S. Lewis.

- **Funeral Eschatology.** Christian preachers who don't believe that Jesus has 'returned" (come) and received his first disciples into heaven (John 14:1-3), assure the family and friends at a Christian funeral that the dearly departed believer is better off than those there assembled because he/she is in heaven with Jesus, right now. Call it "funeral eschatology," but while comforting, it's totally inconsistent. Many educated Christians rightly recognize a no-one-in-heaven-yet dilemma in the classroom (see John 3:13; 13:33, 36). Yet they conveniently choose to ignore it at the funeral home. Which is it? Do believers today immediately go to heaven upon physical death? Or, do they still have to wait in Hades or somewhere else until Jesus finishes preparing the place and "returns" to receive them?

"It is certainly the most embarrassing verse in the Bible .... The one exhibition of error and the one confession of ignorance grow side by side."
– C.S. Lewis

Are We So Blind or Ashamed?

Are we so blind to see or ashamed to admit the implications of nonoccurrence? These informed critics use Jesus' own words against us. Their attacks should, at the least, stir some sober reflections (1 Pet. 3:15; 2 Tim. 4:2-4). But we need to do more than that. Why? Because modern scholarship has been reinventing the historical Jesus. For instance, the book, *Jesus Under Fire*, reports that the liberal and well-publicized group, the "Jesus Seminar," claims that "less than two percent of the sayings of Jesus in the Gospels were actually spoken by him and another fourteen percent are similar to what Jesus said."[14] You can read about the latest reinvention attack in a New York Times Bestseller book titled, *Misquoting Jesus: The Story Behind Who Changed the Bible and Why* (HarperOne, 2007).

Many educated Christians rightly recognize a no-one-in-heaven-yet dilemma in the classroom . . . . Yet they conveniently choose to ignore it at the funeral home.

Consequently, growing numbers of critics are publicly proclaiming that "the Bible cannot be trusted because Jesus was wrong about the timing of His coming."[15] Equally, embarrassing, they emphasize, is the long and growing list of his zealous followers who have been equally in error about the time of this same supposed event.

How then should we respond to these scholarly critics and skeptics—whether they are atheists, liberals, Jews, Muslims, or just plain scoffers—who have denigrated Christ, the Bible, and Christian faith in general? To date, and in this author's opinion, we have done a poor and pathetic job. Saying Jesus is coming back again some time in the future to finish what He started two-thousand years ago is hardly a convincing argument. As theologian Gary DeMar points out, this quasi defense "has led to the shipwreck of the faith of many former believers" and "many people are turned off by a constant rehearsing of end-time speculations that never come to pass."[16]

Another regrettable example is bestselling author Lee Strobel's book, *The Case for Faith*. In it, Strobel names and addresses what he calls "'The Big Eight' objections to Christianity."[17] As the book's subtitle states, these are billed as "the toughest objections to Christianity" and termed "the eight most convincing arguments against Christian faith."[18] They are—see if you can detect a biggie that is missing:[19]

1) If there's a loving God, why does this pain-wracked world groan under so much suffering and evil?
2) If the miracles of God contradict science, then how can any rational person believe that they're true?
3) If God is morally pure, how can he sanction the slaughter of innocent children as the Old Testament says he did?
4) If God cares about the people he created, how could he consign so many of them to an eternity of torture in hell just because they didn't believe the right things about him?
5) If Jesus is the only way to heaven, then what about the millions of people who have never heard of him?
6) If God really created the universe, why does the evidence of science compel so many to conclude that the unguided process of evolution accounts for life?
7) If God is the ultimate overseer of the church, why has it been rife with hypocrisy and brutality throughout the ages?
8) If I'm still plagued by doubts, then is it still possible to be a Christian?

Conspicuously missing from this list, as well as from Strobel's other bestselling book, *The Case for Christ*, is any recognition of or defense against the main argument used by the above critics and skeptics, alike, to discredit the deity of Christ and the inerrancy of Scripture.

During the past two centuries, critics and skeptics have made a strong case *against* Christ and attacked the Christian faith at its weakest point—i.e. the many embarrassing statements of Jesus to "return" and fulfill all things within the lifetime of his contemporaries. In the same vein, the apocalyptic expectations of every New Testament writer are accused of failing. Once again, this so-called "problem of nonoccurrence" has been the most damaging evidence against the deity of Christ, the authority of the Bible, and the inspiration of every New Testament writer. To date, no effective defense has been provided. Most, if not all, evangelical Christian apologists have left Christ in the jaws of his liberal/skeptic prosecutors. Even Josh McDowell's classic and apologetic book, *Evidence That Demands a Verdict*, did not address this vital issue at all.

Consequently, in America, especially over the past 50-75 years, denomination after denomination, seminary after seminary, church after church, as well as, believer after believer have fallen victim to the liberal/skeptic attack on the Bible and on the integrity and deity of Christ. It is called the "battle for the Bible." And again, the focal point of this attack has been and continues to be upon the eschatological statements of Jesus to "return" within the lifetime of his contemporaries and the imminency expectations of the New Testament writers that He would do just that.

In the first chapter of his book, *Jesus and the Last Days*, George R. Beasley-Murray cites example after example of liberal scholars attacking the supposed failure of eschatological events to occur within the lifetime of Jesus' 1st-century generation as the "fundamental error" which "shows that his [Jesus'] system is discredited."[20]

Reformed theologian R.C. Sproul, Sr. concurs:

> In seminary I was exposed daily to critical theories espoused by my professors regarding the Scriptures. What stands out in my memory of those days is the heavy emphasis on biblical texts regarding the return of Christ, which were constantly cited as examples of errors in the New Testament and proof that the text had been edited to accommodate the crisis in the early church caused by the so-called parousia-delay of Jesus.[21]

Sproul terms this two-century-old assault by liberal scholarship on the Bible and on Jesus Himself "one of the most critical issues that the Church faces today." He further relates that "I have never been satisfied that the evangelical community has dealt with the problems of the time-frame references that are set forth in the New Testament about the near-term expectations . . . things that were to happen within the first century."[22] In another book, Sproul warns that "we must take seriously the skeptic's critique of the time-frame references of New Testament prophecy, and we must answer them convincingly."[23] Also according to Sproul, we evangelicals have not answered them convincingly.

Fact is, and as we shall further see in our next chapter, Jesus made clear, concrete, future predictions about his coming in glory that seemingly did not come to pass, or so we have been told. Liberal and skeptic criticism, especially, concentrates on that point. Their weighty criticism, truly, should be a "cause for pause" for anyone who believes in the inspiration and authority of Scripture. After all, the integrity of Christ and all the New Testament writers is at stake.

"we must take seriously the skeptic's critique of the time-frame references of New Testament prophecy, and we must answer them convincingly."
– R.C. Sproul, Sr.

Robert P. Carroll, for example, in his book titled, *When Prophecies Failed,* discusses "the phenomenon of disconfirmed expectation." He charges that this tendency was not "particular to Marxian thought or limited to modern political structures." To the contrary, it went "back much further in time and thought to the early centuries of Christianity when various Christian communities struggled to come to terms with the failure of the parousia . . . ." This then "gave rise to the need for interpretation of the traditions so as to justify them in light of what had *not* happened."[24]

Kurt Aland in his book, *A History of Christianity*, first confirms that "it was the definite conviction not only of Paul, but of all Christians of that time, that they themselves would experience the return of the Lord."[25] Later, he discloses that "around the middle of the second century . . . the Shepherd of Hermas thinks he has found a solution . . . the Parousia—the Lord's return—has been postponed for the sake of Christians themselves . . . . At first, people looked at it as only a brief postponement, as the Shepherd of Hermas clearly expresses . . . . But soon . . . it was conceived of as a longer and longer period, until finally—this is today's situation . . . ."[26]

Brian E. Daley in *The Hope of the Early Church* rationalizes that eschatology is often seen as a "by-product of failed eschatological hope – a way of coping intellectually with the non-fulfillment of first-century apocalyptic fantasies." And since "the fulfillment of their early hopes was surely delayed," it "required" a "reorientation of the time-line of its eschatological hope."[27]

Jaroslav Pelikan saw it this way in his first volume of *The Christian Tradition: A History of Development of Doctrine.* "When the consummation was postponed," this necessitated "the reinterpretation of biblical passages that had carried eschatological connotation . . . toward a more complex description of the life of faith . . . in the development of Christian eschatology."[28]

Do you *hear* what these informed critics and skeptics and even the revered C.S. Lewis are saying? They are saying Jesus was *literally wrong* when He made numerous time-restrictive predictions and statements regarding his coming, his so-called "return." Perhaps, the embarrassment belongs to C.S. Lewis, et al. But this perceived weakness was, and still is, the crack that let the liberals in the door to begin their systematic criticism and dismantling of Scripture with its inevitable bankrupting of the faith.

Moreover, these informed critics of the Christian faith have had no trouble seeing though the postponement theories, biblical inconsistencies, and poor scholarship of conservative attempts to cover-up for Jesus' predictions to "return" or come again within the lifetime of his contemporaries. Not only have cover-up attempts directly contradicted the teachings of Jesus and the no-delay declarations of Scripture (Hab. 2:3; Heb. 10:37), they just add ammunition to numerous claims opposing Jesus' divinity and the authority of the Bible.

How can conservative evangelicals "answer them convincingly," as R.C. Sproul, Sr. has admonished? Certainly, it's not with the postponement theories of the past, or by changing the meaning of commonly understood and normally used words, or by any of the other side-stepping devices defenders have been forced to employ. Nor can we continue to ignore these attacks hoping they will go away. They haven't and they won't.

An Inerrant Defense, the Ultimate Apologetic

Perhaps the most obvious solution has been staring us in the face all these centuries. The *only solution* to the problem of "nonoccurrence" is *occurrence!* It's the only biblically *consistent solution* and *inerrant defense* that can stop the liberal/skeptic/critic attack dead in its tracks. Without it, conservative Christians are left with no credible response.

Truly, exactness in the form of timely and precise fulfillment is the most Christ-honoring, Scripture-authenticating, and faith-validating of all the various end-time views in the historic church. It is also, in this writer's opinion, the ultimate apologetic supporting God's demonstrated attribute of divine perfection.

The *only solution* to the problem of "nonoccurrence" is *occurrence*! It's the only biblically *consistent solution* and *inerrant defense* that can stop the liberal/skeptic/critic attack dead in its tracks.

First and foremost, let us affirm that the foundational doctrine of the *parousia* and coming on the clouds (not "return" or "second coming" as we shall see) of Jesus Christ is non-negotiable. Again, the very credibility of Jesus and the authority of Scripture are at stake. But we must come to grips with the inspired time-frame parameters and Jesus' inclusion of these two elements within the context of his "all these things." And only one time in human history is, was, or will be the correct time, and only one generation is, was, or will be the generation to experience this age-ending coming of Jesus.

In our next chapter, we'll examine seven demanding, scriptural, and historical evidences why Jesus *did come in this way and manner* and within the generation that was alive during his earthly ministry, *just as and when He said He would,* and *as and when every New Testament writer and his first followers expected—under the guiding of the Holy Spirit (John 16:13).* Is this too frightening to consider? Truth is often frightening. But once again, the divinity of Jesus and the trustworthiness of Scripture hang in the balance.

So, "Come now, let us reason together" (Isa. 1:18). As we do, I implore you not to dismiss any of this evidence prematurely. Read through it all. Ponder it. Test it thoroughly (1 Thess. 5:21). As we reexamine what the Bible actually says and teaches, be prepared to unlearn anything you've received by tradition which won't stand up to an honest test of *sola scriptura,* or "only the Scriptures."

Chapter 11

Seven Demanding Evidences of Jesus' Timely Coming on the Clouds

If Jesus is a failed prophet, then his critics have won the day. But if there is evidence that Jesus did come "on the clouds" in age-ending judgment and consummation of God's plan of redemption—exactly *as* and *when* He said He would—then we *should* be speaking out boldly and loudly in his defense, not blindly following the blind. Below are seven demanding evidences to be carefully considered that He did just that.

Evidence 1. The Emphatic Time Statements of Jesus. The strongest possible evidence that Jesus came on the clouds within the lifetime of his contemporaries is his own time-restrictive statements. He left no doubts. Frequently, He confirmed the certainty and faithfulness of his big, end-time coming and set its time parameter. His words were clear, concise, and unequivocal. He didn't say "maybe" or "possibly" or "someday" or "one day" or "in 2,000 years" or "in 10,000 years." Jesus spoke in a plain, straightforward manner to the ordinary people of his day, not in a complex manner only understood by trained theologians or linguists. When taken at face value, his words concerning this coming are some of the clearest in the New Testament. If forced to mean something else, they become puzzling. As you read the following verses, imagine yourself being one of his 1st-century disciples. How would *you* have understood Jesus' words, especially concerning the *time* of his coming?

Matthew 26:64. Quoting from the prophet Daniel, Jesus responded to and forewarned Caiaphas, the high priest, and the Sanhedrin saying, *". . . In the future you will see the Son of Man sitting at the right hand of the Mighty One, and coming on the clouds of heaven."*

When Jesus said "you," He meant the people He was speaking to. He spoke in the first person directly to Caiaphas, the high priest, and to all present. They were familiar with this apocalyptic language, and would be the ones who would "see" (meaning to recognize) his coming in catastrophic judgment. How could Jesus possibly have been describing an event some 2,000 years later? The text demands fulfillment in their lifetime, not deferment to a people far removed or to times hundreds or thousands of years later. That would have meant nothing to them.[1]

Jesus spoke in a plain, straightforward manner to the ordinary people of his day, not in a complex manner only understood by trained theologians or linguists.

Matthew 10:23. While talking with his disciples, Jesus promised, *"When you are persecuted in one place, flee to another, I tell you the truth, you will not finish going through the cities of Israel before the Son of man comes."*

Was Jesus lying or misleading them here? Was this part of a clever way of keeping them faithful and devoted by giving them false hope? Or were these words spoken to real people in that "you" group living in the 1st century? They were the ones to evangelize those cities of Israel. Jesus' obvious intent was not to deceive but to assure his disciples that during the persecution that was soon to come upon them, they would not run out of places to flee for safety before He came in this way. Furthermore, didn't Jesus' words have to be fulfilled before Israel ceased to exist as a nation circa A.D. 70? If He was inspired and telling the truth, they were.[2]

Matthew 16:27-28. He informed his disciples, *"For the Son of Man is going to come in his Father's glory with his angels, and then he will reward each person according to what he has done. I tell you the truth, some who are standing here will not taste death before they see the Son of Man coming in his kingdom."*

Here again, Jesus is describing the same, singular event with a definite time-frame limitation. A 40-year period was to transpire between his ascension into heaven and this "coming in his kingdom" (also see 2 Tim. 4:1). During that time some of his disciples died, but others remained alive. If this event has yet to take place, then shouldn't we have people living today who are almost 2,000 years old? But this is ridiculous. Rather, why not accept Jesus' words at face value and leave this coming in the time-context in which He clearly and emphatically placed it? Yet many Bible commentators have violently resisted the plain and common-sense meaning of these words.[3]

Matthew 24:3, 27, 30, 34. As we've seen, Jesus divinely linked the time of his coming to the destruction of the Temple. *'Tell us,' they said, 'when will this happen, and what will be the sign of your coming and of the end of the age . . . so will be the coming of the Son of Man . . . . At that time the sign of the Son of Man [Jesus] will appear in the sky, and all the nations of the earth will mourn. They will see the Son of Man coming on the clouds of the sky, with power and great glory. . . . I tell you the truth, this generation will certainly not pass away until all these things have happened."*

Jesus inseparably named his coming as a part of "all these things." He used the very same time phrase his disciples had just heard Him speak to the scribes and Pharisees when He told them the guilt of the blood of the righteous would fall upon "this generation" (Matt. 23:35-36). In all its seventeen other uses in the New Testament, the phrase "this generation" is consistent in its meaning. Jesus meant his contemporaries, not some unborn generation centuries removed, and not a race or type of people. There are no exceptions.[4] And no justification exists for excluding his *parousia* (coming) from the context of "all these things."

John 21:22. *Jesus answered, "If I want him to remain alive until I return (NIV is a bad translation), what is that to you? You must follow me."*

Here Jesus suggested that the Apostle John could be, but not necessarily would be, alive when He returned (the better translation is "till I come" KJV). It's yet another confirmation that a 1st-century timeframe is the only one Jesus ever intended. As far as is known, John was the only original Apostle who survived beyond the destruction of Jerusalem. The point is clear. Can you seriously doubt that any of Jesus' disciples or hearers would have placed his coming in glory outside of the lifetime of some then present? A well-established pattern and consistency of 1st-century imminency dominates Jesus' words. It perfectly harmonizes with the literal, exact, chronological, and sequential fulfillment of Daniel's two time prophecies (covered in chapters five and six), which also pinpointed 1st-century fulfillment, with no gaps, no interruptions, and no exegetic gimmicks.

These statements of Jesus concerning the imminence of his coming have proven especially perplexing for all postponement traditionalists. But why fight them? Why twist them? Why not just take Jesus' time-restricted words at face value, literally and naturally? Every New Testament writer, the early Church believers, and even the unbelieving Jews did exactly that. They never imagined that Jesus might be referring to a distant event 2,000 some years out in the future. So why can't we just take Jesus at his word and leave this magnificent eschatological event in its proper timeframe where it rightly belongs?

Thus, the 1st century should confirm when everything Jesus promised either did or didn't come to pass. If He was wrong, then He was neither inspired, a Prophet of God (Deut. 18:21-22), nor the Messiah. There is no valid escape from this predicament. The texts demand it. Even appealing to the unknown time statement, "No one knows about that day or hour" (Matt. 24:36; 25:13) doesn't mean knowing the time was a futile task. Nor does this excuse override the nearness and time-restriction imposed by Jesus Himself. No one knows the day or hour of the birth of a baby following a nine-month gestation period either. And Jesus compared this coming to just that (Matt. 24:8). But that's why He gave signs. By watching for these signs and obeying his instructions to flee, his disciples could know that the tough times of unequalled tribulation would not last forever and that this coming and their deliverance was very close.

Once more, we'd be well-advised to consider the words of the old hymn, *Tis So Sweet* (see again chapter eight, p-167). Unfortunately, the overwhelming majority of Christians since Bible times have not been willing to just take Jesus at his word. They no more believe that Jesus' words of imminence applied to the time of his first disciples than did the scoffers of that day. So we've employed every means imaginable to side-step, distort, and explain away their natural and time-restricted meaning. The fact is, these manipulations are necessitated by our preconceived notions about the nature of this coming. Since we haven't seen anything resembling what we've been told to look for, we've abandoned a literal-time hermeneutic and postponed occurrence to the future—now 19 centuries and counting.

Ironically, profound things can be simple. And apparently Jesus wanted to keep his statements simple. Otherwise, why say them? We know that "the common people heard Him gladly" (Mark 12:37 KJV). But the traditions of men can and have made the word of God of little or no effect (Mark 7:13; Matt. 15:6). It was true back then. It's still true today. Think about it, though. Why complicate Jesus' words? Why not keep them simple and just honor their plain meaning and adjust our notions of the nature of fulfillment. Maybe, just maybe, Jesus Christ knew in what generation He would come in this manner and taught that very thing using words and meanings his hearers could easily grasp. And maybe, just maybe, it's the uninspired historic Church, its creeds, and our favorite theologians who have made the mistake. Remember, Jesus said it was the "evil servant" who says, "My Lord delayeth his coming" (Matt. 24:48 KJV). And the Church has been preaching "delay" for 19 centuries and counting.[5]

We should be able to stop here and rest our case. If you had heard Jesus' teachings first-hand, how would you have understood his words? Who would you have thought He was talking to and about? Then why should we believe any differently today? Why must we make excuses for Him? If Jesus said it, shouldn't we believe it and that settles it? This is our first evidence. Even if it isn't sufficient to "prove" our point, there's more evidence—much more.

Evidence 2. Equally Inspired and Emphatic Imminency Statements and Expectations of Every New Testament Writer. In addition to taking Jesus at his word, we'd be well advised to take the New Testament writers at their word, too. Bible scholars generally agree that every New Testament writer, the Apostles, and members of the 1st-century Church expected that Christ's *parousia* coming would occur within their lifetime. And why wouldn't they? 1) The Lord told them so. 2) Possessing the promised Holy Spirit, their expectations were evidently guided by the Spirit's disclosing work: "But when he, the Spirit of truth, comes, he will guide you into all truth. He will not speak on his own; he will speak only what he hears, and he will tell you what is to come" (John 16:13; 14:25; also see 1 John 2:20).

If Jesus' Apostles and first disciples were wrong or misguided in their Spirit-guided expectations of this coming of the Lord, what else might they have been mistaken about? How then could we trust them to convey other aspects of the faith along to us accurately, such as the requirements for salvation? After all, whose expectations should we trust? Theirs? The historic Church's? The creeds'? Or ours today?

In the following selected examples, these New Testament writers were declaring inspired truth just as emphatically as Jesus. Again, if their expectations failed to come to pass, as all postponement traditions are constrained to admit, they weren't inspired. There is no other valid option. If the Holy Spirit lied to them, misled them, or did an inadequate job, we would find that intolerable.

If Jesus' Apostles and first disciples were wrong or misguided in their Spirit-guided expectations of this coming of the Lord, what else might they have been mistaken about?

- **James.** Ten years before Jerusalem was destroyed, James declared that he was living "in the last days" (Jas. 5:3) and that "the Judge is standing at the door" (Jas. 5:9; also see Matt. 24:33). He admonished the 1st-century followers of Christ to be patient "until the coming of the Lord" (Jas 5:7). Then he proclaimed "the Lord's coming is at hand" (Jas. 5:8 NAS).

James' words are some of the strongest in the Bible indicating the nearness of the Lord's coming just ten years later. James' sense of the closeness of "the time of the end" agrees with Jesus' teachings.

The same language was used to announce the arrival of the kingdom of God. John the Baptist proclaimed it "at hand" (Matt. 3:2 KJV, the Greek word *eggizo* from *engys* or *eggus*, means "graspable, seizible, there for the taking, or almost there"). It was inaugurated within months (Mark 1:14-15). Jesus used the same idiomatic phrase when speaking of proximity ("behold, he is at hand that doth betray me" [Matt. 26:46 KJV]), and immediacy ("My time is at hand," [Matt. 26:18 KJV]). For Jesus' other uses of this "at hand" idiom, see: Mark 1:15; Matt. 4:17; 10:7; 26:45; John 2:13; 6:4; 7:2; 11:55 KJV.

James' readers did not interpret nor understand his "at hand" time terminology as a 2,000-years-or-longer period, as many of us have been taught today. Nor was James deceiving his audience with a different specialized meaning of known and ordinary words. He issued no disclaimers. His "at hand" demands the same "right there" or "almost right there" immediacy as other scriptures. "At hand" is the ultimate imminency idiom of Scripture. It means there or real soon, and certainly not centuries later.

Some interpreters attempt to cover for God by claiming He has a different view of time than we humans have. Hence, they rationalize a long delay or elongation of the Bible's numerous imminency statements by ascribing to God a time scale different from our own, such as the oft-cited "a day is like a thousand years" (2 Pet. 3:8).[6] Not only does this tactic strip Scripture of a meaning we can grasp, it gives it a character of deception rather than revelation. It's the classic reason so much confusion prevails. God's Word does *not* speak to we humans according to our understanding of time, and then act according to a different scale. For God to inspire men to write words that meant nearness and imminence to humankind, but in reality meant a long time [many centuries], would be confusing and grossly inconsistent with God's character.

The good news is that we can trust God's time and imminency statements. We can be assured that God inspired the writers of Scripture to communicate time in a language that would be clearly understood in its plain literal sense by the common person. When God meant a long time, however, He used those words indicating just that. In Daniel 8:26, 10:14; and 12:2-9, a "distant future" was 400-600 years. In Jeremiah 29:10 and 28, a "long time" was 70 years. In Numbers 24:17, the Redeemer was "not near" (He was some 1,500 years away). On the other hand, when God meant a "short time," He inspired writers to use plain, ordinary words like "at hand," "near," "at the door," "soon," and "shortly." These are all well-understood, human terms that God inspired to communicate time truths to human beings. In the Bible, "near" never means "far" nor does "far" mean "near." Neither can words and phrases indicating imminency be stretched 2,000 years or so in order to protect a theological bias or postponement agenda. No principle of interpretation can justify twisting such plain statements of time. Indeed, it is tragically regrettable that so many scholars would seek to mitigate and nullify these simple words to protect their postponement traditions.

- **The Writer of Hebrews.** In A.D. 65 the author of Hebrews stated, "In just a very little while, He who is coming will come and will not delay" (Heb. 10:37). He was quoting from Habakkuk's "appointed time . . . of the end" prophecy (Hab. 2:3). The entire book of Hebrews conveys this same sense of urgency and imminency. For example, "as you see the Day approaching" (Heb. 10:25), and other statements like it, cannot be ignored, twisted, or lightly brushed aside. They are indicative of the nearness and certainty of the Lord's coming on the clouds. When Hebrews was written, the early Church was undergoing intense persecution from the Jews and the Roman Emperor Nero. These believers were eagerly awaiting the Lord's promised coming. How could they "see the Day approaching" if it was two millennia later? The popular notion that the Lord has delayed his coming directly contradicts these scriptures.

Let's recall that 2,000 years is over 400 years longer than the covenant nation of Israel even existed. That amount of time surely must be considered a "delay" by any one's vernacular. In essence, this "delay" would make the end longer than the period it is ending! Furthermore, what comfort would a distant-future fulfillment be to those suffering, then and there? All of Jesus' parables about his coming again included an interval, but one that nevertheless concluded within the lifetime of its hearers, and not long after their deaths. Remember that it was an evil servant who said "My Lord delayeth his coming" (Matt. 24:48 KJV).

- **Paul.** Paul also led his contemporaries to believe that some of them ("we" and "you," not "those" centuries removed from then) would still be alive on planet Earth when Jesus came (1 Thess. 4:15). Their "whole spirit, soul and body" [physical, *soma* bodies] would be "kept blameless at [until] the coming of the Lord (1 Thess. 5:23-24). If they *all* died without receiving Paul's promise, and their bodies weren't kept but decayed in graves, hasn't his inspiration failed, too? Paul further told Timothy to "keep this commandment . . . until the appearing of our Lord Jesus Christ" (1 Tim. 6:14). He did *not* tell Timothy to keep it until he (Timothy) died. Around A.D. 57, Paul described the Corinthian believers as "eagerly" awaiting Christ's coming at "the end" (1 Cor. 1:7-8) and declared that "the time is short" (1 Cor. 7:29). In all his writings, Paul evidently had no need to clarify that he was referring to the nearness of any other coming, or end, different from that taught by Jesus in his Olivet Discourse. Paul anticipated the imminent coming of Christ in his lifetime (had he not been killed) and in the lifetime of his hearers and first readers. The plain grammatical meaning of Paul's often-used pronoun "we" (1 Thess. 4:15-17; 1 Cor. 15:51-52), and the saturation of his epistles with nearness expectations and exhortations allow no other conclusion than a contemporary one, if we're honest readers (Rom. 13:11-12; Phil. 4:5; Gal. 4:4; 1 Cor. 7:29, 31; 2 Thess. 1:7). Did Paul mislead God's 1st-century people? Of course not. They, not we, were to find rest, vindication, and deliverance from their persecutions when Christ came in vengeance upon his enemies. If these hopes failed to materialize and their expectations ended in disappointment, how can we believe anything Paul said or wrote?

- **Peter.** In his two epistles, Peter similarly admonished his hearers and first readers, exhorting them to live holy lives and hang in there for "a little while" (1 Pet. 1:6; 5:10; compare with Jesus' "a little while" in John 16:16-19, which was only one week in length). This was to be "until the coming of the salvation that is ready to be revealed in the last time" (1 Pet. 1:5) of "these last times" (1 Pet. 1:20). Peter is referring to the identical, 1st-century timeframe for fulfillment, as do all the other New Testament passages. That's why, throughout his epistles, Peter employs the personal pronoun "you." Peter wasn't using this "you" editorially, as some argue (i.e., applying it to just anyone at anytime). It's bad hermeneutics to take personal pronouns in the New Testament letters—including Peter's letters—to refer to some other and distant group who would experience these events. The imminency statements were addressed to people then present, and they meant what they said in that context. Peter also said that "the end of all things is at hand" (1 Pet. 4:7 KJV), Jesus was "ready to judge the living and the dead" (1 Pet. 4:5), and "it is time for judgment to begin with the family of God" (1 Pet. 4:17). What had once been seen as far off by the ancient prophets was now ready to be revealed to the "you" group in that "last time" (1 Pet. 1:5, 12; also Acts 3:24).

- **Like a Thief.** Jesus' coming was often compared to the entrance of a "thief" (Matt. 24:43; 1 Thess. 5:2, 4; 2 Pet. 3:10; Rev. 3:3; 16:15), and therefore presumed by many to be a completely unpredictable event. But the reason for the thief metaphor was that, even though no one could know the precise time—i.e., the literal day or hour when the point of desolation would be finally reached—Jesus' followers were *not* to be caught off guard (1 Thess. 5:4). His disciples could watch and see "the day" approaching by discerning the signs (Heb. 10:25; 1 Thess. 5:5-6). A second reason for the thief metaphor is that no one concerns himself about a thief coming in the distant future, but anyone would be concerned about a thief coming in his lifetime, which the Bible sets at 70 to 80 years (Psa. 90:10). A 2,000-year delay violates both the imagery, sense of urgency, and contemporary significance of this descriptive phrase.

Both Paul and Peter admonished 1st-century believers to not let the day overtake them as a thief. Most of the people received these scriptures and believed them. Back then, they didn't have religious professionals explaining these inspired words away or telling them that these verses applied to some future generation 2,000 years down the road. They knew it applied to them.

Thus, the New Testament writers were in one accord with Jesus as to his end-time coming. Once again, how many times, in how many ways, and with how many inspired words and phrases must these inspired writers express this 1st-century imminency before we moderns bow our knees in submission and cease persisting in our preconceived, postponement notions? The language of nearness forbids a protracted period of time.

But were the New Testament writers grossly mistaken or falsely led? Or did the Holy Spirit fail to do his job? These options pose an intolerable dilemma.

Without question, the Holy Spirit's guidance is the second strongest argument and demanding evidence that the 1st-century expectations of the early Church and New Testament writers were correct and fulfilled (John 16:13; also 1 John 2:20). If we deny this, aren't we denying the faith? If these severely persecuted people did not live to see the Lord's coming in judgment and deliverance weren't they victims of one of the cruelest hoaxes ever perpetrated on humankind?

---

the New Testament writers were in one accord with Jesus as to his end-time coming.

No, the Spirit of truth did not become the Spirit of falsehood. Jesus' first followers were not kept in the dark. The specific time statements of Jesus and the imminency statements of the inspired New Testament writers confirm the time of this coming as "at hand" back then. Attempts to mitigate the time element of Scripture must be condemned (2 Tim. 2:15).

Evidence 3. Intensification of Nearness Language. Another reason for the heightened air of fulfillment expectancy in the 1st century, and one I think you will find equally compelling is, no Holy-Spirit-guided, New Testament writer ever corrected these 1st-century imminence expectations. Nor did they compromise or contradict Jesus' teachings regarding the timeframe for his age-ending coming on the clouds in judgment and deliverance. In fact, they did just the opposite.

As Jesus' literal, forty-year, "this generation" time period wound down (from A.D. 30 to A.D. 70), the sense of nearness language in the New Testament dramatically ratcheted up.[7] This intensification provides further evidence that Jesus' first followers understood his prophetic words as applying to them, then and there.

Therefore, and approximately nineteen years after Jesus delivered his Olivet Discourse, the writers of the New Testament began writing their epistles, or what we now call the books of the New Testament. The intensification of their nearness language is most evident. To dramatize it, I will provide a recap and countdown by using "T minus" the number of years remaining in Jesus' forty-year, this-generation time period, along with the approximate dates when these works were written.[8] Once again, before you read any further ask yourself, how would you have understood their intensifying words if you had been living back then?

'T _minus_ 40 years' (circa A.D. 30) – Jesus said – "_I tell you the truth, this generation will certainly not pass away until all these things have happened_" (Matt. 24:34). According to Deuteronomy 18:22, "If what a prophet proclaims in the name of the Lord does not take place or come true, that is a message the Lord has not spoken. That prophet has spoken presumptuously. Do not be afraid of him." If Jesus was a true prophet, _what_ He said would happen must happen, but also it must happen _when_ He said.

Yet C. S. Lewis, the respected Christian apologist and author, termed this verse, "the most embarrassing verse in the Bible" and an "exhibition of error."[9] As we shall continue seeing, the embarrassment rightly belongs to C. S. Lewis. Jesus iterated this time-restricted promise to come again in this way several times during his earthly ministry (see again evidence #1).

'T _minus_ 21 years' (circa A.D. 49) – Paul wrote – "_The fullness of time was come_" (Gal. 4:4). What "fullness" of what "time" was Paul talking about nineteen years after Jesus' earthly ministry? If back then was the "fullness," does time ever get more full?

'T *minus* 13 years' (circa A.D. 57) – Paul wrote – *"Time is short"* (1 Cor. 7:29) . . . . *"The world in its present form is passing away"* (1 Cor. 7:31).* We hear this first statement a lot nowadays. But whose time was short and what world was passing away back then? The answer to that question is at the *heart* of what all end-time biblical prophecy is all about. One thing is sure; these words distinctly show that a great crisis was near;

'T *minus* 12 years' (circa A.D. 58) – Paul wrote – *"Understand the present time . . . . because our salvation is nearer now than when we first believed. The night is nearly over; the day is almost here"* (Rom. 13:11-12).* Paul and some of these Romans first believed 20-30 years earlier. Now only 12 years remained until the end of Jesus' literal, forty-year, "this-generation" time period. Something truly significant was about to happen. It doesn't take a modern-day rocket scientist or a computer to do this simple math.

'T *minus* 12 years' (circa A.D. 58) – Paul wrote – *"The God of peace will soon [shortly] crush Satan under your feet"* (Rom. 16:20).* Here is an unmistakable reference to the nearness of a day of deliverance for Christians who were being persecuted by enemies that surrounded them.

'T *minus* 10 years' (circa A.D. 60) – James wrote – *"be patient and stand firm, because the Lord's coming is near (at hand) . . . . The judge is standing at the door!"* (Jas. 5:8-9).* James words are some of the strongest in the Bible indicating the nearness of Jesus' coming in judgment. Jesus had told his disciples in his Olivet Discourse that "when you see all these things, you know it [He] is near, right at the door" (Matt. 24:33), and not nineteen hundred plus years away. Now, with only ten years left in Jesus' forty-year countdown, James writes to real, living, and breathing human beings and admonishes them to have patience as a present-relevant virtue, not a futuristic deception. And then he places Judge Jesus "standing at the door!" James' statements here are unmistakable indications of the nearness of this event, and not just mere expressions of *hope*.

'T *minus* 5 years' (circa A.D. 65) – The writer of Hebrews wrote – *"but in these last days he* [God] *has spoken to us by his Son . . . ."* (Heb. 1:2). By divine inspiration, the writer of Hebrews affixes two specific historical events to the biblical time period known as the "last days": 1) the time of Jesus' earthly ministry and 2) the time in which he was writing. Clearly, he saw himself living in the "last days," back then and there. The question is, those were the "last days" of what? As we have seen, they were the "last days" of the biggest thing that was ending at the time or ever will end on planet Earth and in redemptive and world history.

'T *minus* 5 years' (circa A.D. 65) – The writer of Hebrews wrote – *"In just a very very little while, 'He who is coming will come and will not delay . . . .'"* (Heb. 10:37). Here the Greek word translated as a singular "very" in most translations is actually used twice in the original language. Why? Because, it conveys a double intensification of nearness—"in just a *very very* little while." Thus, the original language is far more expressive than the English. Even more incredible, and in direct contradiction of this verse, the Church has been preaching delay for nineteen centuries and counting. The question is, who is right—the inspired writer of Hebrews or the uninspired Church and its modern-day, prophecy-postponement experts (also see Hab. 2:3; Ezek. 12:21-28)? Also, when we compare this "little while" phrase with Jesus' seven uses of "a little while" in John 16:16-19, we see that Jesus' "a little while" was only a matter of a week or two before He was arrested, tried, and crucified.

The entire book of Hebrews conveys this same sense of nearness. For example, "as you see the Day approaching" (Heb. 10:25), and other statements like it, cannot be ignored, twisted, or lightly brushed aside. When Hebrews was written, the early Church was undergoing intense persecution from the Jews and the Roman Emperor Nero. These believers were eagerly awaiting Jesus' promised coming in judgment. Again, ask yourself, how could they "see the Day approaching" if this Day was two millennia in the future?

Let's also note (I cannot emphasize this enough) that Jesus said it was the "evil servant" who says "My Lord delayeth his coming" (Matt. 24:48 KJV).[10]

'T *minus* 3-5 years' (circa A.D. 65-67) – Peter wrote – *"The end of all things is at hand." (1 Pet. 4:7 KJV).* Peter's words are not "the end of *some* things" or "the *middle* of all things," but "the end of all things." As we've seen, "at hand" in the Greek is the ultimate nearness idiom and means "graspable, seizible, there for the taking, or almost there." "At hand" means "soon," and not centuries later.

Let's also not forget that when we read these words of Peter we are reading someone else's mail. Peter's 1st-century letter was addressed "To God's elect, strangers in the world, scattered throughout Pontus, Galatia, Cappadocia, Asia, and Bithynia" (1 Pet. 1:1). He wasn't writing to them about Christians living in the 21st century. That's taking his words totally out of context. Basic interpretative principles demand audience relevancy. Either "the end of all things" Peter was talking about came upon them, back then and there, or Peter was mistaken and uninspired. Ten verses later Peter explains.

'T *minus* 3-5 years' (circa A.D. 65-67) – Peter wrote – *"For it is time for judgment to begin with the family [the house] of God. . ."* (1 Pet. 4:17 [KJV]). Peter, like Jesus, was emphatic. He did not say it "might be" or "someday will be." He said, "For it is time!" A catastrophe was now imminent. The time for judgment was to begin at the house of God. There is no other legitimate explanation. Peter further revealed that Jesus was also "ready to judge the living and the dead" (1 Pet. 4:5). What had once been seen as far off by the ancient prophets was now ready to be revealed to Peter's "you" group in that "last time" (1 Pet. 1:5, 12; also see Acts 3:24).

'T *minus* 2-3 years' (circa A.D. 67-68) – John wrote – *"Little children, this is the last hour . . . it is the last hour"* (1 John 2:18). Twice, in this one verse, John says this. Written on the eve of the destruction of Jerusalem and the Temple,[11] John, like Peter, does not say "might be" or "someday will be" but *"it is* the last hour." Who can deny it? Christian writer Carl F.H. Henry denies it. Writing in Billy Graham's *Decision* magazine, Henry claims "the very last hour, remains future."[12] But according to John in the New Testament, the "last hour" was upon them, back then in the 1st century. Whom should we believe, the inspired writer John or Carl F.H. Henry? Then, it was the "last hour" of what? Theologian Gary DeMar fittingly protests that many who insist "on interpreting the Bible literally," have literally "turned 'the last hour' . . . into two thousand years of church history."[13]

Next, of course, is the book of Revelation, which I will deal with in a future book. But be assured, it, too, perfectly harmonious with these intensifying expectations and ratcheting-up nearness language.[14]

So let's pause here for a moment and ask ourselves, why were these inspired, Holy-Spirit-guided writers writing like this back then and there? None of their words are complicated words. And the progressive dynamic of their language cannot be ignored or lightly dismissed. How would you have understood their words if you were living back then?

Many Bible scholars admit that no one reading the New Testament on his own would get the idea that Christ would not come again for at least two thousand years. They also agree that the 1st-century Church understood these words in a natural, plain, and literal fashion, and as applying to them, there and then. They expected this coming of Jesus to happen within that first Christian generation.

Clearly, 1st-century expectations of Jesus' coming in judgment were soon and getting sooner. DeMar is right again, "No other interpretation is possible if the words are taken in the 'plain, primary, ordinary, usual, or normal' sense, that is they are interpreted literally."[15] Furthermore, a literal interpretation here is in perfect harmony with a plain, natural, and literal understanding of Jesus' words on this same topic. Is it possible these inspired writers of Scripture were mistaken in their expectations? Has time proven them wrong? Was God careless with inspired language? How can Christianity maintain credibility in the light of so many plain statements if it continues to argue that Christ has not yet come?

Many people in the Church today have been taught that the Lord's coming and other related events (judgment, resurrection, and consummation) are always viewed as being near. Hence, church leaders redefine "nearness" to mean "certainty"—i.e., Jesus' so-called "second coming" and "return" are certain and could happen at any time. Or, they stipulate that fulfillment was delayed and postponed, or that Jesus' and the New Testament writers' words do not really mean what they literally say. If any of this human reasoning is right, then the above-cited time and intensifying nearness statements are meaningless. Fulfillment could still be nineteen centuries away and counting. But how far can we stretch nearness (imminency) before nearness (imminency) loses its value?

Another basic question is, if the New Testament writers *did* want to convey a chronological sense of near and getting nearer, how else could they have said it? How else could they have made it any clearer? Their intensification of nearness language demonstrates that they understood the New Testament's time statements literally, at face value, and did not seek to mitigate, elasticize, or ignore them.

So how much of the content of these above statements was relevant to their original audience? Most Christians say, "none of it was." Some say, "some of it was." Only a few say, "all of it was" relevant and perfectly fulfilled, right on time, back then and there.

Evidence 4. A Long Biblical Precedent. Jesus specified exactly *how* He would come again (i.e., the nature of his *parousia* coming). Twice He said He would come "on the clouds" (Matt. 24:30; 26:64). But what did that mean? If you were a 1st-century Jew raised in the synagogue, you would have known exactly what it meant. How is this so? It's because this type of coming had a long biblical precedent. To appreciate the rich Jewish terminology for cloud-coming, we must enter the mind of a 1st-century Jew. If we look at these things only through 21st-century eyes, we'll become prisoners of what has become the traditional mindset of misunderstanding and confusion.

Christ's "coming on the clouds" is a common metaphor borrowed from Old Testament portrayals of God descending from heaven and coming in power and glory to execute judgment on a people or nation. In all the historic comings of God in judgment, He acted through human armies, or through nature, to bring destruction ("the Lord is a man of war" [Exod. 15:3 KJV]). Each was a direct act of God and each was termed "the day of the Lord." They were always described with figurative language, and empowered by supernatural divine intervention and they brought historical calamity to Egypt, Edom, Assyria, Babylon, and even on Israel itself.

If you were a 1st-century Jew raised in the synagogue, you would have known exactly what it meant.

The Jews of Jesus' day had studied these "day of the Lord" occurrences and were familiar with "cloud-coming" phraseology, as well as the application of one with the other.[16] The Hebrew Scriptures are rich in similes and figurative language that poetically portray a heavenly perspective of God coming among men in judgment:

- See, the Lord rides on a swift *cloud* and is coming to Egypt (Isa. 19:1). (For the earthly fulfillment, see Isaiah 20:1-6)
- Look! He advances like the *clouds,* his chariots come like a whirlwind (Jer. 4:13).
- For the day is near, the day of the Lord is near – a day of *clouds,* a time of doom for the nations (Ezek. 30:3).
- Sing to God, sing praise to his name, extol him who rides on the *clouds . . .* (Psa. 68:4).
- . . . He makes the *clouds* his chariots and rides on the wings of the wind. He makes winds his messengers, flames of fire his servants (Psa. 104:3-4).
- Also see Ezek. 30:18; Psa. 18:9-12; 2 Sam. 22:10-12; Nah. 1:3; Joel 2:1-2; Zeph. 1:14-15).

With familiar cloud-coming imagery Daniel prophesied the coming into heaven of the Son of Man (Dan. 7:13). Jesus, by deriving his "coming on the clouds" phrase directly from Daniel, was revealing Himself as God and the promised Messiah (Matt. 24:30; 26:64). The high priest Caiaphas immediately understood this claim of Jesus to be Deity and responded, "He has spoken blasphemy!" (Matt. 26:65). Jesus was also applying his coming in judgment and power of war in the *same* technical way as the Father had come down from heaven to earth in the spirit realm many times before:

Look! The Lord is coming from his dwelling place; he comes down and treads the high places of the earth (Mic. 1:3).

See, the Lord is coming out of his dwelling to punish the people of the earth for their sins (Isa. 26:21).

But your many enemies will become like fine dust, the ruthless hordes like blown chaff. Suddenly, in an instant the Lord Almighty will come with thunder and earthquake and great noise, with windstorm and tempest and flames of a devouring fire (Isa. 29:5-6).

Add to this the many Old Testament passages where God is said to have "come down" (Gen. 11:5, 8; 18:21; Exod. 3:8; 19:11; Num. 11:16-17; Deut. 33:2; Isa. 31:4; 64:3; Psa. 18:9; also see: Isa. 66:15; Psa. 50:3; 96:13; Hos. 8:1)

Because of this background, Jesus' disciples would have understood what He was talking about in his Olivet Discourse (Matt. 24:30). The high priest understood it. That's why he was so offended by and accused Jesus of blasphemy (Matt. 26:64-65). Let's also note that Jesus made no disclaimers to change the meaning or nature of this type of coming, and neither should we.

Another important factor is that in all these real biblical comings of God in the Old Testament, God was *never physically visible*; He was unseen by human eyes! Thus, cloud-coming is the language of divine imagery. It denotes divine action. In every instance, humans were fully aware of God's Presence and personal intervention in those events of history. Obviously, this Jewish perspective is quite different from the way we moderns have been conditioned to think of Christ's coming on the clouds. We imagine his coming to be spectacularly visible on the tops of literal fluffy cumulus clouds transporting Him down to earth.[17] Yet every biblical instance of a cloud-coming was a real coming of God. Jesus employed the same figure of speech for his end-time prophecies. Thus for Jesus and a 1st-century Jew, coming "on the clouds" was not a claim to come visibly to the human eye.

With this understanding, we can see the Lord Jesus making his appearance, or coming again, in the events of the Roman-Jewish War and the final destruction of Jerusalem in A.D. 66 - 73. Just as the cloud-coming Jehovah God came in Old Testament times, Jesus came "on the clouds." He came utilizing the armies of Rome to deliver his people. And in keeping with the Old Testament pattern, He was not physically seen.

Another important fact to reflect in this judgment event is the change of covenant. Therefore, "the day of the Lord" (Jehovah) of the Old Testament became "the day of Christ" (*Christos* 2 Thess. 2:2; *kurios* 2 Pet. 3:10) in the New Testament.

Look, he is coming with the clouds (Rev. 1:7).

Evidence 5. The Pattern of Other Apocalyptic Language. Jesus and the New Testament writers employed other common apocalyptic language—i.e., graphic images of astronomical and earthly upheavals, which were frequently used by the Old Testament prophets to describe the many catastrophic comings of "the day of the Lord":

- "Collapsing-universe" and signs-in-the-sky language: sun and moon darkened, fire, stars falling, sky rolling up, heavens rotting away.
- Or "earth-moving" language: mountains melting, shaking, etc.

They used this very same language to describe the great and glorious day of Christ's coming again.

Yet, in the history of the fulfillment of this cosmic catastrophic language, we look in vain to find these things literally occurring or visibly happening. The dramatic terminology is figuratively depicting the impending literal but real judgment, the utter devastation, and eclipse of powerful political oppressors and sinful nations who opposed God, and even the punishment of God's own people (Isa. 13, 24, 34; Mic. 1; Zeph. 1; Joel 1-2; Ezek. 7-10; 2 Sam. 22). Sure, it sounds like the end of the world, but none of these acts of God was a universe-destroying or time-ending event. This apocalyptic language transcends its literalism. Its long history of fulfillment teaches us something very important about its nature. Dramatic figurative language was always used to describe the awful magnitude of impending judgment which would involve the direct intervention and unseen Presence of God—events so profound that they could not be described or comprehended in literal language.

Just as the cloud-coming Jehovah God came in Old Testament times, Jesus came "on the clouds."

We have a 1st-century "proof" that the New Testament Christians understood the use of apocalyptic language. The Thessalonians could only have believed that "the day of the Lord" had already come if they had understood the language in a figurative way (2 Thess. 2:1-2). Had they been taught the traditional 21st-century concept you and I have been taught—featuring a visible cosmic cataclysm—no one could have confused them that the Day had already happened. The physical earth and heavens were unchanged during their time of confusion. Moreover, Paul did not correct their understanding of the nature of that event, nor did he use the existence of the physical creation as proof that this "day of the Lord" had not come. Rather, he only corrected the time issue (also see 1 Thess. 5:1-4). Therefore, their concept of a non-visible coming of the Lord must have been right. That would be consistent with familiar use of this apocalyptic language by the prophets and its historical fulfillments. Furthermore, neither Jesus nor any New Testament writer gave any hint that their use of this same language should be interpreted any differently. What, then, causes us to suddenly begin interpreting it differently?

A word of caution is in order. While I have been recommending a literal understanding of God's time and imminency statements, literalism cannot be universally applied in interpreting the nature of fulfillments described in symbolic biblical language. Jesus was always correcting the physical literalism of some peoples' interpretations of his figurative teachings—for example: "the temple of his body," "born again," "a well of water springing up to eternal life," "cutting off hands and poking out eyes" just to mention a few. We would be wise to think like 1st-century Jewish believers. They were Old-Testament-literate and apocalyptic-precedent thinkers. They knew that behind every descriptive symbol, image, or figure of speech was a literal reality. Consequently, whenever the literal reality of a "day of the Lord" came, they expected that it would be unmistakably evident but theophanic in nature, as it had been many times before in their history, and as it was to be again.

Evidence 6. In the Same Way, For the Same Purpose. Jesus did not arrive into the world in the way most 1st-century Jews expected the Messiah to come. Nor did He come again circa A.D. 70 in the way most people since that time expected. Nevertheless, Jesus did come in judgment and vindication against an apostate Judaism that had crucified Him, the Son of God. This coming involved both visible and invisible aspects. Using the language of the Prophets, and comparing this coming with the biblical precedents of a coming "day of the Lord," we can document how Jesus' coming was accomplished. He came in exactly the same *way* ("on the clouds"), for exactly the same *purpose* (judgment), to accomplish exactly the same *thing* (destruction of a nation).

First, history records—quite literally—that Jerusalem and the Temple were destroyed by invading Roman armies in A.D. 70 - 73. "Not one stone [was] left upon another," just as Jesus had said (Matt. 24:2). Jesus had inseparably connected his age-ending coming with this dramatically visible, historical event (Matt. 24:1-34). This linkage of time, event, and place in his Olivet Discourse prophecy cannot be overstated. Even the 1st-century scoffers knew that the Temple's destruction was the corresponding physical event that signaled this coming (2 Pet. 3:3-4).

Second, the prophet Ezekiel said that in the latter days God would come up against Israel "as a cloud to cover the land" (Ezek. 38:9, 16; see also Zech. 12-14). New Testament writers confirmed they were then living in those "last days" (Heb. 1:2; Acts. 2:17; 1 Tim. 4:1; 2 Tim. 3:1; Jas. 5:3; 2 Pet. 3:3; 1 Pet. 1:5, 20; Jude 18; 1 John 2:18). At this time, Isaiah had prophesied, the Messiah would come robed "with the garments of vengeance for clothing" (Isa. 59:17 f; see also Rom. 12:19), and He would proclaim not only salvation, but "the day of vengeance of our God" (Isa. 61:2). Jesus' statement in Luke's account of the Olivet Discourse contains this very wording: "When you [Jesus' present audience] see Jerusalem surrounded by armies, you will know that its desolation is near . . . flee . . . For this is the time of punishment [*these be the days of vengeance*] in fulfillment of all that has been written" (Luke. 21:20-22 [in KJV]). The immediate historical setting and explicit framework for these happenings proved to be the Roman-Jewish War of A.D. 66 – 70. After circa A.D. 70 - 73, the "last days" were over.

Third, Isaiah foretold that during this time Israel would fill up the measure of her sin and she would be destroyed (Isa. 65:6-15) by the Lord, who would come with fire and judgment (Isa. 66:15f). Likewise, Jesus said that this time of filling up would "come upon this generation" (Matt. 23:32-36). That 1st-century apostate Jewish nation, with its city and Temple, had become the great enemy of God's emerging new people, the Church.

Jesus, Ezekiel, Isaiah, and Daniel precisely pinpointed when everything promised would come to pass. If they were wrong, they weren't inspired. There is no valid way to escape this conclusion. As the time approached, James said, "The coming of the Lord is at hand" (Jas. 5:8 NAS). Paul reminded his first readers that "the time is short" (1 Cor. 7:29). Peter proclaimed, "The end of all things is at hand" (1 Pet. 4:7

KJV), and warned, "For the time has come for judgment to begin at the house of God" (1 Pet. 4:17). Urgency permeates Peter's expectations. He is emphatic, "The time has come!" John wrote, "It is the last hour!" (1 John 2:18b). How many "last hours" can there be? How long is short? How could these statements have been any clearer? How many inspired declarations are required before we can believe this inspired imminency?

He came in exactly the same *way* ("on the clouds"), for exactly the same *purpose* (judgment), to accomplish exactly the same *thing* (destruction of a nation).

Fourth, the "sign" of his invisible coming would be:

> Do you see all these things?' he asked. 'I tell you the truth not one stone here will be left on another; every one will be thrown down (Matt. 24:2)

As we've seen, the destruction of Jerusalem and its Temple was the "sign" that signaled Christ's age-ending coming in judgment (Matt. 24:3) and consummation of "the end of all things" (1 Pet. 4:7). The "sign of the Son of Man . . . in the sky [in heaven]" (Matt. 24:30) literally could have been the plumes of smoke arising from the burning fires above the mountain plateau on which Jerusalem sat (Mark 10:33).[18] Once again, the destruction of the Judaic world followed the same pattern and nature of many Old Testament comings of God, or "days of the Lord." Figuratively, Edom's day-of-the-Lord destruction was even described as "its smoke will rise forever" (Isa. 34:10). In every instance of God's intervention, his Presence was evident and his vengeance and judgment glaringly visible. But He, his Person, was never actually seen.

Let's recall that God had set Jerusalem on a high place (Psa. 48:1-2; Isa. 2:2-3) at the crossroads of the world (three continents) and "in the center of the nations, with countries all around her" (Ezek. 5:5-17). He had a definite purpose (see Ezek. 5:8-17). After the fall of A.D. 70, transcontinental traders and travelers from near and far could readily see that something significant had happened. News of the devastation of God's chosen people, their Temple, and the entire nation thus spread rapidly throughout the Roman world.

There is, however, another explanation. The literal Greek for Matthew 24's thirtieth verse reads as follows, "And then will appear the sign of the Son of man in heaven" (Matt. 24:30). Hence, it is argued, "in heaven" does not modify the sign—i.e., it appearing "in the sky," as some versions poorly translate this verse. But rather, the sign defines the locality of the Son of Man—reigning in heaven and from the throne on the Father's right hand (Acts 2:30-36; Matt. 26:64).

Either way, let's note that Jesus did not appear "in person" at this time. His resurrected, ascended, and glorified body did not appear in the sky to signal this special coming, nor will it ever (see John 14:19). Yet his bodily Presence was there, in keeping with the long-standing day-of-the-Lord motif. That's why a sign was needed. A sign isn't the reality; it points to the reality. It's something that is visible and points to something that is currently invisible. The fall of Jerusalem (which was not up "in the sky" but on the earth) was the sign that announced the final "last days" of the Jewish age, not the Christian or Church age for which there is no end. These days were still the *beginning days* of the Christian age.

Thus, Jesus' predictions were all fulfilled. And this historical evidence of divine perfection should be perfectly clear by now, unless you're looking through a futurist veil. There is no need to explain away anything or do a fancy dance around any scripture. Nor should we be surprised that God chose to send Christ in judgment to destroy Jerusalem circa A.D. 70 in the same way He had come out of heaven many times before in Old Covenant times "with myriads of holy ones" (Deut. 33:2). Jesus, who had come, died, arose, and gone back to heaven, came out of heaven to judge the very people upon whom He had spoken seven woes (Matt. 23). The time of grace upon the Jewish nation had elapsed (Matt. 27:25; 2 Thess. 1:7-8; Jude 14; Rom. 11:26; Isa. 59: 20-21; 27:9). It's a fact of biblical and redemptive history.

In all this, Jesus' prophetic words, the imminency statements of every New Testament writer, and the Holy-Spirit-led expectations of the early Church can be plainly understood, in our day, as true, inspired, and perfect. Yet no one except God the Father knew the final day or hour (exact time) of this "time of the end" (Dan. 12:7). Nor can we look back today and reconstruct or know for certain when the literal last day or final hour of desolation was achieved. The exact day or hour is not important, but the destruction of biblical Judaism is highly important. It was prophesied; it was fulfilled, precisely and perfectly.

Evidence 7. The Typology of the Jewish High Priest on the Day of Atonement and Jesus Both Appearing 'a Second Time.' The fall of Jerusalem and demise of the Old Covenant Temple system in A.D. 66 - 73 was no localized judgment event as some suggest, just as the cross was no localized execution event. Yet fewer people knew of Jesus' crucifixion than the destruction of the city. Jesus' coming in judgment circa A.D. 70 was also his appearing "a second time, not to bear sin, but to bring salvation to those who are waiting for him" (Heb. 9:28) and "the coming of the salvation that is ready to be revealed in the last time" (1 Pet. 1:5).[19] If He did not appear this "second time," we have a major problem on our hands.

Curiously, the Bible records that Jesus had already come and appeared *many times* following both his resurrection and ascension (see Jesus' promises of these in John 14:18-19). Then what did this phrase appearing "a second time" mean? To understand this terminology, we must refer to the typology of the Jewish high priest, a figure central to Israel's existence. He was their connection to and mediator with God. Once each year on the Day of Atonement (the annual, sixth Jewish feast as prescribed by the Law), the high priest performed his most sacred duty (Lev. 16). He put on his finery, sacrificed a bull, put its blood in a bowl, tied a rope around his leg (according to tradition), entered into the Holy of Holies, sprinkled the blood on the Mercy Seat of the Ark of the Covenant, and made atonement for himself and his house. Then he came out and appeared before the crowd gathered in front of the Tabernacle (later the Temple), killed a goat, took its blood into the Holy of Holies, made atonement for the congregation of Israel, and reappeared a second time to bless the waiting congregation. Lastly, a second goat—the scapegoat—was released into the wilderness. Time spent by the high priest inside the Holy of Holies was a fearful time for the assembled crowd. But his second reappearance, alive, was the most-awaited and joyful part of this whole ritual. It completed the atonement process and revealed that both sacrifices had been accepted by God and that Israel's sins were forgiven for another year.

Jesus Christ, as our new and superior High Priest of the New Covenant (Heb. 4-10), had to perfectly follow and fulfill this typology (Heb 8:5; 10:1). The Bible tells us that the earthly Jewish Temple was only a copy of the heavenly one (Heb. 9, 10, especially 9:23 ff.). That's why Jesus had to go and *prepare* the heavenly place for his saints to occupy; He did this by going through these same atonement steps (John 14:1-4). Therefore, after Jesus ascended to the Father, He entered the true Holy of Holies and offered up the perfect sacrifice of his spilled blood. But just as the atonement ritual of the Old Covenant was never considered complete with only the slaying of the sacrifice, neither was Jesus' atonement work finished at the cross, or even when He entered into the true Holy of Holies. Partway through is not the place to abandon this atonement typology, as most do. In order for Jesus to perfectly fulfill the high priest typology, He also needed to fulfill the final, inseparable, and essential act of atonement—to appear "a second time" to show that his sacrifice had been accepted, and to fulfill the role of both goats—one dead, one alive.[20]

If this final step has yet to occur, as all futurist schemes claim, we are faced with some big problems! Likewise, if Jesus did not appear a second time, we must live with the following unpalatable facts:

1. 1st-century believers watched, waited, and eagerly expected in vain (1 Pet. 1:5-9; 2:12; Heb. 9:28; 10:25; Luke 21:28; Phil. 3:20; Gal. 5:5; Rom. 13:11-13; 1 Cor. 1:7; Titus. 2:11-13).

2. Their salvation and ours is still incomplete. If no final sign or proof of atonement has been manifested from heaven, we cannot know if Jesus' sacrifice has yet been accepted by God.

3. We can't know for sure if our sins are fully forgiven, if we are totally reconciled to God, if we are back in his Presence (where no one had been since Adam), or were we to die tonight, if we would immediately go to heaven (see again John 3:13; 13:33, 36; 14:1-3).

Jesus appearing "a second time" is essential for complete salvation and heaven being open.[21] This is the climax of the whole salvation event. It's where salvation and end-time prophecy (soteriology and eschatology) are inseparably intertwined. It's why eschatology is the story of our salvation in Christ. If this "salvation that is [was] ready to be revealed in the last time" (1 Pet. 1:5) hasn't occurred in almost 2,000 years, all we can be sure of is that we have the promise of salvation. But if that's all we have, how is the New Covenant any better than the Old in this important regard? If the New doesn't supply what the Old could not provide, where are we? How much salvation do we presently have? How much of Christ's mission to "put away sin" is accomplished? Are we still in limbo (an intermediate state) and not yet in God's Presence?

Please note that any doctrine which says that Jesus has not come on the clouds and fulfilled salvation promises to Israel is actually saying that we don't have full redemption (1 Pet. 1:9-13; Acts 3:24; 26:6-8; Eph. 4:4). There's no way around it. As our High Priest, Jesus had to carefully follow and fulfill all aspects of the sacrificial and atonement typology of the high priesthood pattern on the Day of Atonement. This is the crucial factor and meaning behind his appearing "a second time," and that is what was being "eagerly awaited" by the early Church (Gal. 5:5), as they saw "the Day approaching" (Heb. 10:25).

The good news is that postponement traditions are wrong. There was no 19-centuries-and-counting delay. The atonement process was not interrupted. God's redemptive plan was fulfilled by Christ's appearing "a second time." As our High Priest, He did his atoning work during those "last days." He has been "revealed from heaven" (2 Thess. 1:7; 1 Pet. 1:7; Luke 17:30, 31). The sixth Jewish feast of the Day of Atonement is totally fulfilled and Jesus was and is "able to save completely" or "to the utmost" (Heb 7:25 [KJV]). The next question is, how did He appear?

---

any doctrine which says that Jesus has not come on the clouds and fulfilled salvation promises to Israel is actually saying that we don't have full redemption

---

He appeared by "coming on the clouds" circa A.D. 70.[22] The invisible nature of that particular type of coming was why a "sign" was needed and asked for by his disciples (Matt. 24:3, 30). As we've seen, Jesus clearly and inseparably designated the destruction of Jerusalem and its Temple as the sign of his coming. He said, *"Immediately*, after the distress [tribulation] of those days . . . the sign of the Son of Man will appear . . ."* (Matt. 24:29-30). Immediately after the four sieges of A.D. 66 - 70, the sign appeared. In the final destructive event(s), his Presence was manifested and He was revealed as the Son of God. This sign also signaled God's acceptance of Christ's atonement (Heb. 7:25) and that the way into the Most Holy Place was now open (Heb. 9:8). By this sign we can be sure that Jesus completed everything for our salvation in the generation He named "this generation" (Matt. 24:34). Jesus said, "When you [his audience] see Jerusalem surrounded by armies, you will know that its desolation is near . . . . When these things begin to take place, stand up and lift up your heads, because your redemption is drawing near" (Luke 21:20, 28). No longer do we need to look for Jerusalem to be surrounded by armies. No longer are we living in that waiting period.

Confusion over this eschatological-soteriological issue only comes when we don't understand that the destruction of Jerusalem had major redemptive/spiritual significance. If we lift the salvation process out of its "last-days" context at the end of the Jewish age and shift it to an alleged end of a Christian age, we have confused the very roots of our faith. No scriptural basis exists for removing Christ's appearing a second time from the end-time, last-days framework in history in which his sacrifice occurred—"once for all at the end of the ages to do away with sin" (Heb. 1:2; 9:26). God fully dealt with man's sin problem; redemption is not incomplete. It has been fully resolved.

When Jesus said "Not one jot or one tittle shall in no wise pass from the law until all be fulfilled," or "everything is accomplished" (Matt. 5:18 KJV-NIV), He meant exactly what He said. He came again to do just what He said He would (Matt. 5:17). Who among us would question that a large segment (not a mere jot or tittle!) was passing and did pass away from the Law back in the 1st century (Heb. 8:13; 12:26-28; 1 Cor. 7:31)? The Temple, rituals, genealogies, feasts, the sacrificial system, priesthood, and all they typified are totally fulfilled and gone. They were necessary, but only temporarily. Nothing failed to come to pass. That's why "salvation is of the Jews" and their age (John 4:22 KJV), not of the Gentiles or of an intervening Christian age.

Why then are we still waiting for Jesus to be revealed after almost 2,000 years? Whom should we believe, Jesus or our postponing, futurist brethren? I believe Jesus. How could He be any clearer? Everything was accomplished. The typology is complete. The destruction of Jerusalem and its Temple was the sign of the final event in the consummation of God's plan of redemption. Let us recognize and loudly and boldly proclaim that we have received the goal/end/*telos* of our faith, the ultimate and consummated realization of the promise of the salvation (1 Pet. 1:9). The message is one of fulfilled redemption and completed salvation. What more could we ask for? Yet there is more!

Further Dispelling Visibility

Make no mistake. Jesus' timely coming "on the clouds" circa A.D. 70 was a biggie! It was his real, personal, and bodily coming and ending of the Old Covenant age. But it was not his so-called "return" or "second coming," nor will any of his comings in the future so be. The late-great theologian, George Eldon Ladd, in his highly acclaimed book, *The Blessed Hope*, acknowledged this most significant fact this way:

> . . . the words 'return' and 'second coming' are not properly speaking Biblical words in that the two words do not represent any equivalent Greek words."[23]

Ladd's admission here is huge and leads to major implications. Fact is, we Christians have been hamstrung for centuries with these two non-scriptural expressions and unscriptural concepts. Biblically, the idea that Jesus is off somewhere waiting to come back at some future time, as well as the idea of limiting the comings of Jesus to only two or three times, or to any at all, is man's idea and not God's. The biblical and historical facts are, Jesus never left as He said (Matt. 28:20b). Therefore, return language is inappropriate and never used in proper translations. And He still comes, many times and in many different ways as He has done throughout both the Old and New Testaments. Consequently, the coming of Christ does not refer to *just one or two* historical events. Nor is there such terminology in the Bible as a "final coming" or "last coming" in a world, kingdom, and Christian age that are all without end.

How can we be even more sure of all this? It's as simple as answering the question, Where is Jesus now? Yet it's as complex as asking, why don't we see Him with our physical eyes somewhere on this earth? Since we don't see him, we have decided that Jesus could not have "returned" and be here with us. Paradoxically, Billy Graham confidently declared to a mass crusade audience on September 2, 1997, "This living Christ is in the world today." Well, is He or isn't He? And if He is, where is He?

The answer to this perplexity is simple yet profound. Authentic Christianity does not stand for an absentee Christ absent the entire length of the Christian age! It stands for a present and active Christ who never left and is truly, wholly, and totally here with us. Of course, at one point in history, after his ascension and during the closing period of the Jewish age ("the last days"), He did leave, physically. This departure was required, and it was the decisive factor for the coming of the Holy Spirit (John 14:2-3, 18-19, 28; 16:7; 2 Cor. 5:8; Acts 2:16-17 f). However, He didn't leave to send Himself back.[24] So if He's *now* present, and not off in some distant place waiting to come back, then at some point between his departure and his Presence with us today He either *had to return* or *He never left*. The sequence therefore is either: *present, absence, present* or *present, present, present*. It's *majorly* inconsistent for deferment futurists to say that Jesus is with us today and then claim that He has not "returned."

The correct biblical and historical answer is: Jesus never left, just as He said (Matt. 28:20). Hence, He doesn't need to "return" or come back again from anywhere at the end of the Christian age or at the demise of the material universe, as is commonly asserted—one cannot return to a place one never left. John, in the first chapter of the book of Revelation, affirms this reality. He saw Christ standing in the midst of the lampstands (his Church) clothed in his high priestly garments (Rev. 1:13, 20). His continuing Presence has not changed since that time.

The technical word most often used in the New Testament to speak of Jesus' presence is the Greek word *parousia*.[25] Although it's mostly translated as "coming," its primary meaning is the personal "arrival" or "presence" of one who comes. In most cases these two meanings are not interchangeable, but one or the other based on the context (see 1 Cor. 16:17 for the former meaning and Phil. 2:12 for the latter).

---

one cannot return to a place one never left.

Parousia is derived from two Greek words, *para* meaning "with," and *ousia* meaning "being." It conveys the idea of "being with." As we've seen, Jesus inseparably linked and time-limited his *parousia* coming with the destruction of the Jewish Temple and the end of the Old Covenant Age (Matt. 24:3, 27, 33-34). All attempts to unlink these three events are indefensible and an affront to the veracity of Jesus Himself, the imminency expectations of his disciples and the New Testament writers, as well as to the very soundness and authority of Scripture.

No wonder Jesus' disciples asked Him, "What will be the sign of your coming [i.e., your *presence*]?" (Matt. 24:3). They wanted to be sure He would still be with them after the end of the age (see again Matt. 28:20). They wanted assurance of the continuation of his real, literal, personal, bodily, living, tangible, and abiding but usually invisible Presence, and not anything less. That's exactly what Jesus promised and what continued after the destruction of Jerusalem and the end of the Jewish age—Jesus' *presence* in his fullness—not partially, and not just in the form of the earnest or pledge of the Holy Spirit. Today, He Himself is just as present with us, and in our midst, as He was back then.

What is needed is for us to wean ourselves from the idea that the Presence of Christ must be visible, and to reeducate ourselves on how to better worship, encounter, and enjoy Him in his Presence. Unfortunately, assumptions often blind us to realities. So let's take a closer and broader look at the traditional visibility assumption. This is one area where biblical knowledge, not human speculation, must be applied.

At Pentecost there was no visible or physical appearance of the Holy Spirit. Jesus said that God the Father is "unseen" (Matt. 6:6) and that the Holy Spirit is as well (John 14:17). Regarding the nature of the coming of his kingdom, Jesus also said that it "does not come visibly" (Luke 17:20b; 2 Cor. 4:18). Therefore, why must his "coming in his kingdom" (Matt. 16:28) be visible? Even the rapturists are expecting (mistakenly so) an invisible coming of Christ to remove them from planet Earth. What's more, doesn't biblical faith consist of being "certain of what we do not see" (Heb. 11:1), including being "surrounded by such a great cloud of witnesses" (Heb. 12:1, 22-24)? To top it all, however, Jesus declared that "the world would not see me anymore" (John 14:19, also 14:22). Do we trust his words? Do we believe Him? Just how long is Jesus' "not . . . anymore" anyway? How then can we turn around and preach a universally visible, someday coming? Even Revelation's claim that "every eye will see him" (Rev. 1:7) cannot be used. Let's recall that this "seeing" started in a 1st-century context with "those who pierced him" during his crucifixion. But it also includes every eye of every person who has ever lived, lives now, or *will* live on planet Earth, not just the eyes of those people present on earth at some future time.[26]

Honestly and truly, we moderns need to wean ourselves from the idea that the Presence of Jesus, who is God, must be visible or somehow material. To do so, we will better need to understand the nature of his resurrected, ascended, and glorified body and the practical reality of the spirit realm in which He operates. "For where Two or three come together in my name, there am I with them" (Matt. 18:20). Although unseen, Jesus is truly, fully, and personally present with them, isn't He?

Another example of the reality of the invisible is how Jesus Himself interpreted and explained the Old Testament prophecy of the coming of Elijah (Mal. 4:5-6). This fulfillment preceded the coming and anointing of the Messiah in the Jordan River. But it was not fulfilled by a literal reappearance of the Old Testament prophet Elijah, as the Jews were expecting. Instead, Jesus said that John the Baptist was the predicted Elijah. The invisible spirit and power of Elijah came into and operated through John the Baptist (Luke 1:17; Matt. 11:14; 17:10-13). Also illuminating is Jesus' conditional statement, "And if you are willing to accept it . . . ." (Matt. 11:14). Why did He voice this disclaimer? Because He knew many would not or could not accept the invisible nature of this fulfillment. Jesus also warned that a visible criterion was part of the deception of the elect (Matt. 24:23-36 – more one this in the next chapter). This same unwillingness and deception is paralleled today in the failure of many to understand his age-ending coming "on the clouds" and continuing Presence with us.

The bottom line is, the Christian age was never meant to be a time of Christ's absence. Now, we have the scriptural and historical foundation to affirm that, indeed, Jesus has come and received his disciples unto Himself just as He promised (John 14:1-3), into the previously "off limits" Holy of Holies behind the veil (Heb. 6:19, 20; 9:11-12; 10:19-25, 37), and also us as well into the restored Presence of the living God. The Father, Son, and Holy Spirit are all tabernacling (dwelling) in and among us. This has been true from the time of Christ's *parousia* coming, and will be forever (John 14:18, 23; Rev. 21:3). Never was this divine reality to happen in a rebuilt temple in the modern-day city of Jerusalem.

The bottom line is, the Christian age was never meant to be a time of Christ's absence.

Consequently, the Christian age is also the fulfillment of the seventh Jewish Feast of Booths or Tabernacles (Heb. 9:8; Rev. 21:3; Ezek. 37:26-28) and the restoration of the fellowship that Adam lost (Gen.

3:24). If Christianity does not put us back into the Presence of God, then what does it attain? Or, what good is it? It's that simple and that profound. The tabernacle typology in the book of Hebrews is explicit. It reveals: 1) man's salvation from sin, 2) Christ's preparation of a place (where He is) for his disciples, and 3) restoration into the Presence of God in the Holy of Holies, a place where the Old Covenant could never bring us. Nowadays, all is complete (Heb. 9:8, 9; 10:19). We can now enter the Presence of God, both on earth and in heaven, with all our sins forgiven. It's no less than the bottom line of our faith! This covenantal consummation is the meaning and fullness of Christianity. It is no longer our hope. It's part of our heritage in Christ and the foundation of our faith on which we are to build (Eph. 2:20). It was the goal of redemptive history. "And if I go and prepare a place for you, I will come again and receive you to myself; that where I am, there you may be also" (John 14:3 KJV; see also John 17:24)

What Christ outlined in John 14:1-3 was fulfilled in his end-of-the-age *parousia* coming.[27] To extend this fulfillment to a yet-future timeframe is to leave a vacuum and do irreparable harm to God's redemptive plan. If Christ is still preparing that place and has not "returned" (come), as is popularly taught, then no saint is yet in heaven and John 3:13; 13:33, 36 are still in effect! On the other hand, maintaining that if the Lord came in the fall of Jerusalem we no longer have hope of the coming of Christ is also a big mistake.

Please be assured that the comings (plural) of Christ are multifold and ongoing throughout both the Old Testament and the New Testament, since then, today, and in the future. A discussion of this vital aspect of Christ's Presence and his many countless comings is a subject for a future and forthcoming book about the contemporary Christ.

But his coming to end the Old Covenant age need only to happen ONCE, *as* and *when* He said He would. He doesn't need to come and end that age again. We can now live and dwell in his abiding Presence, in both this life and the next. We can also dwell in the Presence of God the Father, and no veil separates us. The Old Covenant could not achieve this consummated reality. Jesus foretold that "On that day you will realize that I am in my Father, and you are in me and I am in you . . . we will come to him and make our home with him" (John 14:20, 23). After Christ's age-ending coming, God the Father, God the Son, and God the Holy Spirit are "all in all" (1 Cor. 15:28; Eph. 4:6).

All Christians should know about this full reality of complete redemption, celebrate it, and experience it fully. Yet most do not. The blame must be laid at the door of postponing, futuristic, end-time beliefs that rob the present of its vitality.[*]

If Christ is still preparing that place and has not "returned" (come), as is popularly taught, then no saint is yet in heaven and John 3:13; 13:33, 36 are still in effect!

In sum, if we wish to achieve a more responsible apocalypticism, we must take seriously the seven demanding evidences presented in this chapter. We must not diminish or rationalize away the Holy Spirit's 1st-century, disclosing work (John 16:13), and his guiding into "all truth," not into nonoccurrence. We must also honor the time and the imminency statements of Scripture and not fall into the temptation of inserting gaps or delays or manipulating common and well-understood words.

Admittedly, believing that Jesus came "on the clouds" in age-ending judgment in the generation He named and is fully present in our midst today is heretical ("a belief different from the accepted belief").[28] It is also biblical! The historical and scriptural evidence is demanding. Would you now agree?

Sad to say, many churches and Christians may not be willing to admit they've been wrong all these years about our faith's "once-for-all-delivered" and totally fulfilled foundation (see Jude 3). It's too embarrassing for them. But how about you? Perhaps you still have some lingering doubts. In our next chapter we'll deal with and dispel eight, remaining, and challenging objections.

---

[*]We cannot and should not dogmatically preclude a future coming that could be physically visible to the world at large and at the same time. Will it happen? God is sovereign, so it could. But, and here is the crucial and distinguishing point that must be stressed, it doesn't have to happen to fulfill any unfulfilled biblical prophecy. Furthermore, let's not forget Jesus' words, "Before long, the world will not see me anymore" (John 14:19). If a universally visible coming, which many expect, does occur someday, it will be as one of his many and countless comings in his everlasting kingdom.

Chapter 12

Eight Challenging Objections

Are you shocked, flabbergasted, or even upset that Jesus might have kept his word and literally came circa A.D. 70 exactly *as* and *when* He said He would, and exactly *as* and *when* every single New Testament writer and most early Church believer expected? Or are you afraid to admit that we might have missed the obvious truth for so many centuries?

In this chapter we will explore eight remaining and challenging objections that have been raised by those struggling with the possibility and implications of our Lord's timely coming "on the clouds" and fulfillment of "all these things" (Matt. 24:30, 34). They are:

1) I cannot give up my faith in Christ's future 'Second Coming' and 'Return!'
2) Jesus compared his coming to lightning—isn't that visible?
3) What about the 'blessed hope'—'the glorious appearing of our great God and Savior, Jesus Christ' (Titus 2:13)—that's visible and worldwide, isn't it?
4) What about Paul's 'man of sin' who first had to be revealed?
5) What about double fulfillment—circa A.D. 70 and sometime in the future?
6) What about Church creeds and confessionals?
7) Shouldn't Christians stop taking the Lord's Supper (Communion) if Jesus has already come again?
8) Is it really possible the elect have been deceived?

Objection #1. I cannot give up my faith in Christ's future 'Second Coming' and 'Return!' No idea has gripped the human imagination more firmly, saturated the Church more completely, or been proclaimed as the hope of the world more frequently than the idea and doctrine of a "Second Coming/Return" of Jesus Christ. Its influence on the thinking of most Christians and non-church people alike has been a driving force in the world. And yet this belief has been both the bane and chief blind spot of Christianity as its persistent nonoccurrence throughout church history has embarrassed and discredited the faith.

Moreover, this event's supposed occurrence is still the central and pivotal event that drives "one of the most divisive elements in recent Christian history . . . . few doctrines unite and separate Christians as much as eschatology"[1]—i.e., the four competing, confusing, and conflicting end-time views in Christianity today.

Once again, please be assured that I believe every word the Bible says about the end-time coming of Jesus as well as his many comings and promises of many more comings—again, to be the subject of a future and forthcoming book re: the contemporary Christ. But as we have seen, the Bible says *nothing* about a "second coming" or a "return." Nor do the historic creeds of the Church. *Nothing!*

Also, be assured that we simply cannot afford to be misinformed or confused about such an important element of our biblical faith. Unfortunately, "second coming" and "return" terminology implies only two comings of Jesus, one in the past and the other supposedly in the future. But this limitation does not fit with the testimony of Scripture. The idea of limiting the comings of Jesus to only two and calling the later one the "Second Coming" or "Return," or limiting his comings in any way—past, present, or future—is simply a human notion, man-made terminology, and a post-biblical doctrine kept alive by tradition.

---

the many comings of Jesus . . . . we simply cannot afford to be misinformed or confused about such an important element of our biblical faith.

Reluctance to give up the so-called "Second Coming/Return" of Christ idea, doctrine, and terminology must be called for what it truly is: *religious bondage.* In this author's opinion, this area of our faith is also ripe for reform.

First, we should drop the use of this non-scriptural terminology and its unscriptural connotations of limiting Jesus' comings to only two and rendering Him an absentee Lord and Savior. This man-made intrusion has led many astray and greatly nullified "the word of God for the sake of your tradition" (Matt. 15:6; Mark. 7:13). Secondly, we must reeducate ourselves concerning the biblical reality of his ongoing Presence and many countless comings—past, present and future.

Of course, a reformation of this magnitude, though desperately needed, is far easier said and outlined than accomplished. Blind allegiance to entrenched traditions stands in the way. It always has. However, the idea and doctrine of a "second coming/return" has got to go. It simply will not stand up to an honest, sincere, and *sola scriptura* testing of Scripture, as we are commanded to do (1 Thess. 5:21).

The question then becomes, are we willing to abandon tradition when its terminology and concept have been shown to be scripturally erroneous? For many, the answer will be yes, absolutely. Others, I suspect, will kick up their heels and resist the truth of God's Word. But the many comings of Jesus are a beautiful biblical truth and an ongoing reality in his everlasting kingdom. So let's not be intimidated or brainwashed by the traditions of men. The plain, simple, yet precious truth of Christ's coming (singular) is many comings (plural). This revelation must be proclaimed in certain and Scripture-honoring terms. He has been and still is present and active in his creation. His comings are one of his ways. Let's stop limiting his comings! He comes! Come Lord Jesus! Again, I will have much more to say on this topic in a future and forthcoming book.

Objection #2. Jesus compared his coming to lightning—isn't that visible? Yes, Jesus did compare his age-ending, *parousia* coming on the clouds to lightning, saying, "For as lightning comes from the east and flashes to the west, so will be the coming of the Son of Man" (Matt. 24:27). But, no, this powerful simile does *not* prove or necessitate visibility. Nor does it require Him being "seen" everywhere all over the whole world at the same time for several reasons:

- Lightning is associated with a localized weather system and is only seen in a specific locale.
- Lightning that flashes from "east to west" is the intra-cloud variety, not cloud-to-ground type of which we normally think and see.
- 90% of intra-cloud lightning is never seen or never directly seen. It's usually veiled and/or muted by clouds. What's seen are only reflections, results, or effects and not the lightning streak itself.
- Thus, this type of lightning is limited in visibility and does not support a limitless or universal visibility. Quite to the contrary.
- Perhaps by referring to this type of lightning, Jesus meant to symbolically illustrate the power and suddenness of his coming upon a particular people, in a specific locale—(see this usage in regards to divine judgment in the course of Old Testament history by the prophet Zechariah – Zech. 9:14); Or to emphasize the darkness of thunderclouds passing in judgment over Israel; Or to depict the swift advance of the Roman armies that entered Judea from the east and marched westward across the country; Or to underscore that his Presence would not be a secret thing but only indirectly "seen" in the attending circumstances and results [the sign of the judgment that fell on Jerusalem].
- We should also understand that lightning imagery is a common theme and manifestation of God in power and judgment, and is used throughout Scripture (see Nahum 1:3-6, for example).

Once again, just because his coming in judgment circa A.D. 70 was invisible does not mean it was unreal, impersonal, non-literal, non-bodily, or only symbolic or spiritual. Nor does its invisibility lessen its significance. Notably, it was not until the year 1560, in the First Scottish Confession of Faith, that an explicit declaration of a visible "return" was made in any of the historic creeds or confessions of the Church.

Also as we have noted, the fact that a sign ("sign of your coming [*parousia*]" and "sign of the Son of Man in heaven" [Matt. 24:3, 30]) was necessary and asked for should tip us off that this coming would *not* be *visible to the naked-eye*, even though many of his other comings have been and are visible. The "sign" of this coming was not a gigantic, multimedia display of his body up in the sky. It was *the fall of Jerusalem and destruction of the Judaic world in the 1st century.* And it remains a sign for all ages.

Objection #3. What about the 'blessed hope'—'the glorious appearing of our great God and Savior, Jesus Christ' (Titus 2:13)— that's visible and worldwide, isn't it? The Italians have a saying, "traduttore, traditore." It literally means, "translator, traitor." Or more freely, "all translators are traitors." In this vein and case, the NIV, KJV, and AMP translations betray us in this verse. Thankfully, the NAS version correctly translates it in accordance with the literal Greek as: "Looking for the blessed hope and the appearing of the glory of our great God and Savior, Christ Jesus."

Did you catch the difference? The first three translations are poor, if not mistranslations, in which the object to appear is the Person of Jesus. In the original Greek and NAS translation the object to appear is "the glory" of that Person. Big difference! Fact is, "the glory of the Lord" appeared numerous times throughout the Old Testament. But never once was this a literal, bodily, visible, or physical appearance of the Person of God. Rather, the appearance of this "glory" took various forms as: a cloud, a consuming fire, fire, like a rainbow in the clouds, or radiance. (See: Exod. 16:7, 10; 24:16, 17; 40:34, 35; Lev. 9:6, 23, 24; Num. 14:10; 16:19, 42; 20:6; 1 Kgs. 8:11; 2 Chron. 5:14; 7:1-3; Ezek. 1:28; 3:12, 23; 10:4, 18; 11:23; 43:5; 44:4; Also see: Psa. 104:31; 138:5; Isa. 35:2; 40:5; 58:8; 60:1; Luke 2:9; 2 Cor. 3:18).

Numbers 14:21 also states that "the glory of the Lord fills the whole earth." That's not a visible appearance of Deity, either. Remember, Jesus specified that "Yet a little while, and the world seeth me no more" (John 14:19a, KJV).

The Italians have a saying, "traduttore, traditore." It literally means, "translator, traitor." Or more freely, "all translators are traitors."

Objection #4. What about Paul's 'man of sin' who first had to be revealed? Circa A.D. 51, the Apostle Paul wrote that the coming (*parousia*) of the Lord would not take place until the rebellion occurs and the "man of sin" (KJV) or "man of lawlessness" (NIV) was revealed. You can read about it in 2 Thessalonians 2:1-12. This revealing was a definite prerequisite!

The most popular postponement tradition claims that this wicked one is a future "Antichrist" figure that has yet to be revealed. Over the centuries, he has been variously identified as Attila the Hun, Napoleon, the Pope, Martin Luther, Mohammed, Hitler, Mussolini, Stalin, Franklin Roosevelt, Henry Kissinger, and Mikhail Gorbachev. Virtually every unpopular public figure has qualified. Obviously, this tradition has proven totally inept at identifying Paul's "man of sin." Unfortunately, it's a tradition that has not died.

For a number of scriptural and historical reasons, the identity of Paul's "man of sin" should not be arbitrarily lifted out of its 1st-century context. So here's my pick. He was definitely a contemporary of Paul's who fulfilled Paul's prophetic prediction and fit his destructive description to a tee. The following is a condensed version of an apologetic presented in *The Man of Sin of II Thessalonians 2*, by Evangelist John L. Bray:[2]

The Man of Sin. A study of 2 Thessalonians 2:1-12.

<u>Verses 1-2.</u> *"Concerning the coming (parousia) of our Lord Jesus Christ and our being gathered to him, we ask you, brothers, not to become easily unsettled or alarmed by some prophecy, report or letter supposed to have come from us, saying that the day of the Lord has already come."*

If the understanding of the nature of the coming of the Lord by Paul's first readers was in keeping with most traditional, modern-day notions of a rapture-removing, visible, world-seeing, or world-ending coming, they could not have been led to believe that it had already happened.

<u>Verses 3-4.</u> *"Don't let anyone deceive you in any way, for that day will not come until the rebellion occurs and the man lawlessness [man of sin] is revealed, the man doomed to destruction [son of*

perdition – KJV]. He opposes and exalts himself over everything that is called God or is worshipped, and even sets himself up in God's temple, proclaiming himself to be God."

Paul wrote during the time of a literal, standing, and second Temple. He gave no hint that this event would occur some nineteen or more centuries later in some other "rebuilt" temple. His first readers apparently expected this fulfillment in their lifetime. That's why some feared that that "day of the Lord" had already occurred. Also, let's note how Paul's prophetic words here match up with Jesus' Olivet Discourse (Matt. 24). Both speak of the same set of events, use similar language, and convey a strong sense of imminence.[3]

History records that the Jewish rebellion against Rome and apostasy from the faith was already underway in the early 60s, and reached its climax in the Roman-Jewish War of A.D. 66 - 70. I propose that Paul's "man of sin" was, most likely, a specific person who set himself up in the Temple that was standing when Paul was writing. He could have been (take your pick): Nero, Titus, a Jewish Zealot leader, the corrupt high priest, or a Christian Zealot. All except Nero physically entered the Temple. And although Paul never calls him "antichrist," the Apostle John tells us that there were many "antichrists" at work at that time (1 John 2:18; 4:3). No doubt this "man of sin" was one of them. But he was also a special person who had to come on the scene prior to the Lord's coming circa A.D. 70 and before the Temple was destroyed.

Verses 5-7. *"Don't you remember that when I was with you I used to tell you these things? And now you know what is holding him back, so that he may be revealed at the proper time. For the secret power of lawlessness is already at work; but the one who now holds it back will continue to do so till he is taken out of the way."*

Paul had mentioned this power of lawlessness on other occasions (see 1 Thess. 2:14-16; 1 Tim. 4:1). Starting around A.D. 66 the Jews began revolting against Rome and rejecting the sacred practice of biblical Judaism. Some followers of Christ who remained zealous for the Temple system were departing from the new faith and falling back into the old ways. Behind it all was "the secret power of lawlessness" that was "already at work," there and then. But something and/or someone, or both, was holding the "man of sin" back at the time Paul wrote this letter (circa A.D. 51). Whatever that was, Paul reminded his first readers that they already knew both its/his identity. So Paul didn't have to tell them. And he didn't. Since they knew both who and what it was, it could not possibly have been something or someone that would not exist for some nineteen or more centuries. But who or what was it?

Throughout Church history endless speculation has revolved around the identity of this restrainer. However, we also do know that this restraint was in force when Paul wrote, and was actively holding back a "man of sin" alive at that time. This fact is a time indicator and should answer the question of *when*. Some have suggested that the "who" was Nero or the Roman government, which held back Jewish persecution of the early Jewish Christians. Futurists say it's the gospel, the Church, the Holy Spirit, or an angel. But if any of these is what was really meant, why did the writer use such veiled language? And yet, none of these things is ever portrayed in Scripture as restraining lawlessness or being removed from the world.

The best answer—in this author's opinion—is that it was both an office (the "what") and a person (the "one who" or "he"). More specifically, it was the institution of the Jewish priesthood. In A.D. 66, the priesthood was led by Ananus as the high priest. It opposed the Jewish, Zealot-led rebellion. And Ananus wanted peace with Rome. As long as he and the priesthood stood in the way, the lawlessness of the Jewish Zealots was held back, the "work of Satan"

> **Since they knew both who and what it was, it could not possibly have been something or someone that would not exist for some nineteen or more centuries.**

couldn't reach its full realization, and the "man of sin" couldn't appear on the scene and cause the final destruction. In A.D. 68, however, Jewish Zealots, with the assistance of the Idumaeans, murdered Ananus and over 12,000 other priests and left their bodies unburied—a violation of the Jewish Law. Thus, the priesthood was "taken out of the way."[4] Appropriately, Josephus wrote of this removal in his history of the fall of the city:

> I should not mistake if I said that the death of Ananus was the beginning of the destruction of the city, and that from this very day may be dated the overthrow of her walls, and the ruin of her affairs, whereon they saw their high-priest, and the procurer of their preservation; slain in the midst of their city . . . for he was thoroughly sensible that the Romans were not to be conquered. He also foresaw that of necessity a war would follow, and that unless the Jews made up matters with them very dexterously, they would be destroyed: to say all in a word, if Ananus had survived that would have certainly compounded matters . . . and I cannot but think that it was because God had doomed this city to destruction, as a polluted city, and was resolved to purge his sanctuary by fire, that he cut off these great defenders and wellwishers.[5]

Verses 8-10. *"And then the lawless one will be revealed whom the Lord Jesus will overthrow with the breath of his mouth and destroy by the splendor of his coming [parousia]. The coming [parousia] of the lawless one will be in accordance with the work of Satan displayed in all kinds of counterfeit miracles, signs and wonders, and in every sort of evil that deceives those who are perishing. They perish because they refused to love the truth and so be saved!"*

All this happened in the very Temple that was occupied and standing until A.D. 70. As the war between the Jews and Rome developed, a strong leader of the Jewish Zealots emerged who would fulfill Paul's prophecy. He would soon become the key man in inciting the Jews against Rome, in bringing abominations into the Temple area, and in causing the final destruction of Jerusalem and the Temple. After Ananus' murder and the removal of the priesthood, Josephus records that a man named John, the son of Levi, fled to Jerusalem from the Roman-conquered area of Gischala in Galilee and became the treacherous leader of the Jewish Zealots in control of the Temple area. As Josephus wrote, "Now this was the work of God, who therefore preserved this John, that he might bring on the destruction of Jerusalem."[6]

Josephus also records that before this John of Gischala, the son of Levi, was established as the Zealot leader in control of the Temple area (there were three Zealot factions), the power of Satan was already doing his deceitful and treacherous work. Then, this John physically entered the Temple, presented himself to the Zealots as a God-sent ambassador,[7] and persuaded them to defy the laws of Rome and go to war to gain independence. He had also instigated the calling in the Idumaeans to keep the Jewish sympathizers from submitting to Rome[8] and ordered the death of Ananus and the removal of the priesthood. After these atrocities, he became the official leader of the Zealot group in control of the Temple area—"John held the temple"[9]—and began disregarding the laws of Rome, God, and man, and promising deliverance from the Romans. Then he broke off from the Zealots and began "setting up a monarchial power."[10] He "set on fire those houses that were full of corn, and of all other provision . . . which would have been sufficient for a siege of many years."[11] He deceived the Jews about the power of the Roman armies.[12] In possession of the Temple and the adjoining parts, he cut the throats of anyone suspected of wanting to go over to the Romans.[13] He performed many sacrileges, such as melting down the golden and sacred utensils used in Temple service, and defiled the Temple.[14] In short, this John established himself in the Temple, the one standing when Paul wrote, and put himself above Rome and above God, thereby taking the place of God in the Temple. All this happened, right then and there, and exactly as Paul had said the "man of sin" would do.

All this happened in the very Temple that was occupied and standing until A.D. 70.

After the coming of the Lord and the destruction of Jerusalem and the Temple in A.D. 70, John of Gischala was "condemned to perpetual imprisonment" by the Roman authorities.[15] Thus was fulfilled Paul's prophetic and symbolic language that this man would be destroyed by "the spirit of his [Jesus'] mouth and brightness of his [*parousia*] coming" (see Isa. 11:4; 30:27-33; Hos. 6:5; also Dan. 7:8, 19-28).

Verses 11-12. *"For this reason God sends them a powerful delusion so that they will believe the lie and so that all will be condemned who have not believed the truth but delighted in wickedness."*

Josephus further recorded that the Roman General Titus had no intention of destroying the Temple. The Romans wanted to preserve it as a trophy and monument of their conquest. Josephus also personally pleaded with John of Gischala to surrender. But such a "madness"[16] swept through John and his Jewish followers that they taunted the powers of Rome and refused to listen. This man, John, through the power of Satan and the delusion sent by God upon the Jewish people, forced the Roman armies to act. Instead of accepting Jesus as Messiah, King, and Deliverer, the unbelieving Jews placed their hopes in this false messiah, a man of deceit and wickedness. They looked to the "man of sin" to lead them to victory and independence. The priesthood, which stood in their way, had been removed. And by August or September of A.D. 70, Paul's entire "man of sin" prophecy of 2 Thessalonians 2:1-12 was fulfilled. The city and the Temple were burned and destroyed. The covenant nation of Israel and biblical Judaism were forever finished.

Only within this 1st-century context does the Apostle Paul's "man of sin" prophecy make sense and have its greatest significance. No justification exists for separating Paul's words from either the Temple standing at the time of his writing or the end of the Jewish age. John of Gischala, the son of Levi, was a contemporary of Paul. He is a strong candidate for being Paul's "man of sin." The eyewitness account of Josephus, a Jewish-Roman historian, truthfully and impartially documents his treachery and his critical role in Jerusalem's demise. No one else in history—Gaius Caesar, Nero, Titus, or Domitian—comes as close to fulfilling this prophecy as this most influential and deceiving Zealot leader. John of Gischala took over the forces of iniquity. He stood in the Temple itself and exalted himself above all that is called God. He put himself above both God and Caesar. He regarded neither the laws of God nor those of man (Rome). He therefore "set himself up" in the Temple, taking the place of God.

In dramatic parallel fashion, Scripture gives this "man of sin"—John of Gischala, the son of Levi—the name of "the one doomed to destruction" or "the son of perdition." This was same name given only to one other infamous betrayer, Judas Iscariot (compare John 17:12 with 2 Thess. 2:3 KJV). Both appeared in the same "last days" timeframe of the Old Covenant age. *Judas betrayed Jesus. John of Gischala betrayed the Jews.*

Thus, was fulfilled Paul's "man of sin" prophecy to a tee. In this author's opinion, John of Gischala was that 1st-century man who had to be revealed before the day of Christ circa A.D. 70, and who was destroyed when it came. No future "man of sin" need come and fulfill this prophecy; it has already been fulfilled.

Objection #5. What about double fulfillment—circa A.D. 70 and sometime in the future? Many Christians have been taught that biblical prophecies often have a double fulfillment. Reformed theologian R.C. Sproul, Sr. exemplifies this dualism. While he admits that "the destruction of the Jerusalem in A.D. 70 was *a* parousia or coming of Christ" and that "Jesus really did come in judgment at this time, fulfilling his prophecy in the Olivet Discourse," he argues that "it was not *the* parousia . . . . not the final or ultimate coming of Christ."[17]

This mixed dualism is referred to in various ways such as: double fulfillment, double sense, double application, partial fulfillment, preliminary fulfillment, ultimate fulfillment, final fulfillment, types, antitypes, prophetic perspective, prophetic foreshortening, foreshadowments, prophetic telescoping, near and far, distant mountaintops, telescoping effect, or even "multiple fulfillments"[18] or "multiple meanings."[19]

This interpretative device of double fulfillment is used to dilute or discredit a past-fulfillment view and to get around the time factor. It is justified by pointing to the Bible's recognized use of types and antitypes. Some of the proof-texts offered as examples include: the virgin birth (Isa. 7:11-14f, Matt. 1:21-23), a ruler of Israel coming from Bethlehem and Jesus being born in Bethlehem (Mic. 5:2; Matt. 2:1-12), the weeping and lamenting following Herod's slaughter of infants in Bethlehem (Jer. 31:15; cited in Matt. 2:17-18), the calling of Israel and Jesus out of Egypt (Hos. 11:1; Matt. 2:13-15), or the rock that the Israelites drank from in the wilderness—"that rock was Christ" (1 Cor. 10:4).

Because of these inspired typologies, some non-inspired interpreters feel this gives them a license to apply this "principle" (or rather "theory") liberally in the field of eschatology. They claim, for example, that Joel 2's prophecy was only partially fulfilled at Pentecost (Acts 2) and that the coming of Elijah before the dreadful day of the Lord was only figuratively fulfilled (Matt. 17:10-13). In their view, both await a future, literal fulfillment. Likewise, they maintain that the circa A.D. 70 destruction of Jerusalem does not exhaust the details given by Christ in the three versions of his Olivet Discourse. Therefore, there "must be" two destructions—one of Jerusalem fulfilled circa 70 A.D. and another of Jerusalem and/or the world in the future. Consequently, some also insist that Daniel's fourth empire (the Roman Empire) must be revived for this complete fulfillment to be attained—"in the days of those kings" (Dan. 2:44).

Of course, a double, duplicated, or mirco-macro-fulfillment approach is mandatory in order to maintain a futuristic "Second Coming" scenario. And double fulfillment or double sense is the view most accepted. But it is highly problematic.

First, where do we find scriptural proof for double fulfillment beyond what Jesus said would take place in his "this generation?" And who makes this call?

Secondly, upon what hermeneutical principle or textual basis does one decide which Bible prophecies have double fulfillment and which do not? Is this not pure speculation, assumption, and assertion?

Thirdly, accepting the idea of double fulfillment or double meanings opens the door for all sorts of strange interpretations and influences. For instance, why not double fulfillment of Christ's crucifixion, or his resurrection, or even his birth? Moreover, why stop at double? Why can't these have triple, quadruple, or more fulfillments? On what textual basis or by what exegetical warrant can we preclude this extrapolation? If we allow double fulfillment in one Messianic act, such as his *parousia* coming, what reason of interpretation would enable us to exempt it from other acts?

Someone, however, might argue that the crucifixion was scripturally stated to have been a "once-for-all" event (Heb. 9:26; 10:10; 1 Pet. 3:18). I, in turn, would argue that when it comes to *any* of the redemptive works or acts of the Messiah, there is no scriptural proof, authority, or even a hint of a double sense of fulfillment. Rather, all of the Messiah's redemptive acts were "once-for-all" events. Furthermore, partial or double fulfillment of these prophecies with an ultimate fulfillment yet to occur not only has no foundation in the text but is totally arbitrary and based on a gratuitous theological presupposition. Of course, this includes Jesus' *parousia* and eschatological coming in a day of the Lord judgment circa A.D. 70. Yet some interpreters apply a double-sense typology to the day of the Lord whenever it is mentioned in the Old Testament—one back then and the ultimate day of the Lord sometime in the future. They claim the ultimate fulfillment will be at the yet-future and so-called "final judgment of God (day of the Lord)." Hence, they diminish the eschatological significance of circa A.D. 70 and strip it of its consummatory nature. But as we have seen, there is no such phraseology used or concept presented in Scripture as "final" or "last judgment" after which there will be no more judgment.[20] Fact is, their future double fulfillment is driven by their equally fallacious and unscriptural future paradigm of an "end of time."

Gary DeMar, on the other hand, makes a cogent point regarding the A.D. 70 day of the Lord noting that it "was a first-century indictment of a single generation of Jews" and quotes another theologian Demarest in saying that "we have no right to lay the sins of the Jews of the first century or any other century on Jewish people today."[21] But this double-sense tendency persists.

Fourthly, only the divinely inspired writers of the New Testament had the authority to determine what were types and antitypes. No one else had or has this authority, inspiration, or capability. Milton S. Terry, whose book, *Biblical Hermeneutics*, was the textbook of choice for most seminaries through 1970s, confronts and counters the application of types/antitypes into theory of double fulfillment, head-on and quite effectively:

> Some writers have confused this subject by connecting it with the doctrine of type and antitype. As many persons and events of the Old Testament were types of greater ones to come, so the language respecting them is supposed to be capable of double sense . . . . But it should be seen that in the case of types the language of the Scripture has no double sense. The types themselves are such because they prefigure things to come, and this fact must be kept distinct from the question of the sense of language used in any particular passage . . . . The twenty-fourth of Matthew, often appealed to in support of this theory, is explicable by a much simpler method.[22]

.

Terry, nevertheless, does concede that "the judgment of Babylon, or Nineveh, or Jerusalem may, indeed, be a type of every other similar judgment . . . but this is very different from saying that the language in which that judgment was predicted was fulfilled only partially . . . and is yet awaiting its complete fulfillment." He rightly warns that "double sense" meanings "introduce an element of uncertainty and confusion into biblical interpretation."[23] And even though he considered Isaiah's birth of a child as "a type of the Messiah," he claims it "did not involve the doctrine of a double sense."[24] Moreover, some of these types were "not a prediction at all."[25]

Walter C. Kaiser, Jr. also has it right when he observes about the day of the Lord, which ran throughout history, that "it occurred in each particular judgment as evidence of its complete fulfillment which was near and approaching."[26]

---

only the divinely inspired writers of the New Testament had the authority to determine what were types and antitypes.

In summary, double fulfillment is simply a speculative theory and an arbitrary, uncontrollable, and uninspired extrapolation that evades and obscures truth. Its use in conjunction with the events of circa A.D. 70 makes Jesus' words mean both less and more than He literally said. His words simply meant what they said. Consequently, double fulfillment must be discarded.

The employment of this hermeneutical device shows, once again, how far some interpreters are willing to go to avoid the plain, straight-forward, common-sense, and literal understanding of Jesus' most dramatic prophecy. They *don't want* to believe it, despite what the text plainly says.

Objection #6. What about Church creeds and confessions? Don't the major creeds and the formal confessions of the historic Church, all held in high esteem and written several centuries after the fall of Jerusalem, speak of Christ's "return" in futuristic terms and therefore teach that He has not yet returned?

So it may initially appear. However, below are five important points to consider when using the creeds to determine the eschatological issue of the Lord's coming/"return:"

1) Scripture has authority, and final authority, over all creeds, confessions, traditions, and belief statements written by men. This is what *sola scriptura* is all about. Scripture must be the final test of orthodoxy, not the creeds. Even the Westminster Confession of Faith admits that the creeds can be in error:

> "31.3 All synods or councils, since the apostles' times, whether general or particular, may err; and many have erred. Therefore they are not to be made the rule of faith, or practice; but to be used as a help in both.

2) It's also true that no Church council after A.D. 70 referred to a past fulfillment of Christ's coming or "return" (*parousia*).
3) The framers of the creeds were primarily interested in setting down or reflecting the basics of the Christian faith *without interpretation*.
4) Two interpretative aspects were not addressed by the creedal framers—the issues of timing and the nature of fulfillment. They did not devote any significant attention to eschatology. They only wanted to reflect the essence of Scripture and nothing more. That's why, for example, the phrase "second coming" is not found in any of the creeds.
5) Because the framers used a direct-lifting procedure to stay close to Scripture, the future tense in Scripture is carried over. The Lord's coming/"return" was future at the time the New Testament was written. The framers thus repeated this language of imminency. As a result, Jesus' supposed "failure" to "return" *as* and *when* He said He would and was expected to has been an embarrassment to the Church for centuries.

For these five reasons, the view we have been exploring in this book that Christ did come on the clouds in age-ending judgment, *as* and *when* He said He would and was expected to circa A.D. 70, and continues to come in many ways, is not in conflict with, but *honors* the major creeds of the undivided Church.[27] But more importantly, this view is biblical. It plainly explains and harmonizes difficult passages, and makes the Bible come alive and applicable in ways the Church has rarely before imagined. Thus, anyone subscribing to this past-fulfillment view of the Lord's consummatory coming and his ongoing comings can wholeheartedly subscribe to the eschatological portions of the major creeds. All we have done in this book is put his climactic, age-ending coming back into its proper biblical and historical context. This change, therefore, is only a matter of the interpretation of timing, and not of content.

But more importantly, this view is biblical.

Amazingly, no creed teaches, recognizes, or even hints that any kind of judgment or coming occurred circa A.D. 70. Yet Eusebius, a 4th-century Christian leader and writer who is often called "the father of Church history," affirmed that Jesus "came" in the fall of Jerusalem and in fulfillment of Zechariah's end-time prophecy.[28] (**Bolds** are mine.)

> For so it was prophesied concerning the destruction of the royal glory of the Jewish nation . . . . Yea, in return for their insults to the Lord who thus prophesied, there has not failed for them lamentation, mourning and wailing. And it was only after our Saviour **came** . . . . laying their Temple low, and driving them from their country, to serve their enemies in a hostile land; wherefore even now every house and every soul is a prey to lamentation . . . . It is impossible to argue that this was fulfilled previously to the period of the Romans, in whose time the Jewish Temple was burnt for the second time . . . and their city from then till now has been inhabited by foreign nations.[29]

> When, then, we see what was of old foretold for the nations fulfilled in our own day, and when the lamentation and wailing that was predicted for the Jews, and the burning of the Temple and its utter destruction, can also be seen even now to have occurred according to the prediction, surely we must also agree that the King who was prophesied, the Christ of God, **has come**, since the **signs** of His **coming** have been shewn in each instance I have treated to have been **clearly fulfilled**.[30]

Athanasius, also writing in the 4th century, declared that Christ came again and fulfilled all of Daniel's 70 weeks prophecy (Dan. 9:24-27):

> And Jerusalem is to stand **till his coming**, and thenceforth, prophet and vision cease in Israel . . . And this was why Jerusalem **stood till then**—namely that there they might be exercised in the types as a preparation for the reality . . . but from that time forth all prophecy is sealed and the city and temple taken, why are they so irreligious and so perverse as to see what has happened, and yet to deny Christ, Who **has brought it all to pass**? . . . What then has not come to pass, that the Christ must do? What is left unfulfilled, that the Jews should now disbelieve with impunity?[31]

These writings of Eusebius and Athanasius suggest some understanding among early-Church fathers of the fulfillment of Jesus' coming *(parousia)* circa A.D. 70. R.C. Sproul, Sr., a renowned Reformed theologian of our day, adds: ". . . the destruction of Jerusalem . . . certainly spelled the end of a crucial redemptive-historical epoch. It must be viewed as the end of some age. It also represents a significant visitation of the Lord in judgment and a vitally important 'day of the Lord.' Whether this was the *only* day of the Lord about which Scripture speaks remains a major point of controversy . . . ."[32]

So whom should we believe—Jesus and the inspired writers of Scripture, or the uninspired framers of the creeds? Elevating these man-made documents to too lofty a position puts us in danger of committing the same sin for which Jesus condemned the Pharisees and scribes: "You have let go of the commands of God and are holding on to the traditions of men . . . You have a fine way of setting aside the commands of God in order to observe your own traditions! . . . Thus you nullify the word of God by your tradition that you have handed down. And you do many things like that" (Mark 7:8-13).

These writings of Eusebius and Athanasius suggest some understanding among early-Church fathers of the fulfillment of Jesus' coming *(parousia)* circa A.D. 70.

Let's be as blunt as Jesus. If any of God's Word is in error on this matter, the position of the creeds (and confessions) is worthless. R.C. Sproul, Sr. put it this way: ". . . skeptical criticism of the Bible has become almost universal in the world. And people have attacked the credibility of Jesus. Maybe some church fathers made a mistake. Maybe our favorite theologians have made mistakes. I can abide with that. I can't abide with Jesus being a false prophet, because if I am to understand that Jesus is a false prophet, my faith is in vain."[33]

Within our traditions, let's agree to support the view which best maintains the honor and integrity of Christ and confirms the inspired and authoritative Word of God. The creeds, confessions, and other "traditions of men" are secondary to the supremacy of inspired Scripture. Creeds and confessions can be mistaken and must be tested by *sola scriptura* (1 Thess. 5:21). After all, if the creeds had it all right, what was the 16th-century Reformation about? And hasn't our understanding of Scripture been improving over the centuries as we've developed and refined our interpretive skills? What's more, the Reformers proclaimed, "The Church is reformed and always reforming." In this process of continuing reform, only Scripture can be trusted and used to determine true orthodoxy, not the creeds or confessions.

So what shall we do with the creeds? I recommend that their eschatological sections be revised—lest we be enslaved to an incorrect and uninspired interpretation of Scripture. And all the creeds have been revised before, some many times. Our rule of faith and practice should be as follows: *Jesus, in numerous places, clearly stated that his coming on the clouds in consummating judgment would occur within the lifetime of his contemporaries. Every New Testament writer utilized urgent, imminent, and intensifying language confirming the immediacy of this coming. We cannot overlook a biblical and time-restricted fulfillment in favor of man-made creeds and confessions.*

Bible scholar, Edward E. Stevens, has aptly questioned, "Which is the greater offense? To question the accuracy of *uninspired* creeds, or to declare that the *inspired* time statements of the Apostles were mistaken? Which would you rather throw out the window, the New Testament writings, or the creeds? And that is exactly the dilemma here."[34] For me, your author, I've been much more comfortable supporting the integrity of what Jesus and the New Testament writers said and wrote, and reexamining my concept of the so-called "second coming" and "return."

Objection #7. Shouldn't Christians stop taking the Lord's Supper (Communion) if Jesus has already come again? The Apostle Paul's instructions for taking the Lord's Supper were that it be done "in remembrance of me [Jesus]" and included the verse, "For whenever you eat this bread and drink this cup, you proclaim the Lord's death **until he comes**" (1 Cor. 11: 23-26f). But if Jesus has already come again/"returned," the argument goes, doesn't this obsolete this sacrament and follow that we should no longer take communion?

In 2005, I participated in a special study group of approximately seventy scholars at the Annual Meeting of the Evangelical Theological Society. Their topic was "The Lord's Supper." One of the presenters addressed this above passage but made no mention of this issue. So in the Q and A portion following his presentation I publicly asked him this series of questions:

"Dr. _____, in your theological understanding, how many comings of Jesus have there been since Paul penned these words?"

"Oh, many," he replied with a glib smile.

"Then why do we still take the Lord's Supper?" I followed up.

"Because this is speaking of his (future) *parousia*," he quickly retorted.

"How do you know that to be true?" I immediately pressed on.

He paused. And you could have heard pins drop around the room. "Well, that's what everyone says it is," he lamely offered as he quickly called on another raised hand from the floor. (The Greek word translated as "coming" in the verse is not *parousia*, but *erchomai*.)

Sad to say, that's how quickly sound arguments or objections can be ignored and dismissed by those indoctrinated to the contrary. So let's re-explore this issue a little more here.

"Well, that's what everyone says it is," he lamely offered . . . .

First, Paul's "until" does not necessarily teach that communion observance would cease upon Christ's consummatory coming. More importantly, Paul's teaching was only an interim instruction that he had received from the Lord (1 Cor. 11:23). He was passing it on to the

Corinthians during the transitionary period of A.D. 30 - 70. But Jesus also said concerning the taking of the Lord's Supper:

- *I tell you, I will not drink of this fruit of the vine from now on until that day when I drink it anew with you in my Father's kingdom (Matt. 26:29).*
- *. . . until it finds fulfillment in the kingdom of God (Luke 22:16).*
- *. . . until the kingdom of God comes (Luke 22:18).*

Secondly, that day came when Jesus came on the clouds and the kingdom was "taken away" from the Old Covenant Jews and "given to a people who will produce its fruit" (Matt. 21:40, 43). From that time on, Christians no longer needed to take communion in a somber, memorialized fashion, "in remembrance of" Him who had departed (John 14:1-3). Post A.D. 70, we take it "anew" with Him "in my Father's kingdom" and in joyous celebration.

This word "anew" has great significance. We have a parallel event in biblical history when new meaning was taken on. In the Old Covenant, the Jewish Passover supper was instituted before Israel's deliverance from Egyptian bondage and was observed throughout the forty-year wilderness period. Likewise, the Lord's Supper was instituted before Jesus' death and observed during the interim forty-year period of A.D. 30 - 70 as a somber observance commemorative of his death, their deliverance from sin, and a longing for his consummatory coming. But after entering the Promised Land, the Jews continued this Passover supper observance—no longer in anticipation of, but in *celebration* of entering. In a similar manner, after A.D. 70, the Lord's Supper was no longer to be a solemn, memorialized remembrance of Him, but a glorious and victorious feast with Him, anew in his full Presence, at his table, and in our new inheritance—the new promised land of the kingdom of God (Matt. 25:34).

Because Jesus kept his Word and came on the clouds *as* and *when* He said He would, the Lord's Supper has even more meaning and purpose today. Like the Passover supper, it has changed from one of anticipation to one of fulfillment and celebration. What's more, the Lord's Supper is an eternal celebration because the kingdom in which it is taken is eternally established (Isa. 9:7; Luke 1:33).

Objection #8. Is it really possible the elect have been deceived? Jesus warned his disciples of deception. He said that there would be "false prophets . . . to deceive even the elect—if that were possible" (Matt. 24:24). If this deception of the elect was not possible, why would Jesus even bring it up? He also said that insistence on a visible criterion (nature) for his end-time *parousia* coming was (and still is) part of this deception:

> At that time if anyone says to you, 'Look, here is the Christ!' or, 'There he is!' do not believe it . . . So if anyone tells you, 'There he is, out in the desert' do not go out; or, 'Here he is, in the inner rooms,' do not believe it (Matt. 24: 23, 26).

Some of "the elect" today (the saints in the Church), as well as back then, have succumbed to this visible-criterion deception. Thus, they, too, have been falsely prophesying. How so?

First, by their paralleled misunderstanding of the invisible nature for his promised and time-restricted coming (Matt. 24:3, 30, 34; John 14:19, 22). Hence, many saints today are still waiting for a physically visible sighting of Jesus in Person, in bodily form, in the sky, in the Israeli desert, in an inner room of a rebuilt temple in Jerusalem, or in some other geographic location to which they can definitely point and in like manner say, "There He is!"

Secondly, by their professing and proclaiming a half-truth faith in a world filled with competing religions and secular ideologies. The truthful half is that the promised Messiah (Jesus) came, lived, died, rose from the dead, and ascended to heaven exactly *as* and *when* prophesied. The untruthful part is that Jesus has not come again to finish the work He started, *as* and *when* He said He would and *as* and *when* He was expected to by his Spirit-guided, first followers and every New Testament writer (John 16:13).

Thus, for 19 centuries and counting, the Church has been attempting to side-step and downplay this time-restricted, 1st-century "failure" and "nonoccurrence." As a result, it has been forced to settle for a faith that has *not* been "once for all delivered to the saints" (Jude 3) and whose "end of all things" was *not* "at hand" in that same 1st-century context in which these inspired words were penned (1 Pet. 4:7 KJV).

Consequently, and since the fall of Jerusalem circa A.D.70, most of the Church has been proclaiming a half-truth faith. We must therefore ask, if this half-truth faith has been as effective as God has allowed it to be, how much more effective and God-empowered would be the proclamation and practice of a whole-truth faith—one that really "was [past tense] once for all delivered to the saints" (Jude 3)?

If this deception of the elect was not possible, why would Jesus even bring it up?

I believe it's time for this reform to take place and for God's people to come out of their 19-centuries-and-counting "deception of the elect." In every generation except one, the Church has wrongly proclaimed the imminence of our Lord's climactic coming on the clouds in age-ending judgment and consummation. No more. Perhaps we should now expand our Easter proclamation to say:

> He's arisen! He's arisen, indeed!
> He's come! He's come, indeed!
> He's with us! He's with us, indeed!
> He still comes! He still comes, indeed!

What We're Contending For

This book is not talking about something "new." We should have taken our Lord at his word long ago. Lest there be any misunderstanding, let me reiterate the positive view being presented herein. I, and hopefully you by now, are contending:

For . . . a world "without end" (Eph. 3:21 KJV) and a *terra firma* earth that "endures [remains] forever" (Eccl. 1:4).

For . . . "the faith that was once for all delivered to the saints" (Jude 3) in the 1st century—not one with any portion yet to be delivered—just as Christ died "once for all" (1 Pet. 3:18; Heb. 10:10; see also Heb. 9:12, 26; Rom. 6:10).

For . . . an imminent "end of all things" which was "at hand," fulfilled in that same time-context (1 Pet. 4:7 KJV), and is not still future.

For . . .the Lord's anointing, crucifixion, resurrection, and coming "on-the-clouds," all of which were precisely foretold, time-specified, and time-restricted by Scripture, with no delays, gaps, nonoccurrences, failures, unmet expectations, excuses, or side-stepping-exegetic gimmicks. And He remains with us forever.

For . . . the Holy Spirit who did *not* obscure Christ's truth, and did *not* become the spirit of falsehood to 1st-century believers, but who guided their expectations, correctly and perfectly (John 16:13).

For . . . the end of the age of Moses, the full atoning (salvation) work of Christ, and the consummated reality of our faith, which is finished and available, and no longer our *hope* but our *heritage*. This is the *sure foundation* upon which Bible-believing Christians are to build (Eph. 2:20).

Lastly . . . *for* a literal day in August or September of A.D. 70 as a third most important day in human history, along with Christ's birth day and his resurrection day. Perhaps, we could call it Parousia, or Consummation Day, or something. It would be a commendable sacred holiday for the Church to instate and future Christians to celebrate as the anniversary of the perfect ending *for* the world.[35] Dare we make any less of it? And just wait until you see what else fully arrived, back then and there.

PART V: THE NEW CREATION

Chapter 13

The New Heaven and New Earth —Are They Really a Sequel?[*]

S omething most Bible readers *do not know* is—*three different entities* in the Bible are called "heaven and earth." One entity would never pass away. Another had already passed away. A third would soon pass away and be made new.

If this sounds like a riddle, perhaps, it is. It is also a biblical and historical fact and truth. But, sadly . . .

Confusion Prevails

"God has *not* created the new heaven and new earth yet," a pastor-friend of mine insisted. With a wave of his hand out the window, he leaned back in his chair and sighed, "I believe the Bible says that there will be an end to all this someday." But will there so be?

Of course, this pastor's two classic assertions came before he read the contents of this book and chapter.

---

[*] Much of the material in this chapter was first presented in a paper by the author at the Evangelical Theological Society's Midwestern Regional Meeting in March 1997 in Chicago, Illinois, at the Moody Bible Institute.

The Frank & Earnest cartoon featured in chapter two (p-57) captures the heart of the issue. Is God really planning a sequel? If He is, here are three sobering implications for us to ponder:

1) If the present universe (consisting of heaven, the heavens, the earth, and much more) is destroyed in a final cataclysmic disaster when God brings human history to a close (as many believe the Bible predicts), will God replace all of it with a new one?

2) If the current cosmos is purified through a fiery renovation (as others believe the Bible says), will those who have already gone to heaven come back and spend eternity with Jesus on a renewed or recycled Earth? If so, does this mean that they will no longer "dwell in the house of the Lord forever" (i.e., dwell in heaven) as the Psalmist claims (Psa. 23:6)? Wouldn't this mean that our citizenship is not in heaven, as the Bible states (Phil. 3:20)—i.e., that the heaven of today is only a temporary resting place and humankind's eternal destiny is ultimately an earthly one?

3) Alas, is this truly the "end of our world?" If either of these two popular and futuristic views is correct, shouldn't we just write off this present planet and start looking forward to the new one?

Not so fast! Both views—a future destruction or cataclysmic renovation of the planet and cosmos—are in contextual conflict with Peter's 1st-century statement that "the end of all things is at hand" (1 Pet. 4:7 KJV); as well as with other consummatory scriptures (see Luke. 21:20-22, 32; 1 Cor. 7:29, 31; 10:11; 1 Pet. 4:17; 1 John 2:18). Did Peter really mean what he said, or did he only mean that the end of *some* things was at hand back then? Taking such liberty with Scripture is unacceptable for those of us who believe in its Spirit-guided inspiration and authority. Something has to give.

In this final chapter let's explore ten revelational insights which should help us gain a better understanding of Peter's prophetic words and how they also applied to the coming of the Bible's "new heaven and new earth." I believe you'll find these ten insights most compelling. But please don't jump ahead; read them in sequence. They build upon each other and escalate in breadth and depth.

Ten Revelational Insights

One faithful day over nineteen centuries ago, on the small island of Patmos in the Mediterranean Sea, Jesus gave John a breathtaking vision of a new heaven and a new earth:

> Then I saw a new heaven and a new earth, for the first heaven and the first earth had passed away, and there was no longer any sea. I saw the Holy City, the new Jerusalem, coming down out of heaven from God, prepared as a bride beautifully dressed for her husband (Rev. 21:1-2).

What was John seeing? Did he see a sequel to our planet and a re-do of outer space, or something else? The practical fact is, the meaning of this biblical phrase "heaven and earth" cannot simply be found in a dictionary or casually assumed. But if we are sincere in seeking a responsible apocalypticism (i.e., a view or expectation of the end), we must be willing to lay aside our preconceived ideas and carefully determine the identity and nature of this biblical reality, and to do so within its historical time constraints and contextual framework.

The following ten revelational insights will enable us to identify the three different "heaven-and-earth" entities mentioned in this chapter's opening paragraph. Most likely, these insights will require you to rethink and readjust your traditional understanding of the fulfillment of John's "a new heaven and a new earth." And surely God's truth is more precious to you than man's tradition?

The primary hermeneutical (interpretative) question to keep in mind during this our last exploratory adventure of this book is: Does time determine nature, or does nature determine time? This question is critical, so pause for a moment and think about your answer. Traditionalists assume the latter. And since they haven't seen what they expect to see (i.e, nature of fulfillment), they must adjust the time factor. And time can only be adjusted in one direction—out into the future.

This book, to the contrary, takes the view that *time determines nature*. Throughout, I've proposed that the *time* and *imminency* statements of Scripture must be naturally and literally honored. Like a jigsaw puzzle, they provide the straight-edge, border pieces (historical framework) in which all the other pieces properly fit. Therefore, it's our understanding of the *nature of fulfillment* which must be adjusted, and not the time factor.

Let's begin our final exploration with the first insight supporting the case for a past fulfillment of John's prophesied "a new heaven and a new earth."

Insight 1. Jesus Tied the Passing Away of Heaven and Earth to the Passing of the Law of Moses.

> Do not think that I have come to abolish the Law or the Prophets; I have not come to abolish them but to fulfill them. I tell you the Truth, until heaven and earth disappear [pass away], not the smallest letter, not the least stroke of a pen [one jot or one tittle], will by any means disappear [pass away] from the Law until everything is accomplished [all be fulfilled]. (Matt. 5:17-18 NIV [KJV])

For Jesus Christ, not the smallest component of the Law would disappear or pass away until two key events took place: 1) "heaven and earth disappear" (pass away), and 2) "everything is accomplished" (all be fulfilled). How could words be spoken more plainly? All three eschatological events are hereby interconnected. They stand or fall together. The Law system of the Old Covenant would disappear at the same time this "heaven and earth" passed away and when "everything is accomplished."

Jesus began these prophetic words by saying that He came "to fulfill the Law and the Prophets." His statement includes the entire Mosaic, Old Covenant system (Exod. 19:3-8; 20:1-23:19). He did not come to bring new prophecy, and neither did any of the writers of the New Testament.[1] Later in his earthly ministry He added, "When you see Jerusalem surrounded by armies . . . this is the time of punishment in fulfillment of all that has been written" (Luke 21:20, 22). "All that has been written" refers to "everything . . . that is written about me [Jesus] in the Law of Moses, the Prophets and the Psalms" (Luke 24:44).[2] In other words, it was the whole Old Testament. This would certainly include Isaiah's promise of a passing of "heaven and earth" (Isa. 51:6-16) and the creation of "the new heavens and a new earth" (Isa. 65:17-18; 66:22).[3] And the historical reality is, neither the Law nor biblical Judaism has been practiced for over 1,900 years. Why not? Because they disappeared. If Jesus' words are to be trusted, then the "heaven and earth" He had in mind and mentioned must have disappeared as well. Would you agree?

As we have seen and in perfect correlation with this passing, Jesus placed the destruction of the Jewish Temple and Jerusalem within the generation then present—Jesus' "this generation" (Luke 21:32; Matt. 24:34). And the demise of the Temple and its vital institutions of the Law were much more than a "jot" or a "tittle," or "the smallest letter" or "least stoke of a pen." It was the entire system of biblical Judaism. Therefore, are we not forced to conclude that *all* was fulfilled? Don't we have absolute confirmation that circa A.D. 70 was when that Law system was finally and completely put out of business?[4] Also, if the Law passed away at the end of that age (Matt. 24:3; 33-34), whatever "heaven and earth" Jesus was referring to back then must also have passed away and *cannot* now exist, wouldn't you now agree?

However, if Jesus was referring to the physical universe and the *terra firma* Earth, which has not passed away, then everything hasn't been accomplished and fulfilled yet, for they and the Law were supposed to pass away together. That would mean something quite stunning—the Law of Moses is still in effect, God's people are still under its authority, and we should be performing animal sacrifices, celebrating Jewish feasts and rituals, observing Jewish dietary laws, and honoring the Jewish priesthood. But neither the Christian Church nor the orthodox Jews have practiced these elements in almost 2,000 years. Such a literal interpretation simply doesn't make sense. To the contrary, and as we saw in chapter three, the Bible declares that the physical earth and the whole material universe are "without end" and eternally established. If Jesus was referring to the material heaven and earth in the passage above, He contradicted the Bible as well as Himself.

It's a case of all or nothing. Either *all* was fulfilled, or *nothing* was fulfilled. All passed away, or nothing passed away.

Of course, we cannot side-step the plain meaning of Jesus' words. He joined together the passing of the Law, the passing of the old heaven and earth, and the accomplishment and fulfillment of everything. And what Jesus "has joined together, let not man separate" (Matt. 19:6). As we shall see, the heaven and earth that Jesus was talking about did indeed pass away and was superseded by a new heaven and a new earth. And it all came to pass precisely *as* and *when* He had said it would.

It's a case of all or nothing. Either *all* was fulfilled, or *nothing* was fulfilled. All passed away, or nothing passed away. If there is a single Old Testament promise or prophecy unfulfilled, and if the old heaven and earth did not disappear, then the Old Covenant and its Law system are still in effect. Ridiculous, you say? Exactly. But it's this simple: if the Old Covenant system passed away, then the "heaven and earth" that Jesus named has also passed away. There is no legitimate escape from this conclusion. The problem disappears, however, when we understand that Jesus' use of "heaven and earth" language here is a figurative name for a real spiritual reality, and not a reference to the material universe and earth. Let's see if there is valid biblical support for this understanding.

Insight 2. The Words Heaven and Earth Are Found in a Book that Abounds with Signs and Symbols.

Since the "a new heaven and a new earth" terminology is contained in the apocalyptic book of Revelation that is filled with signs and symbols, it is not unreasonable to deduce that this expression also may be a sign and symbol. And a sign and symbol is not the reality but points to a reality beyond itself—in this case something other than the physical creation (Rev. 21:1). If indeed it is a sign and a symbol, then its meaning, or clues to its meaning, will be provided in that book itself or elsewhere in the Bible. Once again, the interpretative principle of letting "Scripture interpret Scripture" is a valid method for determining the meaning of any apocalyptic sign or symbol used in the Bible, and works especially well for those found in the book of Revelation.

Whatever the "a new heaven and a new earth" symbol represents, it is also part of the whole prophecy of the book of Revelation. That whole prophecy, from first to last, was affirmed by that book itself as being "at hand," "obeyable," "not to be sealed up," and certain to "shortly come to pass" (Rev. 1:1, 3; 22:6-10 KJV). These clear time statements are unequivocal and undeniable, and must be honored. They serve as hermeneutical guideposts or reference points for contextualizing the fulfillment of the entire prophecy. We cannot avoid them, stretch them like a rubber band nineteen centuries and counting, or change their natural meaning just because they may not fit our nature-of-fulfillment notions. They were given by the angel of Revelation as a guide for interpreting the rest of that book's content. Therefore, every sign and symbol in Revelation must be understood within this time-restricted framework. We can be certain of this because of the angel's instructions to leave the book open.[5]

If Jesus had meant for the prophecy of Revelation to become relevant 1,900 years or so later, the angel should have told John to "reseal the book." He had told Daniel to seal up the prophetic sayings of his book "till the time of the end," which was six hundred years away from the time of his writing (Dan. 12:4). But John was told to leave his book unsealed (Rev. 22:10). Why? Because its end-time events were to happen soon—soon enough to fulfill Jesus' prophecy within his "this generation."[6] There is no room for a 1,900-year-and-counting gap before all that was "at hand" was fulfilled, established, and forever made available.

Admittedly, Jesus' first disciples did not always understand his allegorical messages and manner of speech. But "the loud voice from the throne" gave an even greater sense of urgency and force to his apocalyptic message of "a new heaven and a new earth" by saying the word "now." Let's emphasize this "nowness" from the ensuing verses of Revelation 21:3-7:

> Now ... the dwelling of God is with men, and he will live
>   with them. They will be his people, and God
>   himself will be with them and be their God.
> [Now] ... He will wipe every tear from their eyes.
> [Now] ...There will be no more death or mourning or crying or
>   pain, for the old order of things has passed away.
> [Now] ... I am making everything new.
> [Now] ... These words are trustworthy and true.
> [Now] ... 'It is done.'
> [Now] ... To him who is thirsty I will give to drink without cost from
>   the spring of the water of life.
> [Now] ... He who overcomes will inherit all this."

What was to be inherited "now?" Everything He was describing, including "a new heaven and a new earth . . . and . . . the new Jerusalem"—then and there, not someday in the distant future.

The interpretative speculation that lifts these end-time events out of the period to which they belong does gross injustice to their imminent, 1st-century, and fulfillment nature. A responsible interpretation—one using sound hermeneutic principles—will recognize and honor the time context the book of Revelation imposes upon itself, and the normal meaning of the time-sensitive words employed in establishing that context. Anything less does violence to the text.

If this "loud voice from the throne" was not referring to the physical creation, what did He mean by "a new heaven and a new earth?"

Insight 3. Biblical Use of Both Literal and Figurative Meanings.

The Bible, from beginning to end, contains not only literal language, but also symbolic or figurative language. Many things are described both ways. The term "heaven and earth" is a good example. Throughout the Bible, it is used both literally and figuratively.

The first ten words in the Bible speak of a literal, physical heavens and earth. "In the beginning God created the heavens and the earth" (Gen. 1:1). God spoke his physical creation into existence (Gen. 1:3ff). Since He is sovereign, He could, no doubt, speak it out of existence, or into a different form, any time He so desires. But He hasn't. And, as we shall see, He doesn't have to in order to fulfill any unfulfilled promise or prophecy. Why? Because the "heaven and earth" terminology also has a figurative usage and meaning. For example:

- The Song of Moses in the book of Deuteronomy begins with the exhortation, "Listen, O heavens . . . Hear, O earth" (Deut. 32:1). Isaiah started his Old Testament book with the same words, "Hear, O heavens! Listen, O earth" (Isa. 1:2a). To what or to whom were these two prophets directing their messages? Did they expect the actual physical stars and planets to hear, and the global Earth to listen and take note? Of course not. Isaiah tells us that "O heavens" and "O earth" are simply other names for God's "children," or "my people" of Israel (see Isa. 1:2b-3). They were the ones who could and were to hear and listen.

- God used this same symbolism in simile form in his promise to Abraham: "I will make your offspring like the dust of the earth"

(Gen. 13:16). "Look at the heavens and count the stars . . . so shall your offspring be" (Gen. 15:5; also 22:17; Dan. 12:3). The Apostle Paul stated that "we have this treasure in earthen vessels" (2 Cor. 4:7 KJV) and appealed to Genesis 2:7, where it is written, "And the Lord God formed man of the dust of the ground" (1 Cor. 15:45). Let's face it: we are earth! We "live in houses of clay whose foundations are in the dust" (Job 4:19).

- God spoke again through Isaiah saying, "Turn to me and be saved, all you ends of the earth; for I am God, and there is no other" (Isa. 45:22). "Be silent before me, you islands" (Isa. 41:1). These "ends of the earth" and "islands" are people, not *terra firma*.

- "Lift up your heads, O you gates." Here the Psalmist calls us gates! "Be lifted up, you ancient doors" (Psa. 24:7, 9). We are those doors! "Tremble before him, all the earth" (Psa. 96:9). Here we are called earth again!

- Isaiah also refers to people as trees ("they will be called oaks of righteousness, a planting of the Lord for the display of his splendor" [Isa. 61:3]), and as grass ("the sons of men, who are but grass" [Isa 51:12]). The Psalmist and Jeremiah use similar "tree" similes (Psa. 1:3; Jer. 17:8). Jude refers to some people as "clouds without rain . . . autumn trees . . . wild waves of the sea . . . wandering stars" (Jude 12-13). The angel in Revelation interpreted, "The waters you saw . . . are people" (Rev. 17:15). And lastly, even God Himself is referred to as "the Rock" (Deut. 32:4, 15, 18, 30, 31), and Jesus as "that Rock" (1 Cor. 10:4).

- Jesus talked metaphorically of cutting off hands and feet and plucking out eyes (Matt. 5:29, 30), and spoke of "streams of living water" when referring to "the Spirit" (John 7:38, 39). In the book of Revelation, Christ holds seven stars in his hand, explaining to John that they are the seven messengers (angels or leaders) of the seven churches (Rev. 1:16, 20; see also Dan. 8:15-26). He's even the bright Morning Star (Rev. 22:16: see also Num. 24:17). Many more scriptural examples could be cited to illustrate this point. It shouldn't be surprising, then, to realize that the fleeing of earth and sky from the Presence of the Lord in Revelation 20:11f, which precedes the new heaven and new earth prophecy, most probably symbolizes the judgment of people and does not refer to the destruction of the physical/material earth and sky. After all, why would God judge the ground, the stars, the moon, or the planets? Inanimate matter can't sin. It can't choose to follow or not follow God or obey or disobey Him. How would God's judgment of these objects serve any redemptive purpose?

Understanding the biblical pattern of figurative terminology, especially in the Old Testament, lets us begin to see how 1st-century Jews would have understood these familiar symbols of "heaven and earth" to stand for humanity. But this scriptural phrase, in its apocalyptic, eschatological usage, symbolized more than just individual people.

Insight 4. Heaven and Earth Symbolized the Israelites' World.

During the time of the Law and the Prophets, Israel and its people had no special meaning apart from their covenant-determined "world." In a similar fashion, we use the word "world" today, not just to refer to planet Earth, but figuratively when we speak of the sports world, sales world, religious world, workaday world, or society as a whole.

We also find the word "heavens" used in the Bible in a figurative, corporate way to symbolize governments or people in authority. For example, recall Joseph's prophetic dream. He saw the heavenly bodies of the sun, moon, and stars bowing down to him. They represented the leaders of the nation of Egypt, or perhaps the heads of the tribes of Israel (Gen. 37:9). "Earth," (Greek *ge*) when used collectively, can refer to a nation or nations and the people, as well as to the "land" of Israel itself.

Incredibly and for our benefit, the following short passage in Isaiah contrasts God's establishment of two different meanings for the Bible's "heaven and earth" terminology. Isaiah writes by inspiration: "And forgettest the Lord thy maker, that hath stretched forth the **heavens**, and laid the foundations of the **earth** . . ." (Isa. 51:13a KJV). Here God, through his prophet, uses the past perfect form of the verbs translated "stretched" (*natah*) and "laid" (*suwm*) in recounting his creation of the physical heavens and *terra firma* Earth. But notice what happens just a few verses later when the verb form switches to the infinitive: "But I am the Lord thy God, that divided the sea, whose waves roared: The Lord of Hosts is his name. And I have put my words in thy mouth; I have covered thee in the shadow of mine hand, that I may plant the **heavens**, and lay the foundations of the **earth**, and may say unto Zion, 'Thou art my people'" (Isa. 51:15-16 KJV – **bold** is mine).

What a difference. It's a totally different "world" in meaning. In this second portion of this same passage, God is still speaking to Israel. But here He says He gave them his Law ("words in thy mouth") and his covenant protection ("covered thee in the shadow of mine hand"). Next He uses the infinitive form of the verbs (to "plant" [*nata*] and to "lay" [*suwm*]) to speak of forming a "heavens and earth" different from the ones mentioned above in verse 13. This latter "heavens and earth" He forms by the process of delivering his chosen people, the Jews, from Egyptian slavery by parting the Red Sea, giving them the Mosaic Covenant on Mt. Sinai, and protecting them from their enemies.

It's important to emphasize that this second portion of the passage could not be referring to the physical creation (it is improperly translated by the NIV translation[7]), because the material heavens and earth existed long before the first Jewish exodus out of Egypt and the giving of the Mosaic Law on Mt. Sinai. Neither is God saying through Isaiah that He created the *terra firma* Earth for Israel to occupy since Gentiles occupied it as well. What God is saying in these two infinitive purpose clauses is that He gave them the Law to establish a theocratic "heavens and earth." He gave his covenant to the Israelites to create their "world" of biblical Judaism—the Jewish religious system. That's how the Jews became God's covenant people.

God later confirmed this establishment process through another prophet using the same infinitive verb forms: "And at what instant I shall speak concerning a nation, and concerning a kingdom, to build and to plant it" (Jer. 18:9 KJV; see also Jer. 1:10; Eccl. 3:2).

This historic background and apocalyptic framework lets us see more clearly the meaning of Jesus' teaching concerning the disappearing or passing away of the old "heaven and earth" and "the Law." Jesus' consistent usage of a figurative "heaven and earth" was focusing on that same theocratic entity of which Isaiah spoke. He was using those same covenantal terms to represent the people incorporated into the "world" of biblical Judaism.

Furthermore, this understanding perfectly harmonizes with Paul's statement that "this world in its present form is passing away" (1 Cor. 7:31), and whose "time is [was] short" (1 Cor. 7:29). Again, the nature and time questions are crucial here. When Paul wrote these words, around A.D. 57, he was not deluded. Nor was he referring to an end of the material universe or the destiny of the physical planet. As we saw in chapter three, the entire physical creation is established forever. What Paul envisioned did not fail to materialize. He was referring to the Old Testament Law system that was progressively disintegrating and disappearing as well as being transformed into a new order and reality in Christ, right before their very eyes (Heb. 8:13; 9:10). And very soon the Law would be fulfilled and its Old Covenant world annihilated. This end did not require the end of humanity or the demise of the cosmic creation.

The Jewish historian Josephus corroborates this 1st-century Jewish understanding. In his book *The Antiquities of the Jews*,[8] he describes how the Jews of Jesus' time looked upon their Temple as "a Heaven and earth." They believed that their Temple was at the very center of the earth, and saw it as the place where heaven and earth came together, and where God met man. Josephus calls its outer tabernacle "an imitation of the system of the world" and "sea and land, on which men live." By contrast, the inner, Most Holy Place he terms "a Heaven peculiar to God." The veil that separated the two "was very ornamental, and embroidered with all sorts of flowers which the earth produces."

This veil was visible from outside the Temple area. So it's not hard to imagine Jesus sitting on the Mount of Olives (just a short distance across a small valley from the Temple) gesturing toward this Jewish "heaven and earth," and speaking his prophetic words: "Heaven and earth will pass away, but my words will never pass away" (Matt. 24:35; Luke 21:33).

---

the Jews of Jesus' time looked upon their Temple as "a Heaven and earth."

His Jewish audience also might have recalled these other words of the prophet Isaiah and so confirmed that the "world" of heaven and earth which was to be destroyed was the Temple and the Jewish religious system:

> Lift up your eyes to the heavens, look at the earth beneath; the heavens will vanish like smoke, the earth will wear out like a garment and its inhabitants die like flies. But my salvation will last forever, my righteousness will never fail (Isa. 51:6).

The importance of this change of covenant worlds also can be seen in the inspired words of the writer of Hebrews:

> In the beginning, O Lord, you laid the foundations of the earth, and the heavens are the work of your hands. They will perish, but you remain; they will all wear out like a robe; like a garment they will be *changed.* But you remain the same and your years will never end (Heb. 1:10-12; quoting from Psa. 102:25-27—emphasis mine. Also see Deut. 31:26-28).

> By calling this covenant 'new,' he [God] has made the first one obsolete; and what is obsolete and aging will soon disappear (Heb. 8:13).

Today, if you ask an orthodox Jew what the expression "heaven and earth" means to him, most likely, he will respond without hesitation, "the Temple."

So if God destroyed the Old Covenant "heaven and earth"—the world of biblical Judaism—would He not establish a new one to replace the old? Or would He leave a multi-century void? As we shall see, the old "heaven and earth," which God had "planted," prefigured and linked directly into the new one. The old indeed perished, and was "changed." Moreover, this transition and transformation from one covenant world to the other was to occur through a "shaking" process.

Insight 5. Precedent and Type for "the Shaking."

> ". . . In a little while I will once more shake the heavens and the earth, the sea and dry land. I will shake all nations, and the desire of all nations will come, and I will fill this house with glory," says the Lord Almighty (Hag. 2:6-7).

What did this Old Testament, *post*-exilic (post-Babylon captivity) prophet, Haggai, mean by this second shaking? To find the answer we must discover the last time God shook the "heavens and earth." That event will serve as the precedent and type for this next shaking.

As we've previously seen, cosmic-collapsing, light-darkening, and earth-moving apocalyptic language is employed throughout the Old Testament. It was always used to vividly portray and prophesy an impending "day of the Lord," when God would pour out his judgment on a wicked nation or people. A number of these occurrences exist. Unfortunately, many biblical scholars have chosen to willfully ignore these instances in their insistence on a future-coming literal destruction of Planet Earth and the universe. But God once warned through Isaiah, a *pre*-exilic prophet:

> Therefore I will shake the heavens, and the earth shall remove out of her place, in the wrath of the LORD of hosts, and in the day of his fierce anger (Isa. 13:13 KJV).

This *pre*-exilic shaking and removing prophecy chronologically preceded Haggai's *post*-exilic, "once-more"-shaking prophecy. Here, once again, many are tempted to think that a literal destruction of the physical universe is the intended meaning. But this drastic language was employed to show the greatness and completeness of these two judgments. The immediate historical setting for the fulfillment of this Isaiah 13:13 prophecy was God's overthrow and desolation of the Babylonians (see Isa. 13:19-22). Previously, God had foretold through the prophet Habakkuk that He would use the Babylonians to bring chastening upon Judah (the southern kingdom of Israel), to destroy Jerusalem and the Temple, and to deport many Jews into captivity (Hab. 1:5-11). This occurred in the 6th century B.C.

Hence, this first prophesied "shake" and "remove" judgment of Isaiah 13 was against those same Babylonians (Isa. 47:5-10; Jer. 51:6-10; Zeph. 1-3; Hos. 11:5; Amos 6:14; 9:8-10). With God's intervention and support, the Persian army was to be God's instrument of that judgment. It defeated the Babylonians, laid waste their country, and took over the Babylonian empire. Afterwards Cyrus, the Persian king, released the captive Jews to return to their land. The Jews then rebuilt their capital city and the Temple and reinstituted the practices of biblical Judaism.

As devastating as the 587 B.C. fall of Jerusalem and ensuing seventy years of Babylonian captivity were for the Jewish people, they were temporary and mild desolations compared to the greater, cataclysmic judgment yet to come. Furthermore, God's shaking and removal of Babylon was to serve as the *precedent* and *type* for that future, "once-more" shaking and age-ending judgment of Old Covenant Israel. This prior and divine judgment of Babylon was also well ingrained in 1st-century Jewish thought and remembrance.

Early in Israel's history, God had promised that as long as the Israelites kept the covenant, He would bless and protect their nation more than any other. On the other hand, if they broke the covenant He would withdraw his protective Presence, chasten and scatter his people (Lev. 26:14-39; Deut. 28:15-68). Over the course of Jewish history a cycle of apostasy, oppression, repentance, and deliverance was repeated numerous times. As a result of this perpetual, national disobedience, Israel's sin mounted. That's why Jesus not only borrowed the same "shake" judgment language of the Prophets (Matt. 24:29 from Isa. 13:10; 34:4), but confirmed another of Isaiah's prophecies by saying that Israel would "fill up, then, the measure of the sin of your forefathers" (Matt. 23:32; Isa. 65:6-19). This "filling up" would include the rejection of Jesus as the Messiah. When full, Haggai's prophesied "once more" shaking judgment would come—but this time that judgment would be upon the Jews.

The Jewish writer of the New Testament book of Hebrews readily made this connection. Writing around A.D. 65, he warned his readers that he and they were living in "the last days" of which Haggai had prophesied (Heb. 1:2). He quoted Haggai directly and referred to the last major judgment of God upon the Jewish people (Heb. 12:5-7, 25, 26 [i.e., the 587 B.C. destruction of Jerusalem and subsequent 70 years of Babylonian captivity]), but here's how he emphasized the imminency and permanency of that second, "once more" shaking prophecy:

Haggai's prophesied "once more" shaking judgment would come—but this time that judgment would be upon the Jews.

At that time his voice shook the earth, but now he has promised, 'Once more I will shake not only the earth but also the heavens' [from Haggai 2:6]. The words 'once more' indicated the removing of what can be shaken—that is, created things—so that what cannot be shaken may remain (Heb. 12:26-27).

Clearly, the writer tells us that to shake what can be shaken signifies removing it. As we've seen, the Apostle Paul taught the Jews the same thing—that their "world" in its present form was passing away (1 Cor. 7:31; also 1 John 2:17). In Acts 13:40-41, Paul quoted directly from Habakkuk 1:5 and cited God's previous punishment of Israel through the Babylonians some six hundred years earlier. Then he warned that this type of judgment was about to come upon them. No doubt, this is why the Jews in Asia later accused Paul, saying, "This is the man who teaches all men everywhere against our people and our law and this place" (Acts 21:28).

Indeed, a massive judgment was forthcoming. Not only was God going to "shake" and "remove" the Judaic "heavens and earth" world; He was never going to bring them back. Instead, He promised to supersede or transcend them with that which "cannot be shaken." And what was that? The writer of Hebrews explains that it was to be the new kingdom of God, a kingdom that was already in human history.

Therefore, since we are receiving a kingdom (then and there) that cannot be shaken, let us be thankful, and so worship God acceptably with reverence and awe (Heb. 12:28).

Obviously, this second, "once more" shaking was not a promise or prophecy to shake and remove the physical creation. Not one shred of evidence exists that these early Christians expected a destruction of the planet, an end to the cosmos, or the termination of human existence. Instead, God, in total consistency with the prophetic pattern of divine judgment upon nations in Old Testament times, and in line with the prefigured "shaking" and "removing" of the Babylonian "heavens and earth" via the Persian armies, was about to pour out this next judgment. But this time it was to be upon a rebellious and apostate Israel.

So it happened. God removed that Jewish (heaven and earth) world in A.D. 66 - 73. Its institutions were shaken to the ground and totally removed, never to rise again, just as Daniel had long ago prophesied would happen at "the time of the end" (Dan. 12:4) "when the power of the holy people" would be "finally broken" and "all things will be completed" (Dan. 12:7). All these prophecies and many others were fulfilled when the Roman armies, empowered by God, shook, removed, and left desolate the Temple, the city of Jerusalem, and the whole world of biblical Judaism. This was the historical setting for Christ's "coming on the clouds." The impressive parallelism, precedent, and typology of God's similar coming and "shaking" judgment upon the Babylonians must not be missed.

Not one shred of evidence exists that these early Christians expected a destruction of the planet, an end to the cosmos, or the termination of human existence.

Insight 6. Isaiah's New Heavens and New Earth.

The book of Revelation's phrase "a new heaven and a new earth" is not new in scriptural terminology. Isaiah was the first to foresee a coming transformation from the old creation to the new in such radical terms that he twice writes down God's words in speaking of "new heavens and a new earth:"

> Behold, I will create new heavens and a new earth. The former things will not be remembered, nor will they come to mind. But be glad and rejoice forever in what I will create, for I will create Jerusalem to be a delight and its people a joy (Isa. 65:17-18).

> As the new heavens and the new earth that I make will endure [remain] before me," declares the Lord, "so shall your name and descendants [seed] endure [remain] (Isa. 66:22 [KJV]).

Some interpreters think Isaiah's terminology refers to the return of Israel to her land from Babylonian captivity ("a second time" return [see Isa. 11:11], the first being from Egyptian exile), and the restoration of their "world" as an initial, limited, and double fulfillment of entering a "new heavens and new earth." This seems unlikely, however.

Isaiah's "new heavens and new earth" are absolutely Messianic and totally covenantal. They unquestionably are tied into Haggai's "once more" shaking and go hand-in-hand with:

- Jeremiah's and Ezekiel's promises of a New Covenant for Israel (Jer. 31:31-32; 50:4-5; Ezek. 34:25-30; 37:21-28; also Isa. 59:20-21).
- Jesus' conjoined passing of the Law and the old heaven and earth (Matt. 5:17-18; 24:34-35).
- Putting the Law in minds and writing it on hearts (Jer. 31:33).
- The making of a new people of God (Jer. 31:33b ff; Isa. 65:13-16).
- The gift of a new name (Isa. 62:2; 65:15), a new heart, and a new spirit, and the placement of God's Spirit in his people (Ezek. 11:19; 18:31; 36:26-27).
- Doing a new thing (Isa. 43:18-21); and making all things new (Rev. 21:5).

Daniel knew that the ultimate restoration of Israel was not its return to her land following Babylonian captivity. Hence, he prayed for divine insight into the greater and lasting restoration that would occur during the days of the Messiah and conclude at the "time of the end." That time would coincide with the fulfillment of Isaiah's vision of a "new heavens and a new earth," and with the arrival of the Holy City promised to Abraham and his seed through Christ, whose builder and maker is God (Heb. 11:16). In continuity with the old, this new heaven and new earth would also be determined by covenant (Gal. 4:21-31). In contrast, however, it would not be a heaven and earth that could be shaken (Heb. 12:18-29). It was the "world" that Abraham and his descendents (seed) would inherit (Rom. 4:13). Isaiah places this radical transformation in "the last days" (Isa. 2:2-4). The New Testament confirms that they were living in those very "last days," right then and there (Heb. 1:2; Acts 2:17; 1 Tim. 4:1; 2 Tim. 3:1; Jas. 5:3; 2 Pet. 3:3; 1 Pet. 1:5, 20; Jude 18; 1 John 2:18). Therefore, this restoration and the fulfillment of Israel's hopes was consummated circa A.D. 70 - 73 when Israel and its religious institutions and ordinances were destroyed by the armies of Rome. But this eschatological event had both a destructive and a restorative side.

Revelation's phrase "a new heaven and a new earth" was the restorative side. The destructive side was appropriately symbolized by Babylonian imagery (Rev. 17, 18, 19), the biblical precedent and type for this judgment. Such a figurative and symbolic approach neither diminishes its reality or importance, nor disguises its true identity. As we've seen, five times Babylon is called "the great city" (Rev. 18:10, 16, 19; 16:19; 17:18 – see again chapter nine, p-185-186). And there is only one "great city" in Revelation. It's 1st-century Jerusalem. How do we know? Again, Revelation 11:8 tells us that "the great city" was "where also their Lord was crucified." No other city of any other time fits or will fit this description. The new creation was only fully realized and established when the Old Covenant "world" of Judaism was removed at the end of the age of Moses in that 1st century (Matt. 25:34).

A solemn warning: We must not make the mistake of interpreting the prophecy of "a new heaven(s) and new earth" independently from its established imagery, historical context, and scriptural roots. The facts of history and the pattern of terminology used in Scripture provide firm proof for the figurative, but nevertheless real, nature of the "heaven and earth" fulfillment as is being described in this chapter. The Apostle Paul confirmed this truth, thusly:

> For I tell you that Christ has become a servant of the Jews on behalf of God's truth, to confirm the promises made to the patriarchs (Rom. 15:8).

At his birth, Jesus entered into the Old Covenant (heaven and earth) world of biblical Judaism. He came "on the clouds" circa A.D. 70 to complete the Old Covenant and bring the consummation of the promised "new heaven(s) and new earth" in the New Covenant world. The dual use of heaven and earth language indicates a continuity. Both were determined by covenant. And covenantal change—not cosmic cataclysm—is the key to the proper understanding all end-time Bible prophecy (eschatology).

Next, let's see how Peter's vivid description of the destruction of the earth and the universe in 2 Peter 3 uses the same figurative and symbolic language to speak of the same fulfillment events and ensuing reality.

Insight 7. The Destruction of the World in 2 Peter 3.

> But the day of the Lord will come like a thief. The heavens will disappear with a roar; the elements will be destroyed by fire, and the earth and everything in it will be laid bare.
>
> Since everything will be destroyed in this way, what kind of people ought you to be? You ought to live holy and godly lives as you look forward to the day of God and speed its coming. That day will bring about the destruction of the heavens by fire, and the elements will melt in the heat. But in keeping with his promise we are looking forward to a new heaven and a new earth, the home of righteousness (2 Pet. 3:10-13).

No question about it. 2 Peter 3 is the biblical text most often quoted to support a future and universal cataclysm. The futurists see it as the end of time, the close of human history, and the final demise or fiery renovation of planet Earth and the solar system. Contemporary prophecy writers have had a field day applying Peter's language to the horrors of the atomic and nuclear bomb and terrorizing modern-day humanity with the supposed "hopelessness" of our present-day situation. But is a literal and materialistic reading of Peter's "heaven(s)" and "earth" terminology suddenly justified, as countless commentators have assumed? Or do Peter's words speak of the very same 1st-century consummatory event we've been addressing throughout this book? To settle this question, let's investigate a trail of five clues. They should help us arrive at the true meaning of 2 Peter 3's supposed "universe-destroying" text.

Clue 1. Peter's Consistency. This Peter is the same inspired Peter who in his first letter to these same people writes, "The end of all things is at hand" (1 Pet. 4:7 KJV), and "the time is come that judgment must begin at the house of God" (1 Pet. 4:17 KJV). Now in chapter three of his second letter, he refers back to his first epistle and reminds his readers that he is writing on the same theme (2 Pet. 3:1). And Peter is consistent. He is not introducing a new topic. Nor does this chapter stand apart from his first epistle or the earlier part of his second. He uses the same apocalyptic language and style that is used over and over in the Old Testament. Their meanings and historical fulfillments were well-known to the religiously educated people of his day.

Peter does admit, however, that these things, about which Paul also wrote, are "hard to understand" (2 Pet. 3:15-16). In other words, they are not readily apparent. Why not? If this chapter's text is "literal," it would not be hard to understand at all. On the other hand, if it depends on biblical and historical precedent, then its terminology and fulfillment pattern require thought, a historical perspective, and spiritual understanding.

Peter's objective is for his readers to understand both the imminency and the nature of the end that's coming and not be carried away by error. He laments that some people living in those times only want to distort and complicate it (2 Pet. 3:16b-17)—a problem in our times as well. If the many references to and fulfillments of the dissolving, shaking, and darkening of the heavens and earth in the Old Testament are to be taken literally, wouldn't it mean that our material planet and cosmos has been destroyed numerous times? Of course, this is ridiculous. And Peter's letter is no exception. He uses this same language without any qualification that he's using it differently. His language is consistent with this figurative usage elsewhere.

Peter's objective is for his readers to understand both the imminency and the nature of the end that's coming and not be carried away by error.

Clue 2. What Are These "Elements" That Are Burned Up? The Greek word translated "elements," which Peter said were to be "destroyed by fire" and "melt in the heat" [or "with fervent heat"– KJV], are assumed by most interpreters to be either the four physical substances that the ancients believed made up the material world (earth, water, air, and fire) or the modern chemical elements of the universe as they appear on a chemist's periodic table.

Two problems are inherent with these assumptions. First, neither reading properly translates the Greek word in question. A quick glance into a Greek concordance—not into an English dictionary—will dispel any doubt as to the primary meaning of this word for those who first received it. The Greek word for "elements" is *stoicheion*. It means something orderly in arrangement, a principle, or a rudiment. It's derived from the verb *stoicheo*, which means to arrange in regular line, to march in (military) rank (keep step), or, figuratively, to conform to virtue and piety or to walk orderly.

The second problem is that this word is *never* used to refer to the material creation in any other New Testament occurrence or context. As we compare Scripture with Scripture, we find its uses elsewhere in the New Testament will give us a clearer perspective of its intended meaning here. In Hebrews 5:12 and Colossians 2:8, 20, the same Greek word *stoicheion* is translated as "rudiments," "rudimentary and elemental teachings," "elementary principles" or "truths," and "first" or "basic principles" in various Bible translations (such as the KJV, AMP, NAS, and NIV). Paul uses the word twice in his letter to the Galatians (vv. 4:3, 9) to mean elementary teachings, elemental things, or basic principles. He says that under the Law people were held in bondage to these "elements of the world." Paul didn't mean that these Old Covenant Jews were under bondage to the physical substances of the material creation (earth, water, air, fire, or chemical matter). He meant that they were under bondage to the Law system, its institutions, its priesthood, and its sacrificial rituals. Paul then explains, in verses 4-5, that this was why "God sent his Son, born of a woman, born under the law, to redeem those under the law, that we might receive the full rights of sons." He wasn't saying that they would be freed from the physical world. Peter's meaning for "elements" is the same as Paul's. *It has nothing to do with the physical creation.*[9]

This Greek word *stoicheion* could, of course, be used to speak of the four physical parts of which the ancients believed our universe was made. But such a usage would be an isolated exception to the way it is used everywhere else in Scripture. If Peter had intended a different meaning, he would have said so. But he didn't. For us to force a change of meaning from well-established usage is at best arbitrary and presumptuous. Should we presume to determine biblical truth by finding an exception to the normal and consistent meaning of often-used words, and to do so without some overwhelming contextual reason? Of course not. Any time we have to create new or changed definitions for familiar words, something is wrong. We'd be much wiser to keep within this word's primary definition and prevailing usage in Scripture. So what exactly are, or were, these "elements?"

The "elements" Peter is speaking of are the "elementary principles" or "rudiments" of biblical Judaism, that Old Covenant "world" or system which would soon be destroyed in the coming of "the day of the Lord" circa A.D. 70. These "elements" of the old Jewish religion—its forms, institutions and mode of existence—were the types and shadows pointing to the new substance. They had served their purpose and were in the process of passing away. Shortly, they would be dissolved, melted, and destroyed by fire, forever.

But what did Peter mean when he said that the elements would be destroyed by "fire?" What was this fire? It was not a reference to future, nuclear explosions as many have been led to believe. Rather, it was a reference to both the literal conflagration of A.D. 70, and, figuratively, to God Who is "a consuming fire" (Heb. 12:29), and whose Messiah casts judgments with "fire."[10] Fire is often used as a biblical symbol of judgment. This divine "fire" destroyed the Temple, the city, the sacrifices, the priesthood, the genealogies, the tribes, and the whole heart, soul, and physical components of the Jewish religious system and theocracy—forever. Truly, Peter's "world" that was soon to perish was the world of biblical Judaism: Old-Covenant Israel.

Again, not one shred of evidence exists that 1st-century Jews or Jewish Christians were anticipating a cosmic catastrophe that would terminate time, burn up planet Earth, and end human history. Our modern-day view would have shocked any biblically literate Old-Testament Jew, and should give us a jolt, too. We must recognize that the Holy Spirit is consistent with his use of words and concepts in Scripture. The melting and dissolving of Peter's "elements" was a totally covenantal transformation, not a cosmic conflagration. Dare we presume or teach otherwise? Unfortunately, many do. They get away with it because their followers have little or no knowledge of the Greek, do not look in a concordance, or do not compare usages in other passages of Scripture. It's a sad commentary on modern biblical ignorance that many succumb to this erroneous, end-of-the-world sensationalism because of this passage. God has promised not to "destroy" the world again (Gen. 8:21-22; 9:11). And nowhere in the Bible does God say that He'll destroy the entire universe. To the contrary, He states that it is eternal.[11] Peter's "elements" must be interpreted and understood within their biblical, covenantal, and historical setting.

Clue 3. Coattailing on the Prophets. In 2 Peter 3:2, Peter reminds his readers of what the prophets have said concerning the subject he is addressing. Peter's visual description of the coming "day of the Lord" is anchored in what the prophets had foretold. He speaks in their language, a language with which his audience was familiar.

Therefore, Peter prefaces his teaching by mentioning three different heavens and earths in verses 5, 7, and 13—the physical one "destroyed" in Noah's day,[12] the covenantal one ("the present heaven and earth") in Peter's day, and the new one to come. The contrast between the physical heaven and earth and the first covenantal one is exactly the same distinction and in complete harmony with the prophet Isaiah's dual usage detailed in our revelational Insight 4 (Isa. 51:13, 16).

The melting and dissolving of Peter's "elements" was a totally covenantal transformation, not a cosmic conflagration.

The Old Testament prophets never foretold an end of time, of planet Earth, or of human history. Those are *not* biblical subjects. These prophets often used "heavens and earth" as a symbol associated with the downfall of nations or governmental systems by invading armies. Jesus utilized this same terminology in the same way (Matt. 5:17-18; 24:35). Paul affirmed that same thing saying, "this world in its present form is passing away" (1 Cor. 7:31). In an identical manner, Joel foretold the destruction of Jerusalem (Joel 2:30-31). Why then would Peter, a devout Jew, use this language any differently? He didn't. He simply drew on the long biblical tradition of the prophets as it applied to many past fulfillments of "the day of the Lord." After all, this was Peter's theme, a "the day of the Lord" (2 Pet. 3:10), and its soon-coming to bring the demise of the Judaic system. Only those who are unaware of prophetic usage, or who try to interpret outside of historical context, will insist on a literal destruction of the universe, which—as we've seen—is eternally established.

Clue 4. The Promise of the Prophets. If we need further corroboration for a figurative interpretation and understanding, we will find it in the prophets. In 2 Peter 3:13, Peter says, "in keeping with his [God's] promise, we are looking forward to a new heaven and a new earth." As we've seen, Isaiah not only warned of the passing of the old (Isa. 24:1-6; 18-23; 51:6), he also foretold the promised coming of "new heavens and a new earth" in its place (Isa. 65:17-19; 66:22).

As far back as Moses, the Old Covenant people were trained to expect this passing if the Law was broken. They knew that national destruction was part and parcel of the consequences of breaking the Law (Lev. 26; Deut. 28-30). Moses foresaw what would befall Israel in its last days due to its repeated violation of covenant with God. The judgment of 2 Peter 3 is rooted in the fulfillment of the Law and the Prophets. It was a judgment appointed long ago, and, in Peter's day, it was very near. For us today, this particular judgment is past.

After the cross, the Jews were allowed forty years to hear the remaining messengers sent by God and to accept or reject the atonement of Christ as the Passover Lamb and Messiah. God had given them plenty of warning, as far back as Moses. But their continual rebellion and blasphemy, foreknown by God, necessitated God bringing their system—that "heaven and earth" world—to an end. Jesus warned his disciples to be faithful to this "end"—the end of the Jewish age—not the end of the world, a topic He never addressed. Thus Jesus prophesied, "When you see Jerusalem surrounded by armies . . . this is in fulfillment of all that has been written" (Luke 21:20, 22). Old Covenant Israel had failed to recognize the time of its visitation by the Messiah (Luke 19:41-44), and the measure of its sin was filled up in that generation (Matt. 23:31-39; Isa. 65:6-19). Consequently, the Israeli covenant-determined world was dissolved.

Today, we would be wise to interpret and understand the Old Testament Scriptures as Jesus did. This includes every Old Testament prophecy and promise relating to Israel and pertaining to the 1st-century destruction of Jerusalem. The whole of Peter's prophecy, as well as all of eschatology, is grounded in two covenants, two ages, two heavens and earths, and, as we shall soon see, two Jerusalems. The Jewish writer of Hebrews quotes the promise of "a new covenant with the house of Israel" from the prophet Jeremiah (Heb. 8:7-12), then adds:

By calling this covenant 'new,' he [God] has made the first one obsolete; and what is obsolete and aging will soon disappear" (Heb. 8:13).

The Old Covenant did disappear. Paradoxically, on one Sabbath day each and every year, modern-day Jews attending synagogue hear the song of Moses from Deuteronomy 32. It is read as their Torah portion for the week. They think it describes what's going to happen to them in the future if they don't obey the covenant. But this judgment is over. It's past. The ultimate Jewish rebellion against God was the Israelites' rejection of the Messiah. Their "world" was destroyed forevermore, and its "elements" melted in fervent heat. Recognition of this change in "heaven and earth" is the only redemptive-historical perspective through which a responsible apocalypticism can be achieved. It will enable us to biblically adjust our understanding of other "last things" as well.

Clue 5. Imminency Statements. Peter wrote his second letter in the mid 60's (A.D. 65 -67) to the generation of his day. The text makes that clear. Peppered throughout his third chapter are imminency (immediacy) statements (2 Pet. 3:1, 12, 13, 14, 17, 18). Those who hold to a futuristic agenda reason that this passage has not been fulfilled. But these imminency verses cause them a great deal of difficulty. The clarity of the text cries out against the futurists and their position of nonoccurrence. Of course, their side-stepping efforts just provide skeptics and liberal theologians ammunition to attack the inspiration of Scripture. Obviously, a future fulfillment cannot be harmonized with Peter's and Jesus' (and others) imminency statements without violating the integrity of the text. The common practice is to ignore them, but this is a colossal error. They will not go away. If Peter's 1st-century imminency failed, then Peter wasn't inspired. It's that simple.

The question then becomes, was Peter right, wrong, or mistaken? For the honest believer in biblical inspiration there is but one answer. It all happened right on schedule, within the lifetime of the people he addressed. His use of imminency language was accurate. His exhortations for holy living were also right on target, as they are for us today as well. But it was Peter's contemporaries who would soon be involved in this coming "day of the Lord."

Many more examples in the New Testament show that the original readers and hearers were led to believe these climactic "last things" would happen to them, in their lifetime. They weren't misled. As part of the perfect ending that "end" came, the "elements" were burned up, and the old "heaven and earth" disappeared.

Peter, likewise and in this first letter, pinpointed his own contemporaries as the ones who would see imminent fulfillment. In it he talks about how the Old Testament prophets "searched intently and with the greatest care, trying to find out the time and the circumstances to which the Spirit of Christ in them was pointing when he predicted the sufferings of Christ and the glories that would follow" (1 Pet. 1:10-11). Peter tells his readers that these prophets knew that the things they wrote about were not imminent in their day, but would be during his generation—for *you:* "It was revealed to them that they were not serving themselves but you . . ." (1 Pet. 1:12a). Hence, Peter wrote of covenant transition and his 1st-century generation was the group who would see it. The personal pronouns "you" and "we" in both of his letters referred to the saints of his day, not some distant and yet-unborn generation. Peter was admonishing 1st-century believers to be prepared for what was about to happen to them. Is there any more clear way he could have expressed imminency?

Peter also said that scoffers would come in "the last days" (2 Pet. 3:3). Jude, writing just prior to A.D. 70, confirmed that this predicted sign was present and scoffers were dividing the faithful, then and there (Jude 18-19). Without question, that 1st century time was the "last times" referenced in 1 Peter 1:20 and occurring in Jude 18.

The clarity of the imminency statements in 2 Peter 3 should force us to reexamine our beliefs about postponement and an end-of-the-world. How can we continue to trust Scripture if we insist that these verses do not really mean what they say? Many modern-day interpreters lean heavily on 2 Peter 3:8 ("With the Lord a day is like a thousand years, and a thousand years are like a day") to explain away the nearness of all New Testament time and imminency statements, including Peter's. They use this verse to affix a time scale to God different from what we humans understand. This side-stepping device enables them to evade imminency and provides an excuse for a long delay. But it also gives Scripture the character of deception rather than of revelation. God does not obscure truth with his Word.[13] The very next verse clarifies, "The Lord is not slow in keeping his promise, as some understand slowness" (2 Pet. 3:9). This verse confirms the trustworthiness of Peter's and every New Testament writer's time and imminency statements as applicable, then and there, and not 1,900 years removed. Actually, 2 Peter 3:8 (from Psa. 90:4) is a statement portraying God's eternal character—period.

In sum, these five clues tell us that Peter and the other New Testament writers were Jews steeped in Old Covenant history, thought, and language. They didn't suddenly develop a new vocabulary or a new style of expression. The Holy Spirit used their training and guided them to express New Covenant realities in a manner consistent with the prophets of old. Many modern-day Christians need to squarely face the consequences of deferment logic. But once done, we'll see Peter's text in a perfect harmony of convergence and chronological synchronization with all the other time and consummatory statements of the Scriptures. All pinpointed 1st-century fulfillment; such consistency is inescapable. And the fulfillment context is covenantal, not cosmic.

Peter had still another significant thing to say about this new reality. It's the clincher. When we understand this attribute of the nature of the new heaven and earth, we will understand why the ancient prophet Isaiah saw it as the time when the hills would burst into song and the trees clap their hands (Isa. 55:12). You may want to dance and clap as well!

Insight 8. Peter Clinches the New Reality by Defining Its Character.

Peter proclaimed that "righteousness" would dwell (find its home) in "the new heaven and new earth" (2 Pet. 3:13 KJV-NIV). Where this righteousness dwells, and where this home is, is where we will find "the new heaven and new earth." It's the defining and distinguishing characteristic that will enable us to get an unmistakable handle on its true identity, timing, and location.

One thing is certain: this righteousness is not to be found in rocks and dirt—not even in new rocks and new dirt—and certainly not in a revived animal sacrifice system. That Old Covenant system could *not* take away sin (Heb. 10:4). It could not establish righteousness or make anyone righteous (Rom. 8:2-4). Paul emphatically states that ". . . if righteousness come by the law, then Christ is dead in vain" (Gal. 2:21 KJV; see also 3:21). But righteousness came: "God made him [Jesus] who had no sin to be sin for us, so that in him we might become the righteousness of God" (2 Cor. 5:21; also 1 Cor. 1:30).

The same ancient prophet who saw hills dancing and trees clapping had this to further say:

My righteousness draws near speedily, my salvation is on the way . . . .
Lift up your eyes to the heavens, look at the earth beneath; the heavens

will vanish like smoke, the earth will wear out like a garment and its inhabitants die like flies. But my salvation will last forever, my righteousness will never fail . . . . But my righteousness will last forever, my salvation through all generations (Isa. 51:5-6, 8; also 56:1; Jer. 23:5-6).

Isaiah's prophecy here is most revealing. It connects God's righteousness to both salvation and the destruction of the Old Covenant "heavens and earth." If this passage was referring to a cataclysmic end of the world (material cosmos) rather than a covenantal change, no future "generations" would have followed this event—at least on this earth.

Reading carefully, we see that "my salvation is on the way." That means that it was not available in Isaiah's time. It was the coming "everlasting righteousness" spoken of by the prophet Daniel (Dan. 9:24). It was brought into human history, in-breaking, and being revealed in Peter's "last time" (1 Pet. 1:5, 20). It came through the cross. And once established, it would restore humankind back into the Presence of God. Moreover, God and his righteousness fully would come to dwell inside his people—those who received the Messiah, Jesus Christ, as their Lord and Savior. Before then, God's only earthly dwelling was inside the Tabernacle and the Temple. But, as Jesus revealed to the lady at the well, "a time is coming when you will worship the Father neither on this mountain nor in Jerusalem . . . and has now come when the true worshipers must worship in spirit and in truth" (John 4:21, 23). This change of location and dwelling place was part of the promised New Covenant:

I [God] will give you a new heart and put a new spirit in you; I will remove from you your heart of stone and give you a heart of flesh. And I will put my Spirit in you and move you to follow my decrees and be careful to keep my laws (Ezek. 36:26-27; also Jer. 31:33-34; 32:39-40).

I will make a covenant of peace with them; it will be an everlasting covenant. I will establish them and increase their numbers, and I will put my sanctuary among them forever. My dwelling place will be with them; I will be their God, and they will be my people (Ezek. 37:26-27).

In keeping with mistaken futuristic thinking, however, many people today think that we can only experience heaven after we physically die.

They miss out on the heaven we can have right here and now. That's because heaven is not just a place "up there somewhere." It's wherever the omnipresent Spirit of God is. Therefore, another aspect of this New Covenant reality is, we individually become a "new heaven" when God comes to dwell inside us, in our spirit. That's probably why Isaiah prophesied of many new heavens (note his use of the plural). These are the creation of new spirits in his people. The first, or former heaven, is a person's old natural spirit with which he is born. It is at enmity with God. The "new heaven" is the new spirit God gives a person at salvation (1 Cor. 3:16; Eph. 2:6). It is made new by God's Spirit and becomes the dwelling place or tabernacle of God inside the new believer (1 Cor. 3:17; 2 Cor. 6:16; Eph. 2:19-22). Thus the promise is fulfilled:

> Now the dwelling (tabernacle) of God is with men, and he will live with them. They will be his people, and God himself will be with them and be their God (Rev. 21:3).

This promise of a new dwelling place was now, at hand, and not to be sealed up in John's day because it was to take place very soon, according the first and last chapter of Revelation. "For the old order of things has passed away" (Rev. 21:4). A new way of relating to God was there! He and his righteousness dwelled *with* them, and now with us and *in* us! It's a done deal. But there's more.

There is to be a "new earth" as well. Isaiah used "earth" in the singular, probably because we are all made of the same physical stuff. We "have this treasure in earthen vessels" (2 Cor. 4:7 KJV). That means that our former earth consists of our unregenerated physical bodies, and our minds and emotions. This is what the Bible calls our "flesh." As believers, our flesh is our biggest problem. It hampers righteous living. It's where we need to get the victory. After God (the Father, Son and Holy Ghost) comes to dwell within a believer (John 14:23), a process begins wherein Christ is "formed" within that person (Gal. 4:19). Of course, this process requires one's cooperation. But once begun, Christ's redemptive work is enabled to go beyond our renewed spirit dimension to redeem our flesh. Our lives need no longer be dominated by our flesh. We can become wholly redirected by and benefit from the power of God operating in and through us (see Rom. 12:1-2; 13:14). This is how we can truly, fully, and individually become a "new heaven and new earth," "a new creation" or "a new creature," as the Bible says (2 Cor. 5:17; see also Eph. 4:22-24).

Thus, this biblical new heaven and new earth, where righteousness dwells, does not describe some future utopian existence, or redeemed cosmos, or even heaven itself. Rather, it refers to a radically contrasted life of people, individually and corporately, in the New Covenant world of righteousness in Christ. This new "world" cannot be separated from, and has no meaning apart from the full arrival of the New Covenant. No other salvation and no other dwelling place of righteousness remains to be fulfilled. In our day, this righteousness and freedom from sin's domination is available to "everyone (both Jew and Gentile) who calls on the name of the Lord will be saved" (Joel 2:32). Those who call on the name of the Lord are accounted as righteous in God's eyes because of Jesus' righteousness. It's not something we are born with or is naturally in us; rather, it is in Christ, He who comes into us.

> For just as through the disobedience of the one man [Adam] the many were made sinners, so also through the obedience of the one man [Christ] the many will be made righteous (Rom. 5:19).

Putting away sin and bringing in everlasting righteousness were two of God's six ultimate purposes in history (Dan. 9:24; Heb. 9:26). In this manner, "God was reconciling the world to himself in Christ" (2 Cor. 5:19). He redeemed his people through a whole new reality of existence that fully came into being with the passing of the old heavens and earth, exactly as the prophets foretold. It's the central theme of the entire Bible. Such a central, ultimate purpose deserves the metaphorical magnitude of "heaven-and-earth-changing" terminology. All end-time Bible prophecy (eschatology) is anchored to, grounded in, and centered on this redemptive change of covenants and restoration back into the Presence of God.

Jesus said, "Behold, I make all things new" (Rev. 21:5 KJV). And so He has. And so He does. The new substance has come. The old types and shadows are gone. The Old Covenant Mosaic age, which was not able to remove sin and death and was incapable of establishing righteousness, was equated with the heaven and earth which could be shaken and removed. This old order, however, was also superseded by a "new order" (Heb. 9:10; also Gal. 5:5; Rom. 8:19-22), "the new heaven and earth" of the New Covenant kingdom age wherein righteousness dwells. Those who are Christ's are the places where this righteousness now dwells. We are this "home" and the defining and distinguishing characteristic of "the new heaven and new earth."

It's a done deal, and part of God's completed plan of redemption (1 Cor. 1:30; Rom. 1:17; 3:20-21; 5:17; 8:4; 10:4; Phil. 3:9). In this new reality, God dwells with us and in us. This is not an interim plan that will be superseded by something better in the future! Those interpretive schemes that attempt to compromise or postpone this theme are flawed. There is nothing better than the full redemption brought by Christ. It's far too beautiful to miss. It is part of the perfect ending *for* the world!

Thus, this biblical new heaven and new earth, where righteousness dwells, does not describe some future utopian existence, or redeemed cosmos, or even heaven itself. Rather, it refers to a radically contrasted life of people, individually and corporately, in the New Covenant world of righteousness in Christ.

Yet current traditional views that anticipate the annihilation or massive renovation of the material heaven and earth persist and rob God's people of a powerful and available reality. They cause many to miss the mark. We must conclude, therefore, that many have been led astray by a powerful deception.

Insight 9. The Satanic Deception of Cosmic Redemption.

Undoubtedly, God could create a new physical cosmos and/or *terra firma* Earth any time He wanted to. But He hasn't. And the point is, once again, He doesn't have to produce a sequel or massively re-do the present one in order to fulfill any unfulfilled biblical promise or prophecy.

Think about this, however. Satan and his spirit-realm cohorts are smart enough to know that they cannot get Christians to abandon the idea of "a new heaven and a new earth," as promised in the Bible. They also know that Christians long for a better day in a better world. And they know that most are ignorant of Bible history and its precedent fulfillments. So what does that sly ole fox do? He and his legions take God's truths and twist them just enough to make distortions sound plausible.

He says, "Sure, there's going to be a new heaven and a new earth (and a New Jerusalem), and you can live and reign with God in it if that's what you want, and it will be a wonderful paradise, a golden age of peace and plenty . . . but that's all out in the future. In the meantime, it doesn't matter what happens, because God is going to destroy this world anyway someday soon."

Does his deception work? Just look around. Millions of Christians are deeply entrenched in this notion. They are looking for God to deliver more than He has already "once for all delivered" (Jude 3). So they talk about the future dawning of a better day while they drag themselves out of bed each morning and go out to lead defeated lives. People who have a hard time controlling their own lives and who are not about to go out and attempt to expand God's kingdom or do the "works" of Jesus and even "greater works" (John 14:12) talk about reigning and ruling over the whole universe with Jesus someday. What these future-someday-glorified saints plan to reign and rule over isn't clear, since most or all opposition is supposedly wiped out and removed before hand.

Of course, Satan and his spirit-realm cohorts must be thrilled by this diversion. They have gone to elaborate lengths to keep as many of God's people as possible in the dark and grabbing onto these fantasies. Why? I can think of three very good reasons:

1. They know that human beings don't feel nearly the sense of urgency about future hopes and fantasies that they feel about the pressing concerns of their day-to-day lives.
2. They know that if they can keep us in the dark about what God has promised and delivered, they can keep us from reaching our potential in Christ, here and now.
3. They know that once we grasp hold of and enter into the present reality of the new heavens, new earth (and the Holy City, the New Jerusalem), they can never again use the weaknesses of this life to intimidate us. They'll lose control. Such believers would pose a major threat to their strongholds in this world.

I am convinced that a satanic deception lies behind the unbiblical practice of parceling out piecemeal the fulfillment of "all that has been written" (Luke 21:22), giving some to the end of the Jewish age, some to the end of a Christian age, some to the end of a Jewish millennial age, etc.[14] When Scripture is detached from its covenantal framework, it can be used to teach just about anything. It's a classic example of neglecting the context and embracing erroneous pretexts. This is precisely what Satan and his henchmen want. (See again the deception of the elect in our last chapter, pp-274-275.)

Thus, many Christians feel that their redemptive destiny is linked with an environmental renewal. Sure, God is capable of creating or re-creating a new universe to replace this one. That's not the issue. But think again for a moment. What's wrong with our earth is not its plants, animals, rocks, dirt, atmosphere, or the cosmos surrounding it. The problem with this earth is the people who live on it. We are the corrupted; we are the ones in sin who need to be made new. The earth doesn't sin; it can't sin. There is nothing defiling about it. It's God's most beautiful and perfect planet in the universe. Yes, it has become polluted by people's sins and irresponsibility, and it is in need of a good cleansing. But it has proven resilient and can adequately recover on its own without a massive purging by fire.

If we continue following this logic, it stands to reason that the physical stars and other planets are not polluted or affected by human sin. So why would God need to destroy, rejuvenate, replace, or redeem them? To the contrary, "the heavens declare the glory of God" (Psa. 19:1a) and reveal his power and divine nature (Rom. 1:20). Remember, the two symbols go together. It's both "a new heaven (s)" and "a new earth" in which righteousness dwells.

In spite of all this, two of the three postponement and futuristic views of end-time prophecy include the idea of inevitable cosmic destruction in their beliefs.[15] But let's also remember what God promised after the flood which "destroyed" the earth in Noah's day:

> Never again will I curse the ground because of man, even though every inclination of his heart is evil from childhood. And never again will I destroy all living creatures [things], as I have done (Gen. 8:21).

As we discussed in chapter three, some assume that God disclaimed this verse a short time later in Genesis 9:11when He only promises not to destroy all living things by a flood, leaving Him free to destroy it by fire, bowling balls, or anything else. But is God more concerned with methodology than mercy? I think not. On the contrary, we, the inhabitants of this planet, can take this eternal promise of God quite literally and seriously.

Also noteworthy is Peter's comparison of the perishing of the world in Noah's day with his impending "day of the Lord" (2 Pet. 3:6-7). Since the physical earth and universe did not perish in Noah's day, why must it for Peter's? As we have seen, Peter wasn't introducing a new time-ending, universe-destroying event. Peter's event is now past. It was the same Jewish "passing of heaven and earth" that Christ addressed in his Olivet Discourse (Matt. 24:3, 34-35). Something better has come along, and look what's at its center.

Insight 10. The New Jerusalem Is Here!

If all we see in the events of A.D. 70 - 73 is the destruction and desolation of an earthly city, then we've only seen one side of a two-sided event. In addition to this being the setting and sign of the Lord's consummatory coming, the passing of the earthly Jerusalem also signaled the coming of the heavenly Jerusalem. Why so? It's because the New Jerusalem is the city at the center of "the new heaven and new earth."

Unfortunately, most people do not know what a landmark in human history we had in the breakup of the old Judaic system. They do not see that restoration is the immediate flip-side of desolation. So some have bought into what I call "fantasy Christianity." They think will spend eternity in a space city which will someday come down from heaven and hover above the earth. They picture it as a visible cube (perhaps a pyramid) "1,500 miles in length, and as wide and high as it is long" (Rev. 21:16).

But there's a huge problem with this idea: if it's true, then 1 Peter 4:7 is false, and so are all the other consummatory and time-restricted statements we've expounded upon throughout this book. The exact nature of God's Holy City, the New Jerusalem, must be understood within the timeframe and spiritual relevancy of the text. Make no mistake about it; the destiny of the believer in Christ is a life in heaven, not on a new earth and not in a space city hovering above the earth. Heaven is the eternal abode of redeemed people; it is not a temporary and intermediate destiny. If we are "in Christ" now, we already can enjoy a part of heaven here on earth—the covenant-determined New Jerusalem that came *down* from heaven (Rev. 21:2). But it is not heaven, as so many have misconstrued. It exists here on earth, and we can live in it now. Let's prove it using two simple syllogisms:

> **#1 Major premise:** Most Christians believe they can now eat of the "tree of life" (Rev. 2:7; 22:14). On this we agree.

> **#1 Minor premise:** The "tree of life" is located in the New Jerusalem (Rev. 22:2).

> **#1 Conclusion:** The New Jerusalem is a present reality.

~

> **#2 Major premise:** Most Christians believe they can drink freely of the "water of life" (John 4:10, 14; 7:37-39; Rev. 21:6; 22:17). On this we also agree.

> **#2 Minor premise:** The "water of life" is also located in the New Jerusalem (Rev. 22:1).

> **#2 Conclusion:** The New Jerusalem is a present reality.

It is simply not logical to think that these promises are fulfilled spiritual realities in the New Covenant era, and then postpone the arrival of the city in which they are located to sometime in the future. Could God someday speak a physical space city into existence? Of course, He could. But the idea that this is God's plan is pure speculation, since no other Scripture in the Bible confirms this interpretation. Once again, the key here is that God doesn't have to do this in order to fulfill any unfulfilled prophecy or promise of Scripture. Once again, the idea of a coming "New Jerusalem" other than that which we already have in Christ is pure fantasy Christianity.

The full descent of this Holy City, the New Jerusalem, "coming down out of heaven from God" (Rev. 21:2) occurred immediately after the demise of the old Jerusalem (the one Jesus lamented over in Luke 13:34-35). The Old Testament is filled with prophecies of this coming, new, and different Jerusalem.[16] Daniel understood the precise timing for this ultimate and true restoration of Israel. Remember also that Jesus said, "When you see Jerusalem surrounded by armies . . . this is in fulfillment of *all* that has been written" (Luke 21:20-22). The Apostle Paul, in his time, spoke of the old city as "in bondage" (Gal. 4:25 KJV) and the new city as a present, in-breaking reality, "the Jerusalem that is above is free and is our mother" (Gal. 4:26). He contrasted it to the old Judaic system (Gal. 4:21-30).

This soon-coming reality was *part of* the unseen and eternal, spirit-realm reality to which Paul directed the Corinthians:

> For our light and momentary troubles are achieving for us an eternal glory that far outweighs them all. So we fix our eyes not on what is seen, but on what is unseen. For what is seen is temporary, but what is unseen is eternal (2 Cor. 4:17-18).

Abraham looked for a "better country"—a heavenly one—and a heavenly city (Heb. 11:10, 13-16, 39-40) that would be enduring (Heb. 12:22-24; 13:14; Joel 3:14-17). He knew that the Promised Land of Canaan was "a foreign country" (Heb. 11:9). It was only earthly real estate and a type and shadow of the heavenly and true inheritance to come (Heb. 8:5). Abraham's hope for the future was based upon faith in the heavenly realm rather than sight in the earthly realm. That "better country" of Abraham's faith was rooted in the "better promises" of the "better covenant" (Heb. 8:6 KJV) where "in thy seed [offspring] shall all nations of the earth be blessed" (Gen. 22:18 KJV; 26:4; 28:14; Gal. 3:8). What Abraham was seeking was Isaiah's, Peter's, and Revelation's "new heaven(s) and new earth"—the true fulfillment of the real Promised Land. And located at its center is the New Jerusalem, the city from above.

Neither the Law nor a future reestablishment of any portion of it could ever fulfill God's promise to Abraham (Gal. 3:18). Nor could earthly things (Gal. 4:21-31). But the heavenly inheritance of "the new heaven and new earth" and "New Jerusalem" could and did (Heb. 9:23). I cannot emphasize enough that this city is not heaven itself, as some believe (see Revelation chapters 4-6 for that). It comes down from God out of heaven to the earth (Rev. 21:2, 10). And it's not a literal city that comes visibly. Its invisibility, however, does not lessen its actuality or importance. This progressive nature of fulfillment follows perfectly the principle found in 1 Corinthians 15:46: "The spiritual did not come first, but the natural, and after that the spiritual." And the spiritual fulfillment is always the greater reality.

---

the idea of a coming "New Jerusalem" other than that which we already have in Christ is pure fantasy Christianity.

The coming of the New Jerusalem is and was the appropriate conclusion and capstone to the book of Revelation. It symbolizes the end-goal of the entire canon of Scripture and the grand climax of God's plan of redemption "to bring all things in heaven and earth [back] together . . ." (Eph. 1:10). This city is not, however as some assume, the totality of the Church. Rather, it's the beloved community of overcoming saints on earth, here and now, joined together with the "great cloud of witnesses" (Heb. 12:1, 22-24). This climactic and available reality stands in stark covenantal and historical contrast to the old city and the Judaic system that passed away. As long as the theocratic, earthly form of Israel remained, the hope of Israel, the promise of God to Abraham, and Israel's restoration could not be fully realized by either Jew or Gentile (Gal. 3:26-29; Heb. 9:8). But circa A.D. 70, all the old things were fully and finally re-determined and transformed anew "in Christ." This includes the city (Rev. 21:5).

Thus, this fully available, transcendent, and spirit-realm reality of New Covenant life takes place in the New Jerusalem, where God and the Lamb are its light (Rev. 21:23; Psa. 43:3). Unlike the old Jerusalem, there is no temple in the city (Rev. 21:22), because God no longer dwells in temples made with hands (2 Chron. 6:18; Acts 7:48-49; 17:24). His people are its temple (Eph. 2:20-22; 1 Cor. 3:17; 2 Cor. 6:16). You can read a listing of who is in the city in Hebrews 11:22-24 and Revelation

21:7, 27. And yet this heavenly city is the glorious dwelling place of only those believers who not only keep God's commandments on this earth but also overcome the opposition talked about in the Bible's last book of Revelation. It is the exclusive right of the overcoming saints. According to the Bible, these world-conquering saints, and only these, are the ones who inherit all this, and not nominal or defeatist Christians (Rev. 21:7; Gal. 3:29). The overcomers are the city on a hill (Matt. 5:14), the bride (Rev. 21:9-10), and the new people of God (1 Pet. 2:9-10) born by a new birth (John 3:3-7). They are the new priesthood (Rev. 1:5-6), they offer new sacrifices (Rom. 12:1-2; Heb. 8:23; 13:15-16; 1 Pet. 2:5f) in "the greater and more perfect tabernacle not man-made" (Heb. 9:11; Rev. 21:22; 1 Cor. 3:16; 6:19), and they operate in new supernatural powers (Heb. 6:5) and they enjoy close, ideal, if not perfect and ultimate, fellowship with God. This is no less than what is depicted. It truly is a high calling and pertains to us, here and now! No rebuilt temple is needed. Nor is this new reality limited to any particular place. It's available everywhere on earth as God tabernacles with his overcoming people, here and now. This is not something to come at the end of the age Christ came and died and came again to establish. It's part and parcel of that age after it reached its fulfillment. Truly today, "this is none other than the house of God; this is the gate of heaven" (Gen. 28:17).

Although God never intended New Covenant life to be either the end of all human difficulties or an escape from the frailties of the physical plane, the Holy City's symbolic description in Revelation 21 and 22 is given to encourage the saints of every generation starting in the 1st century A.D. Let's also and especially note just who and what are located immediately outside this Holy City's walls: "Outside are the dogs, those who practice magic arts, the sexually immoral, the murderers, the idolaters and everyone who loves and practices falsehood" (Rev. 22:15). This realization should be the fatal blow to the popular and appealing but misguided teaching of a future-coming time when there will be no more evil or sin on a new or renewed Planet Earth. This Christian fantasy is one of those "falsehoods." It supposedly occurs when God finally deals with the sin problem after "the last days" by destroying the world and starting over again. Fact is, God has already and finally dealt with the sin problem during "the last days." And He did it without destroying the world. His resolution was not to eliminate sin, but to provide the remedy for sin. That's why we still see evil and sin on earth on the last page of the Bible. Yes, as the scriptures say, Jesus came "to do away with sin by the sacrifice of himself . . . . and he will appear a second time, not to bear sin, but to bring salvation to those who are waiting for him" (Heb. 9:26, 28). Did He fail?

The greater good news is, Jesus did it all—exactly *as* and *when* it was supposed to be done. Hence, we can press on and overcome in the face of all opposition that remains and will continue to remain in this world. We can enter this inheritance and live daily in the bliss and joy of this community of God, here and now. Jesus demonstrated its reality during his stay on earth. The New Jerusalem is the true climax of the Revelation, the goal of the New Covenant lifestyle, and the essence of community for its residents. What's more, "the leaves of . . . [its] tree are for the healing of the nations" (Rev. 22:2). What a wonderful place to live! What a wonderful place to work! What wonderful blessings to bestow and a ministry to have! This verse, like others, once again rebuts two popular "falsehoods": 1) Why would the nations need healing if sin and evil no longer exist on earth? 2) If the new heaven and new earth is really the afterlife place of heaven, are there really nations in heaven? Fact is, all people, all nations, and all Christians alive today on earth—whether they realize it or not—are either inside the gates of the New Jerusalem or outside the gates. Where are you?

The greater good news is, Jesus did it all—exactly *as* and *when* it was supposed to be done.

Who would want to miss out on what we have now in favor of futuristic fantasies and postponement theologies? Yet some may cynically ask, *"Is this all there is?"* Certainly, this understanding of the new heaven and earth and the New Jerusalem is far removed from what most Christians have been taught and led to believe. And, naturally, there is a certain excitement in a science-fiction, planetary destruction and recreation. But who could prefer that to the glories of the Christian age as the Bible fully describes them—if we allow these Scriptures to speak for themselves in a straightforward and properly contextualized manner? Or, who would want to go back to a revived, old Judaic, animal-sacrifice system, when we have the hope and the promise of the something better that replaced it? Let us lay aside all distractions and deceptions and enter the city.

This inheritance is more glorious, more powerful, and far more joyful than most of us sons and daughters of God have been led to believe. It's an incomparable inheritance, and it's here and available in Christ. It's the New Jerusalem. It's located at the center of God's "new heaven and new earth." It's part of the "faith that was once for all delivered to the saints" (Jude 3). Please note that we are explicitly warned not to "add to" or "take away from" this prophecy or its established reality, for if we do, we'll be removed from this Holy City and miss its blessings and provisions (Rev. 22:18-19).

The Riddle Resolved

The biblical and historical resolution to the riddle with which we began this chapter is this. The "heaven and earth" that would never pass away is *the physical creation*. The one that had already passed away was *Babylon in the 6th century B.C.* The third one that would soon pass away and be made new was *Old Covenant biblical Judaism*.

Thus, the Bible's new heaven and new earth is not a re-creation of the physical universe. It's the complete arrival of the new covenantal order on Planet Earth. And its Holy City, the New Jerusalem, is the ultimate reality, the ultimate joy, and beloved community for God's overcoming people here on this earth! I suggest you read about it, anew, in Revelation 21 and 22.

Are you inside or outside the city? The New Jerusalem awaits!

Conclusion

Now You Know the Rest of the Story, What's Next?

Most people on Planet Earth today have been told and believe that "the end" for the world and human civilization is related to the physical universe. As we have seen throughout the preceding pages, this is a fundamental mistake.

In this book (Parts II, III, IV, and V) we have confronted, head on, four major hot-button issues of our modern day and time. These issues have caused much confusion and needless anxiety over many centuries. They have also produced irresponsible behaviors and impotent worldviews with social, cultural, political, environmental, and theological consequences.

The greater good news is God created all that exists. He did so with divine perfection in both the macro and the micro creations. And it's his world and universe, not ours. We have only been placed here for a short stay. But He has given us the privilege and responsibility to be the stewards of everything He created. He has also completed his plan of redemption with similar divine perfection. Its "end" (Greek *telos* meaning "goal, destination, not termination") came perfectly not at the end of history, but within history at the turning of the ages with the change of covenants in the 1st century A.D.

Sadly, some may find this final manifestation of divine perfection too uncomfortable or embarrassing to grasp. They may prefer to stay entrenched in their traditional schemes that must resort to gaps, delays, postponements, partial- or double-fulfillments, etc. to explain away all that has been presented herein. Others of you will embrace this additional manifestation of divine perfection and be refreshed, reenergized, and reinvigorated to take greater stewardship responsibility for and in our world.

But for all of you who have traveled the pages of this book with me I hope you have enjoyed your journey of discovery. The choice of whether you agree or disagree, however, is not with me or against me. I'm merely the scribe. Rather, it's a choice to agree with or disagree against the writers of the New Testament and their Holy-Spirit guided expectations (John 16:13). This is the same choice I had to make. Now it's your turn.

So lastly again, let's recall the advice scholars Drs. William W. Klein, Craig L. Blomberg, and Robert L. Hubbard, Jr., have appropriately stated in their book, *Introduction to Biblical Interpretation:*

> The historically defensible interpretation has greatest authority. That is, interpreters can have maximum confidence in their understanding of a text when they base that understanding on historically defensible arguments . . . . We should seek the most likely *time* for the fulfillment of a prophecy in history.[1]

Another thing I hope we can now agree upon is that the contents of this book are well-grounded in Scripture and replete with "historically defensible arguments." This has been the dual methodology or *modus operandi* supporting my two major contentions:

1. Our physical world and cosmos are without end.

2. "The end" proclaimed for the world throughout the Bible (and so frequently and falsely prophesied by so many for centuries) is not near and getting nearer; nor is it hanging over our heads like a guillotine blade poised to drop at any moment and chop off our future. Rather, it already came, perfectly and precisely; it is behind us not ahead of us; past not future. We moderns, consequently and currently, are living on the other side of the end appointed by God for the world—i.e., beyond the end. It's *The Perfect Ending for the World.*

This coming weekend in churches around the world people will again gather to hear a story. For almost two thousand years that story has been told and retold.[2] It's the greatest story ever told, and about a man called Jesus of Nazareth, his birth in 4 B.C., his life, and his death and resurrection in A.D. 30. But now—after centuries of confusion, thousands of failed predictions, and the recent bombardment of millennial madness—you know *the climax for the rest of the greatest story ever foretold*. It's a more responsible apocalypticism based upon the divine perfection of timely and precise fulfillment in God's completion of his plan of redemption for humankind from 4 B.C. through circa A.D. 73. This climax is the end that was. No other end is yet to come. It's not near, but far, and getting farther and farther away with each passing day.

The nationally syndicated cartoon "Speed Bump" captured the essence of this rest of the story quite succinctly (although the cartoonist in 2008 did not have the advantage of this book's contents in mind):[3]

Used by permission.

Consequently, never again should you fear the proverbial end of the world or wonder when will it all end? It won't ever end. The world is without end. Amen. And the one and only "end" proclaimed in the Bible was *for* the world, not *of* the world. That end, foreseen long ago by the prophets, has come. For them it was future, but for us it's history. Its "last days" are behind us, not ahead.

There was only one correct timeframe in human history for the divinely appointed "time of the end." That time certainly came, was not delayed, and did not prove false (Hab. 2:3). It occurred exactly *as* and *when* Daniel and Jesus said it would, and exactly *as* and *when* expected (John 16:13). It arrived right on schedule, "when the power of the holy people . . . [was] finally broken" (Dan. 12:7). Such beautiful harmony of prophetic convergence is no accident. And no other faith, religion, philosophy, or ideology is so soundly grounded and authenticated. Dare we make any less of this divine perfection?

Jesus' first followers lived in that expectation; we live in its completion—beyond the end . . .

Jesus promised, "Then you will know the truth, and the truth will set you free" (John 8:32). But before truth sets you free, it can make you sick. Perhaps, some of you are feeling a little unsettled now. Remember, unlearning is the most difficult part of learning. But if truth sets you free, what do you think error does? Error puts you in bondage. Only when we are set free from futuristic endsaying can we stride "boldly without hindrance" into God's kingdom and the future (Acts 28:31).

Jesus also warned of the disastrous consequences of building a house upon a foundation of sand (Matt. 7:24-27). Futuristic endsaying is a house built on the sand of gaps, gimmicks, delay, twisted meanings, and the deception of the elect. Instead, let us build upon the solid rock of Jesus as the "finisher of our faith" (Heb. 12:2), upon the firm ground of a "once-for-all-delivered" faith (Jude 3), and upon the sure foundation of an "end of all things" (1 Pet. 4:7 KJV) that was "at hand" and perfectly fulfilled in the same historical time-context in which all these inspired words were penned. Jesus' first followers lived in that expectation; we live in its completion—beyond the end—*The Perfect Ending for the World*.

Covenantal, Not Cosmic, Transition

As we have further seen, covenantal transition, not cosmic cataclysm, is the central theme and unifying motif throughout the Bible. This is the point missed by interpreters who use 20th- or 21st-century, cosmic-conflagration glasses. The Old Covenant world was the one burning up and changing, not the material cosmos. If we are sincere in seeking a more responsible apocalypticism, it's paramount that we ascertain the original and divinely-intended timeframe and nature of divine perfection in the fulfillment for end-time biblical prophecies, even if they don't conform to the way we have been led, taught, and believe.

It was by covenant that the nation of Israel came into being. It was by covenant that they produced the Messiah and the canon of Scripture. The ending of that Old Covenant world was pertinent to fulfilling the Law and the Prophets and ushering a new people and a new and everlasting reality fully into being. Such is the identity and nature of the metaphoric and apocalyptic phraseology of "new heaven(s) and new earth."

We can now live, confidently and abundantly, in that fulfillment and in the realization of God's everlasting kingdom, which is another subject for a future and forthcoming book. The passive anticipation of a utopian existence on planet Earth someday pales in comparison to this present-day yet greatly un- and under-realized reality. As fascinating as it may be, there is something dreadfully wrong with what the postponing futurists keep telling us about this reality.

First, they tell us that, as wonderful as this glorious reality is, we can't have it now. They want us to believe that God's most exciting promises are all out in a yet-to-be-fulfilled future, somewhere, someday.

Second, they tell us that this reality consists of literal, physical, and material objects. They want us to believe that God's highest ideal for humankind is a physical, material paradise: a space city, a new Garden of Eden, and a re-Judaized Christianity which we do not yet possess.

Third, they are looking for another or a yet-future end-times "last days" period separate and distinct from the one and only one the Bible proclaims was existing in the 1st century. So they interrupt timeframes, insert gaps, and use other side-stepping devices to explain away clear Bible language and stretch out prophetic fulfillment like a rubber band—now creating a "delay" over 400 years longer than the length of time the covenant nation of Israel even existed. But how could the "last days" of an era last longer than the era itself?

The practical, everyday problem with pushing the fulfillment of this reality out into a protracted future is that it depreciates and devalues the Judeo-Christian faith. Furthermore, it dis-empowers people of faith. As a result, those who should be reigning on this earth with Christ right now are not (Rev. 5:10; Rom. 5:17). They have been led astray by the popular misconception that God must solve our problems by destroying the planet and creating a new one before we can experience complete kingdom realities and victories. In other words, God must end what Christ came and died and came again to establish.

This is a, if not the, major reason why most modern-day versions of Christianity have become pale shadows of the faith and the kingdom that Christ announced, modeled, and conferred. Nowhere is the disparity more obvious than in Revelation 21 and 22, where Jesus described the ultimate and normal state of those who live in the city of the new heaven and new earth. May God open our eyes to this ultimate, available, but greatly un- and under-realized reality. May we learn its lessons and live and thrive in its glory and grandeur. And may we seek to understand what God wants us to accomplish in this world for his glory though it— the healing of the nations.

But Where's the Hope?

If all prophecy has been fulfilled, some may feel that this robs them of their hope and renders the future meaningless. The writer of Proverbs responds to this burning question and understandable feeling by admonishing us that: "Hope deferred make the heart sick, but a longing fulfilled is a tree of life" (Prov. 13:12). The fact is, 19-centuries of deferred hope have made the Church sick and the world as well.

Another fact is, we hope for something we don't have. What we hope is when we have it we will be better off. The Apostle Paul said it like this, "For in this hope we were saved. But hope that is seen is no hope at all. Who hopes for what he already has? But if we hope for what we do not have, we wait for it patiently" (Rom. 8:24-25). Paul and his contemporaries were awaiting the appointed time of the end. We now live in its aftermath. Question: Would you rather still be hoping for the cross and salvation? Of course, not. We have that. We also have everything else that God promised. All of this is termed our "once-for-all-delivered" faith (Jude 3).

Let's stop being distracted by hoping for sensational but unscriptural ideas like: the end of the world, the end of time, a future-coming "Antichrist" and "great tribulation," a re-built temple in Jerusalem, or being "raptured" alive out of this life. After all, didn't Jesus pray in his prayer for all believers that we would not be removed from the world? And isn't his prayer still in effect (see John 17:15, 20)? Instead, we can live daily in the full reality of God's grace, love, and blessings in the Holy City on this earth, here and now.

In this author's opinion, the ultimate hope for which every follower of Christ should be striving is this:

> *Someday hearing the words from Jesus Himself, "Well done, good and faithful servant" (Matt. 25:21, 23).*

Why settle for so much less while passively waiting around for things that are not going to happen?

The Next Reformation—the Prophecy Reformation

We are nearing the end of our journey through this book, but it really is a beginning. Our continuing desire should be to understand more and more about our faith that was "once for all delivered to the saints" (Jude 3). And there is much more to know about end-time prophecy, the apocalyptic, the kingdom, resurrection of the dead, Israel, heaven and hell, the afterlife, the spirit realm, supernatural empowerment, the purpose of evil, rewards and punishment, and the contemporary Christ Himself—all topics for future and forthcoming books.

Today, however, as we stand poised just inside the doorstep of a new millennium, I believe we are also on the threshold of a new reformation and an even greater awakening than has occurred in the past. The words of the 16th-century Reformers couldn't ring more true or louder: (*semper reformanda*) "The Church is reformed and always reforming." According to today's reformed thinkers, "The premise of *semper reformanda* is that the people of God are to be continually reforming and revising their viewpoints ever closer to the teachings of the Scriptures and away from unbiblical formulations and conceptions that have crept into both doctrine and practice."[4]

(*semper reformanda*) "The Church is reformed and always reforming."

Fact is, we moderns have not reached the point where reform is no longer needed. And in this author's opinion, the divisive, defeatist, pessimistic, strained theories, and side-stepping interpretative devices of end-time Bible prophecy (eschatology) is the next major area ripe for reform. These falsehoods have distracted us from our high calling—both an earthly and heavenly calling much higher and greater than we've been led to believe. When realized, it will change the way the Christian life is lived out. No longer will dolefully sitting round waiting for Jesus to come back be acceptable. No longer will watching the culture deteriorate into godlessness be permissible. No longer will 6 to 7 out of every 10 children raised in the faith and leaving the faith by age 23 be tolerable.[5] With this next reformation and reawakening, all this will change.

But reformation can be messy. It always has resisters and attackers. This next reformation will be no exception. Some will keep on preaching and teaching things not found in the Bible simply because they are committed to it, have built their ministries upon it, and would be embarrassed or find it awkward to "change horses in the middle of the stream"—so to speak. Others will come against me and fellow co-reformers. But for many of you, who seek after truth and long for a more firm foundation upon which a genuine biblical faith can be better built, it will be a godsend and a breath of fresh air. This is the further reformed faith that must be re-presented in the Church and taken to the world.

As has been true of other reformations, this one will require a new way of thinking, new perspectives, and a paradigm shift away from some of the traditional and defective positions currently holding sway. As such, we must follow the scriptural admonition to "Test everything. Hold on to the good," (1 Thess. 5:21). Our failure to do this in the past has put us in our current eschatological dilemma of so many failed prophecies and conflicting positions. This is the sad but present-day status of our faith at which much of the world scoffs. But how long can we continue stretching out the biblical "last days" and perpetuating imminency of Jesus' so-called "return" before biblical faith completely loses its meaning and value?

R.C. Sproul, Sr. warns us to listen up in writing:

> The evangelical world cannot afford to turn a deaf ear to the railing voices of skepticism that gut Scripture of its divine authority, that assault the credibility . . . of Christ himself [with their] critique of the time-frame references of New Testament prophecy.[6]

The time for further reform has come. Its potential is huge. A more responsible apocalypticism is within our grasp. In this regard, I am very appreciative and much indebted to Dr. James Earl Massey, Former Sr. Editor of *Christianity Today* magazine and Dean Emeritus of the School of Theology, Anderson University, for his endorsement of my original work and first edition of this book. As he foresees and wrote, "Noē's book just could be the spark that ignites the next reformation of Christianity." Then where do we go from here?

First, we must be willing and have the courage to admit that we were wrong and have misunderstood some very important, foundational aspects of Scripture and our faith. This is a necessary prerequisite. For far too long, far too many have been far too vocal and in far too great a frenzy to get out of here and get the world destroyed. This fear-based, traditional, "orthodox" doctrine has been a fool's paradise. It is an outright misunderstanding, misconception and misrepresentation of God's redemptive plan of the ages. Please be assured, we have nothing to fear from the biblical end that was and last days that were—only positive things to gain, and much to celebrate because of them. Therefore, endsaying with its long record of negative impact upon the Church and the world must be relegated to the ash heap of history.

Next, we must fan the spark of reformation into a flame, and the flame into a raging fire of purification. Our current eschatological system needs a major overhaul. Minor tweaking of the four major, competing, confusing, and conflicting positions will not fix the problem. Like Copernicus' model of planetary motion, which upset the current thinking of his day, we, too, will have to unlearn more things in order to relearn them correctly. Therefore, I propose the following four-step process for this next reformation:

Four Steps to Prophecy Reform

Step #1. Acknowledge that the physical world is never going to end. By "world" I mean planet Earth, the cosmos, and humanity. The *terra firma* and all else has been eternally established, and is sustained by our Creator God. He has charged us with the responsibility of keeping it, protecting it, and passing it along to future generations in better condition (spiritually, physically, socially, culturally, politically, environmentally, and theologically) than we found it.

Step #2. Honor the plain, face-value meaning of all prophetic time statements, timeframes, and imminency expectations—no gaps, no gimmicks, no delays, no twisted meanings, no deceptions. Our fundamental error has been the failure to understand the historical context of the 1st century for the fulfillment of all end-time biblical prophecies. Therefore, we have lifted "the perfect ending for the world" out of its divinely appointed timeframe and exchanged our divinely determined heritage for a hodge-podge of flawed human hopes.

Step #3. "Contend for the faith that was once for all delivered to the saints" (Jude 3). "Once for all" here means exactly the same as it means in Romans 6:10 when applied to Jesus' death; in Hebrews 9:12 with Jesus entering the Most Holy Place to pour out his blood; in Hebrews 9:26 with Jesus' appearance and sacrifice of Himself; in Hebrews 10:10 with us being made holy by the sacrifice of his body; and in 1 Peter 3:18 with Christ dying for our sins.

Hence, the past tense use of this phrase can only mean one thing. Biblical faith is a finished faith; the Messiah's two great works, that of the kingdom and salvation, are complete. This is the firm foundation that must be restored, better understood, and more fully realized. We need to take an honest look at history and see how all promised eschatological events happened and all redemptive realities were completely established and made everlastingly available by the time Jerusalem was destroyed and the Jewish age ended circa A.D. 70 - 73. Nothing more remains to be done.

And just as the Protestant Reformation of the 16th century was fueled by this statement from Habakkuk 2:4, "the just/righteous shall live by his faith," (also see Rom. 1:17b), let this next reformation be fueled by the verse that immediately proceeds it, Habakkuk 2:3:

> "For the revelation awaits an appointed time;
> It speaks of the end
> And will not prove false.
> Though it linger, wait for it;
> It will certainly come and will not delay."

In other words, we must now change "the end" the Bible consistently proclaims from being a *terminus ad quem* (the end to which, a finishing point) to a *terminus a quo* (the end from which, a starting point).

Step #4. Unify the current competing, conflicting, confusing and divisive system of four major eschatological views into one view via a "solution of synthesis." The four major views of end-time prophecy are: preterist, premillennial, amillennial, and postmillennial. Each contains strengths and weaknesses. Thus, each needs to and must participate in this reform. A "solution of synthesis" would keep the strengths and dump the weaknesses of each view and unify the strengths into one meaningful, coherent, and consistent view that is more Christ-honoring, Scripture-authenticating, and faith-validating than any one view in and of itself.

In this book we have begun this four-step reformational process. We've addressed steps one and two, and started on steps three and four. As we go forth, let us remember these still-relevant words of warning from Martin Luther:

No greater mischief can happen to a Christian people, than to have God's Word taken from them, or falsified, so that they no longer have it pure and clear. God grant we and our descendants be not witnesses of such a calamity.[7]

So let us grasp the courage of Luther and rise to the reformational task at hand. As word of this next reformation spreads, may it ignite a new impetus for world mission and bring more effective ways of proclaiming God's grace, mercy, and love. And be aware that this reformation could become as, if not more, significant than the 16th-century Protestant Reformation because it will proclaim the gospel of a finished faith, the everlasting kingdom, and a completely restored relationship between God and humankind. This further-reformed, "full" gospel will require changes in the creeds and confessions of the Church—something the 16th-century Protestant Reformation did not require.

But I believe the time has arrived for each of us to rethink his or her approach to end-time Bible prophecy, commit to inspired truth, and rediscover the fullness of our historic faith. Upon this sure foundation the Prophecy Reformation will go forth—in sharp contrast to the glum predictions, repeated errors, and blatant scriptural manipulations of the endsayers. Sure there is much more to address, explain, and reform.

But listen—do you hear the cry ringing over the land? It's the Prophecy Reformation's cry of a "once-for-all-delivered" faith. Soon it may swell to a chorus, then to a roar. Listen! It's the sound of a faith coming together in a new harmony of divine perfection and empowerment. It's a cry destined to revolutionize biblical faith in our new millennium—changing the way Christianity is preached, practiced, and perceived. What a positive difference its discovery will make.

So will you join with me as we sincerely and literally "contend for the faith that was once for all delivered to the saints" (Jude 3)? A world is waiting to be confronted with a more precise, more powerful, more persuasive, more adept, and unflawed, complete and completed gospel. The days of pessimism, retreat, failed prophecies, and escape are over. Let us sacrifice more of our unscriptural traditions on the altar of Bible faithfulness and enter, "boldly and without hindrance" (Acts 28:31), into this next great reformation and spiritual awakening.

In this updated, revised, expanded, and re-titled new edition, I have tried to speak plainly in order to educate and stir you to action. Of course, we've only scratched the surface. More books are needed and will be forthcoming, as well as your involvement and that of many others. I don't have all the answers and may be wrong on some things. I promise you, therefore, I will not close my mind to any civil criticism or new understandings that might better honor and match up with God's revealed Word. Thus, I challenge my critics. Where am I wrong on any or all of this?

In conclusion, the time is ripe and the climate prime to finally recognize and face up to the fact that Christianity in the modern world is not as strong as it could and should be. This must and can be changed. It starts with getting our faith right. Then teaching and proclaiming a further reformed Christianity throughout the Church and the world. Will you join with me by contributing your talents and resources to help make this happen? If you will, the Church in this new millennium just might be accused of turning "the world upside down," again (Acts 17:6 KJV)! If not, we won't. I believe it's that simple and straightforward. What do you now believe?

On with the Prophecy Reformation!

What's Next?

Twelve more pioneering and next-reformation titles and subtitles have been published or are in development and coming from your author and East2West Press. They are (updated: August 2012):

HELL YES! / HELL NO!
What really is the extent of God's grace and mercy? (pub. 2011)

OFF TARGET
18 bull's-eye exposés (pub. 2012)

THE GREATER JESUS
His glorious unveiling (pub. 2012)

UNRAVELING THE END
A balanced scholarly synthesis of four competing and conflicting end-time views—Unifying 'One of the most divisive elements in recent Christian history' (Est. 2012)

BEHIND 'UNRAVELING THE END'
The author's doctoral dissertation and more (Est. 2012)

A ONCE-MIGHTY FAITH
Whatever happened to the central teaching of Jesus? (Est. 2013)

GOD THE ULTIMATE COMPETITIVE EDGE
Why settle for anything less?
Transcending the limits of self-motivation, self-esteem & self-empowerment in a tough competitive world (Est. 2013-14)

THE ISRAEL ILLUSION
Pulling back the curtain on the 'land of God' (Oz) (Est. 2014-15)

THE ORIGIN AND PURPOSE OF EVIL
Solving the problem of the presence of evil (Est. 2014-15)

THE SCENE BEHIND THE SEEN
A Preterist-Idealist commentary of the book of Revelation—unveiling its fulfillment and ongoing relevance—past, present & future (Est. 2015-16)

LIFE'S LAST GREATEST ADVENTURE
What really happens today immediately after you die?—you may be surprised! (Est. 2016-17)

'WARRIORS OF THE LAST TEMPLE'
The story, theology, and script behind the movie (Pending movie release)

Also see: **PEAK PERFORMANCE PRINCIPLES FOR HIGH ACHIEVERS** (1984, revised edition 2006 – Frederick Fell Publishers)

Former Books Out-of-Print

BEYOND THE END TIMES

SHATTERING THE 'LEFT BEHIND' DELUSION

DEAD IN THEIR TRACKS

TOP TEN MISCONCEPTIONS ABOUT JESUS' SECOND COMING AND THE END TIMES

PEOPLE POWER

THE APOCALYPSE CONSPIRACY

Appendix A

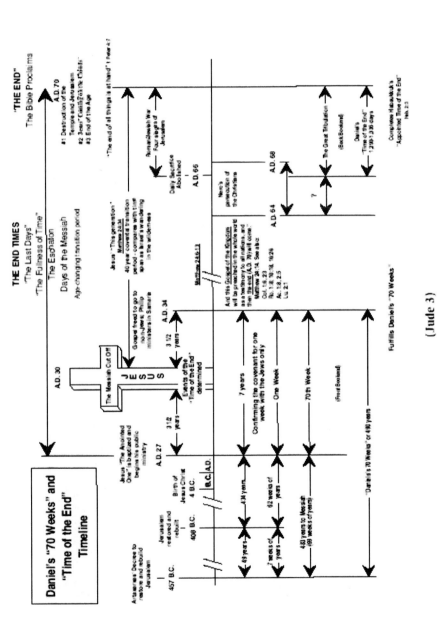

(Jude 3)

Contending… "for the faith that was once for all delivered (entrusted) to the saints"

Appendix B

The Olivet Discourse Cannot Be Divided

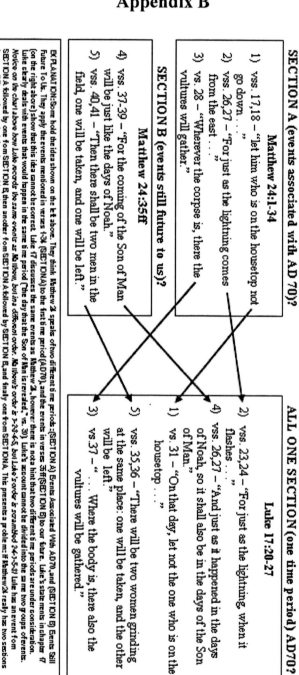

Matthew 24

SECTION A (events associated with AD 70?)

Matthew 24:1-34

1) vss. 17,18 – "let him who is on the housetop not go down. . . ."

2) vss. 26,27 – "For just as the lightning comes from the east . . . ."

3) vs. 28 – "Wherever the corpse is, there the vultures will gather."

SECTION B (events still future to us)?

Matthew 24:35ff

4) vss. 37-39 – "For the coming of the Son of Man will be just like the days of Noah."

5) vss. 40,41 – "Then there shall be two men in the field, one will be taken, and one will be left."

Luke 17

ALL ONE SECTION (one time period) AD70?

Luke 17:20-27

2) vss. 23,24 – "For just as the lightning when it flashes . . . ."

4) vss. 26,27 – "And just as it happened in the days of Noah, so it shall also be in the days of the Son of Man."

1) vs. 31 – "On that day, let not the one who is on the housetop . . . ."

5) vss. 35,36 – "There will be two women grinding at the same place: one will be taken, and the other will be left."

3) vs 37 – ". . . . Where the body is, there also the vultures will be gathered."

EXPLANATION: Some hold the idea shown on the left above. They think Matthew 24 speaks of two different time periods: (SECTION A) Events Associated With AD70, and (SECTION B) Events Still Future To Us. They apply the events mentioned in verses 1-34 (SECTION A) to the first time period (AD70), and the events in verses 35ff (SECTION B) to our future. Luke's statements in chapter 17 (on the right above) show that this idea cannot be correct. Luke 17 discusses the same events as Matthew 24, however there is not a hint that two different time periods are under consideration. Luke clearly deals with events that would happen in the same time period ("the day that the Son of Man is revealed," vs. 30). Luke's account cannot be divided into the same two groups of events. Notice on the chart above how Luke records the same events as Matthew, but in a different order. Matthew's order is 1-2-3-4-5, but Luke's order is scrambled 2-4-1-5-3. Luke has an event from SECTION A followed by one from SECTION B, then another from SECTION A followed by SECTION B, and finally one from SECTION B. This presents a problem: If Matthew 24 really has two sections (or two different time periods) under consideration, then Luke's accounts is incorrect, because he mixes the five events up as if they are all to happen in one time period. Either Luke is mistaken (and therefore uninspired) or its wrong to divide Matthew 24 into two sections. Of course, the solution to this is that both Matthew and Luke speak of the same events which would all happen in the same time period. And, Matthew 24:34 tells us when that time period was to occur :the "generation" alive when it spoke those words (the generation from AD 30-70!)

From the paper "Stevens Response to Gentry" by Edward E. Stevens © 1997, Kingdom Publications p-53, and also his book, What Happened in A.D. 70? (Bradford, PA. :Kingdom Publications, 1997), 18-19

Scripture Index

ENDNOTES

Author's Note

[1] William W. Klein, Craig L. Blomberg, and Robert L. Hubbard, Jr., *Introduction to Biblical Interpretation* (Dallas, TX.: Word Publishing, 1993), 149, 310.

Introduction

[1] Albert Einstein on quantum mechanics, published in the *London Observer*, April 5, 1964; also quoted as "God does not play dice with the world." in *Einstein: The Life and Times*, Ronald W. Clark, New York: World Publishing Co., 1971, p. 19.

[2] Guillermo Gonzalez and Jay W. Richards, *The Privileged Planet: How Our Place in the Cosmos Is Designed for Discovery* (Washington, DC.: Regnery, 2004), *xii.*

[3] Hugh Ross, *The Creator and the Cosmos* (Colorado Springs, CO.: NavPress, 2001), 194.

[4] William Lane Craig, "The Teleological Argument and the Anthropic Principle," www.leaderu.com/offices/billcraig/docs/teleo.html, 1/15/08, p-3.

[5] Comments made by Donald Brownlee, co-author (with Peter D. Ward) of *Rare Earth: Why Complex Life Is Uncommon in the Universe* (no c.s.: Copernicus Books, 2000), in a personal email, 1/28/08.

[6] Ross, *The Creator and the Cosmos*, 180.

[7] Ward and Brownlee, *Rare Earth*, 18.

[8] Illustra Media: *The Privileged Planet,* 60 min., 2004, DVD.

[9] Gonzalez and Richards, *The Privileged Planet*, 6.
[10] Ibid., 4-5.
[11] Ibid., 6.
[12] Ward and Brownlee, *Rare Earth*, 223.
[13] Ibid., 234.
[14] Brownlee, personal email, 1/28/08.
[15] Ward and Brownlee, *Rare Earth*, 53.
[16] Ibid., 264.
[17] Ibid., 265.
[18] Ross, *The Creator and the Cosmos*, 147.
[19] Ibid., 148.
[20] www.aish.com/societywork/sciencenature/The_Anthropic_Principle.asp, 1/16/08, p-1.
[21] Ward and Brownlee, *Rare Earth*, 35.
[22] Gonzalez and Richards, *The Privileged Planet*, x.
[23] Jonathan Wells, *Darwinism and Intelligent Design* (Washington, DC.: Regnery Publishing, 2006), 123-124.
[24] Gonzalez and Richards, *The Privileged Planet*, x. For more, I recommend the two books and DVD referenced above: *The Privileged Planet* and *Rare Earth*, along with the DVD, Illustra Media's DVD: *The Privileged Planet*. Also you can search the Internet under the expressions "the anthropic principle" or "teleology," which is a recently formed field of study (from Greek: *telos*: end, purpose is). Teleology is "the philosophical study of design, purpose, directive principle, or finality in nature or human creations.
[25] www.inplainsite.org/html/anthropic_principles.html., 1/16/08.)
[26] Gonzalez and Richards, *The Privileged Planet*, xiii.
[27] Ibid., *xv*.
[28] Paul Davis, *The Cosmic Blueprint: New Discoveries in Nature's Creative Ability to Order the Universe* (New York, NY.: Touchstone Books, 1989), 203.
[29] Gonzalez and Richards, *The Privileged Planet*, 196.
[30] Illustra Media, *The Privileged Planet*, DVD.
[31] Ross, *The Creator and the Cosmos*, 56.
[32] Ibid., 154.
[33] Ibid., 173.
[34] "For the last four years biochemists have possessed X-ray scanning electron microscopes so powerful they can map complex biological molecules down to the level of the individual atoms that make up the molecules." Ross, *The Creator and the Cosmos*, 140.
[35] Michael Behe, *Darwin's Black Box: The Bio-chemical Challenge of Evolution* (New York: Free Press, 1996).
[36] Ibid., 9.

[37] Ibid., 10.

[38] Charles Darwin, *Origin of Species* (New York , NY.: New York University, 11872, 1998), 154.

[39] Behe, *Darwin's Black Box*, 39.

[40] Ibid.

[41] Ibid.

[42] Ibid., 187.

[43] Ibid., 193.

[44] Ibid., 232.

[45] Ibid., 193.

[46] Ibid., 238.

[47] Ibid., 239.

[48] Ibid., 243.

[49] Ibid., 255.

[50] Ibid., 256.

[51] Ibid., 266.

[52] Ibid., 267.

[53] Ibid., 270.

[54] Charles Colson, *The Good Life* (Wheaton, IL.: Tyndale House Publishers, 2005), 222.

[55] Marvin Olasky, "Darwin slayer," *World* (21 July 2007): 15.

[56] John Piper, "Strange collocation," *World* (24 October 2009): 46.

[57] Billy Graham draws a simple analogy. He argues, "You and I have never met – so how do you know I even exist? You know I exist because you've seen enough evidence to convince you I exist . . . . And the same is true with God." (Billy Graham, "My Answer," *The Indianapolis Star*, 1/3/11.)

[58] A classic and recent example is Stephen Hawking and Leonard Mlodinow's #1 best-seller book, *The Grand Design* (Bantam, 2010).

[59] I will not get into the debate here of how long these days may have been.

[60] See: William Lang Craig, "God Is Not Dead Yet," *Christianity Today* (July, 1008): 22-27. Troy Anderson, "A New Day for Apologetics," ibid., 28-29. Dinesh D'Souze, *What's So Great about Christianity* (Washington, DC.: Regnery, 2007).

[61] Some scholars argue that in Habakkuk 2:3, that which would come was the vision of the end and not the end itself. Daniel's two time prophecies concerning this time and event, however, cannot be so construed.

Chapter 1

[1] *Chicago Tribune*, 14 October 1990, Section 1, p-1, 24.

[2] A *Yandelovich Partners* poll for *Time/CNN* in 1993-APR-28/9.

[3] In article by Jeffrey L. Sheler, "The Christmas Covenant," *U.S. News & World Report* (19 December, 1994): n.p. – reprint.

[4] "The Millennium," www.religioustolerance.org/end_wrl6.htm (9/30/03), 3.

[5] Jeffrey L. Sheler, "Dark Prophecies," *U.S. News & World Report* (15 December 1997): 63.

[6] Conducted by *Princeton Survey Research Associates*, reported in two articles: Kenneth L. Woodward, "The Way the World Ends," and John Leland, "Millennium Madness," *Newsweek* (1 November, 1999): 66-74.

[7] Cathleen Falsani, "With Rapture Index hitting 168, how to avoid being Left Behind," *Chicago Sun-Times*, 13 June 2003, from www.suntimes.com/output/falsani/cst-nws-fals13.html. (6/23/03), 1.

[8] Reported in David Gates, "The Pop Prophets," *Newsweek* (24 May 2004): 48.

[9] Ted Olsen, "Go Figure," *Christianity Today* (October 2006): 26.

[10] www.usatoday.com/news/nation/2006-12-31-year-predictions_x.htm., 10/23/08.

[11] The title of a new book (2009) by end-time pundit, pastor, and author, John Hagee.

[12] Ted Olsen, "Go Figure," 53.

[13] Hippolytus of Rome, *Fragments from Commentaries*, translated in Alexander Roberts and Richard Donaldson, eds., *The Ante-Nicene Fathers*, V (Grand Rapids, MI.: Eerdmans, 1987), 179.

[14] Lactantius, *The Divine Institutes*, Book 7, Chapters 14, 25, in *The Fathers of the Church* (Washington, D.C.: The Catholic University of America Press, 1964), Vol. 49, 509-511, 534.

[15] Richard Erdoes, *A.D. 1000* (San Francisco, CA.: Harper and Row, 1988), 2.

[16] Richard K. Emerson and Bernard McGinn, eds., *The Apocalypse in the Middle Ages* (Ithaca, NY.: Cornell University Press, 1993), 82.

[17] "The Confessions of John Hooper's Faith" in Richard W. Dixon, *History of the Church of England* (New York, NY.: George Routledge and Sons, 1885), 3:219.

[18] Yuri Rubinsky and Ian Wiseman, *A History of the End of the World* (New York, NY.: William Morrow, 1982), 91.

[19] Quoted in Leroy Edwin Froom, *The Prophetic Faith of Our Fathers: The Historical Development of Prophetic Interpretation*, 4 vols. (Washington, D.C.: Review and Herald, 1948), 2:278.

[20] ibid.

[21] Quoted in Jonathan Kirsch, *A History of the End of the World* (New York, NY.: HarperSanFrancisco, 2006), 157.

[22] Quoted in James A. De Jong, *As the Waters Cover the Sea: Millennial Expectations in the Rise of Anglo-American Missions, 1640-1810* (Kampen: J.H. Kok, 1970), 91.

[23] Robert Fuller, *Naming the Antichrist: The History of an American Obsession* (New York, NY.: Oxford University Press, 1995), 64.

[24] P.G. Rogers, *The Fifth Monarchy Men* (New York, NY.: Oxford University Press, 1966), 139.

[25] Fuller, *Naming the Antichrist*, 64.

[26] James Randi, *An Encyclopedia of Claims, Frauds, and Hoaxes of the Occult and Supernatural* (New York, NY.: St. Martin's Press, 1995), 263.

[27] Reginald Stackhouse, *The End of the World?: A New Look at an Old Belief* (Mahwah, NJ.: Paulist Press, 1997), 54.

[28] J.F.C. Harrison, *The Second Coming: Popular Millenarianism 1780—1850* (New Brunswick, NJ.: Rutgers University Press, 1979), 180.

[29] Walter Martin, *The Maze of Mormonism* (Ventura, CA.: Gospel Literature International, 1978), 356.

[30] Catherine Keller, *Apocalypse Now and Then: A Feminist Guide to the End of the World* (Boston, MA.: Beacon Press, 1996), 206.

[31] C.H. Spurgeon, "The Sons of God" sermon, October 7, 1860, Exeter Hall, Strand, cited on www.spurgeon.org/sermons/0339.htm, 12/20/08.

[32] Quoted in Paul Boyer, *When Time Shall Be No More* (Cambridge, MA.: The Belknap Press of Harvard University, 1992), 100-101.

[33] Oswald J. Smith, *Is the Antichrist at Hand?* (Toronto, Canada: The Tabernacle Publishers, 1926), 22-23, 45-48.

[34] Gary Wilburn, "The Doomsday Chic," *Christianity Today* (27 January 1978): 22.

[35] Sales figure reported on *Wikipedia,* "List of best-selling books," 3/15/11.

[36] *Citizen*, Focus on the Family (December 1998): 6.

[37] Claimed in an advertisement for his new book, *Jerusalem Countdown*, in *Charisma* (March 2006): 59.

[38] David Briggs (Associated Press Religion Writer), "Is the Second Coming at hand?" *The Indianapolis Star*, 28 October 1997, A1.

[39] Chris Stampler, "'Feeling a little let down,'" *World*, 15 January 2000, 25.

[40] Tim LaHaye, "The Prophetic Significance of Sept. 11, 2001," lead article on Tim LaHaye Ministries www.timlahaye.com, September 30, 2003.

[41] Tim LaHaye and Greg Dinallo, *Babylon Rising* (New York, NY.: Bantam Books, 2003), 8, 10, 11.

[42] Carol Eisenberg, "Fundamentalists link disasters to 'end times,'" *The Indianapolis Star*, 23 October 2005, sec. 7, p.6.

[43] Harold Camping, *We Are Almost There!* (Oakland, CA.: Family Stations, Inc., 2008), front cover.

[44] "The Prophecies of Nostradamus," www.qsl.net/w5www/nostradamus.html. (2/15/06), p-1-2.

[45] "World War III Predictions Revealed," www.nostradamusonline.com. (2/15/06), p-1-2.

[46] Kiara Windrider, "Prophecies: Prophecy in the Great Pyramid," www.experiencefestival.com/a/Prophecies/id/1934 (2/15/06), p-2.

[47] William M. Alnor, *Soothsayers of the Second Advent* (Old Tappan, NJ.: Fleming H. Revell, 1989), 179-180.

[48] Windrider, "Prophecies: Prophecy in the Great Pyramid," p-2.

[49] Robert S. Boyd, Knight Ridder Newspapers, *The Indianapolis Star*, 12 December 2004, A7.

[50] Steve Hall, "Rocky Horror," *The Indianapolis Star*, 13 February 1997, C1.

[51] "Prophecy," The Summit Lighthouse, www.tsl.org/Prophecy.asp. (2/15/06), p-1.

[52] Some Bibles have this date printed at the top of the first page of Genesis.

[53] In article by Barbara Demick, Knight Ridder Newspapers, in *The Indianapolis Star*, 10 January 1999, A-18.

[54] *Christianity Today* (11 January 1999): 57.

[55] Ad in *The Indianapolis Star*, 12 March 2006, I-4.

[56] Francis X. Gumerlock, *The Day and the Hour: Christianity's Perennial Fascination with Predicting the End of the World* (Power Springs, GA.: American Vision, 2000), 324, 326-327. For more lists of examples, see Gumerlock, *The Day and the Hour* in which he documents two thousand years of erroneous predictions starting in A.D. 41 to the present and beyond. Also see Gary DeMar, *Last Days Madness*, (Brentwood, TN.: Wolgemuth & Hyatt, 1991), chapter one, "The Dating Game," 7-18. Likewise, Tom McIver, *The End of the World: An Annotated Bibliography* (Jefferson, NC. and London: McFarland & Co., 1999) offers a compilation of 3483 writings from the early 2nd century A.D. on that demonstrates "how long, and how often, the End has been predicted, and how certain those who proclaim it are of their beliefs; how wrong many of these beliefs have already turned out to be; how violently these beliefs often contradict each other; and how certain it is that failed predictions do not deter similar predictions, when these too are based on deeply held religious convictions" (p-24). And, Jonathan Kirsch's *A History of the End of the World*.

[57] Bulletin of the Atomic Scientists, "Board Statement," www.thebulletin.org/minutes-to-midnight/board-statements.html. (1/25/2007),

[58] Bulletin of the Atomic Scientists, "Current Time," www.thebulletin.org/doomsday_clock/current_time.htm. (12/1/06), p-1.

Chapter 2

[1] Billy Graham, *Approaching Hoofbeats: The Four Horsemen of the Apocalypse* (Nashville, TN.: W Publishing, 1984), 221.
[2] Marvin Olasky, "Nuke Nightmare," *World* (25 February 1006): 21.
[3] The *Wall Street Journal,* 11 August 1992, front page.
[4] www.history.com/schedule.do?action=daily&date=20081022&time=16000&time., 10/22/08.
[5] Benjamin Anastas, "The Final Days," published July 1, 2007, on www.nytimes.com/2007/07/01/magazine/01world-t.html., 7/1/07.
[6] "Happy New Year, 2012," *Publishers Weekly* (22 Sept. 2008), 34.
[7] G. Jeffrey MacDonald, "Reimagining the Past," *Publishers Weekly* (26 March 2007): S7.
[8] *Publishers Weekly* (31 May, 2010): 33.
[9] Wikipedia.org,, "Harold Camping."
[10] Mark Moring, "It's the End of the World, and We Love It," *Christianity Today* (March 2010), 45.
[11] Line from the film, "JFK," spoken by Jim Garrison as portrayed by actor Kevin Costner.
[12] David Neff, "Second Coming Ecology" *Christianity Today* (July 2008): 34-37.
[13] Quoted in Kirsch, *A History of the End of the World,* 17.
[14] Kevin Phillips, *American Theocracy: The Peril and Politics of Radical Religion, Oil, and Borrowed Money in the 21st Century* (New York, NY.: Viking, 2006), *xiii-xiv.*
[15] Ibid., 100.
[16] Ibid., inside front-cover leaf.
[17] David Neff, *Christianity Today* (17 December 1990): 15.
[18] Gary DeMar, "Chuck Smith's Prophetic Pronouncement Under the Microscope" *American Vision* (Jan/Feb 2008), 14-15.
[19] To be expanded and offered as a future book. See p-333.
[20] Cartoon, *Christianity Today* (14 December 1992): 12.
[21] *The Wall Street Journal,* 29 December 1993.
[22] Yet, "the fear of the Lord is the beginning of wisdom" (Prov. 9:10).
[23] Phillips, *American Theocracy,* 125.

Chapter 3

[1] Billy Graham, "My Answer," *The Indianapolis Star,* 8/29/98, B6.
[2] Ibid., 6/17/98, 12/12/96 and 11/25/94, for example.

---

[3] Ibid., 4/21/10, C13.

[4] The King James Bible also mistranslates the Greek word *aion* as "world" rather than "age" in the phrase "the end of the world (age)" in Matthew 13:39 and 49. Most modern Bible translations clear up this confusion and render it "age." Those who use fear to hold on to people hesitate to give up this translation weapon. What the Bible does say about "the end of the age" and "the time of the end" will be covered in subsequent chapters.

[5] The Greek word *aion* is used for the Hebrew word *olam* in the Septuagint.

[6] Compare with similar idiomatic uses in Heb. 1:8, Rev. 11:15, and Isa. 45:17. A few scholars feel this double use in the idiom does not speak of eternity or endlessness, but of aggregated or compounding periods of time—until all ages have run their course. Most, however, do agree with the explanation given here.

[7] As we shall continue to see (also see Isa. 9:6-7; Ezek. 37:26-28; Dan. 2:44; 7:13-14, 27; Luke 1:33; Heb. 12:28; 13:20; Rev. 11:15f; 14:6).

[8] Washington Irving, one of the most popular American writers of his time, is credited by some historians with making up and popularizing the heroic saga of Columbus battling the flat-Earthers in his 1828 book about the explorer. Others claim that it was the Church which propagated this notion, along with the belief that the earth was the center of the universe.

[9] Some Bible scholars maintain that the book of Ecclesiastes cannot be relied on because the arguments it contains are man's, not God's. The New Testament book of 2 Timothy, however, asserts that "All Scripture [including Ecclesiastes] is useful for teaching, rebuking, correcting, and training in righteousness" (2 Tim. 3:16).

[10] "Great Is Thy Faithfulness" by Thomas O. Chisholm (1866-1960) and William M. Rynyan (1870-1957).

[11] The Greek word translated as "world" here is *kosmos*. In a narrow or wide sense, it can mean the earth, and/or by metonymy, the human race.

[12] For literature concerning the further use of apocalyptic language in the Bible, see: John Joseph Collins, *The Apocalyptic Imagination: An introduction to the Jewish Matrix of Christianity* (New York, NY.: Crossroad, 1984). *The Old Testament Pseudepigrapha*, Vol 1, (New York, NY.: Doubleday, 1983).

[13] ABC News reported on 4/20/98 that the United States has enough nuclear warheads to blow up the world four-times over.

[14] *The World Book Encyclopedia*, 1982, T Volume 19, p-192, states that the laws of thermodynamics "are broad conclusions about the nature of energy, drawn from the results of many experiments."

[15] New evidence presented at the annual winter meeting of the American Astronomical Society, as reported in the *Indianapolis Star*, 1/9/98.

¹⁶ Michael Crichton, *Jurassic Park* (New York, NY.: Ballantine Books, 1990), 367-369.

Chapter 5

¹ See Abraham Cohen, *Everyman's Talmud* (New York, NY.: Schochen Books, 1949), 356.

² This term is used in theological circles and comes from the Greek *eschatos*, meaning "last" or "farthest." The eschaton is variously defined as: the days of the Messiah, the time of consummation of all last things in salvation history, the time of fulfillment of all God's promises, the end times, the "last days," the coming of the kingdom of God in power, and the "time of the end."

³ So did Moses (Deut 31 and 32), Isaiah (Isa. 5:1-7), Zechariah (Zech. 14) and others, but not by using this expression.

⁴ Traditionally and erroneously, Christians have transposed these words to mean that when Jesus returns it will be the end of time, and the end of this material world and universe.

⁵ Some liberal scholars have insisted that all or part of this book was written in the 2nd century B.C. in the time of Antiochus Epiphanes (175-163 B.C.). I, however, agree with the majority of biblical scholars who take Daniel at face value. Daniel states that it was written during the time of Babylonian exile, which was in the 6th century B.C. (Dan. 1:1f.). The historical fact that 1st-century B.C. Qumran Jews viewed Daniel's book as inspired, and made more copies of it than any other Old Testament book is the best evidence for its stated date, and for a refutation of the "contemporary forgery" idea. But even if it was written in the 2nd century B.C., that still leaves an approximate two-century foretelling factor to explain. Many of these same scholars maintain that all of Daniel was fulfilled in the 2nd century B.C. But they fail to explain how the six purpose clauses in Daniel 9:24 were fulfilled at that time.

⁶ J. Daniel Hays, J. Scott Duvall, and C. Marvin Pate, *Dictionary of Biblical Prophecy and End Times* (Grand Rapids, MI.: Zondervan, 2007), 425.

⁷ It's difficult to fix the exact dates for the beginning and ending of the 70 years of Babylonian captivity. Daniel was taken captive in 605 B.C. Another group was deported in 597 B.C., and the final destruction of Jerusalem did not occur until 586 B.C. Likewise, the return from exile was also staggered over a period of years. Contained within this time variance is the actual 70-year period prophesied by Jeremiah.

⁸ Although Ptolemy's chronology—developed in the 2nd century A.D.—is generally accepted by the majority of scholars, not everyone agrees it is correct.

Philip Mauro, in his book, *The Wonders of Bible Chronology* (Reiner Publications, Swengel, PA, 1974) claims that "Ptolemy makes the duration of the Persian Empire more than eighty years too long." Mauro further claims that Ptolemy's chronological statements are "contradicted by the writings of Josephus . . . Persian traditions . . . and by the Jewish National traditions" (p-6). Mauro's chronology is derived from the Bible and recasts the chronology of the last 500 years of the Old Testament era. He, therefore, dates Cyrus' Decree at 457 B.C. Whichever way is correct, both Mauro and this author see 457 B.C. as the appropriate starting date for Daniel's 70 weeks. For readers interested in the details of Mauro's calculations and his proof, I refer you to his book *The Seventy Weeks and the Great Tribulation* (ibid, 1975), and to John C. Whitcomb's book, *Darius the Mede*. All three are well worth one's time and careful consideration.
[9] See again above footnote.
[10] They actually did start rebuilding and inhabiting the city then, too. Also, I'm aware of the difference between the Jewish lunar year of 360 days versus our solar year of 365+ days. However, Israel made adjustments to its calendar on a regular, pre-determined basis to adhere to a solar year of 365¼ days. Otherwise, the cycle of its seven feasts (related to the agricultural seasons) would have quickly gotten way out of synch. If such adjustments were not done, winter months would soon have occurred in the summer and vice versa. Therefore, the use of solar years for Daniel's 490-year timeframe would be the one consistent with the Jews' method of tracking time.
[11] The 444 B.C. date of Artaxerxes' letters is advocated as the starting point by some Bible scholars. But these "letters" are not accorded decree status in Scripture. Next, these scholars use what is termed "prophetic years" of 360 days each. This notion is taken from the use of the Jewish lunar year (see footnote #8 above) and from the idea that the 1,260 days of Revelation 12:6, the "time and times and half a time" of Revelation 12:14, and the 42 months of Revelation 13:5 as all representing a 3½ year period.

Calculation by this method brings scholars close to some of the same 1st-century time dates and events I have presented. But their explanations are not nearly as descriptive and precise. Here is how they figure:

> 444 B.C.
> +
> 173,880   days (483 Years of 360 days each or
>   approximately 476 solar years of 365¼ days to
>   the Messiah)
> A.D. 33

Some Jewish scholars begin Daniel's 70 Weeks with God's decree announcement in Jeremiah 29:10, which supposedly was made in 587 B.C. They end it with the destruction of the Temple in A.D. 70. This raises even more problems, since the time span from 587 B.C. to A.D. 70 is 658 years, not 490.
[12] Later books in the Old Testament give no information about how long this period of rebuilding took to complete.

"According to Barnes and several other trustworthy Bible commentators, the historian Prideaux declared that Nehemiah's last action in rebuilding the city occurred in the 15th year of the Persian ruler Darius Nothus (423-404 B.C.). His 15th year was the 49th year from the 457 B.C. (or 458) decree. Josephus seems to support this idea in his remarks about the death of Nehemiah. This can be viewed as an indication that the 457 B.C. date is correct. But it is possible that some rebuilding continued after that." From, *The Daniel Papers Discovery Series* by Resources For Biblical Communication, Radio Bible Class (Grand Rapids, Michigan, 1994), 15-16.

In the absence of any better information, it is safe to assume that 49 years after the third decree was issued, the work was completed. Difficulty in reconstructing ancient chronology throughout these weeks means that we have to be satisfied with close but approximate dating in confirming what most probably is absolutely accurate to the very year, if not very day.
[13] Anointed" is the Hebrew word *mashiyach* and means "Messiah."
[14] Also, see Daniel 2:44 and 7:15-28.
[15] Daniel uses the Hebrew word (*Karath*), translated as "cut off." This word was used for the death penalty (Lev. 7:20, 21, 25, 27), and often referred to violent death (1 Sam. 17:51; Obad. 9; Nah. 3:15). In Isaiah 53:8, where it is prophesied of the death of Christ, "He was cut off out of the land of the living," the word is *ghzar* and has a nearly identical meaning.
[16] Some scholars feel that Philip's journey to Samaria occurred five to ten years after Christ's crucifixion. The point remains the same, the time restriction had expired.

Chapter 6

[1] See for example: Kenneth L. Gentry, Jr., *Before Jerusalem Fell* (Atlanta, GA.: American Vision, 1998) and John A.T. Robinson, *Redating the New Testament* (Philadelphia, PA.: Westminster Press, 1976).
[2] Of course, Josephus' historical accounts are not inspired and not as reliable as the accounts in the Bible. He is, nevertheless, considered a very reliable source,

and the most accurate and only eye-witness authority of the time for historical information.
[3] Josephus, *The Wars of the Jew,* in William Whiston, trans., *The Works of Josephus* (Peabody, MA.: Hendrickson Publishers, 1987), 2.17.2 (409).
[4] The word "temple" is not in the original language. "Wing" means "pinnacle," "height" or "top most" of the abominations.
[5] Josephus, *Wars,* 5.1.1-3 (1-19).
[6] I recommend these commentaries:
Josephus: The Essential Writings, by Paul L. Maier, Kregel Publications, 1988.
The Topical Josephus, by Cleon L. Rogers, Jr., Zondervan, 1992.

Chapter 7

[1] Kenneth S. Kantzer, ed., "Our Future Hope: Eschatology and Its Role in the Church," *Christianity Today,* 6 February 1987, 1- (I).
[2] The prevailing view attempts to make five world kingdoms out of the four described in Daniel 2 and 7. It's done by spinning off some of the descriptive attributes of the fourth kingdom, inserting a time gap of indeterminable length, and making them into a futuristic, fifth earthly kingdom, which is then called the revived (or revised) Roman Empire. No sound reason exists for taking such latitude. It's totally arbitrary, and is only asserted in order to support a particular futuristic doctrine. Not only does it not fit the picture given by Daniel, Daniel emphatically stated that these visions represented four— not five—earthly kingdoms (Dan. 2:40; 7:17). Their attributes were portrayed by *four* sections of a statue and *four* beasts, and not five. Furthermore, each of the two parallel descriptions of the fourth kingdom fully applies to the old Roman Empire, and was historically and precisely fulfilled. Several scholars have documented the symbolically portrayed attributes of each kingdom, and I will not duplicate their work in this book. But Daniel assured both the king and us that his interpretation was "trustworthy" (Dan. 2:45). All Daniel's prophesied events happened and were fulfilled within this timeframe in history. There is no credible reason to repeat these events or to revive the political, social, and religious conventions of those times.
[3] To date, and in this author's opinion, no futurist has offered a valid justification for interrupting Daniel's 70 weeks timeframe and inserting a time gap—except to assert that their interpretive system "necessitates" this methodology. Some justification attempts I've encountered are:

1) Using Old Testament prophecies that don't specify timeframes as precedents for interrupting those that do—such as Isaiah 9:6 and Zechariah 9:9-10. But these are not analogous.

2) Citing conditional prophetic messages wherein God could change the outcome based upon the response of the people to whom they were given—such as Jonah 3:5 and Jeremiah 18:7-8. But Daniel's were unconditional, and therefore, not analogous.

3) Noting that the Church was a "mystery" in the Old Testament. But jumping from that to an interruption is—at best—a stretch.

4) Reasoning that other interruptions and gaps, also arbitrarily imposed, justify this one—for example, bifurcating (part to the past, part for the future) the book of Revelation, Jesus' Olivet Discourse, and Acts 2:17-21's description of the events of Pentecost. These other intrusions are just as erroneous and without scriptural justification. One misuse cannot be used to justify another in an attempt to be "consistent." This logic is a case of circular error perpetuating itself.

What gap theorists need to prove their case is a clear statement or precedent in Scripture. This is exactly what they don't have. Mere assertion is insufficient justification upon which to hang such an abortive treatment of Scripture. The idea for interruption the timeframe of Daniel's 70 weeks originated in A.D. 1585. A Jesuit priest named Francisco Ribera was the first to separate Daniel's 70th week from the other 69. This was done to deflect apocalyptic heat from the Pope and the Roman Catholic hierarchy, who were being attacked by the Reformers for being the Antichrist and beast of Revelation, respectively. Ribera said that the first 69 weeks (483 years) concluded at the baptism of Jesus in A.D. 27 but that God had extended the 70th week into the future. Thus was born the popular "gap theory." In the early 1800s, J.N. Darby bought into this theory and added the rapture-removal idea. He and Scofield (1900s) popularized this teaching throughout America.

[4] Josephus, *The Antiquities of the Jews*, In William Whiston, trans. *The Works of Josephus* (Peabody, MA.: Hendrickson Publishers, 1987), 18.3.3 (63).

[5] Also, the idea that the beast of Revelation 13 is the Antichrist is purely assumptive. No such connection is ever made in Scripture. We must pay close attention to what the Bible actually says and does not say. But many have not. Hence, for several centuries, Christianity has appeared foolish as the popular endsayers of their day have continually attempted to name the latest global villain as the "biblical Antichrist."

[6] Klein and others, *Introduction to Biblical Interpretation*, 149.

[7] Ibid., 310.

[8] Moisés Silva, *Has the Church Misread the Bible?* (Grand Rapids, MI.: Zondervan, 1987), 8.

[9] A strong case can be made that the book of Revelation was written around A.D. 65-67 and prior to the destruction of Jerusalem in AD 70. See again footnote #1, chapter six.

Chapter 8

[1] Matt. 11:16; 12:41, 42, 45; 23:36; Mark 8:12, 38; Luke 7:31; 11:29, 30, 31, 32, 50, 51; 17:25: Acts 2:40. Also see associated uses: Matt. 12:34, 39; 16:4; 17:17; Mark 9:19; 13:30; Luke 1:50; 9:41; 16:8; Acts 8:33; 13:36; Heb. 3:10.

[2] Not all Bibles do this. Some translators knew better.

[3] This judgment certainly came on that generation of Jews. Whether Jesus' "blood" and God's judgment is still "on us, and on our children" of subsequent generations of Jews post-A.D. 70 is arguable and debatable. I will not be addressing this sensitive point in this book.

[4] Appendix B, "The Olivet Discourse Cannot Be Divided," in *What Happened in A.D. 70?*, (Bradford, PA.: International Preterist Association, 1997), 18-19. Also in Edward E. Stevens, *Stevens Response To Gentry* (Bradford, PA.: International Preterist Association, 2nd ed., 1999), Appendix I, 114.

[5] This misconception is nurtured somewhat by the mistranslation of the Matthew 13: 39, 49; 24:3 phrase "the end of the world" in the King James Version of the Bible. The word "world" in the Greek is *aion* and is better translated as "age." Most later translations agree.

[6] A strong case can be made that all books later included in the New Testament were written prior to A.D. 70. See again footnote #1 in chapter six.

[7] See www.frozenfrontier.com/enochnewtest.htm. / www.stargods.org/EnochQuoted.htm and Quoted2.htm.

Chapter 9

[1] Klein and others, *Introduction to Biblical Interpretation*, 149, 310. For the full quote, see again the Author's Note, footnote #1or the text at end of this chapter.

[2] Eusebius, *Ecclesiastical History*, Book 3, Ch.7, in The Nicene and Post-Nicene Fathers, Vol. 1 (Grand Rapids, MI.: Eerdmans, 1979).

[3] *Ecclesiastical History*, Book 3, Ch.5.

[4] St Augustine, vol. 6.

---

[5] *The Festal Letters*, Letter IV, No. 3-4.

[6] Josephus, *The Antiquities of the Jews*, 10.11.7 (276).

[7] The prophecy does say "armies," not army. Why the use of the plural? Historical accounts reveal that Rome commonly conscripted soldiers from other nations into their fighting ranks. Titus's army below only contained 25,000 Roman soldiers out of approximately 54,000 in the combined armies that came against Jerusalem in A.D. 70.

[8] *Wars*, 5.11.1 (451).

[9] As a man, Jesus did not know the "day or hour" nor everything. By lowering Himself (Phil. 2:6-8), He did not possess all the divine attributes of omniscience. Hence, Luke 2:52 tells us that as a man, "Jesus grew in wisdom and stature, and in favor with God and men."

[10] One can't know the precise day or hour for the birth of a baby either (see Matt. 24:8). This limitation phrase cannot be extrapolated to mean that no one could/can know at all, as is commonly assumed. The only constraint was/is against knowing the "day" and "hour," not week, month, season, year, or generation. The fact is, Jesus never identified a day or hour. Even He did not know (Matt. 24:36). But that was no excuse for not knowing when it was time to flee.

[11] *Ecclesiastical History*, Book III, V. 86.

[12] "The times of the Gentiles" does not refer to the 1967 Six Days War in which Israel recaptured the city of Jerusalem from Gentile control, as is claimed by some popular futurist interpreters. Either 1st-century Gentile (Roman) armies are meant here (see Mark 10:33 and Rev. 11:2), or "the times of the Gentiles" are a reference to the four Gentile world empires of Daniel 2 and 7 and their control over Palestine and the rebellious Jewish people until the coming of the Messiah and his kingdom. After the giving of the Law, four Gentile kingdoms occupied and ruled over Israel (starting with Babylon) until its desolation and the end of the Jewish age. Either way, this phrase has covenantal significance and limits. It cannot be extended for all time. After circa A.D. 70, God's New Covenant people and the kingdom of God are not and cannot be subject to human rule. Dominion over the kingdom was taken away from these Gentile powers and given to the saints of the new Israel. Thus ended the "times of the Gentiles."

[13] Likewise, meaningless would be Jesus' statements about being "on the roof of his house" or fleeing "in winter or on the Sabbath"—i.e., flat roofs, an agrarian society, foot travel and the shortness of a Sabbath's day journey (Matt. 24:17-20). These distinctives were all and only fitting of and particular to a 1st-century time period and Jewish context.

[14] Eusebius, *Ecclesiastical History*, Book 3, chapter 5; from Edersheim, *Life and Times of Jesus the Messiah*, p. 448, Peabody, Mass.: Hendrickson; reprint of 1886 ed.

[15] *Wars*, 6.5.3 (289-300).

[16] Tacitus, *The Histories*, 1:5-7, 1.2-3.

[17] *Wars*, 6.9.3 (420).

[18] In contrast, the prophet Haggai described the building of the Temple as "one stone was laid upon another" (Hag. 2:15).

[19] Actually, not every stone was removed. Three towers and a portion of the wall that enclosed the city on the west were left. It was used for a Roman encampment (*Wars*, 7.1.1 (1-2) and as a monument for posterity.

[20] The immediate, typological, and historical setting for this fulfillment was the destruction of Jerusalem by the Babylonnians in the 6th century B.C.

[21] *Wars*, 7, 1, 1 (1-4).

[22] John Noē, "An Exegetical Basis for a Preterist-Idealist Understanding of the Book of Revelation, *Journal of the Evangelical Theological Society*, Vol. 49, No. 4, (December 2006):768-769. For more see Don K. Preston, *Who Is This Babylon* (Ardmore, OK.: n.p. n.d.) 208-210. Also see, N.T Wright, *Jesus and the Victory of God*, vol. 2 (London, Great Britain; Society for Promoting Christian Knowledge, 1996) 323, 354.

[23] Eusebius, *Ecclesiastical History*, Book III, V, 138.

[24] Donald Guthrie, *New Testament Theology* (Downers Grove, IL.: Inter-Varsity Press, 1981) 816.

[25] The ongoing relevance of whole of the prophecy of Revelation is also addressed in my *JETS* article (see footnote #22 above, again).

[26] At Jewish weddings a crystal goblet is sometimes broken to commemorate the "breaking" of the Holy Place that occurred in A.D. 70.

[27] *Wars*, 4.3.10 (163).

[28] Ibid., 4.6.3 (386).

[29] Ibid., 5.2.4 (24).

[30] Ibid., 6.3.4 (205-219).

[31] Ibid., 6.6.6 (259).

[32] Ibid., 6.1.1 (6-7).

[33] Some, citing the Jewish writing Yoma 21b as a source, think that God's Presence never entered or dwelled in this second Temple because no manifestation of His Shekinah glory (the glory cloud) was ever witnessed, as it was with the Tabernacle and the Solomon's (the first) Temple.

[34] *Wars*, 5.9.4 (412).

[35] Ibid., 5.13.6 (566); also see 5.13.7 (572); 6.5.3 (288); 7.1.1 (4).

[36] Others feel that Titus was the "ruler" or "prince" and the Romans the "people," since Rome carried out the actual destruction.

[37] Strong's Concordance, #3625.

[38] Eusebius, *Proof of the Gospel*, Bk. I, Ch. 6, 34-35.

[39] Klein, Blomberg, and Hubbard, Jr., *Introduction to Biblical Interpretation*, 149, 310.

Chapter 10

[1] These terms are placed in quotation marks for reasons we will cover in chapters eleven and twelve.

[2] Bertrand Russell, *Why I Am Not a Christian* (London: George Allen & Unwin Ltd., 1957), 11.

[3] Albert Schweitzer, *The Quest of the Historical Jesus* (New York, NY.: Macmillan, 1948), 360.

[4] Aryeh Kaplan (orthodox rabbi), "Jesus and the Bible," in *The Real Messiah* (reprinted from *Jewish Youth*, June 1973, Tammuz 5733, No. 40), 57.

[5] Pinchas Stolper (orthodox rabbi), "Was Jesus the Messiah Let's Examine the Facts," in *The Real Messiah* (reprinted from *Jewish Youth*, June 1973, Tammuz 5733, No. 40), 46-47.

[6] Joseph Klausner (scholar), *Jesus of Nazareth: His Life, Times, and Teaching* (New York, NY.: Macmillan, 1925), 405.

[7] Samuel Levine (educator and debater). *You Take Jesus, I'll Take God: How To Refute Christian Missionaries* (Los Angeles: Hamoroh Press, 1980), 15, 23, 49.

[8] Answering-Christianity.com, "The Ultimate Test of Jesus: Jesus' second coming and 'grace,'" (accessed 20 March 2000); available from http://www.arabianebarzaar.com/ac/second.htm; Internet.

[9] Hava Lazarus-Yafeh, *Intertwined Worlds: Medieval Islam and Bible Criticism* (Princeton, NJ: Princeton University Press, 1992), 19-20.

[10] Neal Robinson, *Christ in Islam and Christianity* (Albany: State University of New York Press, 1991), 78.

[11] Hans Kung and Jurgen Moltmann, eds., *Islam: A Challenge for Christianity* (London: SCM Press, 1994), 108.

[12] Yvonne Yazbeck Haddad and Wadi Z. Haddah, eds., *Christian-Muslim Encounters* (Gainesville: University Press of Florida, 1995), 433.

[13] C.S. Lewis, essay "The World's Last Night" (1960), found in *The Essential C.S. Lewis*, Lyle W. Dorsett, ed., (New York: A Touchstone Book, Simon & Schuster, 1996), 385.

[14] Michael J. Wilkins and J.P. Moreland, *Jesus Under Fire* (Grand Rapids, MI.: Zondervan, 1996) Counterpoints catalogue, Zondervan.

[15] Gary DeMar, "Giving Aid and Comfort to the Enemies of the Gospel, *Biblical Worldview*, December 2006, 22.

---

[16] Ibid.

[17] Lee Strobel, *The Case for Faith* (Grand Rapids, MI.: Zondervan, 2000), 20, 23, 247.

[18] www.amazon.com., 10/29/01.

[19] Strobel, *The Case for Faith*, 20.

[20] George R. Beasley-Murray, *Jesus and the Last Days* (Peabody, MA.: Hendrickson, 1993), 11-12.

[21] R.C. Sproul, Sr., *The Last Days According to Jesus* (Grand Rapids, MI.: Baker Books, 1998) 14-15.

[22] R.C. Sproul, Sr., "Last Days Madness" presentation, Ligonier Ministries' National Conference 1999. Cassette.

[23] Sproul, *The Last Days According to Jesus*, 203.

[24] Robert P. Carroll, *When Prophecies Failed* (New York: A Crossroads Book, 1979), 2.

[25] Kurt Aland, *A History of Christianity* (Philadelphia: Fortress Press, 1980), 87.

[26] Ibid., 91-92.

[27] Brian E. Daley, *The Hope of the Early Church* (Cambridge, MA.: Cambridge University Press, 1991), 3.

[28] Jaroslav Pelikan, *The Christian Tradition: A History of Development of Doctrine* (Chicago: The University of Chicago Press, 1971), Vol. 1, "The Emergence of the Catholic Tradition," 123-124.

Chapter 11

[1] Some interpreters contend that this verse pertains to Jesus' ascension and not to his age-ending coming in judgment circa A.D. 70 to destroy Jerusalem and the Temple. But if this is so, how could Caiaphas, et al. have seen the ascension? Others have postulated that this "seeing" of the coming of Christ is in the "hereafter" and therefore doesn't demand a 1st-century fulfillment.

[2] Some contend that this verse has a more simple and obvious meaning—i.e. that Jesus is talking about rejoining them in their ministry trip. In my opinion, this contention is far too reductionistic in light of the eschatological wording used.

[3] Some feel Matthew 16:28 was fulfilled on the Day of Pentecost (Acts 2). And only in this way during the interim period was Jesus said to be with them until the end of the age (Matt. 28:20). But Jesus did not come in his kingdom at Pentecost. Nor was that "the day the Son of Man is revealed" (Luke 17:30). That day was still future and being waited upon thirty-some years after Pentecost (see Heb. 10:25; 2 Thess. 2:1-3; 2 Tim. 4:1). Also, the outpouring of the Holy Spirit was a separately prophesied event in the Old Testament (Ezek. 36:26-27).

Others claim that this verse was fulfilled at the transfiguration (Matt. 17:1-3), or upon his triumphal entry (Matt. 21:5f), or at any of his post-resurrection appearances, or at his ascension, or even during his coming to John in the Book of Revelation. While the transfiguration was a temporary and partial glimpse of Jesus' divine glory granted to Peter, James, and John, the brother of James, it could not be the fulfillment of this verse. How could judgment and Jesus' rewarding of "every man," spoken of in the previous verse (Matt. 16:27), have taken place then? And where were "his angels" at either of those events, as stated in the previous verse? This same rejoinder is valid for all the previously suggested fulfillment explanations. Also, only six days had elapsed. That's not enough time for Jesus' "some . . . not taste death before . . . ." statement to make any sense. The fact is, all inspired New Testament writers, some twenty and thirty years later, were still looking for a future but imminent coming befitting this description, as we'll see shortly. The fulfillment of this passage does not fit any of these previously noted events, nor was Jesus speaking of two different comings arbitrarily separated by eons of time. Verses 27 and 28 are spoken by Jesus in the same breath and are indivisible! A forty-year interval better suits Jesus' prophetic words, in this author's opinion.

The great preacher, Charles H. Spurgeon, said, "If a child were to read this passage I know what he would think it meant: he would suppose Jesus Christ was to come, and there are some standing there who should not taste death until really and literally he did come. This, I believe, is the plain meaning." Spurgeon later explained away this imminency by claiming, "this tasting of death here may be explained, and I believe it is to be explained, by a reference to the second death, which men will not taste of till the Lord comes." Spurgeon's view is an arbitrary and contrived way of looking at this passage. Why not stick to how a child would understand it? That's how Jesus' disciples understood his words. (Spurgeon's quotes are taken from p-3-6 of *Twelve Sermons on the Second Coming of Christ*, edition 1976, Baker Book House.)

[4] While some interpreters agree that "this generation" is a reference to Jesus' contemporaries, they also contend that "all these things" only cover verses 4-28, and that these events were the only ones which occurred at the destruction of Jerusalem. They point out that in verses 29-31 Jesus drops the use of the personal pronoun "you." Therefore, it's asserted, these events are for a different time, long after the destruction of Jerusalem. Obviously, this contention is an argument from silence. No textual justification exists for extracting verses 29-31 from the context.

[5] The evil servant in this parable wasn't "evil" because he said, "My Lord delayeth his coming." He was evil because of what he did during his absence

(Matt. 24:49 KJV). But he did declare "a delay." That is directly contrary to Scripture (Heb. 10:37; Hab. 2:3). Why shouldn't that statement be considered "evil?" The Church, post A.D. 70, has taken a short period of Jesus' supposed departure and gradually developed it into a longer and longer "delay" idea rather than reexamine its notion of the nature of his Presence and consummating coming. Consequently, every generation except one has wrongly believed that Jesus would "return" in its time. The harm this has done must be "evil." Proverbs 13:12 tells us that "Hope deferred makes the heart sick, but a longing fulfilled is a tree of life." In this chapter, I am contending for the latter portion of this proverb.

[6] This quote from Psalm 90:4 has been used as a "scapegoat" text to void the New Testament's teaching of imminency (i.e., nearness or closeness of fulfillment). It actually describes the character and nature of God, his timelessness, everlastingness, eternalness, changelessness, etc. It's not an encoded time formula. Nor does it address how God thinks of time, as many have mistakenly taken it to mean. If it did, this would render meaningless all prophetic time and imminency statements of the Bible.

[7] Theologians prefer the word "imminency" instead of nearness. But they disagree on what this means. Some say it means an event will take place very soon. Others maintain that it only means that it could happen at any moment or is certain to happen someday.

[8] A strong case can be made that every New Testament book was written prior to 70 A.D. See again Robinson, *Redating the New Testament*.

[9] C. S. Lewis, essay "The World's Last Night" (1960), found in *The Essential C.S. Lewis*, Lyle W. Dorsett, 385.

[10] See again footnote #5 above.

[11] John A.T. Robinson places the date at A.D. 60-65 (Robinson, *Redating the New Testament*, 352.).

[12] Carl F.H. Henry, "The Very Last Day, The Very Last Hour," *Decision*, September 2000, 27.

[13] Gary DeMar, *End Times Fiction: A Biblical Consideration of the Left Behind Theology* (Nashville, TN.: Thomas Nelson, 2001), 141.

[14] Again, for my position on Revelation see my published article – John Noē, "An Exegetical Basis for a Preterist-Idealist Understanding of the Book of Revelation, *Journal of the Evangelical Theological Society*, Vol. 49, No. 4, (December 2006):768-769.

[15] Gary DeMar, in Foreword to Francis X. Gumerlock's, *The Day and the Hour: Christianity's Perennial Fascination with Predicting the End of the World* (Powder Springs, GA.: American Vision, 2000), *xxiv*.

[16] Also, in the Old Testament, God dwelt in, or was present in, a physical and visible Shekhinah glory cloud. This is an entirely different matter and will not be

addressed here. Our interest is in how cloud phraseology is used in a symbolic manner, namely that of swiftness and power of literal judgment.

Some interpreters contend that Acts 1:11's account of Jesus ascending into a cloud and two angels declaring that He would come back in "like manner" or "in the same way you have seen Him go into heaven" requires that He "return" visibly on a physical cloud(s). What's missed here is an equal argument that can be made from this same passage to support the *invisibility* of Christ at his consummating coming, since "a cloud hid him from their sight" (v. 9) before He entered heaven. This cloud was not an application in the same pattern of "cloud-coming" judgment. "Like manner" or "same way" refers to how He comes (i.e., the means of), which is in and out of the spirit realm, manifesting Himself in numerous forms and places for a wide variety of purposes. That has always been the way Jesus' many visible comings happened throughout both the Old and New Testament.

[17] To be consistent, shouldn't we also think of Him coming on a white horse (Rev. 19:11), as riding on a literal four-legged steed?

[18] Some suggest that these clouds of rising smoke compare with the cloud that hid Jesus from his disciples' sight upon his ascension (Acts 1:9-11). In a similar manner, Jesus' coming here was hidden from sight. This is one possible way of interpreting the invisible nature of this coming. Interestingly, Josephus, Eusebius, and the *Talmud* record that angelic armies were visibly seen in the clouds just before Jerusalem's destruction. This also could be interpreted as "the sign of his coming," since Jesus is the commander of the heavenly hosts.

[19] My thanks to Max King of Living Presence Ministries for introducing and explaining this fulfillment concept to me in his many writings and lectures.

[20] Some suggest the typology of the sacrificed goat represents unbelieving Jews filling up their measure of sin. And the scapegoat typifies Christians escaping out of Judaism. These two goats may symbolize Jesus being dead and then alive. Also, all the high priest's work had to be performed while smoke filled the Temple. This may be a connection with the cloud at Christ's ascension and clouds of smoke circa A.D. 70.

[21] Paul was not contradicting Jesus' statements about heaven not being open yet in either Philippians 1:21-24 and 2 Corinthians 5:8. He was only expressing his desire, a yearning, or a preference about dying and being present with the Lord. He only said, "I *desire* to depart and be with Christ," not "I *know* I can depart and be with Christ." Likewise, in the latter verse, he only said "would prefer," not that he "could." Let's not make more of this than what Paul did. Furthermore, Paul's words here must be understood within his previously stated futuristic context of "a deposit, guaranteeing what is to come" (2 Cor 5:5).

Hence and at best, it's a stretch to claim that Paul was teaching a then-present reality that if he died he would immediately go to heaven.

[22] Some argue that this occurred on the day of Jesus' resurrection or at his ascension. His appearances after those events are viewed as fulfilling the "second time" typology. One huge problem exists—the inspired writer of Hebrews, as well as 1 Peter 1 and other New Testament writers, writing some 20 to 30 years later, never acknowledged either as this fulfillment. To the contrary, they were still anticipating this appearing as yet-future.

[23] George Eldon Ladd, *The Blessed Hope* (Grand Rapids, MI.: Eerdmans, 1956), 69.

[24] Some postulate that He "returned" in the sending of the Holy Spirit at Pentecost. But this is scripturally impossible. Not only was the outpouring of the Spirit a separate and distinctly-prophesied event in the Old Testament, but no New Testament text acknowledges this event as that fulfillment. Rather, all New Testament writers were still anticipating Christ's age-ending coming as future.

[25] Matt. 24:3, 27, 37, 39; 1 Cor. 15:23; 1 Thess. 2:19; 3:13; 4:15; 5:23; 2 Thess. 2:1, 8, 9; Jas. 5:7, 8; 2 Pet. 1:16; 3:4, 12; 1 John 2:28. *Erchomai* is sometimes used: Matt. 24:30, 48; 26:64; Mark 13:26; 14:62; Luke 21:27. *Erchomai* means "comes and/or goes," and applies to and/or shares aspects with many other and different types of comings. In these verses it refers to his *parousia* coming as well. Its use, most likely, reflects this coming's other aspect of a coming and going in judgment.

[26] For more, see my paper, "The Many Comings of Jesus," presented at the 49th Annual Meeting of the Evangelical Theological Society in November of 1997 in Santa Clara, California.

[27] Some preterist scholars feel that Christ's Parousia was not a one-day event but lasted 3 ½ or more years to bring about the full divine judgment of the Roman-Jewish War A.D. 66-70 and possibly lasted until the last stone was removed circa 73.

[28] *The World Book Dictionary*, 1982 Edition, Doubleday & Company.

Chapter 12

[1] Kantzer, ed., "Our Future Hope: Eschatology and Its Role in the Church," 1-(I).

[2] For a copy of this booklet write: Evangelist John L. Bray
                                          John L. Bray Ministry, Inc.
                                          P.O. Box 90129
                                          Lakeland, FL 33804

³ Compare: <u>Matthew 24</u>   to   <u>2 Thessoloians 2</u>

vv. 11-12	v. 3
v. 15	vv. 4-5
v. 24	v. 9
vv. 21-22	v. 2-8
v. 30	v. 8
v. 31	v. 1
v. 34	vv. 6-7

⁴ Josephus, *Wars*, 4.5.1-2 (305-318). Many modern-day futurists teach that this is still future, and what must be removed is the Holy Spirit. But if Paul meant the "Holy Spirit" why didn't he say so? His words had specific, inspired, and relevant meaning for the hearers and readers of his day.

⁵ Ibid., 4.5.2 (318-323).

⁶ Ibid., 4.2.3 (104).

⁷ Ibid., 4.3.14 (216-219).

⁸ Ibid., 4.4.1-2 (224-235).

⁹ Ibid., 5.6.1 (254).

¹⁰ Ibid., 4.7.1 (389-390).

¹¹ Ibid., 5.1.4 (24-25).

¹² Ibid., 4.3.1 (121-127).

¹³ Ibid., 4.6.3 (377-378); 5.10.1 (420-423).

¹⁴ Ibid., 5.13.6 (562).

¹⁵ Ibid., 6.9.4 (434).

¹⁶ Ibid., 5.13.6 (566); 7.1.1 (4).

¹⁷ Sproul, *The Last Days According to Jesus*, 158.

¹⁸ Klein and others, Introduction to Biblical Interpretation, 305.

¹⁹ Ibid., 120f.

²⁰ Judgment, grace, love, etc. are all part of God's unending kingdom (Isa. 9:7, Luke 1:33).

²¹ Gary DeMar, *Last Days Madness*, 3ʳᵈ ed., (Smyrna, GA.: American Vision, 1997), 265 – in quoting Gary W. Demarest.

²² Milton S. Terry, *Biblical Hermeneutics* (Eugene, OR.: Wipf and Stock, 1890, 1999), 383-384.

²³ Terry, Biblical Hermeneutics, 385.

²⁴ Ibid., 333.

²⁵ Ibid., 399.

²⁶ Walter C. Kaiser, *Toward an Old Testament Theology*, (Grand Rapids, MI.: Zondervan, 1991), 188.

---

[27] The confessions and catechisms of the divided Church (Catholic-Protestant) are another issue. Almost everyone in Reformed circles takes some exception to them. And strict conformity is not justifiable. So why must this book's view conform? These will not be addressed. But one point should be mentioned. While the 16th-century Reformers didn't devote any significant attention to eschatology either, they did use it as a tool to demonize the Pope and the Roman Catholic hierarchy, thereby fueling reformation fervor.

[28] Eusebius, *The Proof of the Gospel*, Book VIII, chapter 4 (Grand Rapids, Mi.: Baker Books, 1981): 144-6 – his discussion on Zechariah 14:1-5.

[29] Eusebius, W.J. Ferrar, ed., *The Proof of the Gospel*, Book 7, Ch. 4, 144, 146 – his discussion on Zechariah 14:1-5.

[30] Ibid., 147.

[31] Athanasius' *On the Incarnation of the Word*, Section 39 Verse 3, Section 40 Verses 1-8.

[32] Sproul, *The Last Days According to Jesus*, 203.

[33] R.C. Sproul, Sr., at the 1993 Covenant Eschatology Symposium in Mt. Dora, Florida. From *Steven's Response To Gentry* booklet, by Edward E. Stevens, Kingdom Publications, 1997, p-52.

[34] Also the president of the International Preterist Association, in a 9/23/98 fax to me.

[35] Every August, some Jews remember the destruction of Jerusalem with a fast day, the Fast of Av. Also, at some Jewish weddings, drinking glasses are broken beneath the feet in remembrance of the shattering of Israel in A.D. 70 A.D. and "the end of biblical Judaism." According to Josephus, the Roman army burned the Temple on August 30, 70— "one cannot but wonder at the accuracy of this period thereto relating; for the same month and day were now observed . . . wherein the holy house was burnt formerly by the Babylonians" (*Wars*, 6.4.8 (268); 6.4.5 (250). By the end of September, the whole city was in Titus' hands (*Wars*, 6.8.1-5 (374-408)). Over the next three years, the Temple stones were dismantled to the ground, after which the area was plowed over.

Chapter 13

[1] Many believe that the New Testament ushered in a new set of promises and prophecies. It did not. The New Testament simply amplified and elaborated upon prophecies made in the Old Testament.

[2] Some futurists while agreeing that Jesus' expression, "all that has been written," refers to prophecies and promises in the Old Testament, argue that new prophecies and promises in the New Testament books and even Jesus' words

themselves—none of which had been written down at the time Jesus spoke these words—refer to a yet-future final fulfillment at the "end of time." (See again footnote #1 above) But the Apostle Paul who wrote most of the New Testament books said it well—he preached *nothing* but the hope of Israel found in Moses and the prophets (see for instance: Acts 26:21-23; 24:14-15).

[3] "Incredulous," one critic writes to this author's original paper and lecture presentation of this material, "that anyone could think that what happened in 70 A.D. was a fulfillment of 'all things that are written.' This is only in reference to the days of vengeance, i.e. the tribulation of Israel; not in reference to everything promised in the Bible . . . . There is an indefinite period of time between verses 24 and 25 in Luke 21 and between verses 28 and 29 of Matthew 24, which has not ended yet." With all due respect to my critic, this is a classic example of allowing nature to determine time. This theologian's notion of the nature of fulfillment dictates a postponement of time out into the future.

[4] Actually, the Law itself was transformed not eliminated (see. Jer. 31:31-33).

[5] Again, for my position on Revelation see my published article – John Noē, "An Exegetical Basis for a Preterist-Idealist Understanding of the Book of Revelation, *Journal of the Evangelical Theological Society*, Vol. 49, No. 4, (December 2006):768-769.

[6] The evidence for the early date for the writing of the book of Revelation (A.D. 65 to 68) is far superior to that for a late date (A.D. 95 to 98) in this author's opinion. See again footnote #1 in chapter six. This dating debate will not be addressed in this book, however.

[7] KJV, AMP and NAS translate it properly. Perhaps the grammatically correct way didn't make sense to the NIV translators. But the more difficult and correct rendering does make sense when we understand what God is conveying here.

[8] Josephus, *The Antiquities of the Jews*, 3.6.4 (122-126); also see 3.7.7 (180-3).

[9] Reformed scholar, Peter J. Leithart agrees. He writes that *"stoicheia . . . refers to the life of Israel under the dietary, sacrificial and purity regulations imposed by the Torah . . . . meant adherence to animal sacrifice, the keeping of days, the avoidance of contamination."* Peter J. Leithart, *Defending Constantine* (Downers Grove, IL.: IVP Academic, 2010), 324-325.

[10] Luke 12:49; 3:9, 16; Heb. 10:26-31; 1 Cor. 3:13-15; see also Lam. 2:3; Psa. 46:6; 50:3; 97:3; Isa. 4:4; 29:6; 30:27-28, 30, 33; 66:15-16, 24; Mal. 3:1-5; 4:1.

[11] Eccl. 1:4; Psa. 78:69; 89:36-37; 93:1; 96:10; 104:5; 119:90; 148:4, 6; Eph. 3:21 KJV.

[12] Some interpreters feel this first "world" that was "destroyed" or "perished" in the flood was the wicked system of things. Either way, the physical real estate of our globe remained intact. See insight 9 for more on this.

[13] If "one day" equals "a thousand years," and we're consistent, then did Jesus fast for 40,000 years? Was He in the grave 3,000 years before his resurrection?

Or vice versa, is the thousand year reign in Revelation 20 only 24 hours long? How ridiculous is this kind of logic? It misses the intended application.

[14] See author's book, *The Apocalypse Conspiracy* (Nashville, TN.: Wolgemuth & Hyatt/Word), 1991.

[15] Amillennialism and Postmillennialism posit "the end of time." The Premillennial view does not.

[16] Isa. 4:2-6; 11; 12; 25; 26:1-4; 30:18-26; 35:3-10; 49; 52; 60; 61; 62; 65:17-25; 66:10-24; Jer. 3:12-18; Ezek. 40-48; Joel 2:28-32; 3:1-21; Mic. 4:1-13; Zeph. 3:8-20; Zech. 2:1-13; 8:1-8; 12:1-3; 14:1-21; Mal. 3:1-6. Jerusalem is often used as a metonym for Israel, the Jewish people, and/or the Judaic Old Covenant system. This is similar to how Washington, D.C. is used by extension to represent the national identity of the United States. The earthly city of Jerusalem in Bible times was the very heart and core of Israel's world.

Conclusion

[1] Klein and others, *Introduction to Biblical Interpretation*, 149, 310.

[2] Opening lines of PBS Special, *"From Jesus to Christ: The First Christmas,"* aired April 6, 1998.

[3] Speed Bump, *The Indianapolis Star*, January 31, 2008.

[4] "Reforming or Deforming," Martin G. Selbrede, Bio, Sept/Oct. 2009, www.chalcedon.edu/articles/print.php, 9/17/09.

[5] See for example: Leslie Leyland Fields, "The Myth of the Perfect Parent," *Christianity Today*, January 2010, 24.

[6] Sproul, *The Last Days According to Jesus*, back flap.

[7] *Table Talk*, chapter one, section 12, translated by William Hazilitt, published in Philadelphia, PA, by the Lutheran Publication Society.

CPSIA information can be obtained at www.ICGtesting.com
Printed in the USA
BVOW08s1327150913

331122BV00001B/82/P

9 780983 430308